Data Visualisation

SAGE was founded in 1965 by Sara Miller McCune to support the dissemination of usable knowledge by publishing innovative and high-quality research and teaching content. Today, we publish over 900 journals, including those of more than 400 learned societies, more than 800 new books per year, and a growing range of library products including archives, data, case studies, reports, and video. SAGE remains majority-owned by our founder, and after Sara's lifetime will become owned by a charitable trust that secures our continued independence.

Los Angeles | London | New Delhi | Singapore | Washington DC | Melbourne

Data Visualisation

A Handbook for Data Driven Design

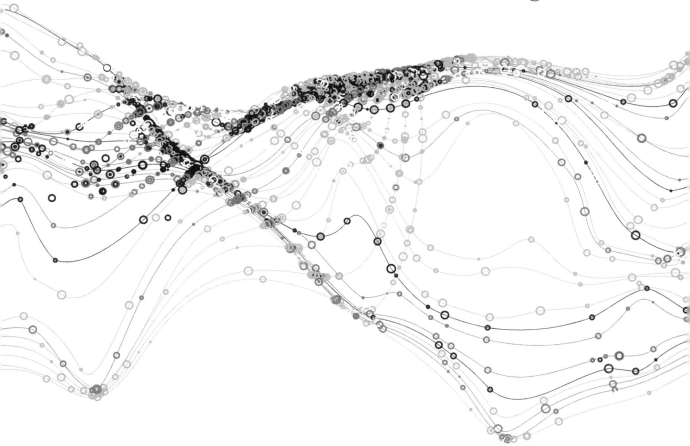

Andy Kirk

Los Angeles | London | New Delhi
Singapore | Washington DC | Melbourne

Los Angeles | London | New Delhi
Singapore | Washington DC | Melbourne

SAGE Publications Ltd
1 Oliver's Yard
55 City Road
London EC1Y 1SP

SAGE Publications Inc.
2455 Teller Road
Thousand Oaks, California 91320

SAGE Publications India Pvt Ltd
B 1/I 1 Mohan Cooperative Industrial Area
Mathura Road
New Delhi 110 044

SAGE Publications Asia-Pacific Pte Ltd
3 Church Street
#10-04 Samsung Hub
Singapore 049483

Editor: Mila Steele
Editorial assistant: Alysha Owen
Production editor: Ian Antcliff
Marketing manager: Sally Ransom
Cover design: Shaun Mercier
Typeset by: C&M Digitals (P) Ltd, Chennai, India
Printed and bound in Great Britain by Ashford
Colour Press Ltd.

Library of Congress Control Number: 2015957322

British Library Cataloguing in Publication data

A catalogue record for this book is available from
the British Library

ISBN 978-1-4739-1213-7
ISBN 978-1-4739-1214-4 (pbk)

FSC
www.fsc.org
MIX
Paper from
responsible sources
FSC® C011748

At SAGE we take sustainability seriously. Most of our products are printed in the UK using FSC papers and boards.
When we print overseas we ensure sustainable papers are used as measured by the PREPS grading system.
We undertake an annual audit to monitor our sustainability.

Contents

List of Figures with Source Notes

Acknowledgements

This book has been made possible thanks to the unwavering support of my incredible wife, Ellie, and the endless encouragement from my Mum and Dad, the rest of my brilliant family and my super group of friends.

From a professional standpoint I also need to acknowledge the fundamental role played by the hundreds of visualisation practitioners (no matter under what title you ply your trade) who have created such a wealth of brilliant work from which I have developed so many of my convictions and formed the basis of so much of the content in this book. The people and organisations who have provided me with permission to use their work are heroes and I hope this book does their rich talent justice.

About the Author

Andy Kirk is a freelance data visualisation specialist based in Yorkshire, UK. He is a visualisation design consultant, training provider, teacher, researcher, author, speaker and editor of the award-winning website visualisingdata.com

After graduating from Lancaster University in 1999 with a BSc (hons) in Operational Research, Andy held a variety of business analysis and information management positions at organisations including West Yorkshire Police and the University of Leeds.

He discovered data visualisation in early 2007 just at the time when he was shaping up his proposal for a Master's (MA) Research Programme designed for members of staff at the University of Leeds.

On completing this programme with distinction, Andy's passion for the subject was unleashed. Following his graduation in December 2009, to continue the process of discovering and learning the subject he launched visualisingdata.com, a blogging platform that would chart the ongoing development of the data visualisation field. Over time, as the field has continued to grow, the site too has reflected this, becoming one of the most popular in the field. It features a wide range of fresh content profiling the latest projects and contemporary techniques, discourse about practical and theoretical matters, commentary about key issues, and collections of valuable references and resources.

In 2011 Andy became a freelance professional focusing on data visualisation consultancy and training workshops. Some of his clients include CERN, Arsenal FC, PepsiCo, Intel, Hershey, the WHO and McKinsey. At the time of writing he has delivered over 160 public and private training events across the UK, Europe, North America, Asia, South Africa and Australia, reaching well over 3000 delegates.

In addition to training workshops Andy also has two academic teaching positions. He joined the highly respected Maryland Institute College of Art (MICA) as a visiting lecturer in 2013 and has been teaching a module on the Information Visualisation Master's Programme since its inception. In January 2016, he began teaching a data visualisation module as part of the MSc in Business Analytics at the Imperial College Business School in London.

Between 2014 and 2015 Andy was an external consultant on a research project called 'Seeing Data', funded by the Arts & Humanities Research Council and hosted by the University of Sheffield. This study explored the issues of data visualisation literacy among the general public and, among many things, helped to shape an understanding of the human factors that affect visualisation literacy and the effectiveness of design.

Introduction

I.1 The Quest Begins

In his book *The Seven Basic Plots*, author Christopher Booker investigated the history of telling stories. He examined the structures used in biblical teachings and historical myths through to contemporary storytelling devices used in movies and TV. From this study he found seven common themes that, he argues, can be identifiable in any form of story.

One of these themes was 'The Quest'. Booker describes this as revolving around a main protagonist who embarks on a journey to acquire a treasured object or reach an important destination, but faces many obstacles and temptations along the way. It is a theme that I feel shares many characteristics with the structure of this book and the nature of data visualisation.

You are the central protagonist in this story in the role of the data visualiser. The journey you are embarking on involves a route along a design workflow where you will be faced with a wide range of different conceptual, practical and technical challenges. The start of this journey will be triggered by curiosity, which you will need to define in order to accomplish your goals. From this origin you will move forward to initiating and planning your work, defining the dimensions of your challenge. Next, you will begin the heavy lifting of working with data, determining what qualities it contains and how you might share these with others. Only then will you be ready to take on the design stage. Here you will be faced with the prospect of handling a spectrum of different design options that will require creative and rational thinking to resolve most effectively.

The multidisciplinary nature of this field offers a unique opportunity and challenge. Data visualisation is not an especially difficult capability to acquire, it is largely a game of decisions. Making better decisions will be your goal but sometimes clear decisions will feel elusive. There will be occasions when the best choice is not at all visible and others when there will be many seemingly equal viable choices. Which one to go with? This book aims to be your guide, helping you navigate efficiently through these difficult stages of your journey.

You will need to learn to be flexible and adaptable, capable of shifting your approach to suit the circumstances. This is important because there are plenty of potential villains lying in wait looking to derail progress. These are the forces that manifest through the imposition of restrictive creative constraints and the pressure created by the relentless ticking clock of timescales. Stakeholders and audiences will present complex human factors through the diversity of their needs and personal traits. These will need to be astutely accommodated. Data, the critical raw material of this process, will dominate your attention. It will frustrate and even disappoint at times, as promises of its treasures fail to materialise irrespective of the hard work, love and attention lavished upon it.

Your own characteristics will also contribute to a certain amount of the villainy. At times, you will find yourself wrestling with internal creative and analytical voices pulling against each other in opposite directions. Your excitably formed initial ideas will be embraced but will need taming. Your inherent tastes, experiences and comforts will divert you away from the ideal path, so you will need to maintain clarity and focus.

The central conflict you will have to deal with is the notion that there is no *perfect* in data visualisation. It is a field with very few 'always' and 'nevers'. Singular solutions rarely exist. The comfort offered by the rules that instruct what is right and wrong, good and evil, has its limits. You can find small but legitimate breaking points with many of them. While you can rightly aspire to reach as close to perfect as possible, the attitude of aiming for *good enough* will often indeed be good enough and fundamentally necessary.

In accomplishing the quest you will be rewarded with competency in data visualisation, developing confidence in being able to judge the most effective analytical and design solutions in the most efficient way. It will take time and it will need more than just reading this book. It will also require your ongoing effort to learn, apply, reflect and develop. Each new data visualisation opportunity poses a new, unique challenge. However, if you keep persevering with this journey the possibility of a happy ending will increase all the time.

I.2 Who is this Book Aimed at?

The primary challenge one faces when writing a book about data visualisation is to determine what to leave in and what to leave out. Data visualisation is big. It is too big a subject even to attempt to cover it all, in detail, in one book. There is no single book to rule them all because there is no one book that can cover it all. Each and every one of the topics covered by the chapters in this book could (and, in several cases, do) exist as whole books in their own right.

The secondary challenge when writing a book about data visualisation is to decide how to weave all the content together. Data visualisation is not rocket science; it is not an especially complicated discipline. Lots of it, as you will see, is rooted in common sense. It is, however, certainly a complex subject, a semantic distinction that will be revisited later. There are lots of things to think about and decide on, as well as many things to do and make. Creative and analytical sensibilities blend with artistic and scientific judgments. In one moment you might be checking the statistical rigour of your calculations, in the next deciding which tone of orange most elegantly contrasts with an 80% black. The complexity of data visualisation manifests itself through how these different ingredients, and many more, interact, influence and intersect to form the whole.

The decisions I have made in formulating this book's content have been shaped by my own process of learning about, writing about and practising data visualisation for, at the time of writing, nearly a decade. Significantly – from the perspective of my own development – I have been fortunate to have had extensive experience designing and delivering training workshops and postgraduate teaching. I believe you only truly learn about your own knowledge of a subject when you have to explain it and teach it to others.

I have arrived at what I believe to be an effective and proven pedagogy that successfully translates the complexities of this subject into accessible, practical and valuable form. I feel well qualified to bridge the gap between the large population of *everyday* practitioners, who might identify themselves as beginners, and the superstar technical, creative and academic minds that are constantly pushing forward our understanding of the potential of data visualisation. I am not going to claim to belong to that latter cohort, but I have certainly been the former – a beginner – and most of my working hours are spent helping other beginners start their journey. I know the things that I would have valued when I was starting out and I know how I would have wished them to be articulated and presented for me to develop my skills most efficiently.

There is a large and growing library of fantastic books offering many different theoretical and practical viewpoints on the subject of data visualisation. My aim is to bring value to this existing collection of work by taking on a particular perspective that is perhaps under-represented in other texts – exploring the notion and practice of a visualisation design process. As I have alluded to in the opening, the central premise of this book is that the path to mastering data visualisation is achieved by making better decisions: effective choices, efficiently made. The book's central goal is to help develop your capability and confidence in facing these decisions.

Just as a single book cannot cover the whole of this subject, it stands that a single book cannot aim to address directly the needs of all people doing data visualisation. In this section I am going to run through some of the characteristics that shape the readers to whom this book is primarily targeted. I will also put into context the content the book will and will not cover, and why. This will help manage your expectations as the reader and establish its value proposition compared with other titles.

Domain and Duties

The core audiences for whom this book has been primarily written are undergraduate and postgraduate-level students and early career researchers from social science subjects. This reflects a growing number of people in higher education who are interested in and need to learn about data visualisation.

Although aimed at social sciences, the content will also be relevant across the spectrum of academic disciplines, from the arts and humanities right through to the formal and natural sciences: any academic duty where there is an emphasis on the use of quantitative and qualitative methods in studies will require an appreciation of good data visualisation practices. Where statistical capabilities are relevant so too is data visualisation.

Beyond academia, data visualisation is a discipline that has reached mainstream consciousness with an increasing number of professionals and organisations, across all industry types and sizes, recognising the importance of doing it well for both internal and external benefit. You might be a market researcher, a librarian or a data analyst looking to enhance your data capabilities. Perhaps you are a skilled graphic designer or web developer looking to take your portfolio of work into a more data-driven direction. Maybe you are in a managerial position and not directly involved in the creation of visualisation work, but you need to coordinate or commission others who will be. You require awareness of the most efficient approaches, the range of options and the different key decision points. You might be seeking generally to improve the sophistication of the language you use around commissioning visualisation work and to have a better way of expressing and evaluating work created for you.

Basically, anyone who is involved in whatever capacity with the analysis and visual communication of data as part of their professional duties will need to grasp the demands of data visualisation and this book will go some way to supporting these needs.

Subject Neutrality

One of the important aspects of the book will be to emphasise that data visualisation is a portable practice. You will see a broad array of examples of work from different industries, covering very different topics. What will become apparent is that visualisation techniques are largely subject-matter neutral: a line chart that displays the ebb and flow of favourable opinion towards a politician involves the same techniques as using a line chart to show how a stock has changed in value over time or how peak temperatures have changed across a season in a given location. A line chart is a line chart, regardless of the subject matter. The context of the viewers (such as their needs and their knowledge) and the specific meaning that can be drawn will inevitably be unique to each setting, but the role of visualisation itself is adaptable and portable across all subject areas.

Data visualisation is an entirely global concern, not focused on any defined geographic region. Although the English language dominates the written discourse (books, websites) about this subject, the interest in it and visible output from across the globe are increasing at a pace. There are cultural matters that influence certain decisions throughout the design process, especially around the choices made for colour usage, but otherwise it is a discipline common to all.

Level and Prerequisites

The coverage of this book is intended to serve the needs of beginners and those with intermediate capability. For most people, this is likely to be as far as they might ever need to go. It will offer an accessible route for novices to start their learning journey and, for those already familiar with the basics, there will be content that will hopefully contribute to fine-tuning their approaches.

For context, I believe the only distinction between beginner and intermediate is one of breadth and depth of critical thinking rather than any degree of difficulty. The more advanced techniques in visualisation tend to be associated with the use of specific technologies for handling larger, complex datasets and/or producing more bespoke and feature-rich outputs.

This book is therefore not aimed at experienced or established visualisation practitioners. There may be some new perspectives to enrich their thinking, some content that will confirm and other content that might constructively challenge their convictions. Otherwise, the coverage in this book should really echo the practices they are likely to be already observing.

As I have already touched on, data visualisation is a genuinely multidisciplinary field. The people who are active in this field or profession come from all backgrounds – everyone has a different entry point and nobody arrives with all constituent capabilities. It is therefore quite difficult to define just what are the right type and level of pre-existing knowledge, skills or experiences for those learning about data visualisation. As each year passes, the savvy-ness of the type of audience this book targets will increase, especially as the subject penetrates more into the mainstream. What were seen as bewilderingly new techniques several years ago are now commonplace to more people.

That said, I think the following would be a fair outline of the type and shape of some of the most important prerequisite attributes for getting the most out of this book:

- Strong numeracy is necessary as well as a familiarity with basic statistics.
- While it is reasonable to assume limited prior knowledge of data visualisation, there should be a strong desire to want to learn it. The demands of learning a craft like data visualisation take time and effort; the capabilities will need nurturing through ongoing learning and practice. They are not going to be achieved overnight or acquired alone from reading this book. Any book that claims to be able magically to inject mastery through just reading it cover to cover is over-promising and likely to under-deliver.
- The best data visualisers possess inherent curiosity. You should be the type of person who is naturally disposed to question the world around them or can imagine what questions others have. Your instinct for discovering and sharing answers will be at the heart of this activity.
- There are no expectations of your having any prior familiarity with design principles, but a desire to embrace some of the creative aspects presented in this book will heighten the impact of your work. Unlock your artistry!
- If you *are* somebody with a strong creative flair you are very fortunate. This book will guide you through when and crucially when *not* to tap into this sensibility. You should be willing to increase the rigour of your analytical decision making and be prepared to have your creative thinking informed more fundamentally by data rather than just instinct.
- A range of technical skills covering different software applications, tools and programming languages is not expected for this book, as I will explain next, but you will ideally have some knowledge of basic Excel and some experience of working with data.

I.3 Getting the Balance
Handbook vs Tutorial Book

The description of this book as being a 'handbook' positions it as being of practical help and presented in accessible form. It offers direction with comprehensive reference – more of a city guidebook for a tourist than an instruction manual to fix a washing machine. It will help you to know what things to think about, when to think about them, what options exist and how best to resolve all the choices involved in any data-driven design.

Technology is the key enabler for working with data and creating visualisation design outputs. Indeed, apart from a small proportion of artisan visualisation work that is drawn by hand, the reliance on technology to create visualisation work is an inseparable necessity. For many there is a understandable appetite for step-by-step tutorials that help them immediately to implement data visualisation techniques via existing and new tools.

However, writing about data visualisation through the lens of selected tools is a bit of a minefield, given the diversity of technical options out there and the mixed range of skills, access and needs. I greatly admire those people who have authored tutorial-based texts because they require astute judgement about what is the right level, structure and scope.

The technology space around visualisation is characterised by flux. There are the ongoing changes with the enhancement of established tools as well as a relatively high frequency of new entrants offset by the decline of others. Some tools are proprietary, others are open source; some are easier to learn, others require a great deal of understanding before you can even consider embarking on your first chart. There are many recent cases of applications or services that have enjoyed fleeting exposure before reaching a plateau: development and support decline, the community of users disperses and there is a certain expiry of value. Deprecation of syntax and functions in programming languages requires the perennial updating of skills.

All of this perhaps paints a rather more chaotic picture than is necessarily the case but it justifies the reasons why this book does not offer teaching in the use of any tools. While tutorials may be invaluable to some, they may also only be mildly interesting to others and possibly of no value to most. Tools come and go but the craft remains. I believe that creating a practical, rather than necessarily a technical, text that focuses on the underlying craft of data visualisation with a tool-agnostic approach offers an effective way to begin learning about the subject in appropriate depth. The content should be appealing to readers irrespective of the extent of their technical knowledge (novice to advanced technicians) and specific tool experiences (e.g. knowledge of Excel, Tableau, Adobe Illustrator).

There is a role for all book types. Different people want different sources of insight at different stages in their development. If you *are* seeking a text that provides in-depth tutorials on a range of tools or pages of programmatic instruction, this one will not be the best choice. However, if you consult *only* tutorial-related books, the chances are you will likely fall short on the fundamental critical thinking that will be needed in the longer term to get the most out of the tools with which you develop strong skills.

To substantiate the book's value, the digital companion resources to this book will offer a curated, up-to-date collection of visualisation technology resources that will guide you through the most common and valuable tools, helping you to gain a sense of what their roles are and where these fit into the design workflow. Additionally, there will be recommended exercises and many further related digital materials available for exploring.

Useful vs Beautiful

Another important distinction to make is that this book is not intended to be seen as a beauty pageant. I love flicking through those glossy 'coffee table' books as much as the next person; such books offer great inspiration and demonstrate some of the finest work in the field.

This book serves a very different purpose. I believe that, as a beginner or relative beginner on this learning journey, the inspiration you need comes more from understanding what is behind the thinking that makes these amazing works succeed and others not.

My desire is to make this the most *useful* text available, a reference that will spend more time on your desk than on your bookshelf. To be useful is to be used. I want the pages to be dog-eared. I want to see scribbles and annotated notes made across its pages and key passages underlined. I want to see sticky labels peering out above identified pages of note. I want to see creases where pages have been folded back or a double-page spread that has been weighed down to keep it open. In time I even want its cover reinforced with wallpaper or wrapping paper to ensure its contents remain bound together. There is every intention of making this an elegantly presented and packaged book but it should not be something that invites you to 'look, but don't touch'.

Pragmatic vs Theoretical

The content of this book has been formed through many years of absorbing knowledge from all manner of books, generations of academic papers, thousands of web articles, hundreds of conference talks, endless online and personal discussions, and lots of personal practice. What I present here is a pragmatic translation and distillation of what I have learned down the years.

It is not a deeply academic or theoretical book. Where theoretical context and reference is relevant it will be signposted as I do want to ground this book in as much evidenced-based content as possible; it is about judging what is going to add most value. Experienced practitioners will likely have an appetite for delving deeper into theoretical discourse and the underlying sciences that intersect in this field but that is beyond the scope of this particular text.

Take the science of visual perception, for example. There is no value in attempting to emulate what has already been covered by other books in greater depth and quality than I could achieve. Once you start peeling back the many different layers of topics like visual and cognitive science the boundaries of your interest and their relevance to data visualisation never seem to arrive. You get swallowed up by the depth of these subjects. You realise that you have found yourself learning about what the very concept of light and sight is and at that point your brain begins to ache (well, mine does at least), especially when all you set out to discover was if a bar chart would be better than a pie chart.

An important reason for giving greater weight to pragmatism is because of people: people are the makers, the stakeholders, the audiences and the critics in data visualisation. Although there are a great deal of valuable research-driven concepts concerning data visualisation, their practical application can be occasionally at odds with the somewhat sanitised and artificial context of the research methods employed. To translate them into real-world circumstances can sometimes be easier said than done as the influence of human factors can easily distort the significance of otherwise robust ideas.

I want to remove the burden from you as a reader having to translate relevant theoretical discourse into applicable practice. Critical thinking will therefore be the watchword, equipping you with the independence of thought to decide rationally for yourself what the solutions are that best fit your context, your data, your message and your audience. To do this you will need an appreciation of all the options available to you (the different things you *could* do) and a reliable approach for critically determining what choices you should make (the things you *will* do and *why*).

Contemporary vs Historical

This book is not going to look too far back into the past. We all respect the ancestors of this field, the great names who, despite primitive means, pioneered new concepts in the visual display of statistics to shape the foundations of the field being practised today. The field's lineage is decorated by the influence of William Playfair's first ever bar chart, Charles Joseph Minard's famous graphic about Napoleon's Russian campaign, Florence Nightingale's Coxcomb plot and John Snow's cholera map. These are some of the totemic names and classic examples that will always be held up as the 'firsts'. Of course, to many beginners in the field, this historical context is of huge interest. However, again, this kind of content has already been superbly covered by other texts on more than enough occasions. Time to move on.

I am not going to spend time attempting to enlighten you about how we live in the age of 'Big Data' and how occupations related to data are or will be the 'sexiest jobs' of our time. The former is no longer news, the latter claim emerged from a single source. I do not want to bloat this book with the unnecessary reprising of topics that have been covered at length elsewhere. There is more valuable and useful content I want you to focus your time on.

The subject matter, the ideas and the practices presented here will hopefully not date a great deal. Of course, many of the graphic examples included in the book will be surpassed by newer work demonstrating similar concepts as the field continues to develop. However, their worth as exhibits of a particular perspective covered in the text should prove timeless. As more research is conducted in the subject, without question there will be new techniques, new concepts, new empirically evidenced principles that emerge. Maybe even new rules. There will be new thought-leaders, new sources of reference, new visualisers to draw insight from. New tools will be created, existing tools will expire. Some things that are done and can only be done by hand as of today may become seamlessly automated in the near future. That is simply the nature of a fast-growing field. This book can only be a line in the sand.

Analysis vs Communication

A further important distinction to make concerns the subtle but significant difference between visualisations which are used for analysis and visualisations used for communication.

Before a visualiser can confidently decide what to communicate to others, he or she needs to have developed an intimate understanding of the qualities and potential of the data. This is largely achieved through exploratory data analysis. Here, the visualiser and the viewer are the same person. Through visual exploration, different interrogations can be pursued 'on the fly' to unearth confirmatory or enlightening discoveries about what insights exist.

Visualisation techniques used for analysis will be a key component of the journey towards creating visualisation for communication but the practices involved differ. Unlike visualisation for communication, the techniques used for visual analysis do not have to be visually polished or necessarily appealing. They are only serving the purpose of helping you to truly learn about your data. When a data visualisation is being created to communicate to others, many careful considerations come into play about the requirements and interests of the intended or expected audience. This has a significant influence on many of the design decisions you make that do not exist alone with visual analysis.

Exploratory data analysis is a huge and specialist subject in and of itself. In its most advanced form, working efficiently and effectively with large complex data, topics like 'machine learning', using self-learning algorithms to help automate and assist in the discovery of patterns in data, become increasingly relevant. For the scope of this book the content is weighted more towards methods and concerns about communicating data visually to others. If your role is in pure data science or statistical analysis you will likely require a deeper treatment of the exploratory data analysis topic than this book can reasonably offer. However, Chapter 4 will cover the essential elements in sufficient depth for the practical needs of most people working with data.

Print vs Digital

The opportunity to supplement the print version of this book with an e-book and further digital companion resources helps to cushion the agonising decisions about what to leave out. This text is therefore enhanced by access to further digital resources, some of which are newly created, while others are curated references from the endless well of visualisation content on the Web. Included online (book.visualisingdata.com) will be:

- a completed case-study project that demonstrates the workflow activities covered in this book, including full write-ups and all related digital materials;
- an extensive and up-to-date catalogue of over 300 data visualisation tools;
- a curated collection of tutorials and resources to help develop your confidence with some of the most common and valuable tools;
- practical exercises designed to embed the learning from each chapter;
- further reading resources to continue learning about the subjects covered in each chapter.

I.4 Objectives

Before moving on to an outline of the book's contents, I want to share four key objectives that I hope to accomplish for you by the final chapter. These are themes that will run through the entire text: challenge, enlighten, equip and inspire.

To **challenge** you I will be encouraging you to recognise that your current thinking about visualisation may need to be reconsidered, both as a creator and as a consumer. We all arrive in visualisation from different subject and domain origins and with that comes certain baggage and prior sensibilities that can distort our perspectives. I will not be looking to eliminate these, rather to help you harness and align them with other traits and viewpoints.

I will ask you to relentlessly consider the diverse decisions involved in this process. I will challenge your convictions about what you perceive to be good or bad, effective or ineffective visualisation choices: arbitrary choices will be eliminated from your thinking. Even if you are not necessarily a beginner, I believe the content you read in this book will make you question some of your own perspectives and assumptions. I will encourage you to reflect on your previous work, asking you to consider how and why you have designed visualisations in the way that you have: where do you need to improve? What can you do better?

It is not just about creating visualisations, I will also challenge your approach to reading visualisations. This is not something you might usually think much about, but there is an important role for more tactical approaches to consuming visualisations with greater efficiency and effectiveness.

To **enlighten** you will be to increase your awareness of the possibilities in data visualisation. As you begin your discovery of data visualisation you might not be aware of the whole: you do not entirely know what options exist, how they are connected and how to make good choices. Until you know, you don't know – that is what the objective of enlightening is all about.

As you will discover, there is a lot on your plate, much to work through. It is not just about the visible end-product design decisions. Hidden beneath the surface are many contextual circumstances to weigh up, decisions about how best to prepare your data, choices around the multitude of viable ways of slicing those data up into different angles of analysis. That is all before you even reach the design stage, where you will begin to consider the repertoire of techniques for visually portraying your data – the charts, the interactive features, the colours and much more besides.

This book will broaden your visual vocabulary to give you more ways of expressing your data visually. It will enhance the sophistication of your decision making and of visual language for any of the challenges you may face.

To **equip** is to ensure you have robust tactics for managing your way through the myriad options that exist in data visualisation. The variety it offers makes for a wonderful prospect but, equally, introduces the burden of choice. This book aims to make the challenge of undertaking data visualisation far less overwhelming, breaking down the overall prospect into smaller, more manageable task chunks.

The structure of this book will offer a reliable and flexible framework for thinking, rather than rules for learning. It will lead to better decisions. With an emphasis on critical thinking you will move away from an over-reliance on gut feeling and taste. To echo what I mentioned earlier, its role as a handbook will help you know what things to think about, when to think about them and how best to resolve all the thinking involved in any data-driven design challenge you meet.

To **inspire** is to give you more than just a book to read. It is the opening of a door into a subject to inspire you to step further inside. It is about helping you to want to continue to learn about it and expose yourself to as much positive influence as possible. It should elevate your ambition and broaden your capability.

It is a book underpinned by theory but dominated by practical and accessible advice, including input from some of the best visualisers in the field today. The range of print and digital resources will offer lots of supplementary material including tutorials, further reading materials and suggested exercises. Collectively this will hopefully make it one of the most comprehensive, valuable and inspiring titles out there.

I.5 Chapter Contents

The book is organised into four main parts (A, B, C and D) comprising eleven chapters and preceded by the 'Introduction' sections you are reading now.

Each chapter opens with an introductory outline that previews the content to be covered and provides a bridge between consecutive chapters. In the closing sections of each chapter the most salient learning points will be summarised and some important, practical tips and tactics shared. As mentioned, online there will be collections of practical exercises and further reading resources recommended to substantiate the learning from the chapter.

Throughout the book you will see sidebar captions that will offer relevant references, aphorisms, good habits and practical tips from some of the most influential people in the field today.

Introduction

This introduction explains how I have attempted to make sense of the complexity of the subject, outlining the nature of the audience I am trying to reach, the key objectives, what topics the book will be covering and not covering, and how the content has been organised.

Part A: Foundations

Part A establishes the foundation knowledge and sets up a key reference of understanding that aids your thinking across the rest of the book. Chapter 1 will be the logical starting point for many of you who are new to the field to help you understand more about the definitions and attributes of data visualisation. Even if you are not a complete beginner, the content of the chapter forms the terms of reference that much of the remaining content is based on. Chapter 2 prepares you for the journey through the rest of the book by introducing the key design workflow that you will be following.

Chapter 1: Defining Data Visualisation

Defining data visualisation: outlining the components of thinking that make up the proposed definition for data visualisation.

The importance of conviction: presenting three guiding principles of good visualisation design: trustworthy, accessible and elegant.

Distinctions and glossary: explaining the distinctions and overlaps with other related disciplines and providing a glossary of terms used in this book to establish consistency of language.

Chapter 2: Visualisation Workflow

The importance of process: describing the data visualisation design workflow, what it involves and why a process approach is required.

The process in practice: providing some useful tips, tactics and habits that transcend any particular stage of the process but will best prepare you for success with this activity.

Part B: The Hidden Thinking

Part B discusses the first three preparatory stages of the data visualisation design workflow. 'The hidden thinking' title refers to how these vital activities, that have a huge influence over the eventual design solution, are somewhat out of sight in the final output; they are hidden beneath the surface but completely shape what is visible. These stages represent the often neglected contextual definitions, data wrangling and editorial challenges that are so critical to the success or otherwise of any visualisation work – they require a great deal of care and attention before you switch your attention to the design stage.

Chapter 3: Formulating Your Brief

What is a brief?: describing the value of compiling a brief to help initiate, define and plan the requirements of your work.

Establishing your project's context: defining the origin curiosity or motivation, identifying all the key factors and circumstances that surround your work, and defining the core purpose of your visualisation.

Establishing your project's vision: early considerations about the type of visualisation solution needed to achieve your aims and harnessing initial ideas about what this solution might look like.

Chapter 4: Working With Data

Data literacy: establishing a basic understanding with this critical literacy, providing some foundation understanding about datasets and data types and some observations about statistical literacy.

Data acquisition: outlining the different origins of and methods for accessing your data.

Data examination: approaches for acquainting yourself with the physical characteristics and meaning of your data.

Data transformation: optimising the condition, content and form of your data fully to prepare it for its analytical purpose.

Data exploration: developing deeper intimacy with the potential qualities and insights contained, and potentially hidden, within your data.

Chapter 5: Establishing Your Editorial Thinking

What is editorial thinking?: defining the role of editorial thinking in data visualisation.

The influence of editorial thinking: explaining how the different dimensions of editorial thinking influence design choices.

Part C: Developing Your Design Solution

Part C is the main part of the book and covers progression through the data visualisation design and production stage. This is where your concerns switch from *hidden* thinking to *visible* thinking. The individual chapters in this part of the book cover each of the five layers of the data visualisation anatomy. They are treated as separate affairs to aid the clarity and organisation of your thinking, but they are entirely interrelated matters and the chapter sequences support this. Within each chapter there is a consistent structure beginning with an introduction to each design layer, an overview of the many different possible design options, followed by detailed guidance on the factors that influence your choices.

The production cycle: describing the cycle of development activities that take place during this stage, giving a context for how to work through the subsequent chapters in this part.

Chapter 6: Data Representation

Introducing visual encoding: an overview of the essentials of data representation looking at the differences and relationships between visual encoding and chart types.

Chart types: a detailed repertoire of 49 different chart types, profiled in depth and organised by a taxonomy of chart families: categorical, hierarchical, relational, temporal, and spatial.

Influencing factors and considerations: presenting the factors that will influence the suitability of your data representation choices.

Chapter 7: Interactivity

The features of interactivity:

- Data adjustments: a profile of the options for interactively interrogating and manipulating data.
- View adjustments: a profile of the options for interactively configuring the presentation of data.

Influencing factors and considerations: presenting the factors that will influence the suitability of your interactivity choices.

Chapter 8: Annotation

The features of annotation:

- Project annotation: a profile of the options for helping to provide viewers with general explanations about your project.
- Chart annotation: a profile of the annotated options for helping to optimise viewers' understanding your charts.

Influencing factors and considerations: presenting the factors that will influence the suitability of your annotation choices.

Chapter 9: Colour

The features of colour:

- Data legibility: a profile of the options for using colour to represent data.
- Editorial salience: a profile of the options for using colour to direct the eye towards the most relevant features of your data.
- Functional harmony: a profile of the options for using colour most effectively across the entire visualisation design.

Influencing factors and considerations: presenting the factors that will influence the suitability of your colour choices.

Chapter 10: Composition

The features of composition:

- Project composition: a profile of the options for the overall layout and hierarchy of your visualisation design.
- Chart composition: a profile of the options for the layout and hierarchy of the components of your charts.

Influencing factors and considerations: presenting the factors that will influence the suitability of your composition choices.

Part D: Developing Your Capabilities

Part D wraps up the book's content by reflecting on the range of capabilities required to develop confidence and competence with data visualisation. Following completion of the design process, the multidisciplinary nature of this subject will now be clearly established. This final part assesses the two sides of visualisation literacy – your role as a creator and your role as a viewer – and what you need to enhance your skills with both.

Chapter 11: Visualisation Literacy

Viewing: Learning to see: learning about the most effective strategy for understanding visualisations in your role as a viewer rather than a creator.

Creating: The capabilities of the visualiser: profiling the skill sets, mindsets and general attributes needed to master data visualisation design as a creator.

Part A
Foundations

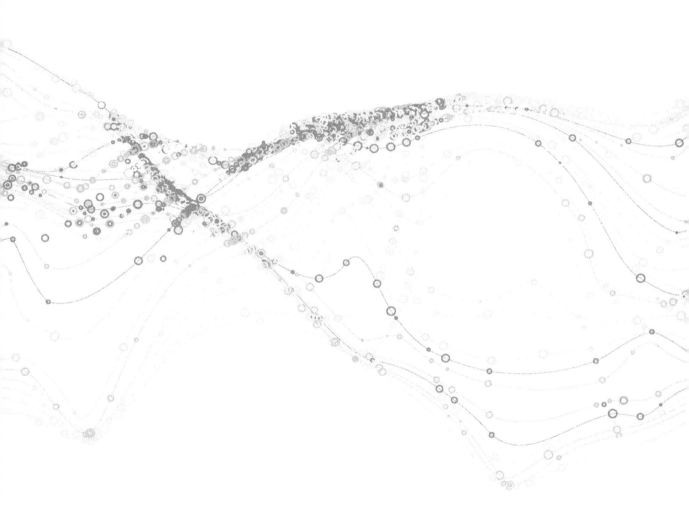

1

Defining Data Visualisation

This opening chapter will introduce you to the subject of data visualisation, defining what data visualisation is and is not. It will outline the different ingredients that make it such an interesting recipe and establish a foundation of understanding that will form a key reference for all of the decision making you are faced with.

Three core principles of good visualisation design will be presented that offer guiding ideals to help mould your convictions about distinguishing between effective and ineffective in data visualisation.

You will also see how data visualisation sits alongside or overlaps with other related disciplines, and some definitions about the use of language in this book will be established to ensure consistency in meaning across all chapters.

1.1 The Components of Understanding

To set the scene for what is about to follow, I think it is important to start this book with a proposed definition for data visualisation (Figure 1.1). This definition offers a critical term of reference because its components and their meaning will touch on every element of content that follows in this book. Furthermore, as a subject that has many different proposed definitions, I believe it is worth clarifying my own view before going further:

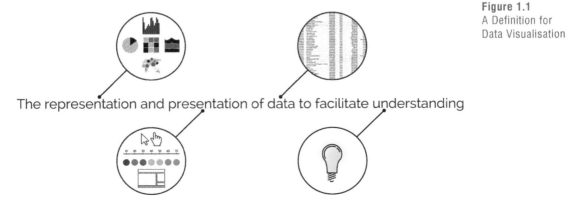

Figure 1.1
A Definition for
Data Visualisation

The representation and presentation of data to facilitate understanding

At first glance this might appear to be a surprisingly short definition: isn't there more to data visualisation than that, you might ask? Can nine words sufficiently articulate what has already been introduced as an eminently complex and diverse discipline?

I have arrived at this after many years of iterations attempting to improve the elegance of my definition. In the past I have tried to force too many words and too many clauses into one statement, making it cumbersome and rather undermining its value. Over time, as I have developed greater clarity in my own convictions, I have in turn managed to establish greater clarity about what I feel is the real essence of this subject. The definition above is, I believe, a succinct and practically useful description of what the pursuit of visualisation is truly about. It is a definition that largely informs the contents of this book. Each chapter will aim to enlighten you about different aspects of the roles of and relationships between each component expressed. Let me introduce and briefly examine each of these one by one, explaining where and how they will be discussed in the book.

Firstly, **data**, our critical raw material. It might appear a formality to mention data in the definition for, after all, we are talking about data visualisation as opposed to, let's say, cheese visualisation (though visualisation of data using cheese has happened, see Figure 1.2), but it needs to be made clear the core role that data has in the design process. Without data there is no visualisation; indeed there is no need for one. Data plays the fundamental role in this work, so you will need to give it your undivided attention and respect. You will discover in Chapter 4 the importance of developing an intimacy with your data to acquaint yourself with its physical properties, its meaning and its potential qualities.

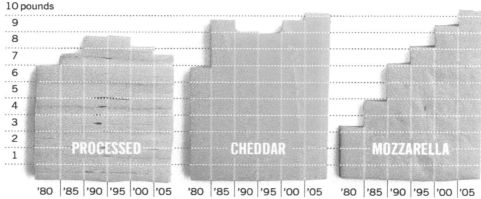

Figure 1.2 Per Capita Cheese Consumption in the US

Data is names, amounts, groups, statistical values, dates, comments, locations. Data is textual and numeric in format, typically held in datasets in table form, with rows of records and columns of different variables.

This tabular form of data is what we will be considering as the raw form of data. Through tables, we can *look* at the values contained to precisely read them as individual data points. We can look up values quite efficiently, scanning across many variables for the different records held.

However, we cannot easily establish the comparative size and relationship between multiple data points. Our eyes and mind are not equipped to translate easily the textual and numeric values into quantitative and qualitative meaning. We can look at the data but we cannot really see it without the context of relationships that help us compare and contrast them effectively with other values. To derive understanding from data we need to see it represented in a different, visual form. This is the act of **data representation**.

This word *representation* is deliberately positioned near the front of the definition because it is the quintessential activity of data visualisation design. Representation concerns the choices made about the form in which your data will be visually portrayed: in lay terms, what chart or charts you will use to exploit the brain's visual perception capabilities most effectively.

When data visualisers create a visualisation they are representing the data they wish to show visually through combinations of *marks* and *attributes*. Marks are points, lines and areas. Attributes are the appearance properties of these marks, such as the size, colour and position. The recipe of these marks and their attributes, along with other components of apparatus, such as axes and gridlines, form the anatomy of a chart.

In Chapter 6 you will gain a deeper and more sophisticated appreciation of the range of different charts that are in common usage today, broadening your visual vocabulary. These charts will vary in complexity and composition, with each capable of accommodating different types of data and portraying different angles of analysis. You will learn about the key ingredients that shape your data representation decisions, explaining the factors that distinguish the effective from the ineffective choices.

Beyond representation choices, the **presentation** of data concerns all the other visible design decisions that make up the overall visualisation anatomy. This includes choices about the possible applications of interactivity, features of annotation, colour usage and the composition of your work. During the early stages of learning this subject it is sensible to partition your thinking about these matters, treating them as isolated design layers. This will aid your initial critical thinking. Chapters 7–10 will explore each of these layers in depth, profiling the options available and the factors that influence your decisions.

However, as you gain in experience, the interrelated nature of visualisation will become much more apparent and you will see how the overall design anatomy is entirely connected. For instance, the selection of a chart type intrinsically leads to decisions about the space and place it will occupy; an interactive control may be included to reveal an annotated caption; for any design property to be even visible to the eye it must possess a colour that is different from that of its background.

The goal expressed in this definition states that data visualisation is about **facilitating understanding**. This is very important and some extra time is required to emphasise why it is such an influential component in our thinking. You might think you know what *understanding* means, but when you peel back the surface you realise there are many subtleties that need to be acknowledged about this term and their impact on your data visualisation choices. Understanding 'understanding' (still with me?) in the context of data visualisation is of elementary significance.

These are not just synonyms for the same word, rather they carry important distinctions that need appreciating. As you will see throughout this book, the subtleties and semantics of language in data visualisation will be a recurring concern.

When consuming a visualisation, the viewer will go through a process of understanding involving three stages: *perceiving*, *interpreting* and *comprehending* (Figure 1.3). Each stage is dependent on the previous one and in your role as a data visualiser you will have influence but not full control over these. You are largely at the mercy of the viewer – what they know and do not know, what they are interested in knowing and what might be meaningful to them – and this introduces many variables outside of your control: where your control diminishes the influence and reliance on the viewer increases. Achieving an outcome of understanding is therefore a collective responsibility between visualiser and viewer.

Figure 1.3
The Three Stages of Understanding

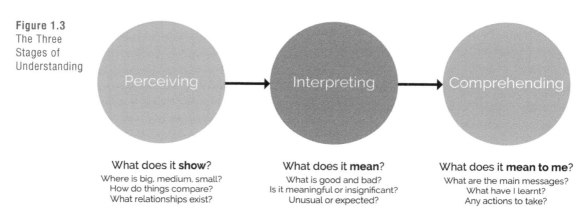

What does it **show**?
Where is big, medium, small?
How do things compare?
What relationships exist?

What does it **mean**?
What is good and bad?
Is it meaningful or insignificant?
Unusual or expected?

What does it **mean to me**?
What are the main messages?
What have I learnt?
Any actions to take?

Let's look at the characteristics of the different stages that form the process of understanding to help explain their respective differences and mutual dependencies.

Firstly, *perceiving*. This concerns the act of simply being able to read a chart. What is the chart showing you? How easily can you get a sense of the values of the data being portrayed?

- Where are the largest, middle-sized and smallest values?
- What proportion of the total does that value hold?
- How do these values compare in ranking terms?
- To which other values does this have a connected relationship?

The notion of understanding here concerns our attempts as viewers to efficiently decode the representations of the data (the shapes, the sizes and the colours) as displayed through a chart, and then convert them into perceived values: estimates of quantities and their relationships to other values.

Interpreting is the next stage of understanding following on from perceiving. Having read the charts the viewer now seeks to convert these perceived values into some form of meaning:

- Is it good to be big or better to be small?
- What does it mean to go up or go down?
- Is that relationship meaningful or insignificant?
- Is the decline of that category especially surprising?

The viewer's ability to form such interpretations is influenced by their pre-existing knowledge about the portrayed subject and their capacity to utilise that knowledge to frame the implications of what has been read. Where a viewer does not possess that knowledge it may be that the visualiser has to address this deficit. They will need to make suitable design choices that help to make clear what meaning can or should be drawn from the display of data. Captions, headlines, colours and other annotated devices, in particular, can all be used to achieve this.

Comprehending involves reasoning the consequence of the perceiving and interpreting stages to arrive at a personal reflection of what all this means *to them, the viewer*. How does this information make a difference to what was known about the subject previously?

- Why is this relevant? What wants or needs does it serve?
- Has it confirmed what I knew or possibly suspected beforehand or enlightened me with new knowledge?
- Has this experience impacted me in an emotional way or left me feeling somewhat indifferent as a consequence?
- Does the context of what understanding I have acquired lead me to take action – such as make a decision or fundamentally change my behaviour – or do I simply have an extra grain of knowledge the consequence of which may not materialise until much later?

Over the page is a simple demonstration to further illustrate this process of understanding. In this example I play the role of a viewer working with a sample isolated chart (Figure 1.4). As you will learn throughout the design chapters, a chart would not normally just exist floating in isolation like this one does, but it will serve a purpose for this demonstration.

Figure 1.4 shows a clustered bar chart that presents a breakdown of the career statistics for the footballer Lionel Messi during his career with FC Barcelona.

The process commences with *perceiving* the chart. I begin by establishing what chart type is being used. I am familiar with this clustered bar chart approach and so I quickly feel at ease with the prospect of reading its display: there is no learning for me to have to go through on this occasion, which is not always the case as we will see.

I can quickly assimilate what the axes are showing by examining the labels along the x- and y-axes and by taking the assistance provided by colour legend at the top. I move on to scanning, detecting and observing the general physical properties of the data being represented. The eyes and brain are working in harmony, conducting this activity quite instinctively without awareness or delay, noting the most prominent features of variation in the attributes of size, shape, colour and position.

Figure 1.4
Demonstrating
the
Process of
Understanding

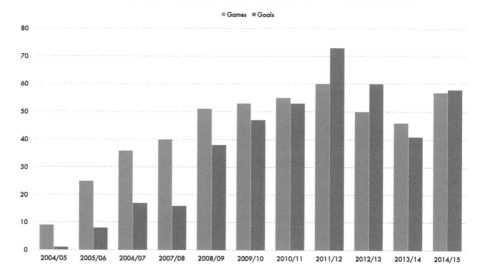

Lionel Messi: Games and Goals for FC Barcelona

I look across the entire chart, identifying the big, small and medium values (these are known as stepped magnitude judgements), and form an overall sense of the general value rankings (global comparison judgements). I am instinctively drawn to the dominant bars towards the middle/right of the chart, especially as I know this side of the chart concerns the most recent career performances. I can determine that the purple bar – showing goals – has been rising pretty much year-on-year towards a peak in 2011/12 and then there is a dip before recovery in his most recent season.

My visual system is now working hard to decode these properties into estimations of quantities (amounts of things) and relationships (how different things compare with each other). I focus on judging the absolute magnitudes of individual bars (one bar at a time). The assistance offered by the chart apparatus, such as the vertical axis (or y- axis) values and the inclusion of gridlines, is helping me more quickly estimate the quantities with greater assurance of accuracy, such as discovering that the highest number of goals scored was around 73.

I then look to conduct some relative higher/lower comparisons. In comparing the games and goals pairings I can see that three out of the last four years have seen the purple bar higher than the blue bar, in contrast to all the rest. Finally I look to establish proportional relationships between neighbouring bars, i.e. by how much larger one is compared with the next. In 2006/07 I can see the blue bar is more than twice as tall as the purple one, whereas in 2011/12 the purple bar is about 15% taller.

By reading this chart I now have a good appreciation of the quantities displayed and some sense of the relationship between the two measures, games and goals.

The second part of the understanding process is *interpreting*. In reality, it is not so consciously consecutive or delayed in relationship to the perceiving stage but you cannot get here without having already done the perceiving. Interpreting, as you will recall, is about converting perceived 'reading' into meaning. Interpreting is essentially about orientating your assessment of what you've read against what you know about the subject.

As I mentioned earlier, often a data visualiser will choose to – or have the opportunity to – share such insights via captions, chart overlays or summary headlines. As you will learn in Chapter 3, the visualisations that present this type of interpretation assistance are commonly described as offering an 'explanatory' experience. In this particular demonstration it is an example of an 'exhibitory' experience, characterised by the absence of any explanatory features. It relies on the viewer to handle the demands of interpretation without any assistance.

As you will read about later, many factors influence how well different viewers will be able to interpret a visualisation. Some of the most critical include the level of interest shown towards the subject matter, its relevance and the general inclination, in that moment, of a viewer to want to read about that subject through a visualisation. It is also influenced by the knowledge held about a subject or the capacity to derive meaning from a subject even if a knowledge gap exists.

Returning to the sample chart, in order to translate the quantities and relationships I extracted from the perceiving stage into meaning, I am effectively converting the reading of value sizes into notions of *good* or *bad* and comparative relationships into *worse than* or *better than* etc. To interpret the meaning of this data about Lionel Messi I can tap into my passion for and knowledge of football. I know that for a player to score over 25 goals in a season is very good. To score over 35 is exceptional. To score over 70 goals is frankly preposterous, especially at the highest level of the game (you might find plenty of players achieving these statistics playing for the Dog and Duck pub team, but these numbers have been achieved for Barcelona in La Liga, the Champions League and other domestic cup competitions). I know from watching the sport, and poring over statistics like this for 30 years, that it is very rare for a player to score remotely close to a ratio of one goal per game played. Those purple bars that exceed the height of the blue bars are therefore remarkable. Beyond the information presented in the chart I bring knowledge about the periods when different managers were in charge of Barcelona, how they played the game, and how some organised their teams entirely around Messi's talents. I know which other players were teammates across different seasons and who might have assisted or hindered his achievements. I also know his age and can mentally compare his achievements with the traditional football career arcs that will normally show a steady rise, peak, plateau, and then decline.

Therefore, in this example, I am not just interested in the subject but can bring a lot of knowledge to aid me in interpreting this analysis. That helps me understand a lot more about what this data means. For other people they might be passingly interested in football and know how to read what is being presented, but they might not possess the domain knowledge to go deeper into the interpretation. They also just might not care. Now imagine this was analysis of, let's say, an NHL ice hockey player (Figure 1.5) – that would present an entirely different challenge for me.

In this chart the numbers are irrelevant, just using the same chart as before with different labels. Assuming this was real analysis, as a sports fan in general I would have the capacity to understand the notion of a sportsperson's career statistics in terms of games played and goals

Figure 1.5
Demonstrating
the Process of
Understanding

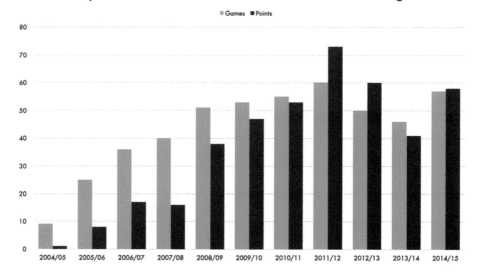

Wayne Kane: Games and Points for Toronto Rangers

scored: I can read the chart (*perceiving*) that shows me this data and catch the gist of the angle of analysis it is portraying. However, I do not have sufficient domain knowledge of ice hockey to determine the real meaning and significance of the big–small, higher–lower value relationships. I cannot confidently convert 'small' into 'unusual' or 'greater than' into 'remarkable'. My capacity to interpret is therefore limited, and besides I have no connection to the subject matter, so I am insufficiently interested to put in the effort to spend much time with any in-depth attempts at interpretation.

Imagine this is now no longer analysis about sport but about the sightings in the wild of *Winglets* and *Spungles* (completely made up words). Once again I can still read the chart shown in Figure 1.6 but now I have absolutely no connection to the subject whatsoever. No knowledge and no interest. I have no idea what these things are, no understanding about the sense of scale that should be expected for these sightings, I don't know what is good or bad. And I genuinely don't care either. In contrast, for those who do have a knowledge of and interest in the subject, the meaning of this data will be much more relevant. They will be able to read the chart and make some sense of the meaning of the quantities and relationships displayed.

To help with *perceiving*, viewers need the context of scale. To help with *interpreting*, viewers need the context of subject, whether that is provided by the visualiser or the viewer themself. The challenge for you and I as data visualisers is to determine what our audience will know already and what they will need to know in order to possibly assist them in interpreting the meaning. The use of explanatory captions, perhaps positioned in that big white space top left, could assist those lacking the knowledge of the subject, possibly offering a short narrative to make the interpretations – the meaning – clearer and immediately accessible.

We are not quite finished, there is one stage left. The third part of the understanding process is *comprehending*. This is where I attempt to form some concluding reasoning that translates into

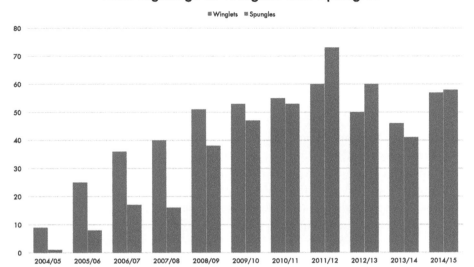

Total Sightings of Winglets and Spungles

■ Winglets ■ Spungles

Figure 1.6
Demonstrating
the Process of
Understanding

what this analysis means for *me*. What can I infer from the display of data I have read? How do I relate and respond to the insights I have drawn out as through interpretation? Does what I've learnt make a difference to me? Do I know something more than I did before? Do I need to act or decide on anything? How does it make me feel emotionally?

Through consuming the Messi chart, I have been able to form an even greater appreciation of his amazing career. It has surprised me just how prolific he has been, especially having seen his ratio of goals to games, and I am particularly intrigued to see whether the dip in 2013/14 was a temporary blip or whether the bounce back in 2014/15 was the blip. And as he reaches his late 20s, will injuries start to creep in as they seem to do for many other similarly prodigious young talents, especially as he has been playing relentlessly at the highest level since his late teens?

My comprehension is not a dramatic discovery. There is no sudden inclination to act nor any need – based on what I have learnt. I just feel a heightened impression, formed through the data, about just how good and prolific Lionel Messi has been. For Barcelona fanatics who watch him play every week, they will likely have already formed this understanding. This kind of experience would only have reaffirmed what they already probably knew.

And that is important to recognise when it comes to managing expectations about what we hope to achieve amongst our viewers in terms of their final comprehending. One person's 'I knew that already' is another person's 'wow'. For every 'wow, I need to make some changes' type of reflection there might be another 'doesn't affect me'. A compelling visualisation about climate change presented to Sylvie might affect her significantly about the changes she might need to make in her lifestyle choices that might reduce her carbon footprint. For Robert, who is already familiar with the significance of this situation, it might have substantially less immediate impact – not indifference to the meaning of the data, just nothing new, a shrug of the shoulders. For James, the hardened sceptic, even the most indisputable evidence may have no effect; he might just not be receptive to altering his views regardless.

What these scenarios try to explain is that, from your perspective of the visualiser, this final stage of understanding is something you will have relatively little control over because viewers are people and people are complex. People are different and as such they introduce inconsistencies. You can lead a horse to water but you cannot make it drink: you cannot force a viewer to be interested in your work, to understand the meaning of a subject or get that person to react exactly how you would wish.

Visualising data is just an agent of communication and not a guarantor for what a viewer does with the opportunity for understanding that is presented. There are different flavours of comprehension, different consequences of understanding formed through this final stage. Many visualisations will be created with the ambition to simply inform, like the Messi graphic achieved for me, perhaps to add just an extra grain to the pile of knowledge a viewer has about a subject. Not every visualisation results in a Hollywood moment of grand discoveries, surprising insights or life-saving decisions. But that is OK, so long as the outcome fits with the intended purpose, something we will discuss in more depth in Chapter 3.

Furthermore, there is the complexity of human behaviour in how people make decisions in life. You might create the most compelling visualisation, demonstrating proven effective design choices, carefully constructed with very a specific audience type and need in mind. This might clearly show how a certain decision really needs to be taken by those in the audience. However, you cannot guarantee that the decision maker in question, while possibly recognising that there is a *need* to act, will be in a *position* to act, and indeed will know *how* to act.

It is at this point that one must recognise the ambitions and – more importantly – realise the limits of what data visualisation can achieve. Going back again, finally, to the components of the definition, all the reasons outlined above show why the term **to facilitate** is the most a visualiser can reasonably aspire to achieve.

It might feel like a rather tepid and unambitious aim, something of a cop-out that avoids scrutiny over the outcomes of our work: why not aim to 'deliver', 'accomplish', or do something more earnest than just 'facilitate'? I deliberately use 'facilitate' because as we have seen we can only control so much. Design cannot change the world, it can only make it run a little smoother. Visualisers can control the output but not the outcome: at best we can expect to have only some influence on it.

1.2 The Importance of Conviction

The key structure running through this book is a data visualisation design process. By following this process you will be able to decrease the size of the challenge involved in making good decisions about your design solution. The sequencing of the stages presented will help reduce the myriad options you have to consider, which makes the prospect of arriving at the *best* possible solution much more likely to occur.

Often, the design choices you need to make will be clear cut. As you will learn, the preparatory nature of the first three stages goes a long way to securing that clarity later in the design stage. On other occasions, plain old common sense is a more than sufficient guide. However, for more nuanced situations, where there are several potentially viable options presenting themselves, you need to rely on the guiding value of good design principles.

> 'I say begin by learning about data visualisation's "black and whites", the rules, then start looking for the greys. It really then becomes quite a personal journey of developing your conviction.'
> **Jorge Camoes, Data Visualization Consultant**

For many people setting out on their journey in data visualisation, the major influences that shape their early beliefs about data visualisation design tend to be influenced by the first authors they come across. Names like Edward Tufte, unquestionably one of the most important figures in this field whose ideas are still pervasive, represent a common entry point into the field, as do people like Stephen Few, David McCandless, Alberto Cairo, and Tamara Munzner, to name but a few. These are authors of prominent works that typically represent the first books purchased and read by many beginners.

Where you go from there – from whom you draw your most valuable enduring guidance – will be shaped by many different factors: taste, the industry you are working in, the

> 'My key guiding principle? Know the rules, before you break them.' **Gregor Aisch, Graphics Editor, The *New York Times***

topics on which you work, the types of audiences you produce for. I still value much of what Tufte extols, for example, but find I can now more confidently filter out some of his ideals that veer towards impractical ideology or that do not necessarily hold up against contemporary technology and the maturing expectations of people.

The key guidance that now most helpfully shapes and supports my convictions comes from ideas outside the boundaries of visualisation design in the shape of the work of Dieter Rams. Rams was a German industrial and product designer who was most famously associated with the Braun company.

In the late 1970s or early 1980s, Rams was becoming concerned about the state and direction of design thinking and, given his prominent role in the industry, felt a responsibility to challenge himself, his own work and his own thinking against a simple question: 'Is my design *good* design?'. By dissecting his response to this question he conceived 10 principles that expressed the most important characteristics of what he considered to be good design. They read as follows:

1. Good design is innovative.
2. Good design makes a product useful.
3. Good design is aesthetic.
4. Good design makes a product understandable.
5. Good design is unobtrusive.
6. Good design is honest.
7. Good design is long lasting.
8. Good design is thorough down to the last detail.
9. Good design is environmentally friendly.
10. Good design is as little design as possible.

Inspired by the essence of these principles, and considering their applicability to data visualis-ation design, I have translated them into three high-level principles that similarly help me to answer my own question: 'Is my visualisation design *good* visualisation design?' These princi-ples offer me a guiding voice when I need to resolve some of the more seemingly intangible decisions I am faced with (Figure 1.7).

Figure 1.7
The Three
Principles
of Good
Visualisation
Design

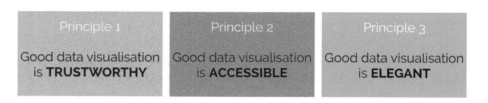

In the book *Will it Make the Boat Go Faster?*, co-author Ben Hunt-Davis provides details of the strategies employed by him and his team that led to their achieving gold medal success in the Men's Rowing Eight event at the Sydney Olympics in 2000. As the title suggests, each decision taken had to pass the 'will it make the boat go faster?' test. Going back to the goal of data visualisation as defined earlier, these design principles help me judge whether any decision I make will better aid the facilitation of understanding: the equivalence of 'making the boat go faster'.

I will describe in detail the thinking behind each of these principles and explain how Rams' prin-ciples map onto them. Before that, let me briefly explain why there are three principles of Rams' original ten that do not entirely fit, in my view, as *universal* principles for data visualisation.

Good design is innovative: Data visualisation does not need always to be innovative. For the majority of occasions the solutions being created call upon the tried and tested approaches that have been used for generations. Visualisers are not conceiving new forms of representation or implementing new design techniques in every project. Of course, there are times when innovation is required to overcome a particu-lar challenge; innovation generally materialises when faced with problems that current solutions fail to overcome. Your own desire for innovation may be aligned to per-sonal goals about the development of your skills or through reflecting on previous pro-jects and recognising a desire to rethink a solution. It is not that data visualisation is never about innovation, just that it is not always and only about innovation.

'I'm always the fool looking at the sky who falls off the cliff. In other words, I tend to seize on ideas because I'm excited about them without thinking through the consequences of the amount of work they will entail. I find tight deadlines energizing. Answering the question of "what is the graphic try-ing to do?" is always helpful. At minimum the work I create needs to speak to this. Innovation doesn't have to be a wholesale out-of-the box approach. Iterating on a previous idea, moving it forward, is innovation.' **Sarah Slobin, Visual Journalist**

Good design is long lasting: The translation of this principle to the context of data visualisation can be taken in different ways. 'Long lasting' could be related to the desire to preserve the ongoing functionality of a digital project, for example. It is quite demoralising how many historic links you visit online only to find a project has now expired through a lack of sustained support or is no longer functionally supported on modern browsers.

Another way to interpret 'long lasting' is in the durability of the technique. Bar charts, for example, are the *old reliables* of the field – always useful, always being used, always there when you need them (author wipes away a respectful tear). 'Long lasting' can also relate to avoiding the temptation of fashion or current gimmickry and having a timeless approach to design. Consider the recent design trend moving away from *skeuomorphism* and the emergence of so-called *flat* design. By the time this book is published there will likely be a new movement. 'Long lasting' could apply to the subject matter. Expiry in the relevance of certain angles of analysis or out-of-date data is inevitable in most of our work, particularly with subjects that concern current matters. Analysis about the loss of life during the Second World War is timeless because nothing is now going to change the nature or extent of the underlying data (unless new discoveries emerge). Analysis of the highest grossing movies today will change as soon as new big movies are released and time elapses. So, once again, this idea of long lasting is very context specific, rather than being a universal goal for data visualisation.

Good design is environmentally friendly: This is, of course, a noble aim but the relevance of this principle has to be positioned again at the contextual level, based on the specific circumstances of a given project. If your work is to be printed, the ink and paper usage immediately removes the notion that it is an environmentally friendly activity. Developing a powerful interactive that is being hammered constantly and concurrently by hundreds of thousands of users puts an extra burden on the hosting server, creating more demands on energy supply. The specific judgements about issues relating to the impact of a project on the environment realistically reside with the protagonists and stakeholders involved.

A point of clarity is that, while I describe them as *design* principles, they actually provide guidance long before you reach the design thinking at the final stage of this workflow. Design choices encapsulate the critical thinking undertaken throughout. Think of it like an iceberg: the design is the visible consequences of lots of hidden preparatory thinking formed through earlier stages.

Finally, a comment is in order about something often raised in discussions about the principles for this subject: that is, the idea that visualisations need to be memorable. This is, in my view, not relevant as a universal principle. If something is memorable, wonderful, that will be a terrific by-product of your design thinking, but in itself the goal of achieving memorability has to be isolated, again, to a contextual level based on the specific goals of a given task and the capacity of the viewer. A politician or a broadcaster might need to recall information more readily in their work than a group of executives in a strategy meeting with permanent access to endless information at the touch of a button via their iPads.

Principle 1: Good Data Visualisation is Trustworthy

The notion of trust is uppermost in your thoughts in this first of the three principles of good visualisation design. This maps directly onto one of Dieter Rams' general principles of good design, namely that good design is honest.

Trust vs Truth

This principle is presented first because it is about the fundamental integrity, accuracy and legitimacy of any data visualisation you produce. This should always exist as your primary concern above all else. There should be no compromise here. Without securing trust the entire purpose of doing the work is undermined.

There is an important distinction to make between trust and truth. Truth is an obligation. You should never create work you know to be misleading in content, nor should you claim something presents the truth if it evidently cannot be supported by what you are presenting. For most people, the difference between a truth and an untruth should be beyond dispute. For those unable or unwilling to be truthful, or who are ignorant of how to differentiate, it is probably worth putting this book away now: my telling you how this is a bad thing is not likely to change your perspective.

If the imperative for being truthful is clear, the potential for there being multiple different but legitimate versions of 'truth' within the same data-driven context muddies things. In data visualisation there is rarely a singular view of the truth. The glass that is half full is also half empty. Both views are truthful, but which to choose? Furthermore, there are many decisions involved in your work whereby several valid options may present themselves. In these cases you are faced with choices without necessarily having the benefit of theoretical influence to draw out the *right* option. You decide what is right. This creates inevitable biases – no matter how seemingly tiny – that ripple through your work. Your eventual solution is potentially comprised of many well-informed, well-intended and legitimate choices – no doubt – but they will reflect a subjective perspective all the same. All projects represent the outcome of an entirely unique pathway of thought.

'Every number we publish is wrong but it is the best number there is.' **Andrew Dilnott, Chair of the UK Statistics Authority**

You can mitigate the impact of these subjective choices you make, for example, by minimising the amount of assumptions applied to the data you are working with or by judiciously consulting your audience to best ensure their requirements are met. However, pure objectivity is not possible in visualisation.

Rather than view the unavoidability of these biases as an obstruction, the focus should instead be on ensuring your chosen path is trustworthy. In the absence of an objective truth, you need to be able to demonstrate that *your* truth is trustable.

Trust has to be earned but this is hard to secure and very easy to lose. As the translation of a Dutch proverb states, 'trust arrives on foot and leaves on horseback'. Trust is something you can build by eliminating any sense that your version of the truth can be legitimately disputed. Yet, visualisers only have so much control and influence in the securing of trust. A visualisation can be truthful but not viewed as trustworthy. You may have done something with the best of intent behind your decision making, but it may

'Good design is honest. It does not make a product appear more innovative, powerful or valuable than it really is. It does not attempt to manipulate the consumer with promises that cannot be kept.'
Dieter Rams, celebrated Industrial Designer

ultimately fail to secure trust among your viewers for different reasons. Conversely a visualisation can be trustworthy in the mind of the viewer but not truthful, appearing to merit trust yet utterly flawed in its underlying truth. Neither of these are satisfactory: the latter scenario is a choice we control, the former is a consequence we must strive to overcome.

Let's consider a couple of examples to illustrate this notion of trustworthiness. Firstly, think about the trust you might attach respectively to the graphics presented in Figure 1.8 and Figure 1.9. For the benefit of clarity both are extracted from articles discussing issues about home ownership, so each would be accompanied with additional written analysis at their published location. Both charts are portraying the same data and the same analysis; they even arrive at the same summary finding. How do the design choices make you feel about the integrity of each work?

Both portrayals are truthful but in my view the first visualisation, produced by the UK Office for National Statistics (ONS), commands greater credibility and therefore far more trust than the second visualisation, produced by the *Daily Mail*. The primary reason for this begins with the colour choices. They are relatively low key in the ONS graphic: colourful but subdued, yet conveying a certain assurance. In contrast, the *Daily Mail*'s colour palette feels needy, like it is craving my attention

Percentage of each age group that are home owners[5], England, 1981 to 2012

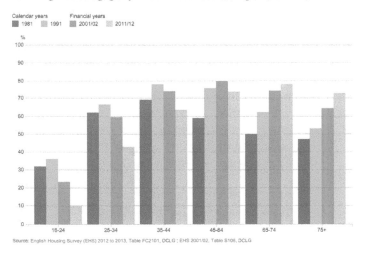

Figure 1.8   Housing and Home Ownership in the UK (ONS)

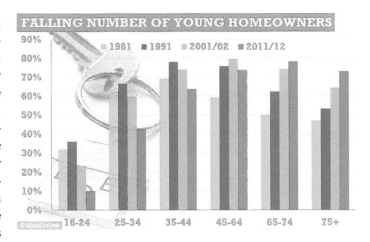

Figure 1.9   Falling Number of Young Homeowners (*Daily Mail*)

with sweetly coloured sticks. I don't care for the house key imagery in the background but it is relatively harmless. Additionally, the typeface, font size and text colour feel more gimmicky in the second graphic. Once again, it feels like it is wanting to shout at me in contrast to the more polite nature of the ONS text. Whereas the *Daily Mail* piece refers to the ONS as the source of the data, it fails to include further details about the data source, which is included on the ONS graphic alongside other important explanatory features such as the subtitle, clarity about the yearly periods and the option to access and download the associated data. The ONS graphic effectively 'shows all its workings' and overall earns, from me at least, significantly more trust.

Another example about the fragility of trust concerns the next graphic, which plots the number of murders committed using firearms in Florida over a period of time. This frames the time around the enactment of the 'Stand your ground' law in the Florida. The area chart in Figure 1.10 shows the number of murders over time and, as you can see, the chart uses an inverted vertical y-axis with the red area going lower down as the number of deaths increases, with peak values at about 1990 and 2007. However, some commentators felt the inversion of the y-axis was deceptive and declared the graphic not trustworthy based on the fact they were perceiving the values as represented by an apparent rising 'white mountain'. They mistakenly observed peak values around 1999 and 2005 based on them seeing these as the highest points. This confusion is caused by an effect known as *figure-ground* perception whereby a background form (white area) can become inadvertently recognised as the foreground form, and vice versa (with the red area seen as the background).

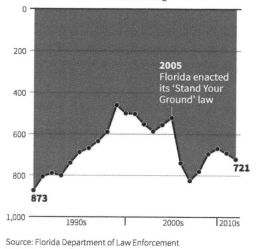

Figure 1.10   Gun Deaths in Florida

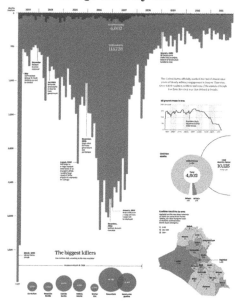

Figure 1.11   Iraq's Bloody Toll

The key point here is that there was no intention to mislead. Although the approach to inverting the y-axis may not be entirely conventional, it was technically legitimate. Creatively speaking, the effect of dribbling blood was an understandably tempting metaphor to pursue. Indeed, the graphic attempts to emulate a notable infographic from several years ago showing the death toll during the Iraq conflict (Figure 1.11). In the case of the Florida graphic, on reflection maybe the data was just too 'smooth' to convey the same dribbling effect achieved in the Iraq piece. However, being inspired and influenced by successful techniques demonstrated by others is to be encouraged. It is one way of developing our skills.

Unfortunately, given the emotive nature of the subject matter – gun deaths – this analysis would always attract a passionate reaction regardless of its form. In this case the lack of trust expressed by some was an unintended consequence of a single, innocent design: by reverting the y-axis to an upward direction, as shown in the reworked version in Figure 1.12, you can see how a single subjective design choice can have a huge influence on people's perception.

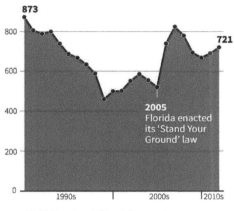

Figure 1.12 Reworking of 'Gun Deaths in Florida'

The creator of the Florida chart will have made hundreds of perfectly sound visualisations and will make hundreds more, and none of them will ever carry the intent of being anything other than truthful. However, you can see how vulnerable perceived trust is when disputes about motives can so quickly surface as a result of the design choice made. This is especially the case within the pressured environment of a newsroom where you have only a single opportunity to publish a work to a huge and widespread audience. Contrast this setting with a graphic published within an organisation that can be withdrawn and reissued far more easily.

Trust Applies Throughout the Process

Trustworthiness is a pursuit that should guide all your decisions, not just the design ones. As you will see in the next chapter, the visualisation design workflow involves a process with many decision junctions – many paths down which you could pursue different legitimate options. Obviously, design is the most visible result of your decision making, but you need to create and demonstrate complete integrity

'My main goal is to represent information accurately and in proper context. This spans from data reporting and number crunching to designing human-centered, intuitive and clear visualizations. This is my sole approach, although it is always evolving.' **Kennedy Elliott, Graphics Editor, The Washington Post**

in the choices made across the entire workflow process. Here is an overview of some of the key matters where trust must be at the forefront of your concern.

Formulating your brief: As mentioned in the discussion about the 'Gun Crimes in Florida' graphic, if you are working with potentially emotive subject matter, this will heighten the importance of demonstrating trust. Rightly or wrongly, your topic will be more exposed to the baggage of prejudicial opinion and trust will be precarious. As you will learn in Chapter 3, part of the thinking involved in 'formulating your brief' concerns defining your audience, considering your subject and establishing your early thoughts about the purpose of your work, and what you are hoping to achieve. There will be certain contexts that lend themselves to exploiting the emotive qualities of your subject and/or data but many others that will not. Misjudge these contextual factors, especially the nature of your audience's needs, and you will jeopardise the trustworthiness of your solution. As I have shown, matters of trust are often outside of your immediate influence: cynicism, prejudice or suspicion held by viewers through their beliefs or opinions is a hard thing to combat or accommodate. In general, people feel comfortable with visualisations that communicate data in a way that fits with their world view. That said, at times, many are open to having their beliefs challenged by data and evidence presented through a visualisation. The platform and location in which your work is published (e.g. website or source location) will also influence trust. Visualisations encountered in already-distrusted media will create obstacles that are hard to overcome.

Working with data: As soon as you begin working with data you have a great responsibility to be faithful to this raw material. To be transparent to your audience you need to consider sharing as much relevant information about how you have handled the data that is being presented to them:

- How was it collected: from where and using what criteria?
- What calculations or modifications have you applied to it? Explain your approach.
- Have you made any significant assumptions or observed any special counting rules that may not be common?
- Have you removed or excluded any data?
- How representative it is? What biases may exist that could distort interpretations?

'Data and data sets are not objective; they are creations of human design. Hidden biases in both the collection and analysis stages present considerable risks [in terms of inference].' **Kate Crawford, Principal Researcher at Microsoft Research NYC**

Editorial thinking: Even with the purest of intent, your role as the curator of your data and the creator of its portrayal introduces subjectivity. When you choose to do one thing you are often choosing to not do something else. The choice to focus on analysis that shows how values have changed over time is also a decision to not show the same data from other viewpoints such as, for example, how it looks on a map. A decision to impose criteria on your analysis, like setting date parameters or minimum value thresholds, in order to reduce clutter, might be sensible and indeed legitimate, but is still a subjective choice.

Data representation: A fundamental tenet of data visualisation is to never deceive the receiver. Avoiding possible misunderstandings, inaccuracies, confusions and distortions is of primary concern. There are many possible features of visualisation design that can lead to varying degrees of deception, whether intended or not. Here are a few to list now, but note that these will be picked up in more detail later:

- The size of geometric areas can sometimes be miscalculated resulting in the quantitative values being disproportionately perceived.
- When data is represented in 3D, on the majority of occasions this represents nothing more than distracting – and distorting – decoration. 3D should only be used when there are legitimately three dimensions of data variables being displayed and the viewer is able to change his or her point of view to navigate to see different 2D perspectives.
- The bar chart value axis should never be 'truncated' – the origin value should always be zero – otherwise this approach will distort the bar size judgements.
- The aspect ratio (height vs width) of a line chart's display is influential as it affects the perceived steepness of connecting lines which are key to reading the trends over time – too narrow and the steepness will be embellished; too wide and the steepness is dampened.
- When portraying spatial analysis through a thematic map representation, there are many different mapping projections to choose from as the underlying apparatus for presenting and orienting the geographical position of the data. There are many different approaches to flatten the spherical globe, translating it into a two-dimensional map form. The mathematical treatment applied can alter significantly the perceived size or shape of regions, potentially distorting their perception.
- Sometimes charts are used in a way that is effectively corrupt, like using pie charts for percentages that add up to more, or less, than 100%.

Data presentation: The main rule here is: if it looks significant, it should be, otherwise you are either misleading or creating unnecessary obstacles for your viewer. The undermining of trust can also be caused by what you decline to explain: restricted or non-functioning features of interactivity.

- Absent annotations such as introduction/guides, axis titles and labels, footnotes, data sources that fail to inform the reader of what is going on.
- Inconsistent or inappropriate colour usage, without explanation.
- Confusing or inaccessible layouts.
- Thoroughness in delivering trust extends to the faith you create through reliability and consistency in the functional experience, especially for interactive projects. Does the solution work and, specifically, does it work in the way it promises to do?

Principle 2: Good Data Visualisation is Accessible

This second of the three principles of good visualisation design helps to inform judgments about how best to facilitate your viewers through the process of understanding. It is informed by three of Dieter Rams' general principles of good design:

2 Good design makes a product useful.
4 Good design makes a product understandable.
5 Good design is unobtrusive.

Reward vs Effort

The opening section of this chapter broke down the stages a viewer goes through when forming their understanding about, and from, a visualisation. This process involved a sequence of perceiving, interpreting and then comprehending. It was emphasised that a visualiser's control over the viewer's pursuit of understanding diminishes after each stage. The objective, as stated by the presented definition, of 'facilitating' understanding reflects the reality of what can be controlled. You can't force viewers to understand, but you can smooth the way.

To facilitate understanding for an audience is about delivering accessibility. That is the essence of this principle: to remove design-related obstacles faced by your viewers when undertaking this process of understanding. Stated another way, a viewer should experience minimum friction between the *act* of understanding (effort) and the *achieving* of understanding (reward).

This 'minimising' of friction has to be framed by context, though. This is key. There are many contextual influences that will determine whether what is judged inaccessible in one situation could be seen as entirely accessible in another. When people are involved, diverse needs exist. As I have already discussed, varying degrees of knowledge emerge and irrational characteristics come to the surface. You can only do so much: do not expect to get all things right in the eyes of every viewer.

'We should pay as much attention to understanding the project's goal in relation to its audience. This involves understanding principles of perception and cognition in addition to other relevant factors, such as culture and education levels, for example. More importantly, it means carefully matching the tasks in the representation to our audience's needs, expectations, expertise, etc. Visualizations are human-centred projects, in that they are not universal and will not be effective for all humans uniformly. As producers of visualizations, whether devised for data exploration or communication of information, we need to take into careful consideration those on the other side of the equation, and who will face the challenges of decoding our representations.' **Isabel Meirelles, Professor, OCAD University (Toronto)**

That is not to say that attempts to accommodate the needs of your audience should just be abandoned, quite the opposite. This is hard but it is essential. Visualisation is about human-centred design, demonstrating empathy for your audiences and putting them at the heart of your decision making.

There are several dimensions of definition that will help you better understand your audiences, including establishing what they know, what they do not know, the circumstances surrounding their consumption of your work and their personal characteristics. Some of these you can accommodate, others you may not be able to, depending on the diversity and practicality of the requirements. Again, in the absence of perfection optimisation is the name of the game, even if this means that sometimes the least worst is best.

The Factors Your Audiences Influence

Many of the factors presented here will occur when you think about your project context, as covered in Chapter 3. For now, it is helpful to introduce some of the factors that specifically relate to this discussion about delivering accessible design.

Subject-matter appeal: This was already made clear in the earlier illustration, but is worth logging again here: the appeal of the subject matter is a fundamental junction right at the beginning of the consumption experience. If your audiences are not interested in the subject – i.e. they are indifferent towards the topic or see no need or relevance to engage with it there and then – then they will not likely stick around. They will probably not be interested in putting in the effort to work through the process of understanding for something that might be ultimately

> 'Data visualization is like family photos. If you don't know the people in the picture, the beauty of the composition won't keep your attention.' **Zach Gemignani, CEO/ Founder of Juice Analytics**

> Many of the ideas for this principle emerged from the Seeing Data visualisation literacy research project (seeingdata.org) on which I collaborated.

irrelevant. For those to whom the subject matter is immediately appealing, they are significantly more likely to engage with the data visualisation right the way through.

Dynamic of need: Do they need to engage with this work or is it entirely voluntary? Do they have a direct investment in having access to this information, perhaps as part of their job and they need this information to serve their duties?

Subject-matter knowledge: What might your audiences know and not know about this subject? What is their capacity to learn or potential motivation to develop their knowledge of this subject? A critical component of this issue, blending existing knowledge with the capacity to acquire knowledge, concerns the distinctions between complicated, complex, simple and simplified. This might seem to be more about the semantics of language but is of significant influence in data visualisation – indeed in any form of communication:

- *Complicated* is generally a technical distinction. A subject might be difficult to understand because it involves pre-existing – and probably high-level – knowledge and might be intricate in its detail. The mathematics that underpinned the Moon landings are complicated. Complicated subjects are, of course, surmountable – the knowledge and skill are acquirable – but only achieved through time and effort, hard work and learning (or extraordinary talent), and, usually, with external assistance.
- *Complex* is associated with problems that have no perfect conclusion or maybe even no end state. Parenting is complex; there is no rulebook for how to do it well, no definitive right or wrong, no perfect way of accomplishing it. The elements of parenting might not be necessarily complicated – cutting Emmie's sandwiches into star shapes – but there are lots of different interrelated pressures always influencing and occasionally colliding.
- *Simple*, for the purpose of this book, concerns a matter that is inherently easy to understand. It may be so small in dimension and scope that it is not difficult to grasp, irrespective of prior knowledge and experience.
- *Simplified* involves transforming a problem context from either a complex or complicated initial state to a reduced form, possibly by eliminating certain details or nuances.

Understanding the differences in these terms is vital. When considering your subject matter and the nature of your analysis you will need to assess whether your audience will be

'Strive for clarity, not simplicity. It's easy to "dumb something down," but extremely difficult to provide clarity while maintaining complexity. I hate the word "simplify." In many ways, as a researcher, it is the bane of my existence. I much prefer "explain," "clarify," or "synthesize." If you take the complexity out of a topic, you degrade its existence and malign its importance. Words are not your enemy. Complex thoughts are not your enemy. Confusion is. Don't confuse your audience. Don't talk down to them, don't mislead them, and certainly don't lie to them.' **Amanda Hobbs, Researcher and Visual Content Editor**

immediately able to understand what you are presenting or have the capacity to learn how to understand it. If it is a subject that is inherently complex or complicated, will it need to be simplified? If you are creating a graphic about taxation, will you need to strip it down to the basics or will this process of simplification risk the subject being oversimplified? The final content may be obscured by the absence of important subtleties. Indeed, the audience may have felt sufficiently sophisticated to have had the capacity to work out and work with a complicated topic, but you denied them that opportunity. You might reasonably dilute/reduce a complex subject for kids, but generally my advice is don't underestimate the capacity of your audience. Accordingly, clarity trumps simplicity as the most salient concern about data visualisation design.

What do they need to know? The million-dollar question. Often, the most common frustration expressed by viewers is that the visualisation 'didn't show them what they were most interested in'. They wanted to see how something changed over time, not how it looked on a map. If you were them what would you want to know? This is a hard thing to second-guess with any accuracy. We will be discussing it further in Chapter 5.

Unfamiliar representation: In the final chapter of this book I will cover the issue of visualisation literacy, discussing the capabilities that go into being the most rounded creator of visualisation work and the techniques involved in being the most effective consumer also. Many people will perhaps be unaware of a deficit in their visualisation literacy with regard to consuming certain chart types. The bar, line and pie chart are very common and broadly familiar to all. As you will see in Chapter 6, there are many more ways of portraying data visually. This deficit in knowing how to read a new or unfamiliar chart type is not a failing on the part of the viewer, it is simply a result of their lack of prior exposure to these different methods. For visualisers a key challenge lies with situations when the deployment of an uncommon chart may be an entirely reasonable and appropriate choice – indeed perhaps even the 'simplest' chart that could have been used – but it is likely to be unfamiliar to the intended viewers. Even if you support it with plenty of 'how to read' guidance, if a viewer is overwhelmed or simply unwilling to make the effort to learn how to read a different chart type, you have little control in overcoming this.

Time: At the point of consuming a visualisation is the viewer in a pressured situation with a lot at stake? Are viewers likely to be impatient and intolerant of the need to spend time learning how to read a display? Do they need quick insights or is there some capacity for them to take on exploring or reading in more depth? If it is the former, the immediacy of the presented information will therefore be a paramount requirement. If they have more time to work through the process of perceiving, interpreting and comprehending, this could be a more conducive situation to presenting complicated or complex subject matter – maybe even using different, unfamiliar chart types.

Format: What format will your viewers need to consume your work? Are they going to need work created for a print output or a digital one? Does this need to be compatible with a small display as on a smartphone or a tablet? If what you create is consumed away from its intended native format, such as viewing a large infographic with small text on a mobile phone, that will likely result in a frustrating experience for the viewer. However, how and where your work is consumed may be beyond your control. You can't mitigate for every eventuality.

Personal tastes: Individual preferences towards certain colours, visual elements and interaction features will often influence (enabling or inhibiting) a viewer's engagement. The semiotic conventions that visualisers draw upon play a part in determining whether viewers are willing to spend time and expend effort looking at a visualisation. Be aware though that accommodating the preferences of one person may not cascade, with similar appeal, to all, and might indeed create a rather negative reaction.

Attitude and emotion: Sometimes we are tired, in a bad mood, feeling lazy, or having a day when we are just irrational. And the prospect of working on even the most intriguing and well-designed project sometimes feels too much. I spend my days looking at visualisations and can sympathise with the narrowing of mental bandwidth when I am tired or have had a bad day. Confidence is an extension of this. Sometimes our audiences may just not feel sufficiently equipped to embark on a visualisation if it is about an unknown subject or might involve pushing them outside their comfort zone in terms of the demands placed on their interpretation and comprehension.

The Factors You Can Influence

Flipping the coin, let's look at the main ways we, as visualisers, can influence (positively or negatively) the accessibility of the designs created. In effect, this entire book is focused on minimising the likelihood that your solution demonstrates any of these negative attributes. Repeating the mantra from earlier, you must avoid doing anything that will cause the boat to go slower.

As you saw listed at the start of this section, the selected, related design principles from Dieter Rams' list collectively include the aim of ensuring our work is useful, unob-

> 'The key difference I think in producing data visualisation/infographics in the service of journalism versus other contexts (like art) is that there is always an underlying, ultimate goal: to be useful. Not just beautiful or efficient – although something can (and should!) be all of those things. But journalism presents a certain set of constraints. A journalist has to always ask the question: How can I make this more useful? How can what I am creating help someone, teach someone, show someone something new?'
> **Lena Groeger, Science Journalist, Designer and Developer at ProPublica**

trusive and understandable. Thinking about what *not* to do – focusing on the likely causes of failure across these aims – is, in this case, more instructive.

Your Solution is Useless

- You have failed to focus on *relevant* content.
- It is not *deep* enough. You might have provided a summary-level/aggregated view of the data when the audience wanted further angles of analysis and greater depth in the details provided.

- A complex subject was *oversimplified*.
- It is not fit for the *setting*. You created work that required too much time to make sense of, when immediate understanding and rapid insights were needed.

Your Solution is Obtrusive

- It is visually *inaccessible*. There is no appreciation of potential impairments like colour blindness and the display includes clumsily ineffective interactive features.
- *Its format* is misjudged. You were supposed to create work fit for a small-sized screen, but the solution created was too fine-detailed and could not be easily read.
- It has too many *functions*. You failed to focus and instead provided too many interactive options when the audience had no desire to put in a lot of effort interrogating and manipulating the display.

You Solution is not Understandable

- Complex *subject* or complex *analysis*. Not explained clearly enough – assumed domain expertise, such as too many acronyms, abbreviations and technical language.
- Used a complex *chart* type. Not enough explanation of how to read the graphic or failure to consider if the audience would be capable of understanding this particular choice of chart type.
- Absent *annotations*. Insufficient details like scales, units, descriptions, etc.

Principle 3: Good Data Visualisation is Elegant

Elegance in design is the final principle of good visualisation design. This relates closely to the essence of three more of Dieter Rams' general principles of good design:

3   Good design is aesthetic.
8   Good design is thorough down to the last detail.
10   Good design is as little design as possible.

What is Elegant Design?

Elegant design is about seeking to achieve a visual quality that will attract your audience and sustain that sentiment throughout the experience, far beyond just the initial moments of engagement. This is presented as the third principle for good reason. Any choices you make towards achieving 'elegance' must not undermine the accomplishment of trustworthiness and accessibility in your design. Indeed, in pursuing the achievement of the other principles, elegance may have already arrived as a by-product of trustworthy and accessible design thinking. Conversely, the visual 'look and feel' of your work will be the first thing viewers encounter before experiencing the consequences of your other principle-led thinking. It therefore stands that optimising the perceived appeal of your work will have a great impact on your viewers.

The pursuit of elegance is elusive, as is its definition: what gives something an elegant quality? As we know, beauty is in the eye of the beholder, but how do we really recognise elegance when we are confronted by it?

When thinking about what the pursuit of elegance of means, the kind of words that surface in my mind are adjectives like *stylish*, *dignified*, *effortless* and *graceful*. For me, they capture the timelessness of elegance, certainly more so than *fancy*, *cool* or *trendy*, which seem more momentary. Elegance is perhaps appreciated more when it is absent from or not entirely accomplished in a design. If something feels cumbersome, inconsistent and lacking a sense of harmony across its composition and use of colour, it is missing that key ingredient of elegance.

> 'When working on a problem, I never think about beauty. I think only how to solve the problem. But when I have finished, if the solution is not beautiful, I know it is wrong.' **Richard Buckminster Fuller, celebrated inventor and visionary**

> 'Complete is when something looks seamless, as if it took little effort to produce.' **Sarah Slobin, Visual Journalist**

When it feels like style over substance has been at the heart of decision-making, no apparent beauty can outweigh the negatives of an obstructed or absent functional experience. While I'm loathe to dwell on forcing a separation in concern between form and function, as a beginner working through the design stages and considering all your options, functional judgements will generally need to be of primary concern. However, it is imperative that you also find room for appropriate aesthetic expression. In due course your experience will lead you to fuse the two perspectives together more instinctively.

In his book *The Shape of Design*, designer Frank Chimero references a Shaker proverb: 'Do not make something unless it is both necessary and useful; but if it is both, do not hesitate to make it beautiful.' In serving the principles of trustworthy and accessible design, you will have hopefully covered both the *necessary* and *useful*. As Chimero suggests, if we have served the mind, our heart is telling us that now is the time to think about beauty.

How Do You Achieve Elegance in Design?

There are several components of design thinking that I believe directly contribute to achieving an essence of elegance.

Eliminate the arbitrary: As with any creative endeavour or communication activity, editing is perhaps the most influential skill, and indeed attitude. Every single design decision you make – every dot, every pixel – should be justifiable. Nothing that remains in your

> '"Everything must have a reason"... A principle that I learned as a graphic designer that still applies to data visualisation. In essence, everything needs to be rationalised and have a logic to why it's in the design/visualisation, or it's out.' **Stefanie Posavec, Information Designer**

work should be considered arbitrary. Even if there isn't necessarily a scientific or theoretical basis for your choices, you should still be able to offer reasons for every thing that is included and also excluded. The reasons you can offer for design options being rejected or removed are just as important in evidence of your developing eye for visualisation design.

Often you will find yourself working alone on a data visualisation project and will therefore need to demonstrate the discipline and competence to challenge yourself. Avoid going through the motions and don't get complacent. Why present data on a map if there is nothing spatially relevant about the regional patterns? Why include slick interactive features if they really add no value to the experience? It is easy to celebrate the brilliance of your amazing ideas and become consumed by work that you have invested deeply in – both your time and emotional energy. Just don't be stubborn or precious. If something is not working, learn to recognise when to not pursue it any further and then kill it.

Thoroughness: A dedicated visualiser should be prepared to agonise over the smallest details and want to resolve even the smallest pixel-width inaccuracies. The desire to treat your work with this level of attention demonstrates respect for your audience: you want them to be able to work with quality so pride yourself on precision. Do not neglect checking, do not cut corners, do not avoid the non-sexy duties, and never stop wanting to do better.

> 'You don't get there [beauty] with cosmetics, you get there by taking care of the details, by polishing and refining what you have. This is ultimately a matter of trained taste, or what German speakers call fingerspitzengefühl ("finger-tip-feeling")'.
> **Oliver Reichenstein, founder of Information Architects (iA)**

Style: This is another hard thing to pin down, especially as the word itself can have different meanings for people, and especially when it has been somewhat 'damaged' by the age-old complaints around something demonstrating style over substance. Developing a style – or signature, as Thomas Clever suggests – is in many ways a manifestation of elegant design. The decisions around colour selection, typography and composition are all matters that influence your style. The development of a style preserves the consistency of your strongest design values, leaving room to respond flexibly to the nuances of each different task you face. It is something that develops in time through the choices you make and the good habits you acquire.

> 'I suppose one could say our work has a certain "signature". "Style" – to me – has a negative connotation of "slapped on" to prettify something without much meaning. We don't make it our goal to have a recognisable (visual) signature, instead to create work that truly matters and is unique. Pretty much all our projects are bespoke and have a different end result. That is one of the reasons why we are more concerned with working according to values and principles that transcend individual projects and I believe that is what makes our work recognisable.'
> **Thomas Clever, Co-founder CLEVER°FRANKE, a data driven experiences studio**

Many news and media organisations seek to devise their own style guides to help visualisers, graphics editors and developers navigate through the choppy waters of design thinking. This is a conscious attempt to foster *consistency* in approach as well as create *efficiency*. In these industries, the perpetual pressure of tight timescales from the relentless demands of the news cycle means that creating efficiency is of enormous value. By taking away the burden of having always to think from scratch about their choices, the visualisers in such organisations are left with more room to concern themselves with the fundamental challenge of *what* to show and not just get consumed by *how* to show it. The best styles will stand out as instantly recognisable: there is a reason why you can instantly pick out the work of the *New York Times*, *National Geographic*, Bloomberg, the *Guardian*, the *Washington Post*, the *Financial Times*, Reuters and the *South China Morning Post*.

Decoration should be additive, not negative: The decorative arts are historically considered to be an intersection of that which is useful and beauty, yet the term decoration when applied to

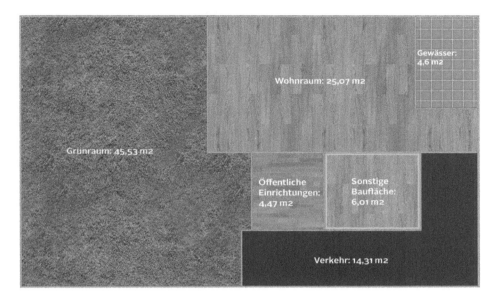

Figure 1.13
If Vienna
Would be an
Apartment

data can often suggest a negative connotation of dressing it up using superfluous devices to attract people, but without any real substance. Visual embellishments are, in moderation and when discernibly deployed, effective devices for securing visual appeal and preserving communicated value. This is especially the case when they carry a certain congruence with the subject matter or key message, such as with the use of the different ground textures in the treemap displayed in Figure 1.13. In this graphic, Vienna is reduced to an illustrative 100m2 apartment and the floor plan presents the proportional composition of the different types of space and land in the city. This is acceptable gratuitousness because the design choices are additive, not negatively obstructive or distracting.

Any design choices you make with the aim of enhancing appeal through novelty or fun need to support, not distract from, the core aim of facilitating understanding. Be led by your data and your audience, not your ideas. There should, though, always be room to explore ways of seeking that elusive blend of being fun, engaging and informative. The bar chart in Figure 1.14 reflects this: using Kit Kat-style fingers of chocolate for each bar and a foil wrapper background, it offers an elegant and appealing presentation that is congruent with its subject.

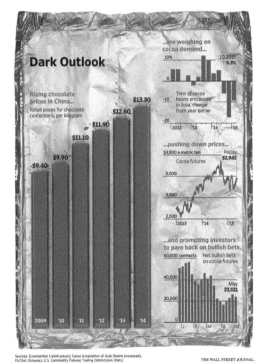

Figure 1.14 Asia Loses Its Sweet Tooth for Chocolate

Allow your personality to express itself in the times and places where such flair is supportive of the aims of facilitating understanding. After all, a singularity of style is a dull existence.

As Groove Armada once sang: 'If everybody looked the same, we'd get tired of looking at each other.'

'I've come to believe that pure beautiful visual works are somehow relevant in everyday life, because they can become a trigger to get people curious to explore the contents these visuals convey. I like the idea of making people say "oh that's beautiful! I want to know what this is about!" I think that probably (or, at least, lots of people pointed that out to us) being Italians plays its role on this idea of "making things not only functional but beautiful".' **Giorgia Lupi, Co-founder and Design Director at Accurat**

Not about minimalism: As expressed by Rams' principle 'Good design is as little design as possible', elegant design achieves a certain invisibility: as a viewer you should not see design, you should see content. This is not to be confused with the pursuit of minimalism, which is a brutal approach that strips away the arbitrary but then cuts deeper. In the context of visualisation, minimalism can be an unnecessarily savage and austere act that may be incongruous with some of the design options you may need to include in your work.

In 'De architectura', a thesis on architecture written around 15 BC by Marcus Vitruvius Pollio, a Roman architect, the author declares how the essence of quality in architecture is framed by the social relevance of the work, not the eventual form or workmanship towards that form. What he is stating here is that good architecture can only be measured according to the value it brings to the people who use it. In a 1624 translation of the work, Sir Henry Wooton offers a paraphrased version of one of Vitruvius's most enduring notions that a 'well building hath three conditions: firmness, commodity, and delight', of which a further interpretation for today might be read as 'sturdy, useful, and beautiful'. One can easily translate these further to fit with these principles of good visualisation design. Trustworthy is sturdy – it is robust, reliable, and has integrity. Useful is accessible – it can be used without undue obstruction. Beautiful is elegant – it appeals and retains attraction.

1.3 Distinctions and Glossary

As in any text, consistency in the meaning of terms or language used around data visualisation is important to preserve clarity for readers. I began this chapter with a detailed breakdown of a proposed definition for the subject. There are likely to be many other terms that you either are familiar with or have heard being used. Indeed, there are significant overlaps and commonalities of thought between data visualisation and pursuits like, for example, infographic design.

As tools and creative techniques have advanced over the past decade, the traditional boundaries between such fields begin to blur. Consequently, the practical value of preserving dogmatic distinctions reduces accordingly. Ultimately, the visualiser tasked with creating a visual portrayal of data is probably less concerned about whether their creation will be filed under 'data visualisation' or 'infographic' as long as it achieves the aim of helping the audience achieve understanding.

Better people than me attach different labels to different works interchangeably, perhaps reflecting the fact that these dynamic groups of activities are all pursuing similar aims and using the same raw material – data – to achieve them. Across this book you will see plenty of references to and examples of works that might not be considered data visualisation design work in the purest sense. You will certainly see plenty of examples of infographics.

The traditional subject distinctions still deserve to be recognised and respected. People are rightfully proud of identifying with a discipline they have expertise or mastery in. And so, before you step into the design workflow chapters, it is worthwhile to spend a little time establishing clarifications and definitions for some of the related fields and activities so all readers are on the same page of understanding. Additionally, there is a glossary of the terms used that will help you more immediately understand the content of later chapters. It makes sense to position those clarifications in this chapter as well.

Distinctions

Data vis: Just to start with one clarification. While the abbreviated term of data visualisation might be commonly seen as 'data vis' (or 'data viz'; don't get me started on the 'z' issue), and this is probably how all the cool kids on the street and those running out of characters on Twitter refer to it, I am sticking with the full *Sunday* name of 'data visualisation' or at the very least the shortened term 'visualisation'.

Information visualisation: There are many who describe data visualisation as information visualisation and vice versa, myself included, without a great deal of thought for the possible differences. The general distinction, if there is any, tends to be down to one's emphasis on the input material (data) or the nature of the output form (information). It is also common that information visualisation is used as the term to define work that is primarily concerned with visualising abstract data structures such as trees or graphs (networks) as well as other qualitative data (therefore focusing more on relationships rather than quantities).

Infographics: The classic distinction between infographics and data visualisation concerns the format and the content. Infographics were traditionally created for print consumption, in newspapers or magazines, for example. The best infographics explain things graphically – systems, events, stories – and could reasonably be termed explanation graphics. They contain charts (visualisation elements) but may also include illustrations, photo-imagery, diagrams and text. These days, the art of infographic design continues to be produced in static form, irrespective of how and where they are published.

Over the past few years there has been an explosion in different forms of infographics. From a purist perspective, this new wave of work is generally viewed as being an inferior form of infographic design and may be better suited to terms like info-posters or tower graphics (these commonly exist with a fixed-width dimension in order to be embedded into websites and social media platforms). Often these works will be driven by marketing intent through a desire to get hits/viewers, generally with the compromising of any real valuable delivery of understanding. It is important not to dismiss entirely the evident – if superficial – value of this type of work, as demonstrated by the occasionally incredible numbers for hits received. If your motive is 'bums on seats' then this approach will serve you well. However, I would question the legitimacy of attaching the term infographic to these designs and I sense the popular interest in these forms is beginning to wane.

Visual analytics: Some people use this term to relate to analytical-style visualisation work, such as dashboards, that serve the role of operational decision support systems or provide instruments of business intelligence. Additionally, the term visual analytics is often used to describe the analytical reasoning and exploration of data facilitated by interactive tools. This aligns with the pursuit of exploratory data analysis that I will be touching on in Chapter 5.

Data art: Aside from the disputes over the merits of certain infographic work, data art is arguably the other discipline related to visualisation that stirs up the most debate. Those creating data art are often pursuing a different motive to pure data visualisation, but its sheer existence still manages to wind up many who perhaps reside in the more 'purest' visualisation camps. For data artists the raw material is still data but their goal is not driven by facilitating the kind of understanding that a data visualisation would offer. Data art is more about pursuing a form of self-expression or aesthetic exhibition using data as the paint and algorithms as the brush. As a viewer, whether you find meaning in displays of data art is entirely down to your personal experience and receptiveness to the open interpretation it invites.

Information design: Information design is a design practice concerned with the presentation of information. It is often associated with the activities of data visualisation, as it shares the underlying motive of facilitating understanding. However, in my view, information design has a much broader application concerned with the design of many different forms of visual communication, such as way-finding devices like hospital building maps or in the design of utility bills.

Data science: As a field, data science is hard to define, so it is easier to consider this through the ingredients of the role of data scientists. They possess a broad repertoire of capabilities covering the gathering, handling and analysing of data. Typically this data is of a large size and complexity and originates from multiple sources. Data scientists will have strong mathematical, statistical and computer science skills, not to mention astute business experience and many notable 'softer' skills like problem solving, communication and presentation. If you find somebody with all these skills, tie them to a desk (legally) and never ever let them leave your organisation.

Data journalism: Also known as *data-driven journalism* (DDJ), this concerns the increasingly recognised importance of having numerical, data and computer skills in the journalism field. In a sense it is an adaption of data visualisation but with unquestionably deeper roots in the responsibilities of the reporter/journalist.

Scientific visualisation: This is another form of a term used by many people for different applications. Some give exploratory data analysis the label *scientific visualisation* (drawing out the scientific methods for analysing and reasoning about data). Others relate it to the use of visualisation for conceiving highly complex and multivariate datasets specifically concerning matters with a scientific bent (such as the modelling functions of the brain or molecular structures).

Glossary

The precision and consistency of language in this field can get caught up in a little too much semantic debate at times, but it is important to establish early on some clarity about its usage and intent in this book at least.

Roles and Terminology

Project: For the purpose of this book, you should consider any data visualisation creation activity to be consistent with the idea of a project. Even if what you are working on is only seen as the smallest of visualisation tasks that hardly even registers on the bullet points of a to-do list, you should consider it a project that requires the same rigorous workflow process approach.

Visualiser: This is the role I am assigning to you – the person making the visualisation. It could be more realistic to use a term like researcher, analyst, creator, practitioner, developer, storyteller or, to be a little pretentious, visualist. Designer would be particularly appropriate but I want to broaden the scope of the role beyond just the design thinking to cover all aspects of this discipline.

Viewer: This is the role assigned to the recipient, the person who is viewing and/or using your visualisation product. It offers a broader and better fit than alternatives such as consumer, reader, recipient or customer.

Audience: This concerns the collective group of people to whom you are intending to serve your work. Within the audience there will be cohorts of different viewer types that you might characterise through distinct personas to help your thinking about serving the needs of target viewers.

Consuming: This will be the general act of the viewer, to consume. I will use more active descriptions like 'reading' and 'using' when consuming becomes too passive and vague, and when distinctions are needed between reading text and using interactive features.

Creating: This will be the act of the visualiser, to create. This term will be mainly used in contrast with *consuming* to separate the focus between the act of the visualiser and the act of the viewer.

Data Terminology

Data is: I'm sorry 'data are' fans, but that's just not how normal people speak. In this book, it's going to be 'data is' all the way. Unless my editor disagrees, in which case you won't even see this passage.

Raw data: Also known as *primary data*, this is data that has not been subjected to statistical treatment or any other transformation to prepare it for usage. Some people have a problem with the implied 'rawness' this term claims, given that data will have already lost its purity having been recorded by some measurement instrument, stored, retrieved and maybe cleaned already. I understand this view, but am going to use the term regardless because I think most people will understand its intent.

Dataset: A dataset is a collection of data values upon which a visualisation is based. It is useful to think of a dataset as taking the form of a table with rows and columns, usually existing in a spreadsheet or database.

Tabulation: A table of data is based on rows and columns. The rows are the records – instances of things – and the columns are the variables – details about the things. Datasets are visualised in order to 'see' the size, patterns and relationships that are otherwise hard to observe. For the purpose of this book, I distinguish between types of datasets that are 'normalised' and others that are 'cross-tabulated'. This distinction will be explained in context during Chapter 5.

Variables: Variables are related items of data held in a dataset that describe a characteristic of those records. It might be the names, dates of birth, genders and salaries of a department of employees. Think of variables as the different columns of values in a table, with the variable name being the descriptive label on the header row. There are different types of variables including, at a general level, quantitative (e.g. salary) and categorical (e.g. gender). A chart plots the relationship between different variables. For example, a bar chart might show the number of staff (with the size of bar showing the quantity) across different departments (one bar for each department or category).

Series: A series of values is essentially a row (or column, depending on table layout) of related values in a table. An example of a series of values would be all the highest temperatures in a city for each month of the year. Plotting this on a chart, like a line chart, would produce a line for that city's values across the year. Another line could be added to compare temperatures for another city thus presenting a further series of values.

Data source: This is the term used to describe the origin of data or information used to construct the analysis presented. This is an important feature of annotation that can help gain trust from viewers by showing them all they need to know about the source of the data.

Big Data: Big Data is characterised by the 3Vs – high volume (millions of rows of data), high variety (hundreds of different variables/columns) and high velocity (new data that is created rapidly and frequently, every millisecond). A database of bank transactions or an extract from a social media platform would be typical of Big Data. It is necessary to take out some of the hot air spouted about Big Data in its relationship with data visualisation. The 'Bigness' (one always feels obliged to include a capitalised B) of data does not fundamentally change the tasks one faces when creating a data visualisation, it just makes it a more significant prospect to work through. It broadens the range of possibilities, it requires stronger and more advanced technology resources, and it amplifies the pressures on time and resources. With more options the discipline of choice becomes of even greater significance.

Visualisation

Chart type: Charts are individual, visual representations of data. There are many ways of representing your data, using different combinations of marks, attributes, layouts and apparatus: these combinations form archetypes of charts, commonly reduced to simply *chart types*. There are some charts you might already be familiar with, such as the bar chart, pie chart or line chart, while others may be new to you, like the Sankey diagram, treemap or choropleth map.

Graphs, charts, plots, diagrams and maps: Traditionally the term *graph* has been used to describe visualisations that display network relationships and *chart* would be commonly used to label common devices like the bar or pie chart. *Plots* and *diagrams* are more specifically attached to special types of displays but with no pattern of consistency in their usage. All these terms are so interchangeable that useful distinction no longer exists and any energy expended in championing meaningful difference is wasted. For the purpose of this book, I will generally stick to the term *chart* to act as the single label to cover all visualisation forms. In some cases, this umbrella label will incorporate maps for the sake of convenience even though they clearly have a unique visual structure that is quite different from most charts. By the way, the noise you just heard is every cartographer reading this book angrily closing it shut in outrage at the sheer audacity of my lumping maps and charts together.

Graphic: The term *graphic* will be more apt when referring to visuals focused more on information-led explanation diagrams (infographics), whereas *chart* will be more concerned with data-driven visuals.

Storytelling: The term *storytelling* is often attached to various activities around data visualisation and is a contemporary buzzword often spread rather thinly in the relevance of its usage. It is a *thing* but not nearly as much a *thing* as some would have you believe. I will be dampening some of the noise that accompanies this term in the next chapter.

Format: This concerns the difference in output form between printed work, digital work and physical visualisation work.

Function: This concerns the difference in functionality of a visualisation, whether it is static or interactive. Interactive visualisations allow you to manipulate and interrogate a computer-based display of data. The vast majority of interactive visualisations are found on websites but increasingly might also exist within apps on tablets and smartphones. In contrast, a static visualisation displays a single-view, non-interactive display of data, often presented in print but also digitally.

Axes: Many common chart types (such as the bar chart and line chart) have axis lines that provide reference for measuring quantitative values or assigning positions to categorical values. The horizontal axis is known as the x-axis and the vertical axis is known as the y-axis.

Scale: Scales are marks on axes that describe the range of values included in a chart. Scales are presented as intervals (10, 20, 30, etc.) representing units of measurement, such as prices, distances, years or percentages, or in keys that explain the associations between, for example, different sizes of areas or classifications of different colour attributes.

Legend: All charts employ different visual attributes, such as colours, shapes or sizes, to represent values of data. Sometimes, a legend is required to house the 'key' that explains what the different scales or classifications mean.

Outliers: Outliers are points of data that are outside the normal range of values. They are the unusually large or small or simply different values that stand out and generally draw attention from a viewer – either through amazement at their potential meaning or suspicion about their accuracy.

Correlation: This is a measure of the presence and extent of a mutual relationship between two or more variables of data. You would expect to see a correlation between height and weight or age and salary. Devices like scatter plots, in particular, help visually to portray possible correlations between two quantitative values.

Summary: Defining Data Visualisation

In this chapter you have learned a definition of data visualisation: 'The representation and presentation of data to facilitate understanding.' The process of understanding a data visualisation involves three stages, namely:

- Perceiving: what can I see?
- Interpreting: what does it mean?
- Comprehending: what does it mean to me?

You were also introduced to the three principles of good visualisation design:

- Good data visualisation is trustworthy.
- Good data visualisation is accessible.
- Good data visualisation is elegant.

Finally, you were presented with an array of descriptions and explanations about some of the key terms and language used in this field and throughout the book.

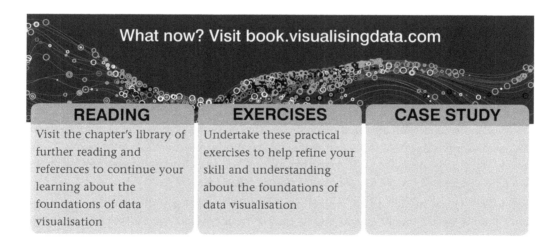

What now? Visit book.visualisingdata.com

READING	EXERCISES	CASE STUDY
Visit the chapter's library of further reading and references to continue your learning about the foundations of data visualisation	Undertake these practical exercises to help refine your skill and understanding about the foundations of data visualisation	

2

Visualisation Workflow

Clear, effective and efficient thinking is the critical difference between a visualisation that succeeds and one that fails. You cannot expect just to land accidentally on a great solution. You have got to work for it.

In this chapter I will outline the data visualisation workflow that forms the basis of this book's structure and content. This workflow offers a creative and analytical process that will guide you from an initial trigger that instigates the need for a visualisation through to developing your final solution.

You will learn about the importance of process thinking, breaking down the components of a visualisation design challenge into sequenced, manageable chunks. This chapter will also recommend some practical tips and good habits to ensure the workflow is most effectively adopted.

2.1 The Importance of Process

As I have already established, the emphasis of this book is on better decision making. There are so many different things to think about when creating a data visualisation, regardless of whether the output will be the simplest of charts or the most ambitious of multi-faceted digital implementations.

The decisions you will face will inevitably vary in the weight of their significance. There will be some big choices – matters like defining your editorial angles and selecting the best fit chart type – and many seemingly small ones – such as picking the precise shade of grey for a chart's axis labels. The process of creating a visualisation generally follows the Pareto principle, whereby 20% of decisions made have implications for about 80% of the final visible design. However, just because some decisions will appear more significant in the final output, as visualisers we need to attend to every single decision equally, caring about detail, precision and accuracy.

To repeat, one of the main mental barriers to overcome for those new to the field is to acknowledge that the pursuit of *perfect* in data visualisation is always unfulfilled. There are better and there are worse solutions, but there is no perfect. Perfect exists in an artificial vacuum. It is free of pressures, has no constraints. That is not real life. There will always be forces pushing and pulling you in different directions. There may be frustrating shortcomings in the data you will have to work with or limitations with your technical capabilities. As discussed, people – your audience members – introduce huge inconsistencies. They – we – are complex, irrational and primarily different. Accepting the absence of perfection helps us unburden ourselves somewhat from the constant nagging sense that we missed out on discovering *the* perfect solution. This can prove quite liberating.

That is not to say our ambitions need to be lowered. Quite the opposite. We should still strive for *best*, the absolute optimum solution given the circumstances we face. To achieve this requires improved effectiveness and efficiency in decision making. We need to make better calls, more quickly. The most reliable approach to achieving this is by following a design process.

The process undertaken in this book is structured around the following stages (Figure 2.1).

Figure 2.1
The Four
Stages of the
Visualisation
Workflow

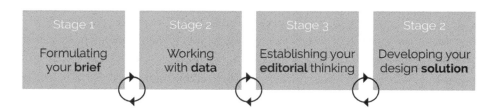

Here are a few observations about this process ahead of its commencement.

Pragmatic: This process aims to provide a framework for thinking, rather than instructions for learning. As described in the Introduction, there are very few universal rules to rely upon. While the comfort provided by rules is what many might seek at the beginning of their learning journey, flexible pragmatism beats dogmatism in any situation. Useful rules do exist in visualisation but are often related to quite micro-level matters. I will come to discuss these in due course.

Reducing the randomness of your approach: The value of the process is that it guides your entry and closing points: where and how to begin your work as well as how and when it will be finished. When you are new to data visualisation, the sheer extent of things to think about can be quite an overwhelming prospect. This workflow approach aims to break down activities into a connected system of thinking that will help to organise and preserve the cohesiveness of your activities. The process incrementally leads you towards developing a solution, with each stage building on the last and informing the next. The core purpose of the approach is to give you a greater sense of the options that exist at each stage and provide you with better information with which to make your choices.

Protect experimentation: The systematic approach I am advocating in this book should not be seen as squeezing out the scope for creativity or eradicating any space for experimentation. It is natural to want to reduce wasted effort, but at the same time it is absolutely vital to seek opportunities – in the right places – for imagination to blossom. In reality, many of the projects you will work on will not necessarily rely on much creative input. There will be projects that have pressures on time – and a need to compromise on experimenting in favour of the desire for efficiency. There will be subjects or datasets that you work with that are just not congruent with overt creative thinking. It is about striking a balance, affording time on those activities that will bring the right blend of value to suit each context.

> 'I truly feel that experimentation (even for the sake of experimentation) is important, and I would strongly encourage it. There are infinite possibilities in diagramming and visual communication, so we have much to explore yet. I think a good rule of thumb is to never allow your design or implementation to obscure the reader understanding the central point of your piece. However, I'd even be willing to forsake this, at times, to allow for innovation and experimentation. It ends up moving us all forward, in some way or another.' **Kennedy Elliott, Graphics Editor, The *Washington Post***

Facilitate adaptability and iteration: This workflow is characterised as a design process rather than a procedure. A good process should facilitate the adaptability and remove the inflexibility of a defined procedure of operation. Although the activities are introduced and presented in this book in a linear fashion, inevitably there is much iteration that takes place. There will be times when you will have to revisit decisions, maybe even redo activities in a completely different way given what you have discovered further down the line. If you make mistakes or bad calls – and everyone does – it is important to fail gracefully but recover quickly. You will need to be able to respond to changes in circumstances and accommodate their impact fast. A good process cushions the impact of situations arising like this.

The first occasion, not the last: It is important to note that the tasks you face at each stage in the process will represent the first occasion you pay attention to these matters, but not the final occasion. There is something of a trickle-down effect here. Many of the concerns you will be faced with at the start of a challenge will likely continue to echo in your thoughts right through to the end. Some things are just not possible to close off that easily. Take the ongoing demands of profiling who your audiences are and what they might need. That thinking starts early and should actually never drop off your radar. The nature of the process gives you the best chance of keeping all the plates spinning that need to be spun, knowing which ones can be left to drop and when.

Always the same process: The range of visualisation challenges you will face in your career will vary. Even if you are producing the same work every month, no two projects will provide the same experience: just having an extra month of data means it has a new shape or size. It is different. Some projects you work on will involve fairly simple data, others will involve hugely complex data. In some cases you will have perhaps two hours or two days to deliver a solution, in others you might have two months. The key thing is that the process you follow will always require the same activities in the same sequence, regardless of the size, speed and complexity of your challenge. The main difference is that any extremes in the circumstances you face will amplify the stresses at each stage of the process and place greater demands on the need for thorough, effective and timely decision making.

'You need a design eye to design, and a non-designer eye to feel what you designed. As Paul Klee said, "See with one eye, feel with the other".' **Oliver Reichenstein, founder of Information Architects (iA)**

Partitioning your mindset: Within each of the sequenced stages listed in Figure 2.1 there will be different demands on your mindset: sometimes you are thinking, sometimes you are doing, sometimes you are making. When you are working alone, especially, it is important to appreciate the activities that will require different mindsets:

- *Thinking:* The duties here will be conceptual in nature, requiring imagination and judgment, such as formulating your curiosity, defining your audience's needs, reasoning your editorial perspectives, and making decisions about viable design choices.
- *Doing:* These are practical tasks that will still engage the brain, obviously, but manifest themselves through more hands-on activities like sketching ideas and concepts, learning about a subject through research, gathering and handling your data.
- *Making:* These involve the constructive and technical activities that specifically relate to the production cycle as you face the challenge of translating promising, well-considered design concepts into effective, working solutions.

2.2 The Process in Practice

Throughout this book I will call out key points of advice in the form of useful tips, tactics or good habits you should be looking to consider employing. Many of these have been informed by interviews with some of the brilliant people working in this field today. As you are about to commence the design workflow here are some pieces of advice that transcend any individual stage of the process.

Managing progress and resources: Good planning, time and resource management keep a process cohesive and progressing. They represent the lubricant. You will rarely have the luxury of working on a project that has no defined end date and so adhering to imposed or self-imposed timescales is especially important. It is very easy to get swallowed up by the demands of certain activities, particularly those involved in the 'working with data' stage. Similarly the production cycle (which takes place during and beyond Part C), as you iterate between idea, prototype and construction, can at times appear never to have an end in sight. As one task is finished, another two always seem to appear. As you get closer to a deadline you will either sink or swim: for some the pressure of time is crippling; others thrive on the adrenaline it brings and their focus is sharpened as a result. Recognising the need to factor in time for some of the broader responsibilities – clerical tasks, arranging demo meetings and skype calls, file management and running backups – will prove hugely beneficial by the end.

Room to think: On the theme of task duration and progress, it is important to build in the capacity to think. The notion of brain 'states' is relevant here, in particular the 'alpha' state which kicks in most commonly when we are particularly relaxed. Being in this state helps to heighten your imagination, learning and thought process. Apologies for the mental image but I do some of my most astute thinking in the shower or bath, and just before going to sleep at night. These are the occasions when I am most likely drifting into a relaxed alpha state and help me to contemplate most clearly the thoughts and ideas I might have. I find train or air travel achieves the same as does lying on a beach. Unfortunately in the latter scenario I just don't care enough about work in that moment to note down my frequent genius ideas (what do you mean 'which ones'?). If I have a task that will take two days of my time but the deadline is further away, I typically try to break down the time I give to it across smaller clusters of three to four hours spread across four days of activity in order to create sufficient opportunities for my brain to tick over during the intervening gaps and hopefully allow good ideas to ferment.

Heuristics to support decisions: As I have discussed, there will be occasions when the *best* choice does not present itself, when time is pressurising you and when you will need to make a call. You might have to occasionally rely on heuristic techniques that help to speed up your decision-making at certain stages. Although this might seem an unsatisfactory tactic to consider, given the previously stated need to eliminate arbitrary choices, heuristics can remain consistent with this desire when they rely on educated, intuitive or common-sense judgements. As you develop your experience, the astuteness of such heuristic judgments will be increasingly reliable to fall back on when the need arises.

Pen and paper: The humble pairing of pen and paper will prove to be a real ally throughout your process. I will not over-sentimentally claim this is the most important tool combination because, unless you are producing artisan hand-drawn work, you will have other technical tools that would probably rise up the importance list. However, the point here is that capturing ideas and creating sketches are a critical part of your process. Do not rely on your memory; if you have a great idea sketch it down. This activity is never about artistic beauty. It does not need you to be an artist, it just needs you to get things out of your head and onto paper, particularly if you are collaborating with others. If you are incredibly fortunate to be so competent with a given tool that you find it more natural than using pen and paper to 'sketch' ideas quickly, then this is of course absolutely fine, as long as it is indeed the quickest medium to do so.

Note-taking: Whether this is via pen and paper, or in Word, or a Google doc, note-taking is a vital habit to get into. This is about preserving records of important details such as:

- information about the sources of data you are using;
- calculations or manipulations you have applied to your data;
- assumptions you have made;
- data descriptions, particularly if explanations have been offered to use verbally by somebody who knows the data well;
- questions you have yet to get answers to;
- the answers you did get to your questions;
- terminology, abbreviations, codes – things you need to remember the meaning and associations in your data;
- task lists and wish lists of features or ideas you would like to consider pursuing;
- issues or problems you can foresee;
- websites or magazines that you saw and gave you a bit of inspiration;
- ideas you have had or rejected.

'Because I speak the language of data, I can talk pretty efficiently with the experts who made it. It doesn't take them long, even if the subject is new to me, for them to tell me any important caveats or trends. I also think that's because I approach that conversation as a journalist, where I'm mostly there to listen. I find if you listen, people talk. (It sounds so obvious but it is so important.) I find if you ask an insightful question, something that makes them say "oh, that's a good point," the whole conversation opens up. Now you're both on the same side, trying to get this great data to the public in an understandable way.' **Katie Peek, Data Visualization Designer and Science Journalist**

Note-taking is easier said than done, and I am among the least natural note-takers to roam this Earth, but I have forced it into becoming a habit and a valuable one at that.

Communication: Communication is a two-way activity. Firstly, it is about listening to stakeholders (clients or colleagues) and your audience: what do they want, what do they expect, what ideas do they have? In particular, what knowledge do they have about your subject? Secondly, communication is about speaking to others: presenting ideas, updating on progress, seeking feedback, sharing your thoughts about possible solutions, and promoting and selling your work (regardless of the setting, you will need to do this). If you do not know the intimate details of your subject matter you will need to locate others who do: find smart people who know the subject better than you or find smart people who do not know the subject but are just smart. You cannot avoid the demands of communicating so do not hide behind your laptop – get out there and speak and listen to people who can help you.

'Research is key. Data, without interpretation, is just a jumble of words and numbers – out of context and devoid of meaning. If done well, research not only provides a solid foundation upon which to build your graphic/visualisation, but also acts as a source of inspiration and a guidebook for creativity. A good researcher must be a team player with the ability to think critically, analytically, and creatively. They should be a proactive problem solver, identifying potential pitfalls and providing various roadmaps for overcoming them. In short, their inclusion should amplify, not restrain, the talents of others.' **Amanda Hobbs, Researcher and Visual Content Editor**

Research: Connected to the need for good communication is the importance of research. This is an activity that will exist as a constant, running along the spine of your process thinking. You cannot know everything about your subject, about the meaning of your data, about the relevant and irrelevant qualities it possesses. As you will see later, data itself can only tell us so much; often it just tells us where interesting things might exist, not what actually explains why they are interesting.

Attention to detail: Like note-taking, this will be something that might not be a natural trait for some but is so important. You cannot afford to carry any errors in your work. Start every project with that commitment. This is such an important ingredient to securing trust in your work. The process you are about to learn is greatly influenced by the concept of 'aggregation of marginal gains'. You need to sweat the small stuff. Even if many of your decisions seem small and inconsequential, they deserve your full attention and merit being done right, always. You should take pride in the fine detail of your design thinking, so embrace the need for checking and testing. If you are so immersed in your work that you become blind to it, get others to help – call on those same smart people you identified above. As someone who once published a graphic stating Iran's population was around 80 billion and not 80 million, I know how one tiny mistake can cause the integrity of an entire project to crumble to the ground. You do not get a second chance at a first impression, somebody once said. I forget who, I wasn't paying attention …

Make it work for you: The only way you will truly find out whether a process works for you is if you practise it, relentlessly. As I have stated, every project will be different even if only in small ways. However, if you just cannot get the approach presented in this book to fit your personality or purpose, modify it. We are all different. Do not feel like I am imposing this single approach. Take it as a proposed framework based on what has worked for me in the past. Bend it, stretch it, and make it work. As you become more experienced (and confident through having experienced many different types of challenges) the many duties involved in data visualisation design will become second nature, by which time you probably will no longer be aware of even observing a process.

Be honest with yourself: Feedback, editing, not doing certain things, are disciplines of the effective visualiser. Honesty with yourself is vital, especially as you are often working on a solo project but need so many different skill

> 'No work is ever wasted. If it's not working, let go and move on – it'll come back around to be useful later.' **Emma Coats, freelance Film Director, formerly of Pixar**

sets and mindsets. As I mentioned in the last section, preciousness or stubbornness that starts to impede on quality becomes destructive. Being blind to things that are not working, or not taking on board constructive feedback just because you have invested so much time in something, will prove to be the larger burden. Do not be afraid to kill things when they are not working.

Learn: Reflective learning is about looking back over your work, examining the output and evaluating your approach. What did you do well? What would you do differently? How well did you manage your time? Did you make the best decisions you could given the constraints that existed? Beyond private reflections, some of the best material about data visualisation on the Web comes from people sharing narratives about their design processes. Read how other people undertake their challenges. Maybe share your own? You will find you truly learn about something when you find the space to write about it and explain it to others. Write up your projects, present your work to others and, in doing so, that will force you to think 'why did I do what I did?'.

Summary: Data Visualisation Workflow

In this chapter you were introduced to the design workflow, which involves four key stages:

1 Formulating your brief: planning, defining and initiating your project.
2 Working with data: going through the mechanics of gathering, handling and preparing your data.
3 Establishing your editorial thinking: defining what you will show your audience.
4 Developing your design solution: considering all the design options and beginning the production cycle.

Undertaking the activities in this workflow require you to partition your mindset:

- Thinking: conceptual tasks, decision making.
- Doing: practical undertakings like sketching, visually examining data.
- Making: technical duties like analysing data, constructing the solution.

Finally, you were presented with some general tips and tactics ahead of putting the process into practice:

- This will be the first time you think about each of the stages and activities, not the last – visualisation design is as much about plate-spinning management as anything else.
- The importance of good project management to manage progress and resources cannot be over-emphasised.
- Create room to think: clear thinking helps with efficiency of effort.
- Pen and paper will prove to be one of your key tools.
- Note-taking is a habit worth developing.
- Communication is a two-way relationship: it is speaking *and* listening.
- Attention to detail is an obligation: the integrity of your work is paramount.
- Make the workflow work for you: practise and adapt the approach to suit you.
- Be honest with yourself, do not be precious and have the discipline not to do things, to kill ideas, to avoid scope-creep.

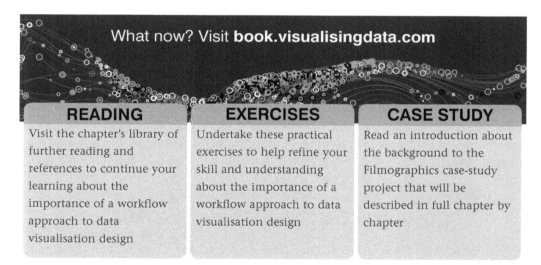

What now? Visit **book.visualisingdata.com**

READING	EXERCISES	CASE STUDY
Visit the chapter's library of further reading and references to continue your learning about the importance of a workflow approach to data visualisation design	Undertake these practical exercises to help refine your skill and understanding about the importance of a workflow approach to data visualisation design	Read an introduction about the background to the Filmographics case-study project that will be described in full chapter by chapter

Part B

The Hidden Thinking

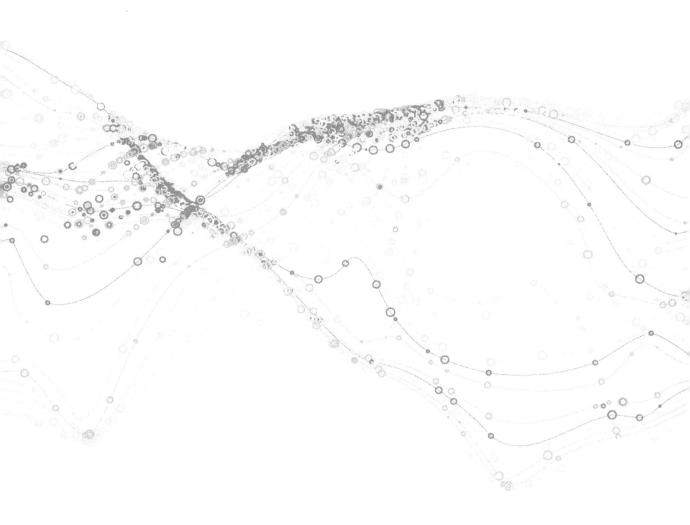

3

Formulating Your Brief

In Chapter 2 you learnt about the importance of process, taking on data visualisation challenges using a design workflow to help you make good decisions. This third chapter initiates the process with formulating your brief.

The essence of this stage is to identify the context in which your work will be undertaken and then define its aims: it is the who, what, why, where, when and how. It can be as formal – and shared with others – or as informal an activity as you need to make it.

The first contextual task will be to consider why you are producing this data visualisation – what is its *raison d'être*? To answer this, you will need to define what triggered it (the origin curiosity) and what it is aiming to accomplish (the destination purpose). Recognising that no visualisation projects are ever entirely free of constraints or limitations, you will also need to identify the circumstances surrounding the project that will shape the scope and nature of the project you're about to undertake.

Following these contextual definitions you will briefly switch your attention to consider a vision for your work. With the origin and intended destination mapped out you will be able to form an initial idea about what will be the best-fit type of design solution. You will be introduced to the purpose map, which provides a landscape of all the different types of visualisation you *could* pursue, helping you establish an early sense of what you *should* pursue. To wrap up the chapter, you will allocate some time to harness the instinctive thoughts you might have had about the ideas, images, keywords and inspirations that you feel could play a role in your work.

Collectively this work will provide you with a solid foundation from which to best inform all your subsequent workflow process stages.

3.1 What is a Brief?

In its simplest form a brief represents a set of expectations and captures all the relevant information about a task or project. It is commonly associated with the parlance of project management or graphic design, but in data visualisation the need to establish clarity about the definitions and requirements of a project is just as relevant. This is about establishing the context of and vision for your work.

When you are working with clients or colleagues it will be in the interests of all parties to have a mutual understanding of the project's requirements and some agreement over the key deliverables. In such situations you may have already been issued with some form of initial brief from these stakeholders. This could be as informal as an emailed or verbal request or as formal as a template-based briefing document. Irrespective of what has been issued you will get more value from compiling your own briefing document to ensure you have sufficient information to plan your upcoming work.

If you are not working for or with others – essentially pursuing work that you have initiated yourself – you clearly will not have been issued with any brief, but once again, it will be to your advantage to compile a brief for yourself. This does not have to be an overly burdensome or bureaucratic task. I use a simple checklist that is not only practically lightweight but also comprehensively helpful, comprising a series of question prompts that I either answer myself or raise with those stakeholders with whom I am working.

For some beginners, this stage can feel somewhat frustrating. On the surface it sounds like a clerical prospect when what you really want is just to get on with the good stuff, like playing with the data and focusing on creativity. Understanding contextual matters, in particular before anything else, is too invaluable a practice to neglect. All the decisions that follow in this workflow will be shaped around the definitions you establish now. There may be changes but you will reap the benefits from gaining as much early clarity as possible.

3.2 Establishing Your Project's Context
Defining Your Origin Curiosity

'Be curious. Everyone claims she or he is curious, nobody wants to say "no, I am completely 'uncurious', I don't want to know about the world". What I mean is that, if you want to work in data visualisation, you need to be relentlessly and systematically curious. You should try to get interested in anything and everything that comes your way. Also, you need to understand that curiosity is not just about your interests being triggered. Curiosity also involves pursuing those interests like a hound. Being truly curious involves a lot of hard work, devoting time and effort to learn as much as possible about various topics, and to make connections between them. Curiosity is not something that just comes naturally. It can be taught, and it can be learned. So my recommendation is: develop your curiosity, educate yourself – don't just wait for the world to come to you with good ideas. Pursue them.' **Professor Alberto Cairo, Knight Chair in Visual Journalism, University of Miami, and Visualisation Specialist**

A worthwhile data visualisation project should commence from the starting point of a curiosity. According to the dictionary definition, curiosity is about possessing 'a strong desire to know or learn something'. This aligns perfectly with the goal of data visualisation, defined in Chapter 1 as being to facilitate understanding. By establishing a clear sense of where your project originated in curiosity terms, the primary force that shapes your decision making will be the desire to respond effectively to this expressed intrigue.

A visualisation process that lacks an initially articulated curiosity can lead to a very aimless solution. After all, what is it you are solving? What deficit in people's understanding are you trying to address? Having the benefit of even just a broad motive can help you tremendously in navigating the myriad options you face.

The nature of the curiosity that surrounds your work will vary depending on where it originated and who it is serving. Consider these five scenarios where the characteristics differ sufficiently to offer different contextual challenges:

Personal intrigue – 'I wonder what ...'

Stakeholder intrigue – 'He/she needs to know ...'

Audience intrigue – 'They will need to know ...'

Anticipated intrigue – 'They might be interested in knowing ...'

Potential intrigue – 'There might be something interesting ...'

Let's work through an illustration of each of these scenarios to explain their differences and influences.

Firstly, there are situations where a project is instigated in response to a curiosity borne out of **personal intrigue**. An example of this type of situation can be found in the case-study project that I have published as a digital companion to this book (book.visualisingdata.com) to help demonstrate the workflow process in practice. The project is titled 'Filmographics' and concerns the ebb and flow of the careers of different movie stars. You can find out more about it by visiting the book's digital resources.

The reason I pursued this particular project was because, firstly, I have a passion for movies and, secondly, I had a particular curiosity about the emergence, re-emergence and apparent disappearance of certain actors. Expressed as a question, the core curiosity that triggered this project was: 'What is the pattern of success or failure in the movie careers of a selection of notable actors?'

This initial question provided me with immediate clarity: the goal of the visualisation would be to deliver an 'answer' to this question, to help me better understand how the career patterns look for the different actors selected. In this case I am the originator of the curiosity and I am pursuing this project for my own interest.

Ultimately, whether this initially defined curiosity remains the same throughout the process does not really matter. Quite often one's initial expression of curiosity shifts considerably once data has been gathered and analysed. When more research is carried out on the subject matter you become more roundly acquainted with the relevance (or otherwise) of the trigger enquiry. You might alter your pursuit when you realise there is something different – and potentially more interesting – to explore. You do not want to be anchored to an enquiry that no longer reflects the most relevant perspective but it does offer at least a clear starting point – an initial motive – from which the process begins.

Sometimes, the nature of the motivation for a personal intrigue-based curiosity is recognition of one's ignorance about an aspect of a subject that should be known (a deficit in 'available' understanding) more than a defined interest in a subject that may not be known (possibly creating new understanding).

Let's consider another scenario, still concerning movie-related subject matter, but to explain a different type of curiosity. Suppose you work for a movie studio and have been tasked by a casting director to compile a one-off report that will profile which actors are potentially the best option to cast in a major sci-fi movie that has just been given the green light to begin production. You have certain criteria to follow: they have to be female, aged 30-45, and must fit the description of 'rising' star. They must not have been in other sci-fi movies, nor can they have any of the 'baggage' that comes with being associated with huge flops. Their fees should be under $2 million. You go away, undertake the analysis, and compile a report showing the career paths of some of the most likely stars who fit the bill.

This scenario has not come about through your own personal curiosity but instead you are responding to the specific curiosity of the casting director. In undertaking this work you effectively inherit – take on – the curiosity of others. They have briefed you to find the data, analyse it, and then present the findings to them. This would be an example of curiosity born out of **stakeholder intrigue**: work commissioned by a stakeholder who is also the target audience (or is the prominent party among the intended audience). There is no *anticipation* of interest here, rather it is known.

For the third scenario, you might work for a business involved in the analysis and commentary of the state of the movie industry. Let's imagine your company specialises in producing a dashboard that is shared with a broad group of users comprising Hollywood executives, studio senior management and casting agents, among others. The dashboard profiles all aspects of the industry, covering current trends and the career fortunes of a wide range different actors, helping users to identify who is hot, who is not, who is emerging, who is declining, who will cost what, who scores well with different audiences, etc.

The various indicators of information you are compiling and presenting on the dashboard are based on the recognised needs of the professional curiosities these people (client users) will have about this subject matter (movie career statuses). Given the diverse permutations of the different measures included, not all the information provided will be of interest all the time to all who consume it, but it is provided and available as and when they do need it. This would be an example of curiosity born out of **audience intrigue** – shaped out of a combination of knowing what *will* be needed and reasonably anticipating what *could* be needed.

What you are working towards in situations like this is ensuring that all the relevant aspects of *possible* curiosity can be brought together in a single place to serve as many needs as possible. There are similarities here with the multitude of dials, displays and indicators in the cockpit of an aircraft. The pilot does not need all that information as an immediate priority all the time, but *may* need access to some of the information in a reactive sense should the situation arise. Additionally, this scenario may be typical of a varied and larger scale audience in contrast to the more bespoke nature of a stakeholder intrigue scenario. You will rarely if ever be able to serve 100% of the audience's potential needs but you can certainly aspire to do your best.

Consider another similar scenario, but with a different setting used to illustrate a more subtle distinction. Suppose I am as a graphics editor working for a newspaper. One of the topics of current attention might concern the relatively late-career breakthrough of a certain actor, who has almost overnight moved from roles in relatively modest TV shows to starring in cinematic blockbusters. It is decided by the assignments editor that I will work on a graphic that examines the fortunes of this actor's career alongside a selection of other actors to provide contrast or draw comparisons with.

On this occasion the trigger is not necessarily emerging from personal intrigue. I have essentially been issued with the requirements: even if I agree with the idea or had a similar thought myself, the organisational relationship decrees that others will instruct me about which tasks to work on. A stakeholder – the assignments editor (or others in the editorial hierarchy) – has determined that this is a topic of interest and worth exploring. However, in contrast to the stakeholder intrigue scenario, here the stakeholder is not the intended audience. It is not necessarily even a curiosity they have themselves. The motive for this work is likely driven by the machinations of current affairs: what is news-

'The best piece of advice, which is "always be curious," came from Steve Duenes, who has led the graphics team at the *New York Times* for more than a decade. Being curious covers the essence of journalism: question everything, never make assumptions, dig. You can't make great visualizations without great information, so make sure your reporting leads you to visual stories that are interesting, surprising, signifi- cant.' **Hannah Fairfield, Sr. Graphics Editor, The *New York Times***

worthy and likely to be of some interest to readers? Therefore, the belief is that this analysis (looking at this actor's career path compared with others) is aligned to the current entertainment news agenda.

This would be an example of curiosity born out of **anticipated intrigue**. The audience has not explicitly asked for this and does not necessarily need it. However, it is perceived to be relevant in the context of the news cycle and informed judgement has been used to anticipate there should be sufficient interest among the target audience about this topic. Sometimes you will work on projects where you have almost to imagine or assume what appetite exists among an audience rather than just respond to an expressed need.

Most of the projects I work on will be driven by stakeholders asking me to create a visualisation to communicate understanding to others (not necessarily them), as per the 'audience' and 'anticipated' intrigue scenarios. The secondary role of the 'filmographics' project, that I defined as emerging from and serving a personal intrigue, will also be to pique the interest of other movie fans. Again, this is based on anticipated intrigue more than known audience intrigue.

The final scenario of curiosity goes back to our role as an individual. Let's say I am interested in data visualisation and also interested in movies and I discover a clean dataset full of rich content about movies and actors. This sounds like a compelling opportunity to do something with it because I am convinced there will be some nuggets of insight locked inside. I might not have determined a specific curiosity yet, as my entry point, but I will be able to establish this later once I have had a closer look at what potential the data offers.

This would be a situation where curiosity is born out of **potential intrigue** – potential because I just do not know explicitly what it will be yet. Sometimes, in your subject of study or in the workplace, perhaps if you work with collections of survey results or findings from an experiment, you might find yourself with the opportunity to explore a dataset without any real prior sense of exactly what it is you are looking to get out of it. You are initially unclear about the precise angle of your enquiry but you will explore the data to acquaint yourself fully with its qualities and generally research the subject. From there you should have a better idea of a more specific curiosity you might pursue. In effect, this scenario would then switch into more personal intrigue (if it remains just for yourself) or anticipated intrigue (if you might share it with others).

The potential intrigue type of curiosity might also extend to situations where you simply have a desire to practise your visualisation skills, experimenting and trying out new techniques with some sample data. In this scenario the incentive is more to learn from a new experience of working through a visualisation process and may not necessarily have the same drivers as when definable audiences exist

This final scenario is the only one whereby the availability of and access to data would arrive before you have articulated a specific curiosity. In all the other scenarios outlined, the data you need will typically be sought as a response to the curiosity. Even in the lattermost scenario about potential intrigue, data itself does not just fall from the sky and into your lap(top). The sheer fact that you have a dataset to work with will be because somebody else, at an earlier moment in time, was interested in measuring an activity, recording it, and making the collected data available. That in itself could only have arisen from their own curiosity.

Why do these different scenarios of curiosity have such an important role to play? Firstly, they provide clarity about the angles of analysis that you might be pursuing. As you will see later, even in the smallest and seemingly simplest dataset, there are many possibilities for conducting different types of analysis. The burden of choosing is somewhat eased by knowing in advance what might be the most interesting and relevant analysis to focus on. Secondly, the different scenarios described all present slightly different characteristics in the dynamics of the people involved. Who are the stakeholders and what is their interest? Who are the intended recipients – the audience – and what is their interest? As you have already seen – and will keep seeing - the involvement of *people* creates such influential forces (good and bad) shaping your visualisation thinking. You therefore need to know about how those forces might materialise from the outset.

Identifying Your Project's Circumstances

Defining your project's circumstances involves identifying all the requirements and restrictions that are inherited by you, imposed *on* you or determined *by* you. These are the different pressure points that establish what you can or cannot pursue and what you should or should not pursue. Much of this contextual thinking is therefore associated with the aim of ambition management.

There are so many hidden variables and influences in a visualisation project that the end viewer never gets to see and often does not appreciate. It is natural for them to assess a project through the lens of an idealised context free of restriction, but there are always limitations, external influences and project-specific factors that affect the shape of the final work.

In order to design a tool, we must make our best efforts to understand the larger social and physical context within which it is intended to function.' **Bill Buxton, Computer Scientist, Designer and Author**, *Sketching User Experiences*

When starting a project you will find that not all the circumstances that could have an influence on your work will prove to be as identifiable, definable or fixed as you might like. Some things change. Some things can only be recognised once you've become a little more acquainted with the nature of your task. As I stated in the previous chapter, doing this activity now is only the first occasion you will be paying attention to these matters, not the last. Of course, the more you *can* define, the greater the clarity your subsequent decisions will be based upon. There are other stages where you can work with uncertainty but, ideally, not here. Your work needs to obtain as much focus as possible.

There are some factors that may not be relevant or do not have any predefined restrictions or set requirements. For example, you might not have any format restrictions (print vs digital, large size vs small size) to contend with, in which case it is entirely up to you how it evolves. Identifying that no format restrictions exist is as valuable as knowing when they do. It gives you control. You might decide there is merit in imposing a restriction yourself. You might appreciate some degree of focus by determining that your target output will be for a printed, poster-sized display.

> 'Context is key. You'll hear that the most important quality of a visualisation is graphical honesty, or storytelling value, or facilitation of "insights". The truth is, all of these things (and others) are the most important quality, but in different times and places. There is no singular function of visualisation; what's important shifts with the constraints of your audience, goals, tools, expertise, and data and time available.' **Scott Murray, Designer**

People

Stakeholders: In project situations where you have been requested/commissioned to do a visualisation by somebody else, it is helpful to establish an understanding of all the different *players* and their involvement. Defining stakeholders will help you anticipate what sort of experience you are going to go through, how enjoyable and smooth it might be, or how much friction and what obstacles might be involved.

For starters, who is the ultimate customer? This might not be the person who has directly commissioned you, nor might it be somebody belonging to the intended audience, rather someone who has influence over the final work. They may not be decision makers, rather decision approvers. They are the people from whom you await the thumbs up. Stakeholders will have an influence on when work is of sufficient quality, in their eyes, to declare it as being on the right path or, ultimately, to signal the completion of the project. In my world, when you might be doing work as a contracted design consultant, they determine when I will get paid. As you have seen, stakeholders might also be the people from whom the origin curiosity emerged, so they will be especially invested in what it is you are able to produce.

Other stakeholders might have a smaller involvement or influence. Their role may be a positive one – offering advice and assistance with a specific domain challenge – or, in a minority of cases, a negative one – hindering progress by influencing design decisions beyond their remit and capability. In this case they become interferers. We don't like interferers because they make life unnecessarily harder (especially, strangely enough, if they are nice people). A primary contact person, who will act as the liaison between parties, will be another important role to identify.

If there are no stakeholders and the project is a solo pursuit there will be much more flexibility for you to dictate matters. You might even be more motivated to go 'above and beyond' if you are driven by a personal intrigue. Conversely there will be fewer channels of guidance and support. This is not to say that one situation is better, it just means they are different and this difference needs to be recognised early.

Audience: What are the characteristics of your viewers? Several different attributes were defined in discussing the principle for 'accessible design' in Chapter 1. You are primarily trying to understand their relationship with the subject matter. How informed are they about a subject and what motivation might they have towards it – is it a passing interest or a definable need? What capacity might they have to make sense of the type of visualisations you may need to create (their graphical literacy)? How could their personal traits influence your design choices? You will never nor should you ever let the spinning plate of concern about your audience drop.

Constraints

Pressures: The primary pressure relates to timescales: how much time have you got to work through the full process and publish a completed solution? The difference in potential ambition between a project that is needed in two days compared with one that is needed in two months is clear. However, the real issue is the relationship between timescales and the estimated duration of your work. Two months might sound great but not if you have three months' work to accomplish. Estimating project duration to any reliable degree is a difficult task. You need experience from working on a diverse range of projects that can inform your expectations for how long each constituent task could take. Even then, seemingly similar projects can end up with very different task durations as a result of the slightest changes in certain circumstances, such as the inclusion of an extra variable of data, or more significant changes like a previously print-only project requiring a bespoke digital interactive solution as well.

> 'What is the LEAST this can be? What is the minimum result that will 1) be factually accurate, 2) present the core concepts of this story in a way that a general audience will understand, and 3) be readable on a variety of screen sizes (desktop, mobile, etc.)? And then I judge what else can be done based on the time I have. Certainly, when we're down to the wire it's no time to introduce complex new features that require lots of testing and could potentially break other, working features.' **Alyson Hurt, News Graphics Editor, NPR, on dealing with timescale pressures**

> Always note down your task durations so you can refine your estimates far better on future projects. These estimates are not just valuable for client work, you will need them to manage your own time regardless of the nature of the project.

In addition to project timescales, you will need to be aware of any other milestones that might have to be met. Work that you are producing for other stakeholders will often require you to present your ideas/progress at various stages. This is a good thing. It gives you the opportunity to check if you are in sync or discover if you have misunderstood certain needs. Note that it can be risky to present under-developed concepts to potentially inexperienced stakeholders who may not be able to extend their imagination to envision how the work will look when completed.

Other pressures may exist in tangible terms through financial restrictions. What time can you afford to spend? This is not just associated with freelancing or studio work, it can be the same for research groups which have finite resources and need to use their time – and their costs – sensibly. It might also have an influence on occasions where you need to outsource parts of your work (e.g. paying for transcription services, third-party data sources) or make purchases (software, hardware, licences for photograph usage).

The final pressure is slightly less tangible but comes in the form of what might be described as market influences. Sometimes you will find your work is competing for attention alongside other work. In this age of plenty, a desire to emulate the best or differentiate from the rest can prove to be a strong motive. For example, if you are working for a charitable organisation, how do you get your message across louder and more prominently than others? If you are working on an academic research project, how do you get your findings heard among all the other studies also looking to create an impact? It might be the internal dynamics within a student group or organisation or the broader competition across entire marketplace and industries, but regardless, considerations like this do introduce an extra ingredient to shape your thinking.

Rules: These are relatively straightforward matters to define and are concerned with any design rules you need to know about and follow. These might be issues around:

- *Layout/size restrictions*: Maximum size and specific shape restrictions might exist with graphics created for articles published in journals or the screen size dimensions for digital outputs that need to work on a tablet/smartphone. Are there printing resolution requirements around dpi (dots per inch)? The commonly used industry standard for printing is 300 dpi.
- *Style guidelines*: In many organisations (and with some media) there are often visual identity branding guides imposed on you that determine the colours, typeface and possibly logos that you need to include. If possible, try to push back on this because they can be unnecessarily restrictive and often the choices imposed are horribly ill-suited to data visualisation. Otherwise, you will have to abide by the style requirements dictated to you. Also check to see if you will need to include any logos. They may take up valuable space and you'll need to think about their impact on the balance of your overall colour palette and composition.
- *Functional restrictions*: The potential requirement to create outputs that are compatible with certain browsers, versions of software or programming languages will be an important consideration to establish early.

Consumption

Frequency: The issue of frequency concerns how often a particular project will be repeated and what its lifespan will be. It might be a regular (e.g. monthly report) or irregular (e.g. election polling graphic updated after each new release) product, in which case the efficiency and reproducibility of your data and design choices will be paramount. If it is a one-off, you will have freedom from this concern but you will have to weigh up the cost–benefit involved. Will there be any future benefits from reusing the techniques and thinking you put into this project? Can you afford to invest time and energy, for example, in programmatically automating certain parts of the creation process or will this be ultimately wasted if it is never reused? What is the trade-off between the amount of work to create it and the expiry of its relevance as time goes by – will it very quickly become out of date as new data 'happens'? Maybe it is a one-off project in creation terms but is to be constantly fed by real-time data updates, in which case the primary concern will be of functional robustness.

'I like to imagine that I have a person sitting in front of me, and I need to explain something interesting or important about this data to them, and I've only got about 10 seconds to do it. What can I say, or show them, that will keep them from standing up and walking away?' **Bill Rapp, Data Visualisation Designer, discussing an audience scenario setting he conceives in his mind's eye**

Setting: This concerns the situation in which your work would be consumed. Firstly, this is judging whether the work is going to be consumed remotely or presented in person (in which case the key insights and explanations can be verbalised). Secondly, is the nature of the engagement one that needs to facilitate especially rapid understanding or does it lend itself to a more extended/prolonged engagement?

I keep four characteristic settings in mind when thinking about the situations in which my work will be consumed by viewers:

- The *boardroom*: A setting characterised by there being limited time, patience or tolerance for what might be perceived as any delay in facilitating understanding: immediate insights required, key messages at a glance.
- The *coffee shop*: A more relaxed setting that might be compatible with a piece of work that is more involving and requiring of viewers to spend more time learning about the subject, familiarising themselves with how to read the display and discovering the (likely) many different parts of the content.
- The *cockpit*: The situation that relates to the instrumentation nature of a visualisation tool or dashboard. There is a need for immediate signals to stand out at a glance whilst also offering sufficient breadth and depth to serve the likely multitude of different potential interests. Another example might be the usage of a reference map that works on all levels of enquiry, from at a glance, high-level orientation through to in-depth detail to aid the operational needs of navigation.
- The *prop*: Here a visualisation plays the role of a supporting visual device to accompany a presenter's verbal facilitation of the key understandings (via a talk) or an author's written account of salient findings (report, article).

Deliverables

Quantity: This concerns establishing the project's workload prospect in terms of quantities. How many *things* am I making? How much, what type, what shape and what size? Is it going to involve a broad array of different angles of analysis or a much narrower and focused view of the data? What are the basic quantities of the outputs? Is it, for example, going to be about producing 12 different graphics for a varied slide deck or a 50-page report that will need two charts for each of the 20 questions in a survey and some further summaries? Perhaps its a web-based project with four distinct sections, each requiring four interactively adjustable views of data. It will not always be possible to determine such dimensions this early on in the process, but even by just establishing a rough estimate this can be helpful, especially for informing your estimate of the project's likely duration.

Format: This concerns the output format: digital, print or physical. You will need a clear understanding of the specific format of the deliverables required to factor in how your design work will be affected:

- Is it intended as a large poster-sized print or something for a standard A4-sized report?
- Will it exist as a website, a video, maybe even a tool or app?
- Is the digital output intended for smartphone, tablet (which ones?) as well as desktop? What ppi (pixels per inch) or resolution will it ideally need to work with?
- Are you handing over to your stakeholder *just* the final design work or will you also be expected to provide all the background files that contributed to the final piece of work?

'I love, love, love print. I feel there is something so special about having the texture and weight of paper be the canvas of the visualisation. It's a privilege to be able to design for print these days, so take advantage of the strengths that paper offers – mainly, resolution and texture. Print has a lot more real estate than screen, allowing for very dense, information packed visualisations. I love to take this opportunity to build in multiple story strands, and let the reader explore on their own. The texture of paper can also play a role in enhancing the visualisation; consider how a design and colour choices might be different on a glossy magazine page versus the rougher surface of a newspaper.' **Jane Pong, Data Visualisation Designer, loves print (I think)**

Resources

Skills: What capabilities exist among those who will have a role to play in the design process? This might just be you, in which case what can you do and what can't you do? What are you good at and not good at? If you have collaborators, what are the blend of competencies you collectively bring to the table? How might you allocate different roles and duties to optimise the use of your resources? To help assess your capabilities, and possibly those across any team you are part of, consider the breakdown presented in Chapter 11 in the 'Seven hats' section.

'The thing is, this world, especially the digital data visualization world, is changing rapidly: new technologies, new tools and frameworks are being developed constantly. So, you need to be able to adapt. But principles are much more timeless. If you know what you want to create, then using technology is just the means to create what you have in mind. If you're too fixed on one type of technology, you may be out of a job soon. So, keep learning new technologies, but more importantly, know your principles, as they will allow you to make the right decisions.' **Jan Willem Tulp, Data Experience Designer**

Technology: As I have described already, there are myriad tools, applications and programming options in the data visualisation space, offering an array of different capabilities. No single package offers everything you will ever need but, inevitably, some offer more and others less. In order to complete the more advanced visualisation projects you will likely require a Swiss-Army-knife approach involving a repertoire of different technology options at each of the preparatory and development stages in this process. The software and technological infrastructure you have access to will have a great influence on framing the ambitions of your work. I will be sharing more information about tools in the digital resources that accompany this book.

A final point to make about circumstances is to recognise the value, in many cases, of limitations and constraint. Often such restrictions can prove to be a positive influence. Consider the circumstances faced by Director Steven Spielberg while filming *Jaws*. The early attempts to create a convincing-looking shark model proved to be so flawed that for much of the film's scheduled production Spielberg was left without a visible shark to work with. Such were the diminishing time resources that he could not afford to wait for a solution to film the action sequences so he had to work with a combination of props and visual devices. Objects being disrupted, like floating barrels or buoys and, famously, a mock shark fin piercing the surface, were just some of the tactics he used to create the suggestion of a shark rather than actually show a shark. Eventually, a viable shark model was developed to serve the latter scenes but, as we all now know, in not being able to show the shark for most of the film, the suspense was immeasurably heightened. This made it one of the most enduring films of its generation. The necessary innovation that emerged from the limited resources and increasing pressure led to a solution that surely transcended any other outcome had there been freedom from restrictions. The key message here is to embrace the constraints you face because they can heighten your creative senses and lead to successful, innovative solutions.

Defining Your Project's Purpose

Identifying the curiosity that motivates your work establishes the project's origin. The circumstances you have just considered will give you a sense of the different factors that will influence your experience on the project and shape your ambitions. The final component of contextual thinking is to consider your intended destination. What is it you specifically hope to accomplish with your visualisation? This involves articulating your project's *purpose*.

You know now that the overriding goal is to facilitate understanding, that is non-negotiable, but the *nature* of this understanding may vary significantly. In Chapter 1, I described how – as viewers – we go through a process of understanding involving the stages of *perceiving, interpreting* and, finally, *comprehending*. The undertaking of the first stage of perceiving is largely controlled by the accessibility of the visualiser's design choices. The second stage of interpreting (establishing meaning from a visualisation) will be influenced by the viewer's capacity to derive meaning *or* by the visualiser providing explanatory assistance to help the viewer form this meaning. The final stage of comprehending is largely determined by the viewer alone as what something means to them is so uniquely shaped by their personal context: what they know or do not know, what their beliefs are and what their intentions are for acquiring this understanding.

This three-stage model of understanding helps demonstrate the importance of defining the purpose of a visualisation upfront. Some visualisations might aim to be quite impactive, attempting to shock or inspire viewers in order to persuade them about a need to change behaviour or make significant decisions. For example. you might be seeking to demonstrate visually compelling evidence of the impact of dietary factors like sugary drinks on the rise of obesity. The purpose might not just be to inform but actively to seek to make a difference, maybe targeting parents to change the foods they allow their kids to eat. To achieve this kind of outcome you might take a more emotive approach in the portrayal of your data to attract the audience's attention in the first place and then strike home the powerful message in a way that resonates more deeply. Affecting people to this degree can be quite ambitious.

In a different context, you might not need to go this deep. Some projects may be more modestly designed to enlighten or simply inform viewers better about a subject, even if the acquired understanding is quite small. There might be recognition that the target viewers should (and maybe are better placed to) reach their own conclusions. Perhaps, if you were revealing the same type of dietary data to health professionals rather than to parents, you might only be serving to confirm what they already might know or at least suspect. They probably will not need convincing about the importance of the message, so the ambitions of the visualisation itself will be considerably different. To achieve the purpose of this project would likely lead to a very different design approach from the one in the previous scenario.

One size does not fit all. No single type of visualisation will be capable of delivering an experience whereby all flavours of understanding are facilitated. Articulating your purpose is your statement of intent: a necessary sense of focus to help inform your design choices and a potential measure to determine whether you accomplish your aims.

Defining your purpose before establishing your trigger curiosity is putting the cart before the horse. A project driven by curiosity is the purest basis for a visualisation project to commence and one most likely to be guided by the clearest thinking. It is the approach that fits best with the sequence of thinking outlined in this workflow. When the desired purpose drives decisions, visualisers can be overly focused on outputs and not inputs. As discussed in Chapter 4, you need to let your data do the talking, not force the data to do your talking. The pressure to reach the desired destination can impact artificially on the data, editorial and design decisions you make.

If you are working with colleagues or for clients who express their requirements from the perspective of an outcome- or purpose-led process, your skill as a visualiser will be to direct the discussions towards a more curiosity-led perspective. Sometimes you will find stakeholders who are primarily motivated by a desire to reach many viewers and their singular measure of success is purely the quantity of eyeballs that will peruse a piece of work. However, I would contest that this does not make it a viable motive for an effective data visualisation, where the measure of success is about facilitating understanding first and foremost. Loads of visitors and social media hits (likes, retweets, upvotes) are a wonderful bonus but should only be seen as a by-product of interest, not an indicator of effectiveness in and of itself. Those who seek a viral success story rarely achieve it because it is so hard to manufacture.

3.3 Establishing Your Project's Vision
The 'Purpose' Map

In compiling definitions about the curiosity, circumstances and purpose, you have helped to initiate your process with a clear idea of the origin of your work, its likely desired destination, and some of the most influencing factors you will have to contend with along the way.

To supplement this contextual thinking you should take the opportunity to consider forming an initial vision for your work. The definition of vision is 'the ability to think about or plan the future with imagination or wisdom' and it has particular relevance for how we might foresee achieving the purpose we have stated.

There are many types of visualisation with many different characteristics. Two of the most significant concern the differences in *tone* and *experience*. Reflecting the diversity of visualisation work being produced, the 'purpose map' (Figure 3.1) offers a high-level view of this landscape shaped by different relationships across those two dimensions.

Figure 3.1
The 'Purpose Map'

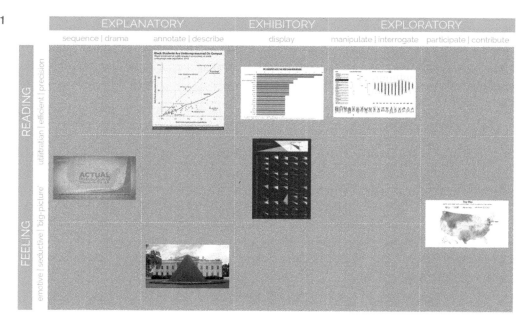

Certain types of visualisation will offer a better fit for your project. Their characteristics, in terms of experience and tone, will offer the right blend to best connect your origin curiosity with destination purpose. What you need to consider here is what can you envision being the most suitable type of visualisation that might be most capable of accomplishing what you intend.

While the more detailed design thinking won't arrive until later in the workflow, even at this early stage it is instructive to put some thought into this matter. Let me explain sequentially the meaning of each of these dimensions and the significance of the different regions within this purpose map.

Experience

The horizontal dimension of this map concerns the experience of the visualisation:

- How will it practically operate as a means of communication?
- Through what functional experience will understanding be achieved by the viewer?

Along this spectrum are three different states against which you may define your intentions: *Explanatory, Exhibitory* or *Exploratory* (for a mnemonic, think about this as being all about the EXs).

Explanatory visualisations are found on the left side of the map. Explanatory in this context essentially means we – as visualisers – will provide the viewer with a visual portrayal of the subject's data *and* will also take some responsibility to bring key insights to the surface, rather than leave the prospect of interpreting the meaning of the information entirely to the viewer. The visualiser here is attempting to assist with the viewers' process of understanding as much as possible, in particular with the interpretation, drawing out the meaning of the data.

The rightmost side of this explanatory region of the map (in the second column, more towards the middle of the map) might be considered the 'mildest' form of explanatory visualisation. Here you find projects that include simple annotation devices like value labels or visual guides that direct the eye to help assist with the task of interpreting the data: the use of colour can be an immediate visual cue to help separate different features of a chart and captions might outline a key message or summary finding. An example of this kind of explanatory visualisation is seen in Figure 3.2, which was published in an article reporting on protests across US schools (in November 2015) regarding the

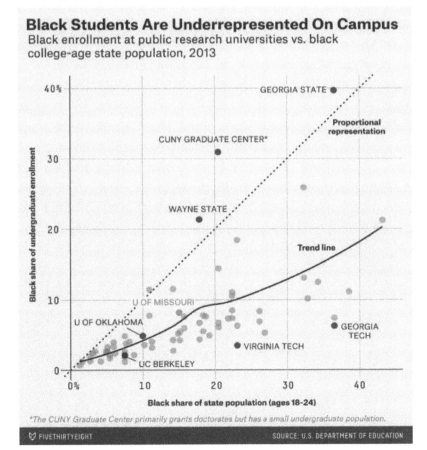

Figure 3.2
Mizzou's Racial Gap Is Typical On College Campuses

underrepresentation of black students. Here you can see a scatter plot comparing the share of enrolled black students for different public research universities (in the vertical axis) with the share of the college-age black populations in the respective states. With protests beginning at the University of Missouri, the chart uses red to highlight this data point within the chart to enable comparison with other schools. Other notable schools are emphasised to draw out some of the main insights. Additionally, using *encoded overlays*, such as the trend line and dotted-line indicating proportional representation, the viewer is assisted beyond just perceiving the data to help them with the stage of interpretation: what does it mean to be higher or lower on this chart? Which locations are considered good/bad or typical/atypical?

The best way to get your head around 'explanatory' visualisations is to consider how you would explain this display of analysis to a viewer if you were sat with that person in front of a screen or with a printout. What features would you be pointing out to them? Which values would you be pointing to as being the most interesting? What things would you not need to explain? The traits of a good explanatory visualisation will accommodate these types of important descriptions, which would otherwise be verbalised, within the design of the chart itself, making it 'stand' alone without the need for in-person explanation.

Towards the leftmost region of the map this is where the experience is about generally more intensive attempts to enlighten an audience's understanding of a subject. This could possibly be through the use of a narrative structured around a compelling sequence of information and/or a dramatic experience. The form of this type of work would be characterised by videos or presentations, or maybe an animated or motion graphic. Some term this 'narrative' visualisation. This is arguably where the most tangible demonstrations of visualisation through storytelling (more on this later) are found. An example that typifies this classification on the map would be characterised by this very powerful and popular video (Figure 3.3) about the issue of wealth inequality in the USA. It employs a semi-animated slideshow sequence to weave together the narrative and is accompanied by an effective and affective voiceover narrating the story.

Figure 3.3
Image taken from 'Wealth Inequality in America'

Across all explanatory visualisations the visualiser will require sufficient knowledge (or the skill and capacity to acquire this) about the topic being shown in order to identify the most relevant, interesting and worthwhile insights to present to the viewer. Creating explanatory visualisations forces you to challenge how well you actually know a subject. If you cannot explain or articulate what is insightful, and why, to others, then this probably means you do not know the reasons yourself.

Fundamentally, explanatory visualisations are the best-fit solution if the specific context dictates that saying nothing is not good enough; leaving viewers with a 'so what?' reaction would be seen as a failure, so in such cases a takeaway message(s) would need to be offered.

Exploratory visualisations differ from explanatory visualisations in that they are focused more on helping the viewer or – more specifically in this case – the *user* find their own insights. Almost universally, these types of works will be digital and interactive in nature. The 'mildest' forms of exploratory works are those that facilitate interrogation and manipulation of the data. You might be able to modify a view of the chart, perhaps by highlighting/filtering certain categories of interest, or maybe change data parameters and switch between different views. You might be able to hover over different features to reveal detailed annotations. All of these operations facilitate understanding to the extent of the *perceiving* stage. The task of *interpreting* and *comprehending* will largely be the responsibility of the viewer to form. This will be suitable if the intended audience have the necessary foundation knowledge for the subject and sufficient interest to translate the general and personal meaning.

An example of this type of visualisation can be seen through the interactive project (Figure 3.4). It was developed to allow users to explore different measures concerning the dimension changes of wood, over time, across selected cities of the world.

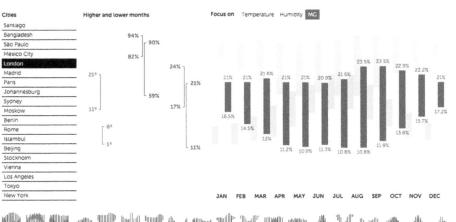

Figure 3.4
Dimensional
Changes in
Wood

There are no captions, no indications of what is significant or insignificant, no assistance to form meaning through the use of colours or markers to emphasise 'good' or 'bad' values. This project is simply a visual window into the analysis of this data that lets users perceive the data values and interact with the different dimensions offered. To form meaning, it is open to them to determine what features of the data resonate with their existing interests, knowledge and needs.

As you look more towards the rightmost edge of the purpose map you reach far deeper exploratory experiences. You might characterise visualisations here as facilitating a more participatory or contributory experience. The prospect of greater control, a deeper array of features and the possibility of contributing one's own data to a visualisation can be very seductive. Users are naturally drawn to challenges like quizzes and projects that allow them to make sense of their place in the world (e.g. how does my salary compare with others; how well do I know the area where I live?) – they are simply too hard to resist! The huge success of the *New York Times'* so-called 'Dialect map' (Figure 3.5), showing the similarity or otherwise of US dialects based on users' responses to 25 questions, is just one example of a contemporary project employing this participatory approach to great effect.

Figure 3.5
How Y'all,
Youse and
You Guys
Talk

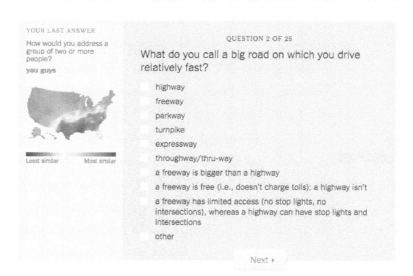

The biggest obstacle to the success of an exploratory visualisation's impact is the 'so what?' factor. 'What do you want me to do with this project? Why is it relevant? What am I supposed to get out of this?' If these are the reactions you are seeing expressed by your intended users then there is a clear disconnect between the intentions of your project and the experience (or maybe expectations) of the audiences using it.

Exhibitory visualisations are found in the final separate 'experience' category within the latitude of the purpose map. They are characterised by being neither explicitly explanatory nor exploratory. With exhibitory visualisations the viewers have to do the work to interpret meaning, relying on their own capacity to make sense of the display of data (to perceive it) and the context of the subject-matter. As well as lacking explanatory qualities, they also do not offer scope for exploratory interrogation. I generally describe them as simply being visual displays of data. Think of this term in relation to exhibiting an artwork: it takes the interpretative capacity of the viewer to be able to understand the *content* of a display as well as the *context* of a display.

When you look across the many different visualisations being published you will find that many projects mistakenly fall into the void of being exhibitory visualisation when they really need to be more supportively explanatory or functionally exploratory.

So you might wonder what the value is of an exhibitory visualisation. Well, sometimes the setting for a visualisation does not need exploration or direct explanation. As I've stated, exhibitory projects rely entirely on and make assumptions about the capacity of and interest among the target audience. If you have a very specific audience whom you know to be sufficiently knowledgeable about the domain and the analysis you have provided, it might not need important insights to be surfaced in the way you would with an explanatory visualisation. An explanatory project will mainly be for audiences who do not have the knowledge, capacity or time to find for themselves the key features of meaning (through interpreting) alone. Furthermore, the extent of the analysis might be so narrow that there is no fundamental need to incorporate ways of manipulating and personalising the experience as you would see with exploratory visualisations.

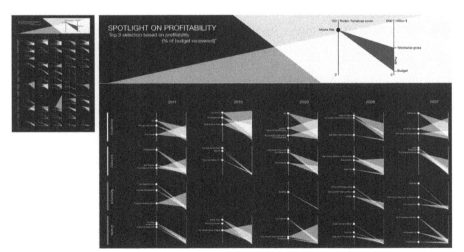

Figure 3.6
Spotlight on
Profitability

In Figure 3.6, the analysis of the top three profitable movies by genre and year is not interactive (and so does not enable any explorations), nor does it bring to the surface any observations about notable movies or conclusions about the relationship between movie ratings and takings.

It is intended as an exhibitory experience – a visual display of this data – that lets you as a user draw your own conclusions, find your own shapes of interest, and look up the movies that you want to see data for.

An exhibitory visualisation might also be a graphic that supports a written article or report. In and of itself it does not explain things in a stand-alone sense but instead exists as a visual prop for referencing. The written passages will therefore provide the explanatory narrative separate but still drawn from the supporting graphic.

I mentioned earlier the scenario of sitting down with someone and explaining a chart to them from a printout or a screen. As I said, the key points verbalised in this setting would, for an explanatory piece, be directly incorporated within the graphic. Conversely, I might use an exhibitory visualisation in a presentation where my narrative, observations and gestures provide the explanatory experience – I perform these myself, in person – rather than these being incorporated within or around the chart(s). This would define the visualisation as *exhibitory* but presented in an *explanatory* setting. Two of the most famous visualisation-based presentations, Al Gore's presentation in *An Inconvenient Truth* and Hans Rosling's 'Gapminder TEDtalk', are excellent demonstrations of this.

> One could argue that the Rosling talk was an explanatory presentation of an exploratory tool, but some of the main narrative was delivered against a more exhibitory animation of data.

Tone

The vertical dimension of the purpose map concerns the intended tone of the visualisation, with *reading* tone positioned towards the top and *feeling* tone towards the bottom. Whereas the experience dimension had two distinct and opposite sides (Explanatory vs Exploratory) with a pivot in the middle (Exhibitory), the tone dimension is much more of a continuum with subtle – and very subjective – variations between the two ends. What you are largely considering here is a judgement of the most suitable perceptual readability of your data.

Whereas the difference between types of experience can be quite distinct once you become familiar with the characteristics of each, defining tone is a slightly harder matter to nail down, especially as a beginner. The general question you are asking yourself is: through what tone of voice in my design will the purpose of this project be accomplished? Let me elaborate by looking closely at the two ends of this continuum.

Reading tone: At the top of the purpose map the tone of your visualisation design choices will be geared towards optimising the ease with which viewers can accurately estimate the magnitude of and relationships between values. There is emphasis on the efficiency of perceiving data. The reading tone would be your best-fit approach when the purpose of your work requires you to facilitate understanding with a high degree of precision and detail. This would also be relevant in situations when there is no need to seduce an audience through your aesthetic treatment. Furthermore, it suits the needs well when the subject matter does not inherently embody or merit any form of visual stimulation to convey the essence of the message more potently. The visual quality created with this tone might be considered rather utilitarian, formed around a style that feels consistent with adjectives like analytical, pragmatic, maybe even no-frills.

Devices like bar charts, as you can see in Figure 3.7, are the poster boys for this type of display. As you will learn later, the perceptual accuracy enabled by using the size of a bar to represent quantitative values makes these charts extremely effective options for visually portraying data in a way that aids both general sense-making and accurate point-reading. That's why they are so ubiquitous.

Most of the visualisations you will ever produce will lean towards this *reading* end of the tonal continuum. Indeed, you might ask why would you ever seek to create anything but the most easily and accurately readable representations of data? Surely anything that compromises on this aim is undermining the principles of trustworthy and accessible design? Well, that's why the definitions around purpose are so significant in their influence and why we need to appreciate other perspectives.

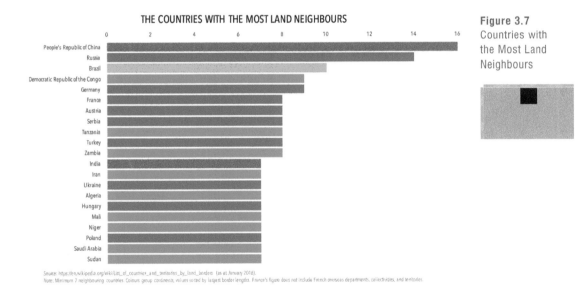

Figure 3.7
Countries with the Most Land Neighbours

Feeling tone: The lower end of this vertical dimension offers a contrasting tone of voice to that of *reading*. When I introduced in Chapter 1 the sequence of understanding – from perceiving to interpreting and through to comprehending – the illustration I gave was

'There's a strand of the data viz world that argues everything could be a bar chart. That's possibly true but also possibly a world without joy.'
Amanda Cox, Editor, *The Upshot*

based on perceiving a bar chart. Here you could easily and confidently estimate the values portrayed by the bar sizes. Sometimes, though, your aims will not necessarily fit with the singular desire to provide such a perceptually precise display: sometimes you might justify placing greater importance on the *feeling* of your data. At this side of the tonal spectrum there is more emphasis placed on determining the *gist* of the big, medium and small values and a general *sense* of the relationships that exist. Sometimes an 'at-a-glance', high-level view is the most suitable way to portray a subject's values.

Again, let me address the likely objections from those spitting their coffee at the very thought of any visualiser not giving the utmost priority to precision, efficiency and accuracy in their work. To appreciate why, on occasion, you might consider a different approach it is worth reflecting again on the motive for visualising data. Visual forms of data unquestionably offer a more revealing and more efficient way to understand the quantities and relationships that exist within data. It cannot be reasonably achieved either effectively or efficiently through non-visual forms. By visualising data you are looking for something more and something different from what, let's say, a table of data can offer. The bar chart, by way of example, offers that. However, on occasion you might need something even more different than this.

In the project illustrated in Figure 3.8, you will see excerpts from an analysis about the small number of families who have most financial clout when it comes to providing funding for presidential candidates. The data quantities are portrayed using Monopoly house pieces as a metaphor of wealth. The red houses represent the small number of families who have contributed nearly half of the initial campaign funding. The green pieces are representative of the total households in the US. You cannot count the pieces, you cannot even remotely estimate their relative proportions, but you get the gist of the scales involved as a proxy illustration of the remarkably disproportionate balance and power of wealth. Furthermore, this use of the Monopoly pieces is a symbolically strong metaphor as well as offering an appealing, almost playful approach to portraying the data.

Figure 3.8
Buying
Power: The
Families
Funding
the 2016
Presidential
Election

There will be times when you will need to consider employing what might be described as aesthetic seduction: some way of creating an appealing form that attracts viewers and encourages them to engage with a subject they might not have otherwise found relevant. This could involve a novel visual 'look' that attracts – but also informs – or a functional feature that attracts – but also performs. The influence of fun cannot be underestimated here. I repeat, we are all humans with occasionally quite base needs. Sometimes viewers crave something that stirs a more upbeat and upfront emotional engagement.

Some may argue that viewers will be encouraged to engage with a visualisation if it is relevant to them, regardless of its appearance, otherwise they should not be considered part of the target audience. That is not true, unfortunately. Perhaps in a business or operational setting, the needs of individuals, roles and groups are much more clear-cut and you can apply a binary perspective like that quite easily. Outside in the real world there are many more nuances. As a viewer your interest in a subject may not materialise until after viewers have engaged with a visualisation. It may be a consequence not the prerequisite. Had they not been somehow attracted to view it in the first place they might never have reached that point.

On a similar note, sometimes you will be working with a subject – like wealth inequality, as we've just seen, or gun crime, as discussed earlier – that has the potential to stir strong emotions. Any visualisation of this data has to contend with decisions about how to handle the perpetual baggage of feeling that comes as standard. Depending on the purpose of your work there might be good reason to encapsulate and perhaps exploit these emotions through your visualisation in a way that arguably a bar chart simply may not be able to achieve. By embodying an emotional sensation (fear,

'I love the idea of Edward Tufte's assertion that "Graphical excellence is that which gives to the viewer the greatest number of ideas in the shortest time with the least ink in the smallest space." But I found that when I developed magazine graphics according to that philosophy, they were most often met with a yawn. The reality is that Scientific American isn't required reading. We need to engage readers, as well as inform them. I try to do that in an elegant, and refined, and smart manner. To that end, I avoid illustrative details that distort the core concept. But I'm happy to include them if the topic could benefit from a welcoming gesture.' **Jen Christiansen, Graphics Editor at** *Scientific American*

'On the one hand we had this great idea of doing something fun – animated lifts racing up and down buildings while the user was on the web page. But on the other hand this is The *Financial Times* and that carries with it a responsibility to do things in a certain way. So we spent time illustrating and designing to give the graphic high production values, and it was then presented alongside an excellent piece of journalism from our manufacturing correspondent. The result? An undeniably fun user experience, but delivered in such a way that met FT subscribers' standards for high quality visuals and high quality journalism.' **John Burn-Murdoch, Senior Data Visualisation Journalist at** *Financial Times*, **having fun visualising the speed of elevators in skyscrapers**

shock, fun, power, inequity) through your display, you might be able to influence how your viewer experiences that most elusive stage of understanding, comprehending. The task of reasoning 'what does this mean to me?' is often a somewhat intangible notion but far less so when an emotional chord is struck. Behaviours can be changed. The making of decisions can be stirred. The taking of actions can be expedited. So long as the audience's needs, interest and setting are aligned this can be an entirely suitable strategy.

For some in the visualisation field, this can be seen as manipulation and, to a certain degree it probably is. As long as you are still faithful to the underlying data and you have not achieved an outcome through superficial, artificial or deceptive means, I believe it is an entirely appropriate motive in the right circumstances. As ever, there is a balance to be struck and you must remind yourself of the influence of the design principles I introduced earlier to ensure that none of the choices you make hinder the overall goal of facilitating the type of understanding your context decrees.

It is important to note that any visualisation work that leans more towards 'feeling' is typically the exception and in a minority. However, a skilled visualisation practitioner needs to have an adaptive view. They need to be able to recognise and respond to those occasions when the purpose does support an exceptional approach and a compromise beyond just serving the most perpetually accurate and efficient reading of data is required.

The Purpose Map in Practice

Since the milestone of 500 executions in 2013 the number has grown significantly. For the purpose of this illustration, for now we will consider the nature of this data as it was at the moment of this milestone.

A simple illustration of the role of the purpose map involves momentarily focusing on a rather grave subject: data about offender executions. In 2013, the State of Texas reached the unenviable milestone of having executed its 500th death-row prisoner since the resumption of capital punishment in 1982. At the time of this landmark I came across a dataset curated by the Texas Department of Criminal Justice and published on its website. This simply structured table of data (Figure 3.9) included striking information about the offenders, their offences and their final statements – a genuinely compelling source of data. Thinking about this subject and the dataset helps to frame the essence of what role this purpose map can play, especially in the tone dimension.

Figure 3.9 Image taken from Texas Department of Criminal Justice Website

Imagine viewing this data from a high vantage point, like in a hot-air balloon. The big picture is that there are 500 prisoners who have been executed. That is the whole. Lowering the viewpoint, as you get a little closer, you might see a breakdown of race, showing 225 offenders were white, 187 black, 86 Hispanic and 2 defined as other. Lower still and you see that 4 offenders originated from Anderson County. Lower again reveals that 112 offenders referred to God in their last statement. Down to the lowest level – the closest vantage point – you see individuals and individual items of data, such as Charles Milton, convicted in Tarrant county, who was aged 34 when executed on 25 June 1985.

The view of the data has travelled from a figurative perspective to a non-figurative one. The former is an abstraction of the data that effectively supresses the underlying phenomena being about people and translates – and maybe reduces it – into statistical quantities. People into numbers. The latter perspective concerns a more literal and realistic expression of what the data actually represents.

> 'Data is a simplification – an abstraction – of the real world. So when you visualize data, you visualize an abstraction of the world.' **Dr Nathan Yau, Statistican and Author of _Data Points_**

Going back to the discussion about judging tone, there are several different potential ways of portraying this executed offenders data depending on the purpose that has been defined.

Suppose you worked at the Texas Department of Criminal Justice as a member of staff responsible for conducting and reporting data analysis. You might be asked to analyse the resource implications of all offenders currently on death row, looking at issues around their cost 'footprint'. In this case you might seek to strip away all the emotive qualities of the data and focus only on its statistical attributes. You would likely aim for a figurative or abstracted representation of the subject, reducing it to fundamental statistical quantities and high-level relationships. Your approach to achieve this would probably fit with the upper end of the tonal dimension, portraying your work with a utilitarian style that facilitates an efficient and precise reading of the data.

A different scenario may now involve your doing some visual work for a campaign group with a pro-capital-punishment stance. The approach might be to demonise the individuals, putting a human face to the offenders and their offences. The motive is to evoke sensation, shock and anger to get people to support this cause. Would a bar chart breakdown of the key statistics accomplish this in tone? Possibly not.

> 'I have this fear that we aren't feeling enough.' **Chris Jordan, Visual Artist and Cultural Activist**

Another situation could see you working for a newspaper that had a particularly liberal viewpoint and was looking to publish a graphic to mark this sober milestone of 500 executions. You might avoid using the stern imagery of the offenders' mug shots and instead focus on some of the human sentiments expressed in their last statements or on case studies of some of the extremely young offenders for whom life was perhaps never going to follow a positive path. To humanise or demonise the individuals involved in this dataset is possible because there is such richness and intimate levels of detail available from the data.

It is worth reinforcing again that a figurative approach (_reading_) is typically what most of your work will involve and require. Only a small proportion will require a non-figurative (_feeling_) approach even with emotive subjects. The whole point about introducing you to the alternative perspective of the feeling tone is to prepare you for those occasions when the desired purpose of your work requires more of a higher-level grasp of data values or a deeper connection with subject matter through its data.

To complete this discussion, here are some final points to make about the purpose map to further clarify and frame its scope.

Format: Firstly, it is important to stress that this map does not define format in terms of print, digital or physical. Exploratory visualisations will almost entirely be digital but exhibitory or explanatory projects could be print or digital.

First thoughts not final commitment: Considering the definitions of experience and tone now simply represents the beginning of this kind of design thinking. As the workflow progresses you might change (or need to change) your mind and pursue an alternative course, especially when you get deeper into data work, the nature of which may reveal a better fit with a completely different type of solution. I will state again that in these early stages the things you will think about will be the first occasion on which you think about them but not the last. The benefit of starting this kind of thinking now is the increased focus it affords from any sense of eliminating potential types of visualisation from your concern that will have no relevance to your context.

Collective visual quality: Decisions around tone may not be solely isolated to how data should be represented. There may be a broader sense of overall visual mood or 'quality' that you are trying to convey across the presentation design choices as well. As you will see, there are other media assets (photos, videos, illustrations, text) that could go towards achieving a certain tone for the project that does not necessarily directly influence the tone of the data.

Not about a singular location: Some projects will involve just a single chart and this makes it a far more straightforward prospect to inform your definition of its best-fit location on this purpose map. However, there will be other projects that you work on involving multiple chart assets, multiple interactions, different pages and deeper layers. So, when it comes to considering your initial vision through the purpose map dimensions, you may recognise separate definitions for each major elements. This will become much clearer as you get deeper into the project – and can actually identify the need for multiple assets.

The mantra proposed by Ben Schneiderman, one of the most esteemed academics in this field – 'Overview first, details on demand' – informs the idea of thinking about different layers of readability and depth in your visualisation work accessed through interactivity. Some of the chart types that you will meet in Chapter 6 can only ever hope to deliver a *gist* of the general magnitude of values (the big, the small and the medium) and not their precise details. A *treemap*, for example, is never going to facilitate the detailed perceiving of values because it uses rectangular areas to represent data values and our perceptual system is generally quite poor at judging different area scales. Additionally, a treemap often comprises a breakdown of many categorical values within the same chart display, so it is very busy and densely packed. However, if you have the capability to incorporate interactive features that allow the user to enter via this first overview layer and then explore beneath the surface, maybe clicking on a shape to reveal a pop-up with precise value labels, you are opening up additional details.

In effect you have moved your viewer's readability up the tonal spectrum that began with more of a general feeling of data and then moved towards the reading of data as a result of the interactive operation. Sometimes a 'gateway' layer is required for your primary view, to seduce your audience or to provide a big-picture overview (feeling), and then you can let the audience move on to more perceptually precise displays of the data (reading) either through interaction or perhaps by advancing through pages in a report or slide-deck sequence.

In the Better Life Index, shown in Figure 3.10, the opening layer is based around a series of charts that look like flowers. This is attractive, intriguing and offers a nice, single-page, at-a-glance

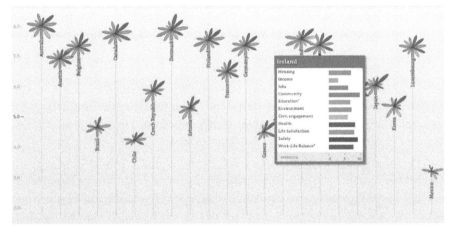

Figure 3.10
OECD Better
Life Index

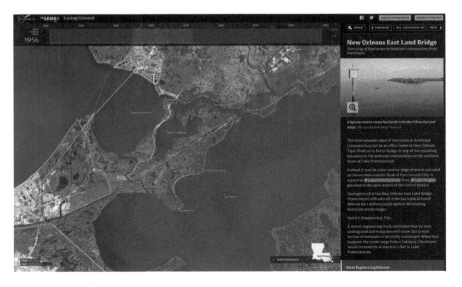

Figure 3.11
Losing Ground

summary. The task of reading the petal sizes with any degree of precision is hard but that is not the intent of this first layer. The purpose is to get a balance between a form that attracts the user and a function that offers a general sense of where the big, medium and small values sit within the data. For those who want to read the values with more precision, they are only a click away (on the flowers) from viewing an alternative display using a bar chart to represent the same values.

Increasingly there is a trend for projects to incorporate both explanatory and exploratory experiences into the same overall project – the term 'explorable explanations' has been coined to describe them. A project like 'Losing Ground' by ProPublica (Figure 3.11) is an example of this as it moves between telling a story about the disappearing coastline of Louisiana and enabling users to interrogate and adjust their view of the data at various milestone stages in the sequence.

Harnessing Ideas

The discussions so far in this chapter have involved practical reasoning. Before you move on to the immediate next stage of the design process – working with data – it can be valuable to briefly allow yourself the opportunity to harness your instinctive imagination.

Alongside your consideration of the purpose map, the other strand of thinking about 'vision' concerns the earliest seeds of any ideas you may have in mind for what this solution might comprise or even look like. These might be mental manifestations of ideas you have formed yourself or influenced or inspired by what you have seen elsewhere.

There are limits to the value of ideas and also to the role they are allowed to play, as I will mention shortly, but your instincts can offer a unique perspective if you choose to allow them to surface. If you have a naturally analytical approach to visualisation this activity might seem to be the wrong way round: how can legitimate ideas be formed until the data has been explored? I understand that, and it is a step that some readers will choose not to entertain until later in the process. However, do not rule it out, see if liberating your imagination now adds value to your analytical thinking later. There are several aspects to the concept and role of harnessing ideas that I feel are valuable to consider at this primary stage:

'I focus on structural exploration on one side and on the reality and the landscape of opportunities in the other ... I try not to impose any early ideas of what the result will look like because that will emerge from the process. In a nutshell I first activate data curiosity, client curiosity, and then visual imagination in parallel with experimentation.' **Santiago Ortiz, founder and Chief Data Officer at DrumWave, discussing the role – and timing – of forming ideas and mental concepts**

Mental visualisation: This concerns the other meaning of visualisation and is about embracing what we instinctively 'see' in our mind's eye when we consider the emerging brief for our task. In *Thinking Fast and Slow*, by Daniel Kahneman, the author describes two models of thought that control our thinking activities. He calls these System 1 and System 2 thinking: the former is responsible for our instinctive, intuitive and metaphorical thoughts; the latter is much more ponderous, by contrast, much slower, and requiring of more mental effort when being called upon. System 1 thinking is what you want to harness right now: what are the mental impressions that form quickly and automatically in your mind when you first think about the challenge you're facing?

You cannot switch off System 1 thoughts. You will not be able to stop mental images formulating about what your mind's eye sees when thinking about this problem instinctively. So, rather than stifling your natural mental habits, this earliest stage of the workflow process presents the best possible opportunity to allow yourself space to begin imagining.

What colours do you see? Sometimes instinctive ideas are reflections of our culture or society, especially the connotations of colour usage. What shapes and patterns strike you as being semantically aligned with the subject? This can be useful not just to inspire but also possibly to obtain a glimpse into the similarly impulsive way the minds of your audience might connect with a subject when consuming the solution.

For example, Figure 3.12 shows the size of production for different grape varieties across the wine industry. It uses a bubble chart to create the impression of a bunch of grapes. You can clearly see how this concept might have been formed in early sketches before the data even arrived, based on the mental visualisation of what the shape of a bunch of grapes looks like. It is consistent with the subject and offers an immediate metaphor that means any viewer looking at the work will immediately spot the connection between form and subject.

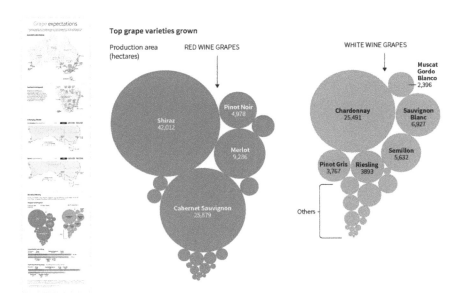

Figure 3.12
Grape
expectations

Keywords: What terms of language come to mind when thinking about the subject or the phenomena of your data? Figure 3.13 shows some notes I made in capturing the instinctive keywords and colours that came to mind when I was forming early thoughts and ideas about a project to do with psychotherapy treatment in the Arctic.

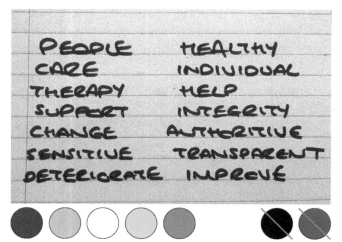

Figure 3.13　Example of Keywords and Colour Swatch Ideas

'I draw to freely explore possibilities. I draw to visually understand what I am thinking. I draw to evaluate my ideas and intuitions by seeing them coming to life on paper. I draw to help my mind think without limitations, without boundaries. The act of drawing, and the very fact we choose to stop and draw, demands focus and attention. I use drawing as my primary expression, as a sort of functional tool for capturing and exploring thoughts.' **Giorgia Lupi, Co-founder and Design Director at Accurat**

The words reflected the type of language I felt would be important to frame my design thinking, establishing a reference that could inform the tone of voice of my work. The colours were somewhat arbitrary and in the end I did not actually use them all, but they were indicative of the tones I was seeking. I did, however, see through my intention to avoid the blacks and blues (as they would carry unwelcome and clichéd connotations in this subject's context).

Sketching: As well as taking notes, sketching ideas is of great value to us here. I mentioned earlier that this is not about being a gifted artist but recognising the freedom and speed when extracting ideas from your mind onto paper. This is particularly helpful if you are working with collaborators and want a low-fidelity sketch for discussing plans, as well as in early discussions with stakeholders to understand better each others' take on the brief. For some people, the most fluent and efficient way to 'sketch' is through their software application of choice rather than on paper.

Regardless of whether your tool is the pen or the computer, just sketch your ideas with whatever is the most

Figure 3.14　Example of a Concept Sketch, by Giorgia Lupi

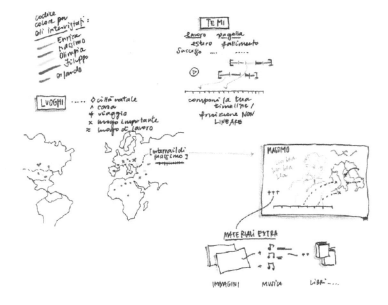

efficient and effective option given your time and confidence (see Figure 3.14). You will likely refine your sketches later on and, indeed, eventually you will move your attention completely away from pen and paper and onto the tools you are using to create the final work.

Research and inspiration: It is important to be sufficiently open to influence and inspiration from the world around you. Exposing your senses to different sources of reference both within and outside of visualisation can only help to broaden the range of solutions you might be able to conceive. Research the techniques that are being used around the visualisation field, look through books and see how others might have tackled similar subjects or curiosities (e.g. how they have shown changes over time on a map).

Beyond visualisation consider any source of imagery that inspires you: colours, patterns, shapes, and metaphors from everyday life whose aesthetic qualities you just like. In addition to your notebook and sketch pad, start a scrapbook or project mood board that compiles the sources of inspiration you come across and helps you form ideas about the style, tone or essence of your project. They might not have immediate value for the current project you are working on but may materialise as useful for future work.

'Recently taking up drawing has helped me better articulate the images I see in my mind, otherwise I still follow up on all different types of design and art outside information design/data visualisation. I try to look at things outside my field as often as I can to keep my mind fresh as opposed to only looking at projects from my field for inspiration.' **Stefanie Posavec, Information Designer**

'Look at how other designers solve visual problems (but don't copy the look of their solutions). Look at art to see how great painters use space, and organise the elements of their pictures. Look back at the history of infographics. It's all been done before, and usually by hand! Draw something with a pencil (or pen … but NOT a computer!) Sketch often: The cat asleep. The view from the bus. The bus. Personally, I listen to music – mostly jazz – a lot.' **Nigel Holmes, Explanation Graphic Designer, on inspirations that feed his approach**

'It is easy to immerse yourself in a certain idea, but I think it is important to step back regularly and recognise that other people have different ways of interpreting things. I am very fortunate to work with people whom I greatly admire and who also see things from a different perspective. Their feedback is invaluable in the process.' **Jane Pong, Data Visualisation Designer**

Limitation of your ideas: There are important limitations to acknowledge around the role of ideas. Influence and inspiration are healthy: the desire to emulate what others have done is understandable. Plagiarism, copying and stealing uncredited ideas are wrong. There are ambiguities in any creative discipline about the boundaries between influence and plagiarism, and the worlds of visualisation and infographic design are not spared that challenge.

Being influenced by the research you do and the great work you see around the field is not stealing, but if you do incorporate explicit ideas influenced by others in your work, at the very least you should do the noble thing and credit the authors, or even better seek them out and ask them to grant you their approval. You do not have to credit William Playfair every time you use the bar chart, but there are certain unique visual devices that will be unquestionably deserving of attribution.

Secondly, data is your raw material, your ideas are not. As you will see later, it is vital that you leave the main influence for your thinking to emerge from the type, size and meaning of your data. It may be that your ideas are ultimately incompatible with these properties of the data, in which case you will need to set these aside, and perhaps form new ones.

Eventually you will need to evolve from ideas and sketched concepts to starting to develop a solution in your tool of choice. These early ideas and sparks of creativity are vital and they should be embraced, but do not be precious or stubborn, always maintain an open mind and recognise that they have a limited role. Try to ignore the voices in your head after a certain period!

Limitation of others' ideas: Finally, there is the diplomatic challenge of being faced with the prospect of taking on board other people's ideas. One of the greatest anxieties I face comes from working with stakeholders who are unequivocally and emphatically clear about what they think a solution should look like. Often your involvement in a project may arrive after these ideas have already been formed and have become the basis of the brief issued by the stakeholders to you ('Can you make this, please?'). This is where your tactful but assured communicator's skill set comes to the fore. The ideas presented may be reasonable and well intended but it is your responsibility to lead on the creation process and guide it away from an early concept that simply may not work out. You can take these idea on board but, as with the limitations of your own ideas, there will be other factors with a greater influence – the nature of the data, the type of curiosities you are pursuing, the essence of the subject matter and the nature of the audience, among many other things. These will be the factors that ultimately dictate whether any early vision of potential ideas ends up being of value.

Summary: Formulating Your Brief

Establishing Your Project's Context

Defining Your Origin Curiosity Why are we doing it: what type of curiosity has motivated the decision/desire to undertake this visualisation project?

- Personal intrigue: 'I wonder what ...'
- Stakeholder intrigue: 'He/she needs to know ...'
- Audience intrigue: 'They need to know ...'
- Anticipated intrigue: 'They might be interested in knowing ...'
- Potential intrigue: 'There should be something interesting ...'

Circumstances The key factors that will impact on your critical thinking and shape your ambitions:

- People: stakeholders, audience.
- Constraints: pressures, rules.
- Consumption: frequency, setting.
- Deliverables: quantity, format.
- Resources: skills, technology.

Defining Your Purpose The 'so what?': what are we trying to accomplish with this visualis-ation? What is a successful 'outcome'?

Establishing Your Project's Vision

'Purpose Map' Plotting your expectation of what will be the best-fit type of solution to facili-tate the desired purpose:

- What kind of experience? Explanatory, exhibitory or exploratory?
- What tone of voice will it offer? The efficiency and perceptibility of reading data vs the high-level, affective nature of feeling data?

Harnessing Ideas What mental images, ideas and keywords instinctively come to mind when thinking about the subject matter of this challenge? What influence and inspiration can you source from elsewhere that might start to shape your thinking?

Tips and Tactics

- Do not get hung up if you are struggling with some circumstantial factors. Certain things may change in definition, some undefined things will emerge, some defined things will need to be reconsidered, some things are just always open.
- Notes are so important to keep about any thoughts you have had that express the nature of your curiosity, articulation of purpose, any assumptions, things you know and do not know, where you might need to get data from, who are the experts, questions, things to do, issues/problems, wish lists …
- Keep a 'scrapbook' (digital bookmarks, print clippings) of anything and everything that inspires and influences you – not just data visualisations. Log your ideas and inspire yourself.
- This stage is about ambition management/skills – it is to your benefit that you treat it with the thoroughness it needs. The negative impact of any corners being cut here will be ampli-fied later on.

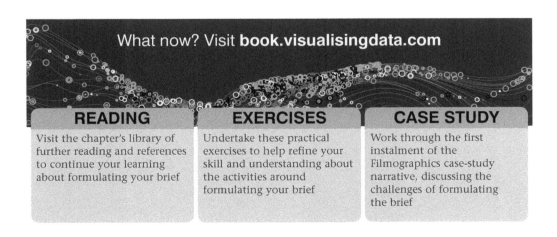

What now? Visit **book.visualisingdata.com**

READING
Visit the chapter's library of further reading and references to continue your learning about formulating your brief

EXERCISES
Undertake these practical exercises to help refine your skill and understanding about the activities around formulating your brief

CASE STUDY
Work through the first instalment of the Filmographics case-study narrative, discussing the challenges of formulating the brief

4

Working With Data

In Chapter 3 the workflow process was initiated by exploring the defining matters around context and vision. The discussion about curiosity, framing not just the subject matter of interest but also a specific enquiry that you are seeking an answer to, in particular leads your thinking towards this second stage of the process: working with data.

In this chapter I will start by covering some of the most salient aspects of data and statistical literacy. This section will be helpful for those readers without any – or at least with no extensive – prior data experience. For those who have more experience and confidence with this topic, maybe through their previous studies, it might merely offer a reminder of some of the things you will need to focus on when working with data on a visualisation project.

There is a lot of hard work that goes into the activities encapsulated by 'working with data'. I have broken these down into four different groups of action, each creating substantial demands on your time:

- Data acquisition: Gathering the raw material.
- Data examination: Identifying physical properties and meaning.
- Data transformation: Enhancing your data through modification and consolidation.
- Data exploration: Using exploratory analysis and research techniques to learn.

You will find that there are overlapping concerns between this chapter and the nature of Chapter 5, where you will establish your editorial thinking. The present chapter generally focuses more on the mechanics of familiarisation with the characteristics and qualities of your data; the next chapter will build on this to shape what you will actually do with it.

As you might expect, the activities covered in this chapter are associated with the assistance of relevant tools and technology. However, the focus for the book will remain concentrated on identifying *which* tasks you have to undertake and look less at exactly *how* you will undertake these. There will be tool-specific references in the curated collection of resources that are published in the digital companion.

4.1 Data Literacy: Love, Fear and Loathing

I frequently come across people in the field who declare their love for data. I don't love data. For me it would be like claiming 'I love food' when, realistically, that would be misleading. I like sprouts but hate carrots. And don't get me started on mushrooms.

At the very start of the book, I mentioned that data might occasionally prove to be a villain in your quest for developing confidence with data visualisation. If data were an animal it would almost certainly be a cat: it has a capacity to earn and merit love but it demands a lot of attention and always seems to be conspiring against you.

I *love* data that gives me something interesting to do analysis-wise and then, subsequently, also visually. Sometimes that just does not happen.

I *love* data that is neatly structured, clean and complete. This rarely exists. Location data will have inconsistent place-name spellings, there will be dates that have a mixture of US and UK formats, and aggregated data that does not let me get to the underlying components.

You don't need to *love* data but, equally, you shouldn't fear data. You should simply respect it by appreciating that it will potentially need lots of care and attention and a shift in your thinking about its role in the creative process. Just look to develop a rapport with it, embracing its role as the absolutely critical raw material of this process, and learn how to nurture its potential.

For some of you reading this book, you might have interest in data but possibly not much knowledge of the specific activities involving data as you work on a visualisation design solution. An assumed prerequisite for anyone working in data visualisation is an appreciation of data and statistical literacy. However, this is not always the case. One of the biggest causes of failure in data visualisations – especially in relation to the principle I introduced about 'trustworthy design' – comes from a poor understanding of these numerate literacies. This can be overcome, though.

'When I first started learning about visualisation, I naively assumed that datasets arrived at your doorstep ready to roll. Begrudgingly I accepted that before you can plot or graph anything, you have to find the data, understand it, evaluate it, clean it, and perhaps restructure it.' **Marcia Gray, Graphic Designer**

I discussed in the Introduction the different entry points from which people doing data visualisation work come. Typically – but absolutely not universally – those who join from the more creative backgrounds of graphic design and development might not be expected to have developed the same level of data and statistical knowledge than somebody from the more numerate disciplines. If you are part of this creative cohort and can identify with this generalisation, then this chapter will ease you through the learning process (and in doing so hopefully dispel any myth that it is especially complicated).

Conversely, many others may think they do not know enough about data but in reality they already do 'get' it – they just need to learn more about its role in visualisation and possibly realign their understanding of some of the terminology. Therefore, before delving further into this chapter's tasks, there are a few 'defining' matters I need to address to cover the basics in both data and statistical literacy.

Data Assets and Tabulation Types

Firstly, let's consider some of the fundamentals about what a dataset is as well as what shape and form it comes in.

When working on a visualisation I generally find there are two main categories of data 'assets': data that exist in tables, known as datasets; and data that exists as isolated values.

Tabulated datasets are what we are mainly interested in at this point. Data as isolated values refers to data that exists as individual facts and statistical figures. These do not necessarily

> For the purpose of this book I describe this type of data as being raw because it has not yet been statistically or mathematically manipulated and it has not been modified in any other way from its original state.

belong in, nor are they normally collected in, a table. They are just potentially useful values that are dispersed around the Web or across reports: individual facts or figures that you might come across during your data gathering or research stages. Later on in your work you might use these to inform calculations (e.g. applying a currency conversion) or to incorporate a fact into a title or caption (e.g. 78% of staff participated in the survey), but they are not your main focus for now.

Tabulated data is unquestionably the most common form of data asset that you will work with, but it too can exist in slightly different shapes and sizes. A primary difference lies between what can be termed *normalised* datasets (Figure 4.1) and *cross-tabulated* datasets (Figure 4.2).

A normalised dataset might loosely be described as looking like lists of data values. In spreadsheet parlance, you would see this as a series of columns and rows of data, while in database parlance it is the arrangement of fields and records. This form of tabulated data is generally the most detailed form of data available for you to work with. The table in Figure 4.1 is an example of normalised data where the columns of variables provide different descriptive values for each movie (or record) held in the table.

CATEGORY	MOVIE TITLE	CRITIC RATING	REVIEW GROUP
Star Wars	Star Wars: Episode IV - A New Hope	8.3	Fresh
Star Wars	Star Wars: Episode V - The Empire Strikes Back	8.7	Fresh
Star Wars	Star Wars: Episode VI - Return of the Jedi	6.8	Fresh
Star Wars	Star Wars: Episode I - The Phantom Menace	5.8	Rotten
Star Wars	Star Wars: Episode II - Attack of the Clones 3D	6.6	Fresh
Star Wars	Star Wars: Episode III - Revenge of the Sith 3D	7.2	Fresh
X-Men	X-Men	7.0	Fresh
X-Men	X2: X-Men United	7.4	Fresh
X-Men	X-Men: The Last Stand	5.9	Rotten
X-Men	X-Men Origins - Wolverine	5.1	Rotten
X-Men	X-Men: First Class	7.4	Fresh
X-Men	The Wolverine	6.3	Fresh
X-Men	X-Men: Days of Future Past	7.6	Fresh
Tolkien	The Lord of the Rings: The Fellowship of the Ring	8.2	Fresh
Tolkien	The Lord of the Rings: The Two Towers	8.5	Fresh
Tolkien	The Lord of the Rings: The Return of the King	8.7	Fresh
Tolkien	The Hobbit: An Unexpected Journey	6.6	Fresh
Tolkien	The Hobbit: The Desolation of Smaug	6.8	Fresh
Tolkien	The Hobbit: The Battle of the Five Armies	6.3	Fresh

Figure 4.1

Example of a Normalised Dataset

Cross-tabulated data is presented in a reconfigured form where, instead of displaying raw data values, the table of cells contain the results of statistical operations (like summed totals, maximums, averages). These values are aggregated calculations formed from the relationship between two variables held in the normalised form of the data. In Figure 4.2, you will see the cross-tabulated result of the normalised table of movie data, now showing a statistical summary for each movie category. The statistic under 'Max Critic Rating' is formed from an aggregating calculation based on the 'Critic Rating' and 'Category' variables seen in Figure 4.1.

Figure 4.2
Example of a
Cross-tabulated
Dataset

CATEGORY	MOVIES	MAX CRITIC RATING	REVIEW: FRESH	REVIEW: ROTTEN
Star Wars	6	8.7	5	1
Tolkien	6	8.7	6	0
X-Men	7	7.6	5	2
SUMMARY	19	8.7	16	3

Typically, if you receive data in an already cross-tabulated form, you do not have access to the original data. This means you will not be able to 'reverse-engineer' it back into its raw form, which, in turn, means you have reduced the scope of your potential analysis. In contrast, normalised data gives you complete freedom to explore, manipulate and aggregate across multiple dimensions. You may choose to convert the data into 'cross-tabulated' form but that is merely an option that comes with the luxury of having access to the detailed form of your data. In summary, it is always preferable, where possible, to work with normalised data.

Data Types

One of the key parts of the design process concerns understanding the different types of data (sometimes known as *levels of data* or *scales of measurement*). Defining the types of data will have a huge influence on so many aspects of this workflow, such as determining:

- the type of exploratory data analysis you can undertake;
- the editorial thinking you establish;
- the specific chart types you might use;
- the colour choices and layout decisions around composition.

In the simplest sense, data types are distinguished by being either qualitative or quantitative in nature. Beneath this distinction there are several further separations that need to be understood. The most useful taxonomy I have found to describe these different types of data is based on an approach devised by the psychologist researcher Stanley Stevens. He developed the acronym NOIR as a mnemonic device to cover the different types of data you may come to work with, particularly in social research: Nominal, Ordinal, Interval, and Ratio. I have extended this, adding onto the front a 'T' – for Textual – which, admittedly, somewhat undermines the grace of the original acronym but better reflects the experiences of handling data today. It is important to describe, define and compare these different types of data.

Textual (Qualitative)

Textual data is qualitative data and generally exists as unstructured streams of words. Examples of textual data might include:

- 'Any other comments?' data submitted in a survey.
- Descriptive details of a weather forecast for a given city.
- The full title of an academic research project.

- The description of a product on Amazon.
- The URL of an image of Usain Bolt's victory in the 100m at the 2012 Olympics.

In its native form, textual data is likely to offer rich potential but it can prove quite demanding to unlock this. To work with textual data in an analysis and visualisation context will generally require certain natural language processing techniques to derive or extract classifications, sentiments, quantitative properties and relational characteristics.

An example of how you can use textual data is seen in the graphic of CEO swear word usage shown in Figure 4.3. This analysis provides a breakdown of the profanities used by CEOs from a review of recorded conference calls over a period of 10 years. This work shows the two ways of utilising textual data in visualisation. Firstly, you can derive categorical classifications and quantitative measurements to count the use of certain words compared to others and track their usage over time. Secondly, the original form of the textual data can be of direct value for annotation purposes, without the need for any analytical treatment, to include as captions.

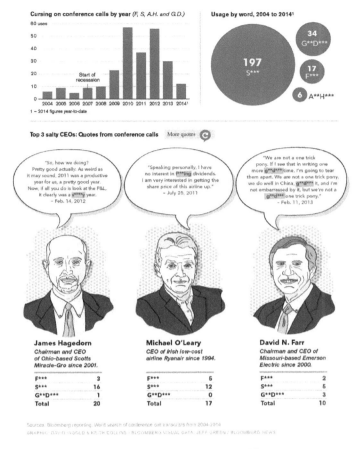

Figure 4.3   Graphic Language: The Curse of the CEO

Working with textual data will always involve a judgement of reward vs effort: how much effort will I need to expend in order to extract usable, valuable content from the text? There are an increasing array of tools and algorithmic techniques to help with this transformational approach but whether you conduct it manually or with some degree of automation it can be quite a significant undertaking. However, the value of the insights you are able to extract may entirely justify the commitment. As ever, your judgment of the aims of your work, the nature of your subject and the interests of your audience will influence your decision.

Nominal (Qualitative)

Nominal data is the next form of qualitative data in the list of distinct data types. This type of data exists in categorical form, offering a means of distinguishing, labelling and organising values. Examples of nominal data might include:

- The 'gender' selected by a survey participant.
- The regional identifier (location name) shown in a weather forecast.
- The university department of an academic member of staff.
- The language of a book on Amazon.
- An athletic event at the Olympics.

Often a dataset will hold multiple nominal variables, maybe offering different organising and naming perspectives, for example the gender, eye colour and hair colour of a class of school kids.

Additionally, there might be a hierarchical relationship existing between two or more nominal variables, representing major and sub-categorical values: for example, a major category holding details of 'Country' and a sub-category holding 'Airport'; or a major category holding details of 'Industry' and a sub-category holding details of 'Company Names'. Recognising this type of relationship will become important when considering the options for which angles of analysis you might decide to focus on and how you may portray them visually using certain chart types.

Nominal data does not necessarily mean text-based data; nominal values can be numeric. For example, a student ID number is a categorical device used uniquely to identify all students. The shirt number of a footballer is a way of helping teammates, spectators and officials to recognise each player. It is important to be aware of occasions when any categorical values are shown as numbers in your data, especially in order to understand that these cannot have (meaningful) arithmetic operations applied to them. You might find logic statements like TRUE or FALSE stated as a 1 and a 0, or data captured about gender may exist as a 1 (male), 2 (female) and 3 (other), but these numeric values should not be considered quantitative values – adding '1' to '2' does not equal '3' (other) for gender.

Ordinal (Qualitative)

Ordinal data is still categorical and qualitative in nature but, instead of there being an arbitrary relationship between the categorical values, there are now characteristics of order. Examples of nominal data might include:

- The response to a survey question: based on a scale of 1 (unhappy) to 5 (very happy).
- The general weather forecast: expressed as Very Hot, Hot, Mild, Cold, Freezing.
- The academic rank of a member of staff.
- The delivery options for an Amazon order: Express, Next Day, Super Saver.
- The medal category for an athletic event: Gold, Silver, Bronze.

Whereas nominal data is a categorical device to help distinguish values, ordinal data is also a means of classifying values, usually in some kind of ranking. The hierarchical order of some ordinal values goes through a single ascending/descending rank from high or good values to low or bad values. Other ordinal values have a natural 'pivot' where the direction changes around a recognisable mid-point, such as the happiness scale which might pivot about 'no feeling' or weather forecast data that pivots about 'Mild'. Awareness of these different approaches to 'order' will become relevant when you reach the design stages involving the classifying of data through colour scales.

Interval (Quantitative)

Interval data is the less common form of quantitative data, but it is still important to be aware of and to understand its unique characteristics. An interval variable is a quantitative and numeric measurement defined by difference on a scale but *not* by relative scale. This means the difference between two values is meaningful but an arithmetic operation such as multiplication is not.

The most common example is the measure for temperature in a weather forecast, presented in units of Celsius. The absolute difference between 15°C and 20°C is the same difference as between 5°C and 10°C. However, the relative difference between 5°C and 10°C is not the same as the difference between 10°C and 20°C (where in both cases you multiply by two or increase by 100%). This is because a zero value is arbitrary and often means very little or indeed is impossible. A temperature reading of 0°C does not mean there is no temperature, it is a quantitative scale for measuring relative temperature. You cannot have a shoe size or Body Mass Index of zero.

Ratio (Quantitative)

Ratio data is the most common quantitative variable you are likely to come across. It comprises numeric measurements that have properties of difference *and* scale. Examples of nominal data might include:

- The age of a survey participant in years.
- The forecasted amount of rainfall in millimetres.
- The estimated budget for a research grant proposal in GBP (£).
- The number of sales of a book on Amazon.
- The distance of the winning long jump at the 2012 Olympics in metres.

Unlike interval data, for ratio data variables zero means something. The absolute difference in age between a 10 and 20 year old is the same as the difference between a 40 and 50 year old. The relative difference between a 10 and a 20 year old is the same as the difference between a 40 and an 80 year old ('twice as old').

Whereas most of the quantitative measurements you will deal with are based on a linear scale, there are exceptions. Variables about the strength of sound (decibels) and magnitude of earthquakes (Richter) are actually based on a logarithmic scale. An earthquake with a magnitude of 4.0 on the Richter scale is 1000 times stronger based on the amount of energy released than an earthquake of magnitude

> If temperature values were measured in kelvin, where there is an absolute zero, this would be considered a ratio scale, not an interval one.

2.0. Some consider these as types of data that are different from ratio variables. Most still define them as ratio variables but separate them as non-linear scaled variables.

Temporal Data

Time-based data is worth mentioning separately because it can be a frustrating type of data to deal with, especially in attempting to define its place within the TNOIR classification. The reason for this is that different components of time can be positioned against almost all data types, depending simply on what form your time data takes:

Textual: 'Four o'clock in the afternoon on Monday, 12 March 2016'

Ordinal: 'PM', 'Afternoon', 'March', 'Q1'

Interval: '12', '12/03/2016', '2016'

Ratio: '16:00'

Note that time-based data is separate in concern to duration data, which, while often formatted in structures such as hh:mm:ss, should be seen as a ratio measure. To work with duration data it is often useful to transform it into single units of time, such as total seconds or minutes.

Discrete vs Continuous

Another important distinction to make about your data, and something that cuts across the TNOIR classification, is whether the data is discrete or continuous. This distinction is influential in how you might analyse it statistically and visually.

The relatively simple explanation is that discrete data is associated with all classifying variables that have no 'in-between' state. This applies to all qualitative data types and any quantitative values for which only a whole is possible. Examples might be:

- Heads or tails for a coin toss.
- Days of the week.
- The size of shoes.
- Numbers of seats in a theatre.

In contrast, continuous variables can hold the value of an in-between state and, in theory, could take on any value between the natural upper and lower limits if it was possible to take measurements in fine degrees of detail, such as:

- Height and weight.
- Temperature.
- Time.

One of the classifications that is hard to nail down involves data that could, on the TNOIR scale, arguably fall under both ordinal and ratio definitions based on its usage. This makes it hard to determine if it should be considered discrete or continuous. An example would be the star system used for rating a movie or the happiness rating. When a star rating value is originally captured, the likelihood is that the input data was discrete in nature. However, for analysis purposes, the statistical operations applied to data that is based on different star ratings could reasonably be treated either as discrete classifications or, feasibly, as continuous numeric values. For both star review ratings or happiness ratings decimal averages could be calculated as a way of formulating average score. (The median and mode would still be discrete.) The suitability of this approach will depend on whether the absolute difference between classifying values can be considered equal.

4.2 Statistical Literacy

If the fear of data is misplaced, I can sympathise with anybody's trepidation towards statistics. For many, statistics can feel complicated to understand and too difficult a prospect to master. Even for those relatively comfortable with stats, it is unquestionably a discipline that can easily become rusty without practice, which can also undermine your confidence. Furthermore, the fear of making mistakes with delicate and rule-based statistical calculations also depresses the confidence levels lower than they need to be.

The problem is that you cannot avoid the need to use *some* statistical techniques if you are going to work with data. It is therefore important to better understand statistics and its role in visualisation, as you must do with data. Perhaps you can make the problem more surmountable by packaging the whole of statistics into smaller, manageable elements that will dispel the perception of overwhelming complexity.

I do believe that it is possible to overstate the range and level of statistical techniques *most* people will need to employ on *most* of their visualisation tasks. The caveats are important as I know there will be people with visualisation experience who are exposed to a tremendous amount of statistical thinking in their work, but it is a relevant point.

It all depends, of course. From my experience, however, the majority of data visualisation challenges will generally involve relatively straightforward *univariate* and *multivariate* statistical techniques. Univariate techniques help you to understand the shape, size and range of quantitative values. Multivariate techniques help you to explore the possible relationships between different combinations of variables and variable types. I will describe some of the most relevant statistical operations associated with these techniques later in this chapter, at the point in your thinking where they are most applicable.

As you get more advanced in your work (and your confidence increases) you might have occasion to employ *inference* techniques. These include concepts such as data modelling and the use of regression analysis: attempting to measure the relationships between variables to explore correlations and (the holy grail) causations. Many of you will likely experience visualisation challenges that require an understanding of probabilities, testing hypotheses and becoming acquainted with terms like confidence intervals. You might use these techniques to assist with forecasting or modelling risk and uncertainty. Above and beyond that, you are moving towards more advanced statistical modelling and algorithm design.

It is somewhat dissatisfactory to allocate only a small part of this text to discussing the role of descriptive and exploratory statistics. However, for the scope of this book, and seeking to achieve a pragmatic balance, the most sensible compromise is just to flag up which statistical activities you might need to consider and where these apply. It can take years to learn about the myriad advanced techniques that exist and it takes experience to know when and how to deploy all the different methods.

There are hundreds of books better placed to offer the depth of detail you truly need to fulfil these activities and there is no real need to reinvent the wheel – and indeed reinvent an inferior wheel. That statistics is just one part of the visualisation challenge, and is in itself such a prolific field, further demonstrates the variety and depth of this subject.

4.3 Data Acquisition

The first step in working with data naturally involves getting it. As I outlined in the contextual discussion about the different types of trigger curiosities, you will only have data in place before now if the opportunity presented by the data was the factor that triggered this work. You will recall this scenario was described as pursuing a curiosity born out of 'potential intrigue'. Otherwise, you will only be in a position to know what data you need after having established your specific or general motivating curiosity. In these situations, once you have sufficiently progressed your thinking around 'formulating your brief', you will need to switch your thinking onto the task of acquiring your data:

- What data do you need and why?
- From where, how, and by whom will the data be acquired?
- When can you obtain it?

What Data Do You Need?

Your primary concern is to ensure you can gather sufficient data about the subject in which you are interested to pursue your identified curiosity. By 'sufficient', I mean you will need to establish some general criteria in your mind for what data you do need and what data you do not need. There is no harm in getting more than you need at this stage but it can result in wasted efforts, waste that you would do well to avoid.

Let's propose you have defined your curiosity to be 'I wonder what a map of McDonald's restaurant openings looks like over time?'. In this scenario you are going to try to find a source of data that will provide you with details of all the McDonald's restaurants that have ever opened. A shopping list of data items would probably include the date of opening, the location details (as specific as possible) and maybe even a closing date to ensure you can distinguish between still operating and closed-down restaurants.

You will need to conduct some research, a perpetual strand of activity that runs throughout the workflow, as I explained earlier. In this scenario you might need first to research a bit of the history of McDonald's restaurants to discover, for instance, when the first one opened, how many there are, and in which countries they are located. This will establish an initial sense of the timeframe (number of years) and scale (outlets, global spread) of your potential data. You might also discover significant differences between what is considered a restaurant and what is just a franchise positioned in shopping malls or transit hubs. Sensitivities around the qualifying criteria or general counting rules of a subject are important to discover, as they will help significantly to substantiate the integrity and accuracy of your work.

Unless you know or have been told where to find this restaurant data, you will then need to research from where the data might be obtainable. Will this type of information be published on the Web, perhaps on the commercial pages of McDonald's own site? You might have to get in touch with somebody (yes, a human) in the commercial or PR department to access some advice. Perhaps there will be some fast-food enthusiast in some niche corner of the Web who has already gathered and made available data like this?

Suppose you locate a dataset that includes not just McDonald's restaurants but *all* fast-food outlets. This could potentially broaden the scope of your curiosity, enabling broader analysis about the growth of the fast-food industry at large to contextualise MacDonald's contribution to this. Naturally, if you have any stakeholders involved in your project, you might need to discuss with them the merits of this wider perspective.

Another judgement to make concerns the resolution of the data you anticipate needing. This is especially relevant if you are working with big, heavy datasets. You might genuinely want and need all available data. This would be considered full resolution – down to the most detailed grain (e.g. all details about all MacDonald's restaurants, not just totals per city or country). Sometimes, in this initial gathering activity, it may be more practical just to obtain a sample of your data. If this is the case, what will be the criteria used to identify a sufficient sample and how will you select or exclude records? What percentage of your data will be sufficient to be representative of the range and diversity (an important feature we will need to examine next)? Perhaps you only need a statistical, high-level summary (total number of restaurants opened by year)?

The chances are that you will not truly know what data you want or need until you at least get something to start with and learn from there. You might have to revisit or repeat the gathering of your data, so an attitude of 'what I have is good enough to start with' is often sensible.

From Where, How and By Whom Will the Data Be Acquired?

There are several different origins and methods involved in acquiring data, depending on whether it will involve your doing the heavy work to curate the data or if this will be the main responsibility of others.

Curated by You

This group of data-gathering tasks or methods is characterised by your having to do most of the work to bring the data together into a convenient digital form.

Primary data collection: If the data you need does not exist or you need to have full control over its provenance and collection, you will have to consider embarking on gathering 'primary' data. In contrast to secondary data, primary data involves you measuring and collecting the raw data yourself. Typically, this relates to situations where you gather quite small, bespoke datasets about phenomena that are specific to your needs. It might be a research experiment you have designed and launched for participants to submit responses. You may manually record data from other measurement devices, such as your daily weight as measured by your bathroom scales, or the number of times you interacted face-to-face with friends and family. Some people take daily photographs of themselves, their family members or their gardens, in order to stitch these back together eventually to portray stories of change. This data-gathering activity can be expensive in terms of both the time and cost. The benefit however is that you have carefully controlled the collection of the data to optimise its value for your needs.

Manual collection and data foraging: If the data you need does not exist digitally or in a convenient singular location, you will need to *forage* for it. This again might typically relate to situations where you are sourcing relatively small datasets. An example might be researching historical data from archived newspapers that were only published in print form and not available digitally. You might look to pull data from multiple sources to create a single dataset: for example, if you were comparing the attributes of a range of different cars and weighing up which to buy. To achieve this you would probably need to source different parts of the data you need from several different places. Often, data foraging is something you undertake in order to finish off data collected by other means that might have a few missing values. It is sometimes more efficient to find

Some data acquisition tasks may be repetitive and, should you possess the skills and have access to the necessary resources, there will be scope for exploring ways to automate these. However, you always have to consider the respective effort and ongoing worth of your approach. If you do go to the trouble of authoring an automation routine (of any description) you could end up spending more time on that than you would otherwise collecting by more manual methods. If it is going to be a regular piece of analysis the efficiency gains from your automation will unquestionably prove valuable going forward, but, for any one-off projects, it may not be ultimately worth it

the remaining data items yourself by hand to complete the dataset. This can be somewhat time-consuming depending on the extent of the manual gathering required, but it does provide you with greater assurance over the final condition of the data you have collected.

Extracted from pdf files: A special subset of data foraging – or a variation at least – involves those occasions when your data is digital but essentially locked away in a pdf file. For many years now reports containing valuable data have been published on the Web in pdf form. Increasingly, movements like 'open data' are helping to shift the attitudes of organisations towards providing additional, fully accessible digital versions of data. Progress is being made but it will take time before all industries and government bodies adopt this as a common standard. In the meantime, there are several tools on the market (free and proprietary) that will assist you in extracting tables of data from pdf files and converting these to more usable Excel or CSV formats.

Web scraping (also known as web harvesting): This involves using special tools or programs to extract structured and unstructured items of data published in web pages and convert these into tabulated form for analysis. For example, you may wish to extract several years' worth of test cricket results from a sports website. Depending on the tools used, you can often set routines in motion to extract data across multiple pages of a site based on the connected links that exist within it. This is known as web crawling. Using the same example (let's imagine), you could further your gathering of test cricket data by programmatically fetching data back from the associated links pointing to the team line-ups. An important consideration to bear in mind with any web scraping or crawling activity concerns rules of access and the legalities of extracting the data held on certain sites. Always check – and respect – the terms of use before undertaking this.

Curated by Others

In contrast to the list of methods I have profiled, this next set of data-gathering approaches is characterised by other people having done most of the work to source and compile the data. They will make it available for you to access in different ways without needing the extent of manual efforts often required with the methods presented already. You might occasionally still have to intervene by hand to fine-tune your data, but others would generally have put in the core effort.

Issued to you: On the occasions when you are commissioned by a stakeholder (client, colleague) you will often be provided with the data you need (and probably much more besides), most commonly in a spreadsheet format. The main task for you is therefore less about collection and more about familiarisation with the contents of the data file(s) you are set to work with.

Download from the Web: Earlier I bemoaned the fact that there are still organisations publishing data (through, for example, annual reports) in pdf form. To be fair, increasingly there are facilities being developed that enable interested users to extract data in a more structured form. More sophisticated reporting interfaces may offer users the opportunity to construct detailed queries to extract and download data that is highly customised to their needs.

System report or export: This is related more to an internal context in organisations where there are opportunities to extract data from corporate systems and databases. You might, for example, wish to conduct some analysis about staff costs and so the personnel database may be where you can access the data about the workforce and their salaries.

Third-party services: There is an ever-increasing marketplace for data and many

'Don't underestimate the importance of domain expertise. At the Office for National Statistics (ONS), I was lucky in that I was very often working with the people who created the data – obviously, not everyone will have that luxury. But most credible data producers will now produce something to accompany the data they publish and help users interpret it – make sure you read it, as it will often include key findings as well as notes on reliability and limitations of the data.' **Alan Smith OBE, Data Visualisation Editor,** *Financial Times* commercial services out there now offer extensive sources of curated and customised data that would otherwise be impossible to obtain or very complex to gather. Such requests might include very large, customised extracts from social media platforms like Twitter based on specific keywords and geo-locations.

API: An API (Application Programme Interface) offers the means to create applications that programmatically access streams of data from sites or services, such as accessing a live feed from Transport for London (TfL) to track the current status of trains on the London Underground system.

When Can the Data Be Acquired?

The issue of *when* data is ready and available for acquisition is a delicate one. If you are conducting analysis of some survey results, naturally you will not have the full dataset of responses to work with until the survey is closed. However, you could reasonably begin some of your analysis work early by using an initial sample of what had been submitted so far. Ideally you will always work with data that is as complete as possible, but on occasions it may be advantageous to take the opportunity to get an early sense of the nature of the submitted responses in order to begin preparing your final analysis routines. Working on any dataset that may not yet be complete is a risk. You do not want to progress too far ahead with your visualisation workflow if there is the real prospect that any further data that emerges could offer new insights or even trigger different, more interesting curiosities.

4.4 Data Examination

After acquiring your data your next step is to thoroughly examine it. As I have remarked, your data is your key raw material from which the eventual visualisation output will be formed. Before you choose what meal to cook, you need to know what ingredients you have and what you need to do to prepare them.

It may be that, in the act of acquiring the data, you have already achieved a certain degree of familiarity about its status, characteristics and qualities, especially if you curated the data yourself. However, there is a definite need to go much further than you have likely achieved before now. To do this you need to conduct an examination of the physical properties and the meaning of your data.

As you progress through the stages of this workflow, your data will likely change considerably: you will bring more of it in, you will remove some of it, and you will refine it to suit your needs. All these modifications will alter the physical makeup of your data so you will need to keep revisiting this step to preserve your critical familiarity.

Data Properties

The first part of familiarising yourself with with your data is to undertake an examination of its physical properties. Specifically you need to ascertain its type, size and condition. This task is quite mechanical in many ways because you are in effect just 'looking' at the data, establishing its surface characteristics through visual and/or statistical observations.

What To Look For?

The *type* and *size* of your data involve assessing the characteristics and amount of data you have to work with. As you examine the data you also need to determine its *condition*: how good is its quality and is it fit for purpose?

Data types: Firstly, you need to identify what data types you have. In gathering this data in the first place you might already have a solid appreciation about what you have before you, but doing this thoroughly helps to establish the attention to detail you will need to demonstrate throughout this stage. Here you will need to refer to the definitions from earlier in the chapter about the different types of data (TNOIR). Specifically you are looking to define each column or field of data based on whether it is qualitative (text, nominal, ordinal) or quantitative (interval, ratio) and whether it is discrete or continuous in nature.

Size: Within each column or field you next need to know what range of values exist and what are the specific attributes/formats of the values held. For example, if you have a quantitative variable (interval or ratio), what is the lowest and the highest value? In what number format is it presented (i.e. how many decimal points or comma formatted)? If it is a categorical variable (nominal or ordinal), how many different values are held? If you have textual data, what is the maximum character length or word count?

Condition: This is the best moment to identify any data quality and completeness issues. Naturally, unidentified and unresolved issues around data quality will come to bite hard later, undermining the scope and, crucially, trust in the accuracy of your work. You will address these issues next in the 'transformation' step, but for now the focus is on identifying any problems. Things to look out for may include the following:

- Missing values, records or variables – Are empty cells assumed as being of no value (zero/nothing) or no measurement (n/a, null)? This is a subtle but important difference.
- Erroneous values – Typos and any value that clearly looks out of place (such as a gender value in the age column).
- Inconsistencies – Capitalisation, units of measurement, value formatting.
- Duplicate records.
- Out of date – Values that might have expired in accuracy, like someone's age or any statistic that would be reasonably expected to have subsequently changed.
- Uncommon system characters or line breaks.
- Leading or trailing spaces – the invisible evil!
- Date issues around format (dd/mm/yy or mm/dd/yy) and basis (systems like Excel's base dates on daily counts since 1 January 1900, but not all do that).

How to Approach This?

I explained in the earlier 'Data literacy' section the difference in asset types (data that exists in tables and data that exists as isolated values) and also the difference in form (normalised data or cross-tabulated). Depending on the asset and form of data, your examination of data types may involve slightly different approaches, but the general task is the same. Performing this examination process will vary, though, based on the tools you are using. The simplest approach, relevant to most, is to describe the task as you would undertake it using Excel, given that this continues to be the common tool most people use or have the skills to use. Also, it is likely that most visualisation tasks you undertake will involve data of a size that can be comfortably handled in Excel.

As you go through this task, it is good practice to note down a detailed overview of what data you have, perhaps in the form of a table of data descriptions. This is not as technical a duty as would be associated with the creation of a data dictionary but its role and value are similar, offering a convenient means to capture all the descriptive properties of your various data assets.

> 'Data inspires me. I always open the data in its native format and look at the raw data just to get the lay of the land. It's much like looking at a map to begin a journey.' **Kim Rees, Co-founder, Periscopic**

Inspect and scan: Your first task is just to scan your table of data visually. Navigate around it using the mouse/trackpad, use the arrow keys to move up or down and left or right, and just look at all the data. Gain a sense of its overall dimension. How many columns and how many rows does it occupy? How big a prospect might working with this be?

Data operations: Inspecting your data more closely might require the use of interrogation features such as sorting columns and doing basic filters. This can be a quick and simple way to acquaint yourself with the type of data and range of values.

Going further, once again depending on the technology (and assuming you have normalised data to start with), you might apply a cross-tabulation or pivot table to create aggregated, summary views of different angles and combinations of your data. This can be a useful approach to also check out the unique range of values that exist under different categories as well as helping to establish how sub-categories may relate other categories hierarchically. This type of inspection will be furthered in the next step of the 'working with data' process when you will undertake deeper visual interrogations of the type, size and condition of your data.

If you have multiple tables, you will need to repeat this approach for each one as well as determine how they are related collectively and on what basis. It could be that just considering one table as the standard template, representative of each instance, is sufficient: for example, if each subsequent table is just a different monthly view of the same activity.

For so-called 'Big Data' (see the glossary definition earlier), it is less likely that you can conduct this examination work through relatively quick, visual observations using Excel. Instead it will need tools based around statistical language that will *describe* for you what is there rather than let you *look* at what is there.

Statistical methods: The role of statistics in this examination stage generally involves relatively basic quantitative analysis methods to help describe and understand the characteristics of each data variable. The common term applied to this type of statistical approach is univariate, because it involves just looking at one variable at a time (the best opportunity to perform the analysis of multiple variables comes later). Here are some different types of statistical analyses you might find useful at this stage. These are not the only methods you will ever need to use, but will likely prove to be among the most common:

- *Frequency counts*: applied to categorical values to understand the frequency of different instances.
- *Frequency distribution*: applied to quantitative values to learn about the type and shape of the distribution of values.

- Measurements of *central tendency* describe the summary attributes of a group of quantitative values, including:

  o the mean (the average value);

  o the median (the middle value if all quantities were arranged from smallest to largest);

  o the mode (the most common value).

- Measurements of *spread* are used to describe the dispersion of values above and below the mean:

  o Maximum, minimum and range: the highest and lowest and magnitude of spread of values.

  o Percentiles: the value below which x% of values fall (e.g. the 20th percentile is the value below which 20% of all quantitative values fall).

  o Standard deviation: a calculated measure used to determine how spread out a series of quantitative values are.

Data Meaning

Irrespective of whether you or others have curated the data, you need to be discerning about how much trust you place in it, at least to begin with. As discussed in the 'trustworthy design' principle, there are provenance issues, inaccuracies and biases that will affect its status on the journey from being created to being acquired. These are matters you need to be concerned with in order to resolve or at least compensate for potential shortcomings.

Knowing more about the physical properties of your data does not yet achieve full familiarity with its content nor give you sufficient acquaintance with its qualities. You will have examined the data in a largely mechanical and probably quite detached way from the underlying subject matter. You now need to think a little deeper about its meaning, specifically what it does – and does not – truly represent.

'A visualization is always a model (authored), never a mould (replica), of the real. That's a huge responsibility.' **Paolo Ciuccarelli, Scientific Director of DensityDesign Research Lab at Politecnico di Milano**

What Phenomenon?

Determining the meaning of your data requires that you recognise this is more than just a bunch of numbers and text values held in the cells of a table. Ask yourself, 'What is it about? What activity, entity, instance or phenomenon does it represent?'.

One of the most valuable pieces of advice I have seen regarding this task came from Kim Rees, co-founder of Periscopic. Kim describes the process of taking one single row of data and using that as an entry point to learn carefully about what each value means individually and then collectively. Breaking down the separation between values created by the table's cells, and then sticking the pieces back together, helps you appreciate the parts and the whole far better.

'Absorb the data. Read it, re-read it, read it backwards and understand the lyrical and human-centred contribution.' **Kate McLean, Smellscape Mapper and Senior Lecturer Graphic Design**

You saw the various macro- and micro-level views applied to the context of the Texas Department for Criminal Justice executed offenders information in the previous chapter. The underlying meaning of this data – its phenomenon – was offenders who had been judged guilty of committing heinous crimes and had faced the ultimate consequence. The availability of textual data describing the offenders' last statements and details of their crimes heightened the emotive potential of this data. It was heavy stuff. However, it was still just a collection of values detailing dates, names, locations, categories. All datasets, whether on executed offenders or the locations of MacDonald's restaurants, share the same properties as outlined by the TNOIR data-type mnemonic. What distinguishes them is what these values mean.

What you are developing here is a more semantic appreciation of your data to substantiate the physical definitions. You are then taking that collective appreciation of what your data stands for to influence how you might decide to amplify or suppress the influence of this semantic meaning. This builds on the discussion in the last chapter about the tonal dimension, specifically the difference between figurative and non-figurative portrayals.

A bar chart (Figure 4.4) comprising two bars, one of height 43 and the other of height 1, arguably does not quite encapsulate the emotive significance of Barack Obama becoming the first black US president, succeeding the 43 white presidents who served before him. Perhaps a more potent approach may be to present a chronological display of 44 photographs of each president in order to visually contrast Mr Obama's headshot in the final image in the sequence with the previous 43. Essentially, the value of 43 is almost irrelevant in its detail – it could be 25 or 55 – it is about there being 'many' of the same thing followed by the 'one' that is'different'. That's what creates the impact. (What will image number 45 bring? A further striking 'difference' or a return to the standard mould?)

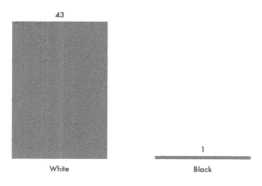

Figure 4.4   US Presidents by Ethnicity (1789 to 2015)

Learning about the underlying phenomena of your data helps you feel its spirit more strongly than just looking at the rather agnostic physical properties. It also helps you in knowing what potential sits inside the data – the qualities it possesses – so you are then equipped the best understanding of how you might want to portray it. Likewise it prepares you for the level of responsibility and potential sensitivity you will face in curating a visual representation of *this* subject matter. As you saw with the case study of the 'Florida Gun Crimes' graphic, some subjects are inherently more emotive than others, so we have to demonstrate a certain amount of courage and conviction in deciding how to undertake such challenges.

> 'Find loveliness in the unlovely. That is my guiding principle. Often, topics are disturbing or difficult; inherently ugly. But if they are illustrated elegantly there is a special sort of beauty in the truthful communication of something. Secondly, Kirk Goldsberry stresses that data visualization should ultimately be true to a phenomenon, rather than a technique or the format of data. This has had a huge impact on how I think about the creative process and its results.' **John Nelson, Cartographer**

Completeness

Another aspect of examining the meaning of data is to determine how representative it is. I have touched on data quality already, but inaccuracies in conclusions about what data is saying have arguably a greater impact on trust and are more damaging than any individual missing elements of data.

The questions you need to ask of your data are: does it represent genuine observations about a given phenomenon or is it influenced by the collection method? Does your data reflect the entirety of a particular phenomenon, a recognised sample, or maybe even an obstructed view caused by hidden limitations in the availability of data about that phenomenon?

Reflecting on the published executed offenders data, there would be a certain confidence that it is representative of the total population of executions but with a specific caveat: it is all the executed offenders under the jurisdiction of the Texas Department of Criminal Justice since 1982. It is not the whole of the executions conducted across the entire USA nor is it representative of all the executions that have taken place throughout the history of Texas. Any conclusions drawn from this data must be boxed within those parameters.

The matter of judging completeness can be less about the number of records and more a question of the integrity of the data content. This executed offenders dataset would appear to be a trusted and reliable record of each offender but would there/could there be an incentive for the curators of this data not to capture, for example, the last statements as they were explicitly expressed? Could they have possibly been in any way sanitised or edited, for example? These are the types of questions you need to pose. This is not aimless cynicism, it is about seeking assurances of quality and condition so you can be confident about what you can legitimately present and conclude from it (as well as what you should not).

Consider a different scenario. If you are looking to assess the political mood of a nation during a televised election debate, you might consider analysing Twitter data by looking at the sentiments for and against the candidates involved. Although this would offer an accessible source of rich data, it would not provide an entirely reliable view of the national mood. It could only offer algorithmically determined insights (i.e. through the process of determining the sentiment from natural language) of the people who have a Twitter account, are watching the debate and have chosen to tweet about it during a given timeframe.

Now, just because you might not have access to a 'whole' population of political opinion data does not mean it is not legitimate to work on a sample. Sometimes samples are astutely reflective of the population. And in truth, if samples were not viable then most of the world's analyses would need to cease immediately.

A final point is to encourage you to probe any absence of data. Sometimes you might choose to switch the focus away from the data you have got towards the data you have not got. If the data you have is literally as

> 'This is one of the first questions we should ask about any dataset: what is missing? What can we learn from the gaps?' **Jer Thorp, Founder of The Office for Creative Research**

much as you can acquire but you know the subject should have more data about it, then perhaps shine a light on the gaps, making that your story. Maybe you will unearth a discovery about the lack of intent or will to make the data available, which in itself may be a fascinating discovery. As transparency increases, those who are not stand out the most.

Any identified lack of completeness or full representativeness is not an obstacle to progress, it just means you need to tread carefully with regard to how you might represent and present any work that emerges from it. It is about caution not cessation.

Influence on Process

This extensive examination work gives you an initial – but thorough – appreciation of the potential of your data, the things it will offer and the things it will not. Of course this potential is as yet unrealised. Furthering this examination will be the focus of the next activity, as you look to employ more visual techniques to help unearth the as-yet-hidden qualities of understanding locked away in the data. For now, this examination work takes your analytical and creative thinking forward another step.

Purpose map 'tone': Through deeper acquaintance with your data, you will have been able to further consider the suitability of the potential tone of your work. By learning more about the inherent characteristics of the subject, this might help to confirm or redefine your intentions for adopting a utilitarian (reading) or sensation-based (feeling) tone.

Editorial angles: The main benefit of exploring the data types is to arrive at an understanding of what you have and have not got to work with. More specifically, it guides your thinking towards what possible angles of analysis may be viable and relevant, and which can be eliminated as not. For example, if you do not have any location or spatial data, this rules out the immediate possibility of being able to map your data. This is not something you could pursue with the current scope of your dataset. If you do have time-based data then the prospect of conducting analysis that might show changes over time is viable. You will learn more about this idea of editorial 'angle' in the next chapter but let me state now it is one of the most important components of visualisation thinking.

Physical properties influence scale: Data is your raw material, your ideas are not. I stated towards the end of Chapter 3 that you should embrace the instinctive manifestations of ideas and seek influence and inspiration from other sources. However, with the shape and size of your data

Figure 4.5   OECD
Better Life Index

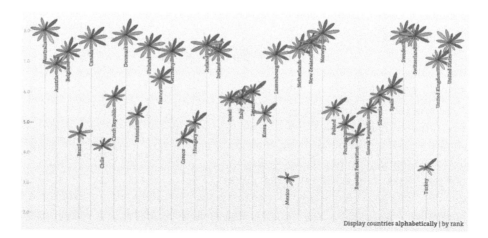

having such an impact on any eventual designs, you must respect the need to be led by your data's physical properties and not just your ideas.

In particular, the range of values in your data will shape things significantly. The shape of data in the 'Better Life Index' project you saw earlier is a good example. Figure 4.5 presents an analysis of the quality of life across the 36 OECD member states. Each country is a flower comprising 11 petals with each representing a different quality of life indicator (the larger the petal, the better the measured quality of life).

'My design approach requires that I immerse myself deeply in the problem domain and available data very early in the project, to get a feel for the unique characteristics of the data, its "texture" and the affordances it brings. It is very important that the results from these explorations, which I also discuss in detail with my clients, can influence the basic concept and main direction of the project. To put it in Hans Rosling's words, you need to "let the data set change your mind set".' **Moritz Stefaner, Truth & Beauty Operator**

Consider this. Would this design concept still be viable if there were 20 indicators? Or just 3? How about if the analysis was for 150 countries? The connection between data range and chart design involves a discerning judgement about 'fit'. You need to identify carefully the underlying shape of the data to be displayed and what tolerances this might test in the shape of the possible design concepts used.

Another relevant concern involves the challenge of elegantly handling quantitative measures that have hugely varied value ranges and contain (legitimate) outliers. Accommodating all the values into a single display can have a hugely distorting impact on the space it occupies. For example, note the exceptional size of the shape for *Avatar* in Figure 4.6, from the 'Spotlight on profitability' graphic you saw earlier. It is the one movie included that bursts through the ceiling, far beyond the otherwise entirely suitable 1000 million maximum scale value. As a single outlier, in this case, it was treated with a rather unique approach. As you can see, its striking shape conveniently trespasses onto the space offered by the two empty rows above. The result emphasises this value's exceptional quality. You might seldom have the luxury of this type of effective resolution, so the key point to stress is always be acutely aware of the existence of 'Avatars' in your data.

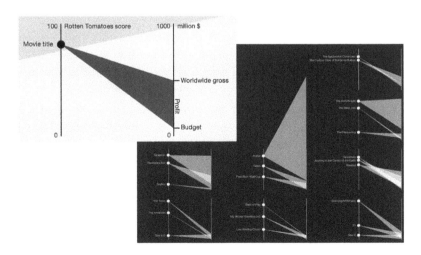

Figure 4.6
Spotlight on
Profitability

4.5 Data Transformation

Having undertaken an examination of your data you will have a good idea about what needs to be done to ensure it is entirely fit for purpose. The next activity is to work on transforming the data so it is in optimum condition for your needs.

At this juncture, the linearity of a book becomes rather unsatisfactory. Transforming your data is something that will take place before, during and after both the examination and (upcoming) exploration steps. It will also continue beyond the boundaries of this stage of the workflow. For example, the need to transform data may only emerge once you begin your 'editorial thinking', as covered by the next chapter (indeed you will likely find yourself bouncing forwards and backwards between these sections of the book on a regular basis). As you get into the design stage you will constantly stumble upon additional reasons to tweak the shape and size of your data assets. The main point here is that your needs will evolve. This moment in the workflow is not going to be the only or final occasion when you look to refine your data.

Two important notes to share upfront at this stage. Firstly, in accordance with the desire for trustworthy design, any treatments you apply to your data need to be recorded and potentially shared with your audience. You must be able to reveal the thinking behind any significant assumptions, calculations and modifications you have made to your data.

Secondly, I must emphasise the critical value of keeping backups. Before you undertake any transformation, make a copy of your dataset. After each major iteration remember to save a milestone version for backup purposes. Additionally, when making changes, it is useful to preserve original (unaltered) data items nearby for easy rollback should you need them. For example, suppose you are cleaning up a column of messy data to do with 'Gender' that has a variety of inconsistent values (such as "M", "Male", "male", "FEMALE", "F", "Female"). Normally I would keep the original data, duplicate the column, and then tidy up this second column of values. I have then gained access to both original and modified versions. If you are going to do any transformation work that might involve a significant investment of time and (manual) effort, having an opportunity to refer to a previous state is always useful in my experience.

There are four different types of potential activity involved in transforming your data: cleaning, converting, creating and consolidating.

Transform to clean: I spoke about the importance of data quality (better quality in, better quality out, etc.) in the examination section when looking at the physical condition of the data. There's no need to revisit the list of potential observations you might need to consider looking out for but this is the point where you will need to begin to address these.

There is no single or best approach for how to conduct this task. Some issues can be addressed through a straightforward 'find and replace' (or remove) operation. Some treatments will be possible using simple functions to convert data into new states, such as using logic formulae that state 'if this, do this, otherwise do that'. For example, if the value in the 'Gender' column is "M" make it "Male", if the value is "MALE" make it "Male" etc. Other tasks might be much more intricate, requiring manual intervention, often in combination with inspection features like 'sort' or 'filter', to find, isolate and then modify problem values.

Part of cleaning up your data involves the elimination of junk. Going back to the earlier scenario about gathering data about McDonald's restaurants, you probably would not need the name of the restaurant manager, details of the opening times or the contact telephone number. It is down to your judgement at the time of gathering the data to decide whether these extra items of detail – if they were as easily acquirable as the other items of data that you really *did* need – may potentially provide value for your analysis later in the process. My tactic is usually to gather as much data as I can and then reject/trim later; *later* has arrived and now is the time to consider what to remove. Any fields or rows of data that you know serve no ongoing value will take up space and attention, so get rid of these. You will need to separate the wheat from the chaff to help reduce your problem.

Transform to convert: Often you will seek to create new data values out of existing ones. In the illustration in Figure 4.7, it might be useful to extract the constituent parts of a 'Release Date' field in order to group, analyse and use the data in different ways. You might use the 'Month' and 'Year' fields to aggregate your analysis at these respective levels in order to explore within-year and across-year seasonality. You could also create a 'Full Release Date' formatted version of the date to offer a more presentable form of the release date value possibly for labeling purposes.

Release Date	Month	Year	Full Release Date
21/06/13	6	2013	Friday, 21 June 2013
26/08/13	8	2013	Monday, 26 August 2013
21/12/12	12	2012	Friday, 21 December 2012
22/12/10	12	2010	Wednesday, 22 December 2010
11/06/09	6	2009	Thursday, 11 June 2009
30/11/10	11	2010	Tuesday, 30 November 2010
29/04/07	4	2007	Sunday, 29 April 2007
14/12/07	12	2007	Friday, 14 December 2007
07/11/06	11	2006	Tuesday, 7 November 2006
20/10/06	10	2006	Friday, 20 October 2006
22/12/06	12	2006	Friday, 22 December 2006
12/11/04	11	2004	Friday, 12 November 2004
20/06/03	6	2003	Friday, 20 June 2003
01/01/98	1	1998	Thursday, 1 January 1998
01/01/03	1	2003	Wednesday, 1 January 2003
29/08/03	8	2003	Friday, 29 August 2003

Figure 4.7 Example of Converted Data Transformation

Extracting or deriving new forms of data will be necessary when it comes to handling qualitative 'textual' data. As stated in the 'Data literacy' section, if you have textual data you will generally always need to transform this into various categorical or quantitative forms, unless its role is simply to provide value as an annotation (such as a quoted caption or label). Some would argue that qualitative visualisation involves special methods for the representation of data. I would disagree. I believe the unique challenge of working with textual data lies with the task of transforming the data: visually representing the extracted and derived properties from textual data involves the same suite of representation options (i.e. chart types) that would be useful for portraying analysis of any other data types.

Here is a breakdown of some of the conversions, calculations and extractions you could apply to textual data. Some of these tasks can be quite straightforward (e.g. Using the LEN function in Excel to determine the number of characters) while others are more technical and will require more sophisticated tools or programmes dedicated to handling textual data.

Categorical conversions:

- Identify keywords or summary themes from text and convert these into categorical classifications.
- Identify and flag up instances of certain cases existing or otherwise (e.g. X is mentioned in this passage).

- Identify and flag up the existence of certain relationships (e.g. A and B were both mentioned in the same passage, C was always mentioned before D).
- Use natural language-processing techniques to determine sentiments, to identify specific word types (nouns, verbs, adjectives) or sentence structures (around clauses and punctuation marks).
- With URLs, isolate and extract the different components of website address and sub-folder locations

Quantitative conversions:

- Calculate the frequency of certain words being used.
- Analyse the attributes of text, such as total word count, physical length, potential reading duration.
- Count the number of sentences or paragraphs, derived from the frequency of different punctuation marks.
- Position the temporal location of certain words/phrases in relation to other words/phrases or compared to the whole (e.g. X was mentioned at 1m51s).
- Position the spatial location of certain words/phrases in relation to other words/phrases or compared to the whole.

A further challenge that falls under this 'converting' heading will sometimes emerge when you are working with data supplied by others in spreadsheets. This concerns the obstacles created when trying to analyse a data that has been formatted visually, perhaps in readiness for printing. If you receive data in this form you will need to unpack and reconstruct it into the normalised form described earlier, comprising all records and fields included in a single table.

Any merged cells need unmerging or removing. You might have a heading that is common to a series of columns. If you see this, unmerge it and replicate the same heading across each of the relevant columns (perhaps appending an index number to each header to maintain some differentiation). Cells that have visual formatting like background shading or font attributes (bold, coloured) to indicate a value or status are useful when observing and reading the data, but for analysis operations these properties are largely invisible. You will need to create new values in actual data form that are not visual (creating categorical values, say, or status flags like 'yes' or 'no') to recreate the meaning of the formats. The data provided to you – or that you create – via a spreadsheet does not need to be elegant in appearance, it needs to be functional.

Transform to create: This task is something I refer to as the hidden cleverness, where you are doing background thinking to form new calculations, values, groupings and any other mathematical or manual treatments that really expand the variety of data available.

A simple example might involve the need to create some percentage calculations in a new field, based on related quantities elsewhere within your existing data. Perhaps you have pairs of 'start date' and 'end date' values and you need to calculate the duration in days for all your records. You might use logic formula to assist in creating a new variable that summarises another – maybe something like (in language terms) IF Age < 18 THEN status = "Child", ELSE status = "Adult". Alternatively, you might want to create a calculation that standardised some quantities' need to source base population figures for all the relevant locations in your data in order to convert some quantities into 'per capita' values. This would be particularly necessary if you anticipate wanting to map the data as this will ensure you are facilitating legitimate comparisons.

Transform to consolidate: This involves bringing in additional data to help expand (more variables) or append (more records) to enhance the editorial and representation potential of your project.

An example of a need to expand your data would be if you had details about locations only at country level but you wanted to be able to group and aggregate your analysis at continent level. You could gather a dataset that holds values showing the relationships between country and continent and then add a new variable to your dataset against which you would perform a simple lookup operation to fill in the associated continent values.

Consolidating by appending data might occur if you had previously acquired a dataset that now had more or newer data (specifically, additional records) available to bring it up to date. For instance, you might have started some analysis on music record sales up to a certain point in time, but once you'd actually started working on the task another week had elapsed and more data had become available.

Additionally, you may start to think about sourcing other media assets to enhance your presentation options, beyond just gathering extra data. You might anticipate the potential value for gathering photos (headshots of the people in your data), icons/symbols (country flags), links to articles (URLs), or videos (clips of goals scored). All of these would contribute to broadening the scope of your annotation options. Even though there is a while yet until we reach that particular layer of design thinking, it is useful to start contemplating this as early possible in case the collection of these additional assets requires significant time and effort. It might also reveal any obstacles around having to obtain permissions for usage or sufficiently high quality media. If you know you are going to have to do something, don't leave it too late – reduce the possibility of such stresses by acting early.

4.6 Data Exploration

The examination task was about forming a deep acquaintance with the physical properties and meaning of your data. You now need to interrogate that data further – and differently – to find out what potential insights and qualities of understanding it could provide.

Undertaking data exploration will involve the use of statistical and visual techniques to move beyond *looking* at data and begin to start *seeing* it. You will be directly pursuing your initially defined curiosity, to determine if answers exist and whether they are suitably enlightening in nature. Often you will not know for sure

'After the data exploration phase you may come to the conclusion that the data does not support the goal of the project. The thing is: data is leading in a data visualization project – you cannot make up some data just to comply with your initial ideas. So, you need to have some kind of an open mind and "listen to what the data has to say", and learn what its potential is for a visualisation. Sometimes this means that a project has to stop if there is too much of a mismatch between the goal of the project and the available data. In other cases this may mean that the goal needs to be adjusted and the project can continue.' **Jan Willem Tulp, Data Experience Designer** whether what you initially thought was interesting is exactly that. This activity will confirm, refine or reject your core curiosity and perhaps, if you are fortunate, present discoveries that will encourage other interesting avenues of enquiry.

To frame this process, it is worth introducing something that will be covered in Chapter 5, where you will consider some of the parallels between visualisation and photography. Before committing to take a photograph you must first develop an appreciation of all the possible viewpoints that are available to you. Only then can you determine which of these is best. The notion of 'best' will be defined in the next chapter, but for now you need to think about identifying all the possible viewpoints in your data – to recognise the knowns and the unknowns.

Widening the Viewpoint: Knowns and Unknowns

At a news briefing in February 2002, the US Secretary of Defense, Donald Rumsfeld, delivered his infamous 'known knowns' statement:

> Reports that say that something hasn't happened are always interesting to me, because as we know, there are known knowns; there are things we know we know. We also know there are known unknowns; that is to say we know there are some things we do not know. But there are also unknown unknowns – the ones we don't know we don't know. And if one looks throughout the history of our country and other free countries, it is the latter category that tend to be the difficult ones.

There was much commentary about the apparent lack of elegance in the language used and criticism of the muddled meaning. I disagree with this analysis. I thought it was probably the most efficient way he could have articulated what he was explaining, at least in written or verbal form. The essence of Rumsfeld's statement was to distinguish *awareness* of what is knowable about a subject (what knowledge exists) from the status of *acquiring* this knowledge. There is a lot of value to be gained from using this structure (Figure 4.8) to shape your approach to thinking about data exploration.

The *known knowns* are aspects of knowledge about your subject and about the qualities present in your data that you are aware of – you are aware that you know these things. The nature of these known knowns might mean you have confidence that the origin curiosity was relevant and the available insights that emerged in response are suitably interesting. You cannot afford to be complacent, though. You will need to challenge yourself to check that these curiosities are still legitimate and relevant. To support this, you should continue to look and learn about the subject through research, topping up your awareness of the most potentially relevant dynamics of the subject, and continue to interrogate your data accordingly.

Additionally, you should not just concentrate on this potentially quite narrow viewpoint. As I mentioned earlier, it is important to give yourself as broad a view as possible across your subject and its data to optimise your decisions about what other interesting enquiries might be available. This is where you need to consider the other quadrants in this diagram.

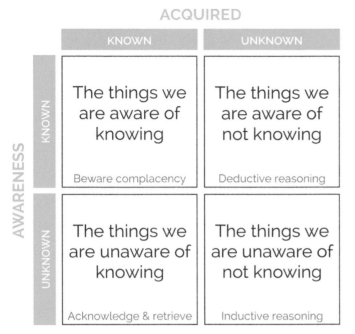

ACQUIRED

Figure 4.8
Making Sense of the *Known Knowns*

On occasion, though I would argue rarely, there may be *unknown knowns*, things you did not realise you knew or perhaps did not wish to acknowledge that you knew about a subject. This may relate to previous understandings that have been forgotten, consciously ignored or buried. Regardless, you need to acknowledge these.

For the knowledge that has yet to be acquired – the *known unknowns* and the even more elusive *unknown unknowns* – tactics are needed to help plug these gaps as far, as deep and as wide as possible. You cannot possibly achieve mastery of all the domains you work with. Instead, you need to have the capacity and be in position to turn as many unknowns as possible into knowns, and in doing so optimise your understanding of a subject. Only then will you be capable of appreciating the full array of viewpoints the data offers.

To make the best decisions you first need to be aware of all the options. This activity is about broadening your awareness of the potentially interesting things you could show – and could say – about your data. The resulting luxury of choice is something you will deal with in the next stage.

Exploratory Data Analysis

As I have stated, the aim throughout this book is to create a visualisation that will facilitate understanding for others. That is the end goal. At this stage of the workflow the deficit in understanding lies with you. The task of addressing the *unknowns* you have about a subject, as well as substantiating what *knowns* already exist, involves the use of exploratory data analysis (EDA). This integrates statistical methods with visual analysis to offer a way of extracting deeper understanding and widening the view to unlock as much of the potential as possible from within your data.

The chart in Figure 4.9 is a great demonstration of the value in combining statistical and visual techniques to understand your data better. It shows the results of nearly every major and many minor (full) marathon from around the world. On the surface, the distribution of finishing times reveals the common bell shape found in plots about many natural phenomenon, such as the height measurements of a large group of people. However, when you zoom in closer the data reveals some really interesting threshold patterns for finishing times on or just before the three-, four- and five-hour marks. You can see that the influence of runners setting themselves targets, often rounded to the hourly milestones, genuinely appeared to affect the results achieved.

Figure 4.9
What Good
Marathons and
Bad Investments
Have in Common

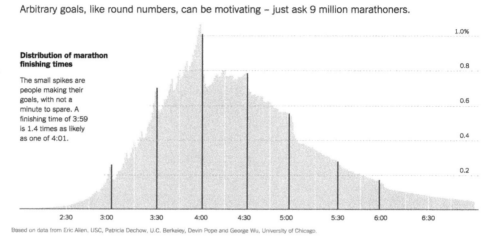

Arbitrary goals, like round numbers, can be motivating – just ask 9 million marathoners.

Distribution of marathon finishing times

The small spikes are people making their goals, with not a minute to spare. A finishing time of 3:59 is 1.4 times as likely as one of 4:01.

Based on data from Eric Allen, USC, Patricia Dechow, U.C. Berkeley, Devin Pope and George Wu, University of Chicago.

Although statistical analysis of this data would have revealed many interesting facts, these unique patterns were only realistically discoverable through studying the visual display of the data. This is the essence of EDA but there is no instruction manual for it. As John Tukey, the father of EDA, described: 'Exploratory data analysis is an attitude, a flexibility, and a reliance on display, not a bundle of techniques'. There is no single path to undertaking this activity effectively; it requires a number of different technical, practical and conceptual capabilities.

Instinct of the analyst: This is the primary matter. The attitude and flexibility that Turkey describes are about recognising the importance of the analyst's traits. Effective EDA is not about the tool. There are many vendors out there pitching their devices as the magic option where we just have to 'point and click' to uncover a deep discovery. Technology inevitably plays a key role in facilitating this endeavour but the value of a good analyst cannot be underestimated: it is arguably more influential than the differentiating characteristics between one tool and the next. In the absence of a defined procedure for conducting EDA, an analyst needs to possess the capacity to recognise and pursue the scent of enquiry. A good analyst will have that special blend of natural inquisitiveness and the sense to know what approaches (statistical or visual) to employ and when. Furthermore, when these traits collide with a strong subject knowledge this means better judgments are made about which findings from the analysis are meaningful and which are not.

Reasoning: Efficiency is a particularly important aspect of this exploration stage. The act of interrogating data, waiting for it to volunteer its secrets, can take a lot of time and energy. Even with smaller datasets you can find yourself tempted into trying out myriad combinations of analyses, driven by the desire to find *the killer* insight in the shadows.

Reasoning is an attempt to help reduce the size of the prospect. You cannot afford to try everything. There are so many statistical methods and, as you will see, so many visual means for seeing views of data that you simply cannot expect to have the capacity to try to unleash the full exploratory artillery. EDA is about being smart, recognising that you need to be discerning about your tactics.

'At the beginning, there's a process of "interviewing" the data – first evaluating their source and means of collection/aggregation/computation, and then trying to get a sense of what they say – and how well they say it via quick sketches in Excel with pivot tables and charts. Do the data, in various slices, say anything interesting? If I'm coming into this with certain assumptions, do the data confirm them, or refute them?' **Alyson Hurt, News Graphics Editor, NPR**

In academia there are two distinctions in approaches to reasoning – deductive and inductive – that I feel are usefully applied in this discussion:

- *Deductive* reasoning is targeted: You have a specific curiosity or hypothesis, framed by subject knowledge, and you are going to interrogate the data in order to determine whether there is any evidence of relevance or interest in the concluding finding. I consider this adopting a detective's mindset (Sherlock Holmes).
- *Inductive* reasoning is much more open in nature: You will 'play around' with the data, based on your sense or instinct about what might be of interest, and wait and see what emerges. In some ways this is like prospecting, hoping for that moment of serendipity when you unearth gold.

In this exploration process you ideally need to accommodate both approaches. The deductive process will focus on exploring further targeted curiosities, the inductive process will give you a fighting chance of finding more of those slippery 'unknowns', often almost by accident. It is important to give yourself room to embark on these somewhat less structured exploratory journeys.

I often think about EDA in the context of a comparison with the challenge of a 'Where's Wally?' visual puzzle. The process of finding Wally feels somewhat unscientific. Sometimes you let your eyes race around the scene like a dog who has just been let out of the car and is torpedoing across a field. However, after the initial burst of randomness, perhaps subconsciously, you then go through a more considered process of visual analysis. Elimination takes place by working around different parts of the scene and sequentially declaring 'Wally-free' zones. This aids your focus and strategy for where to look next. As you then move across each mini-scene you are pattern matching, looking out for the giveaway characteristics of the boy wearing glasses, a red-and-white-striped hat and jumper, and blue trousers.

The objective of this task is clear and singular in definition. The challenge of EDA is rarely that clean. There is a source curiosity to follow, for sure, and you might find evidence of Wally somewhere in the data. However, unlike the 'Where's Wally?' challenge, in EDA you have the chance also to find other things that might change the definition of what qualifies as an interesting insight. In unearthing other discoveries you might determine that you no longer care about Wally; finding him no longer represents the main enquiry.

Inevitably you are faced with a trade-off between spare capacity in time and attention and your own internal satisfaction that you have explored as many different angles of enquiry as possible.

Chart types: This is about seeing the data from all feasible angles. The power of the visual means that we can easily rely on our pattern-matching and sense-making capabilities – in harmony with contextual subject knowledge – to make observations about data that appear to have relevance.

> 'I kick it over into a rough picture as soon as possible. When I can see something then I am able to ask better questions of it – then the what-about-this iterations begin. I try to look at the same data in as many different dimensions as possible. For example, if I have a spreadsheet of bird sighting locations and times, first I like to see where they happen, previewing it in some mapping software. I'll also look for patterns in the timing of the phenomenon, usually using a pivot table in a spreadsheet. The real magic happens when a pattern reveals itself only when seen in both dimensions at the same time.' **John Nelson, Cartographer, on the value of visually exploring his data**

The data representation gallery that you will encounter in Chapter 6 presents nearly 50 different chart types, offering a broad repertoire of options for portraying data. The focus of the collection is on chart types that could be used to communicate to others. However, within this gallery there are also many chart types that help with pursuing EDA. In each chart profile, indications are given for those chart types that be particularly useful to support your exploratory activity. As a rough estimate, I would say about half of these can prove to be great allies in this stage of discovery.

The visual methods used in EDA do not just involve charting, they also involve selective charting – smart charting, 'smarting' if you like? (No, Andy, nobody likes that). Every chart type presented in the gallery includes helpful descriptions that will give you an idea of their role and also what observations – and potential interpretations – they might facilitate. It is important to know now that the chart types are organised across five main families (categorical, hierarchical, relational, temporal, and spatial) depending on the primary focus of your analysis. The focus of your analysis will, in turn, depend on the types of data you have and what you are trying to see.

Research: I have raised this already but make no apology for doing so again so soon. How you conduct research and how much you can do will naturally depend on your circumstances, but it is always important to exploit as many different approaches to learning about the domain and the data you are working with. As you will recall, the middle stage of forming understanding – *interpreting* – is about viewers translating what they have perceived from a display into meaning. They can only do this with domain knowledge. Similarly, when it comes to conducting exploratory analysis using visual methods, you might be able to *perceive* the charts you make, but without possessing or acquiring sufficient domain knowledge you will not know if what you are seeing is meaningful. Sometimes the consequence of this exploratory data analysis will only mean you have become better acquainted with specific questions and more defined curiosities about a subject even if you possibly do not yet have any answers.

The approach to research is largely common sense: you explore the places (books, websites) and consult the people (experts, colleagues) that will collectively give you the best chance of getting accurate answers to the questions you have. Good communication skills, therefore, are vital – it is not just about talking to others, it is about listening. If you are in a dialogue with experts you will have to find an approach that allows you to understand potentially complicated matters and also cut through to the most salient matters of interest.

Statistical methods: Although the value of the univariate statistical techniques profiled earlier still applies here, what you are often looking to undertake in EDA is multivariate analysis. This concerns testing out the potential existence of a correlation between quantitative variables as well as determining the possible causation variables – the holy grail of data analysis.

Typically, I find statistical analysis plays more of a supporting role during much of the exploration activity rather than a leading role. Visual techniques will serve up tangible observations about whether data relationships and quantities seem relevant, but to substantiate this you will need to conduct statistical tests of significance.

One of the main exceptions is when dealing with large datasets. Here the first approach might be more statistical in nature due to the amount of data obstructing rapid visual approaches. Going further, algorithmic approaches – using techniques like machine learning – might help to scale the task of statistically exploring large dimensions of data – and the endless permutations they offer. What these approaches gain in productivity they clearly lose in human quality. The significance of this should not be underestimated. It may be possible to take a blended approach where you might utilise machine learning techniques to act as an initial *battering ram* to help reduce the problem, identifying the major dimensions within the data that might hold certain key statistical attributes and then conducting further exploration 'by hand and by eye'.

Nothings: What if you have found nothing? You have hit a dead end, discovering no significant relationships and finding nothing interesting about the shape or distribution of your data. What do you do? In these situations you need to change your mindset: *nothing* is usually *something*. Dead ends and discovering blind alleys are good news because they help you develop focus by eliminating different dimensions of possible analysis. If you have traits of nothingness in your data or analysis – gaps, nulls, zeroes and no insights – this could prove to be the insight. As described earlier, make the gaps the focus of your story.

'My main advice is not to be disheartened. Sometimes the data don't show what you thought they would, or they aren't available in a usable or comparable form. But [in my world] sometimes that research still turns up threads a reporter could pursue and turn into a really interesting story – there just might not be a viz in it. Or maybe there's no story at all. And that's all okay. At minimum, you've still hopefully learned something new in the process about a topic, or a data source (person or database), or a "gotcha" in a particular dataset – lessons that can be applied to another project down the line.' **Alyson Hurt, News Graphics Editor, NPR**

There is *always* something interesting in your data. If a value has not changed over time, maybe it was supposed to – that is an insight. If everything is the same size, that is the story. If there is no significance in the quantities, categories or spatial relationships, make those your insights. You will only know that these findings are relevant by truly understanding the context of the subject matter. This is why you must make as much effort as possible to convert your *unknowns* into *knowns*.

Not always needed: It is important to couch this discussion about exploration in pragmatic reality. Not *all* visualisation challenges will involve *much* EDA. Your subject and your data might be immediately understandable and you may have a sufficiently broad viewpoint of your subject (plenty of known knowns already in place). Further EDA activity may have diminishing value. Additionally, if you are faced with small tables of data this simply will not warrant multivariate investigation. You certainly need to be ready and equipped with the capacity to undertake this type of exploration activity when it is needed, but the key point here is to judge when.

Summary: Working with Data

This chapter first introduced key foundations for the requisite data literacy involved in visualisation, specifically the importance of the distinction between normalised and cross-tabulated datasets as well as the different types of data (using the TNOIR mnemonic):

- Textual (qualitative): e.g. 'Any other comments?' data submitted in a survey.
- Nominal (qualitative): e.g. The 'gender' selected by a survey participant.
- Ordinal (qualitative): e.g. The response to a survey question, based on a scale of 1 (unhappy) to 5 (very happy).
- Interval (quantitative): e.g. The shoe size of a survey participant.
- Ratio (quantitative): e.g. The age of a survey participant in years.

You then walked through the four steps involved in working with data:

Acquisition Different sources and methods for getting your data.

- Curated by you: primary data collection, manual collection and data foraging, extracted from pdf, web scraping (also known as web harvesting).
- Curated by others: issued to you, downloaded from the Web, system report or export, third-party services, APIs.

Examination Developing an intimate appreciation of the characteristics of this critical raw material:

- Physical properties: type, size, and condition.
- Meaning: phenomenon, completeness.

Transformation Getting your data into shape, ready for its role in your exploratory analysis and visualisation design:

- Clean: resolve any data quality issues.
- Create: consider new calculations and conversions.
- Consolidate: what other data (to expand or append) or other assets could be sought to enhance your project?

Exploration Using visual and statistical techniques to *see* the data's qualities: what insights does it reveal to you as you deepen your familiarity with it?

Tips and Tactics

- Perfect data (complete, accurate, up to date, truly representative) is an almost impossible standard to reach (given the presence of time constraints) so your decision will be when is good enough, good enough: when do diminishing returns start to materialise?

- Do not underestimate the demands on your time; working with data will always be consuming of your attention and effort:

  o Ensure you have built plenty of time into your handling of this data stage.
  o Be patient and persevere.
  o Be disciplined: it is easy to get swallowed up in the potential hunt for discovering things from your data, attempting to explore every possible permutation.

- If your data does not already have a unique identifier it is often worth creating one to track your data preparation process. This is especially helpful if you need to preserve or revert to a very specific ordering of your data (e.g. if the rows have been carefully arranged in order to undertake cross-row calculations like cumulative or sub-totals).

- Clerical tasks like file management are important: maintain backups of each major iteration of data, employ good file organisation of your data and other assets, and maintain logical naming conventions.

- Data management practices around data security and privacy will be important in the more sensitive/confidential cases.

- Keep notes about where you have sourced data, what you have done with it, any assumptions or counting rules you have applied, ideas you might have for transforming or consolidating, issues/problems, things you do not understand.

- To learn about your data, its meaning and the subject matter to which it relates, you should build in time to undertake research in order to equip yourself suitably with domain knowledge.

- Anticipate and have contingency plans for the worst-case scenarios for data, such as the scarcity of data availability, null values, odd distributions, erroneous values, long values, bad formatting, data loss.

- Communicate. If you do not know anything about your data, ask: do not assume or stay ignorant. And then listen: always pay attention to key information.

- Attention to detail is of paramount importance at this stage, so get into good habits early and do not cut corners.

- Maintain an open mind and do not get frustrated. You can only work with what you have. If it is not showing what you expected or hoped for, you cannot force it to say something that is simply not there.

- Exploratory Data Analysis is *not* about design elegance. Do not waste time making your analysis 'pretty', it only needs to inform you.

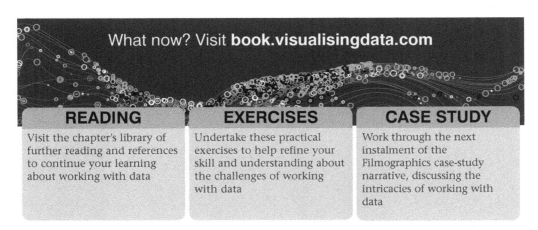

What now? Visit book.visualisingdata.com

READING	EXERCISES	CASE STUDY
Visit the chapter's library of further reading and references to continue your learning about working with data	Undertake these practical exercises to help refine your skill and understanding about the challenges of working with data	Work through the next instalment of the Filmographics case-study narrative, discussing the intricacies of working with data

5

Establishing Your Editorial Thinking

It is very easy to introduce every chapter with claims that each of these reached is *the* important stage but you have really now reached a critical juncture. This is the place in the process where you need to start to commit to a definitive pathway.

The data you gathered during Chapter 4 was shaped by your trigger curiosity. You may have found qualities in the data that you feel reveal relevant insights in response to that pursuit. Alternatively, through exploring your data and researching your subject, you may have discovered new enquiries that might actually offer more interesting perspectives.

Ahead of commencing the design and development of your solution you need to decide what you are actually going to do with this data: what are you going to show your audience? This is where editorial thinking becomes important. In my view it is one of the most defining activities that separates the best visualisers from the rest, possibly even more so than technical talent or design flair.

In this this chapter you will learn about what editorial thinking means, the role it plays, what decisions you need to make and how you might do so.

5.1 What is Editorial Thinking?

You will have noticed the common thread of *curiosity* that weaves its way through the preparatory activities of this workflow process. From the opening curiosity that initiated your work, you then effectively sought, gathered and became acquainted with your data in pursuit of some kind of answer. In this third stage, you will need to make some decisions. The essence of editorial thinking is demonstrating a discerning eye for *what* you are going to portray visually to your audience; the matter of *how* follows next. This stage is the critical bridge between your data work and your design work.

In the first chapter I described how a single context can hold several legitimate views of the truth. The glass that is half full of water is also half empty. It is also half full of air. Its water contents might be increasing or decreasing. Depending on your perspective, there are several legitimate ways of portraying this situation. In a nutshell, editorial thinking is about deciding which of the many viable perspectives offered by your data you will decide to focus on.

To translate this to data visualisation, assume you have data that breaks down total organisational spend across many geographic regions over time. Your profiling of your audience has already informed your thinking that the main interest is in how this has changed over time. But at this point, having looked at the data closely, you have found some really interesting patterns in the spatial analysis. What are you going to do? Are you going to show your audience how this spend compares by region on a map, having now established that this might be of interest to them, or are you going to focus on still showing how it has changed over time by region? Perhaps you could show both. Do you need to show all the regions and include all the available time periods or just focus on some specific key moments? You have got to decide what you are going to do because you are about to face the task of picking chart types, deciding on a layout, possible interactivity, and many other presentation matters.

When trying to explain the role of editorial thinking I find it helpful to consider some of the parallels that exists between data visualisation and photography, or perhaps more specifically, photojournalism. By translating into data visualisation some of the decisions involved in tak-

'A photo is never an objective reflection, but always an interpretation of reality. I see data visualization as sort of a new photojournalism – a highly editorial activity.' **Moritz Stefaner, Truth & Beauty Operator**

ing a photograph, you will find useful perspectives to help shape your editorial thinking. In turn this will have a huge bearing on the design choices that follow. There are three particular perspectives to consider: angle, framing and focus.

Angle

'When the data has been explored sufficiently, it is time to sit down and reflect – what were the most interesting insights? What surprised me? What were recurring themes and facts throughout all views on the data? In the end, what do we find most important and most interesting? These are the things that will govern which angles and perspectives we want to emphasise in the subsequent project phases.' **Moritz Stefaner, Truth & Beauty Operator**

Think of a chart as being a photograph of data. As with a photograph, in visualisation you cannot show everything at once. A panoramic 360° view of data is impossible to display at any moment and certainly not through the window of a single chart. You must pick an angle.

In photography the angle would be formed by the position from where you are standing when taking a shot. In visualisation this relates to the angle of analysis you intend to show:

what are you measuring and by which dimension(s) are you breaking it down? Are you going to show how product sales have changed over time, or how sales look organised by regional hierarchically or how they compare on a map and over time? There are many different angles you could choose. You could also choose to show data from multiple different angles using several charts

'It requires the discipline to do your homework, the ability to quiet down your brain and be honest about what is interesting.' **Sarah Slobin, Visual Journalist**

presented together. Your key consideration in determining each angle is whether it is relevant and sufficient.

Relevant: Why is it worth providing a view of your data from *this* angle and not another one? Why is *this* angle of analysis likely to offer the most relevant and compelling window into the subject for your intended audience? Is it still relevant in light of the context of the origin curiosity – that is, have definitions evolved since familiarising yourself with the data, learning about its potential qualities as well as researching the subject at large?

The judgement of relevance would be similar to the notion of newsworthiness in journalism. In that context, terms like timeliness, proximity, novelty, human interest and current prominence are all ingredients that shape what ultimately becomes news content. The ecosystem in which your work is consumed is likely to be much narrower in size and diversity than it is for a newspaper, for example. Issues of human interest and novelty will seldom have a bearing on your judgement of relevance. Therefore, I believe it is realistic to reduce the list of factors that shape your thinking about relevance to three:

- What does your intended *audience* want or need to know? The various characteristics of your audience's profile, matters discussed in Chapter 1 (accessible design) and Chapter 3 (contextual circumstances), should provide a good sense of this. Sometimes, you can simply ask the members of your intended audience: you might know who they are personally or at least be able to gather information about their needs. On other occasions, with a larger audience, you might need to consider creating personas: a small number of imagined identities that may be demographically representative of the types of viewer you expect to target. Ask yourself, if you were them, what would you want to know?

- What makes something relevant in your context? Part of your judgement will be to consider whether relevance is a product of the normal or the exceptional; often the worthiness of an item of news is based on it being exceptional rather than going through the repeated reporting of normality. Reciting the famous journalistic aphorism, you need to determine if you are reporting news of 'dog bites man!' or 'man bites dog!'. A lack of relevance is a curse that strikes a lot of visualisation work. What you often see is evidence of data that has been worked up into a visual output just because it is available and just because visual things are appealing. There is almost a scattergun approach in hoping that someone, somewhere will find a connection to justify it as relevant.

- What do *you* want your audience to know? You might have the control to decide. Although you respect the possible expressed needs of your audience you might actually be better placed to determine what is truly relevant. Depending on the context, and your proximity to the subject and its data, you might have the autonomy to dictate on what it is you want to say, more so than what you think the audience want to see. Indeed, that audience may not yet know or be sufficiently domain aware to determine for itself what is relevant or otherwise.

Sufficient: This is about judging *how many* angles you need. If a chart (generally) offers a single angle into your data, is that sufficiently representative of what you wish to portray? As I said earlier, you cannot show everything in one chart. Maybe you need multiple charts offering a blend of different angles of analysis to sufficiently represent the most interesting dimensions of the subject matter. Perhaps showing a view of your data over time needs to be supplemented by a spatial view to provide the context for any interpretations.

It is easy to find yourself being reluctant to commit to just a singular choice of angle. Even in a small dataset, there are typically multiple possible angles of analysis you could conduct. It is

'I think this is something I've learned from experience rather than advice that was passed on. Less can often be more. In other words, don't get carried away and try to tell the reader everything there is to know on a subject. Know what it is that you want to show the reader and don't stray from that. I often find myself asking others "do we need to show this?" or "is this really necessary?" Let's take it out.' **Simon Scarr, Deputy Head of Graphics, ThomsonReuters**

often hard to ignore the temptation of wanting to include multiple angles to serve more people's interests.

It is important not to fall into the trap of thinking that if you throw more and more additional angles of analysis into your work you will automatically enrich that work. Just because you have 100 photographs of your holiday, that does not mean you should show me them all. When I reflect on some of the work I have created down the years, I wish I had demonstrated better selection discipline – a greater conviction to exclude angles – to avoid additional content creeping in just because it was available. I often found it far too easy to see everything as being potentially interesting. And I still do (it's the curse of the analyst). The real art is to find just enough of those angles that respond to the core essence of your – or your inherited – curiosity.

Framing

The next perspective to define about your editorial thinking contributes to the refinement of the angles you have selected. This concerns framing decisions. In photographic parlance this relates to choices about the field of view: what will be included inside the frame of the photograph and what will be left out?

Just like a photographer, a visualiser must demonstrate careful judgement about what to show, what not to show, and how to show it. This is effectively a filtering decision concerned with which data to include and exclude:

* All category values, or just a select few?
* All quantitative values or just those over a certain threshold?
* All data or just those between a defined start and end date period?

Naturally, the type and extent of the framing you might need to apply will be influenced by the nature of your trigger curiosity, as well as factors like the complexity of the subject matter and the amount of data available to show. Further considerations like the setting (need rapid insights or OK for deeper, more prolonged engagement?) and output format will also have a bearing on this matter.

One of the key motives of framing is to remove unnecessary clutter – there is only so much that can be accommodated in a single view before it becomes too busy, too detailed, and too small in resolution. There is only so much content your audience will likely be willing and able to process. Inevitably, a balance must be struck to find the most representative view of your content. If you zoom in, filtering away too much of the content, it might hide the important context required for perceiving values. Conversely, if you avoid filtering your content you may fail to make visible the most salient discoveries.

Focus

The third component of editorial thinking concerns what you might choose to focus on. This is not a function of filtering – that is the concern of framing – it is about emphasising what is more important in contrast to what is less important.

The best photographs are able to balance light and colour, not just setting the mood of a situation but illuminating key elements within the frame that help to create depth. They provide a sense of visual hierarchy through their depth as well as the sizing and arrangement of each form.

What needs to be brought into view in the foreground, left in the mid-ground, and maybe relegated to the background simply for context or orientation? What needs to be bigger and more prominent and what can be less so?

Whereas framing judgements were about reducing clutter, this is about reducing noise. If everything in a visualisation is shouting, nothing is heard; if everything is in the foreground, nothing stands out; if everything is large, nothing is dominant.

Decisions about focus primarily concern the development of explanatory visualisations, because creating such a focus – surfacing insights through the astute use of colour or annotated accentuation – is a key purpose for that type of experience. Beyond colour, focus can be achieved through composition choices such as the way elements are more prominently sized and located or the way contents are positioned within a view.

5.2 The Influence of Editorial Thinking

It is important to ground this discussion by explaining practically how these editorial perspectives will apply to your workflow process and, in particular, influence your design thinking.

I described a chart as being like a photograph of the data, displaying a visual answer to a data-driven curiosity. Determining the choice of chart (technically, 'data representation') is just one part of the overall anatomy of a data visualisation. There are choices to be made about four other design layers, namely features of interactivity, annotation, colour and composition.

Your decisions across this visualisation design anatomy are influenced, in a large way, by the editorial definitions you have will make about angle, framing and focus. They might not lead directly or solely to the final choices – there are many other factors to consider, as you have seen – but they will signpost the type of editorial qualities the visualisation will need to accommodate. Let's look at two illustrations of the connection between editorial and design thinking to explain this.

Example 1: The Fall and Rise of US Inequality

The first example (Figure 5.1) is a chart taken from an article published in the 'Planet Money: The Economy Explained' section of the US-based National Public Radio (NPR) website. The article is

Figure 5.1

The Fall and
Rise of U.S.
Inequality, in
Two Graphs

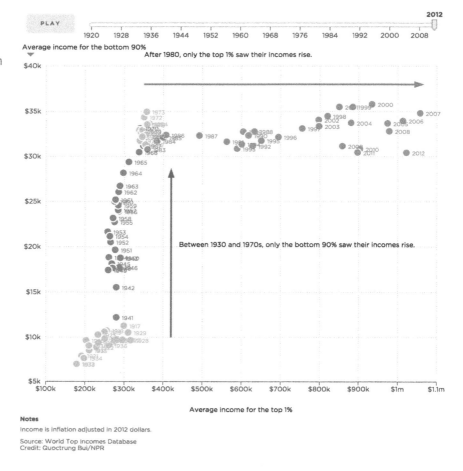

titled 'The Fall and Rise of U.S. Inequality in 2 Graphs'. As the title suggests the full article includes two charts, but I just want to focus on the second one for the purpose of this illustration.

Editorial Perspectives

Let's assess the editorial perspectives of angle, framing and focus as demonstrated by this work.

Angle: The main angle of analysis can be expressed as: 'What is the relationship between two quantitative measures (average income for the bottom 90% and for the top 1% of earners) and how has this changed over time (year)?'. This angle would be considered relevant because the relationship between the *haves* and the *have-nots* is a key indicator of wealth distribution. It is a topical and suitable choice of analysis to include with any discussion about inequality in the USA. As I mentioned there is a second chart presented so it would be reasonable to say that the two sufficiently cover the necessary angles to support the article.

Framing: The parameters that define the inclusion and exclusion of data in the displayed analysis involve filters for time period (1917 to 2012) and country (just for the USA). The starting point of the data commencing from 1917 may reflect a simple arbitrary cut-off point or a significant milestone in the narrative. More likely, it probably represents the earliest available data. One always has a basic desire to always want every chart to include the most up-to-date view of data. While it only reaches as far forward in time as 2012 (despite publication in 2015) the analysis is of such historical depth that it should be considered suitably representative of the subject matter. To just focus on the USA is entirely understandable.

Focus: The visualisation includes a 'time slider' control that allows users to move the focus incrementally through each year, colouring each consecutive yearly marker for emphasis. The colours are organised into three classifications to draw particular attention to two main periods of noticeably different relationships between the two quantitative measures.

Influence on Design Choices

How do these identified editorial perspectives translate directly into design thinking? As you will learn in Chapters 6–10 any visualisation comprises five layers of design. Let's have a look at how they might be influenced by editorial thinking.

Data representation: The *angle* is what fundamentally shapes the data representation approach. In lay terms, it determines which chart type is used. In this example, the defined angle is to show the relationship between two quantitative measures over time (average income for bottom 90% vs. top 1% of earners). A suitable chart type to portray this visually is the scatter plot (as selected). As you will learn in the next chapter, the scatter plot belongs to the 'relational' family of chart types. Given there was also a dimension of time expressed in this angle, a chart type from the 'temporal' family of charts *could* have been used but with the main emphasis being on showing the relationships the scatter plot was the better choice. The *framing* perspective defines what data will be included in the chosen chart: only data for the USA and the time period 1917–2012 is displayed.

Interactivity: As you will discover in Chapter 7, the role of interactivity is to enable adjustments to *what* data is displayed and *how* it is displayed. The sole feature of interactivity in this project is offered through the 'time slider' control, which sequences the unveiling of the data points year by year in either a manual or automated fashion. The inclusion of such interactivity can be influenced by the editorial decisions concerning *focus*: unveiling the yearly values sequences the emphasis on the position – and emerging pattern – of each consecutive value.

Annotation: The primary chart annotations on show here are the two arrows and associated captions, drawing attention to the two prominent patterns that support the general fall and then rise of inequality. Again, the inclusion of the captions would be a consequence of editorial thinking (*focus*) determining these respective patterns in the data should be emphasised to the viewer.

Colour: As you will learn about in Chapter 9, one of the key applications of colour is to support editorial salience – how to emphasise content and direct the eye. As before, editorial *focus* would influence the decision to deploy four colour states within the chart: a default colour to show all points at the start of the animation and then three different emerging colours to separate the three clustered groups visually. Note that the final colour choices of red, green and orange tones are not directly informed by editorial thinking, as the identified value of using four different ones to draw out the focus is what drives this choice.

Composition: This concerns all of the physical layout, shape and size decisions. In this example, the dimensions of editorial thinking have had limited influence over the composition choices. Although, recognising again that there are two charts in the full article, the focus perspective would have likely informed the decision to sequence the ordering of the charts: what made better sense to go first or last and why?

Example 2: Why Peyton Manning's Record Will Be Hard to Beat

In this second example, published on 'TheUpshot' section of the *New York Times* website, there are three charts presented in an article titled 'Why Peyton Manning's Record Will Be Hard to Beat'. Here I will look at all three charts.

Editorial Perspectives

Again, let's assess the editorial perspectives of angle, framing and focus as demonstrated by this work.

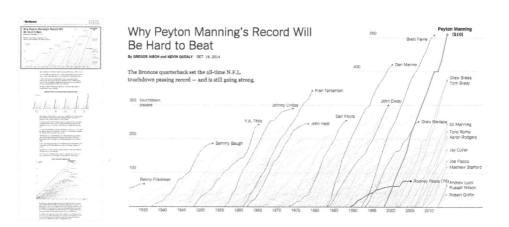

Figure 5.2
Why Peyton Manning's Record Will Be Hard to Beat

Angle: The first chart (Figure 5.2) displays the angle of analysis expressed as 'How have quantitative values (NFL touchdown passes) broken down by category (quarterbacks) changed over time (year)?'. This analysis was relevant at the time due to the significance of Peyton Manning setting a new record for NFL quarterback touchdown passes, an historic moment and, according to the article, 'evidence of how much the passing game has advanced through the history of the game'. Inspired by this achievement, the question posed by this article overall is whether the record will ever be bettered – which would have likely been the origin curiosity that drove the visualisation project in the first place. The article was time relevant because the record had just been achieved. On its own, this analysis would be deemed insufficient to support the overarching enquiry, as evidenced by the inclusion of two further charts that we will look at shortly.

Framing: The parameters that define the inclusion and exclusion framing relate to the time period (1930 to 19 October 2014) and qualifying quantitative threshold (minimum of 30 touchdown passes). It is representative of the truth at the moment of production (i.e. up to 19 October 2014) though clearly the data would no longer be up to date as soon as the next round of games took place. The judgment of the 30 touchdown passes threshold would either be informed by knowledge of the sport (and 30 TDs being a common measure) or more likely influenced by the shape of the data for every quarterback, indicating that it was a logical cut-off value.

Focus: The chart emphasises the record holder as well as the other current players in order to orientate the significance of the achievement and to highlight other contemporary players who *could* have a chance of pursuing this record. It also emphasises previous record holders or noted players to show just how special the new record is. If you want to know the achievements of any other player, their career 'lines' and values come into focus through mouseover-driven interactivity.

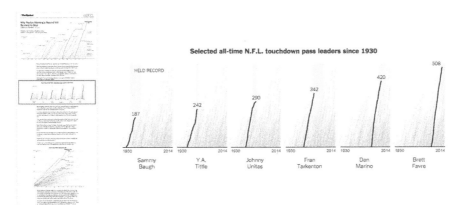

Figure 5.3 Why Peyton Manning's Record Will Be Hard to Beat

In the second chart (Figure 5.3), the same definitions stand for the *angle* and *framing*, but the *focus* has changed. This chart shows the same angle of analysis as seen in the first chart but is now composed of several small repeated charts, each one focusing on the career trajectories of a selected previous record holder.

Focus: Colour is used to emphasise the previous record-holding players' career lines with an illuminating background banding used to display the duration/era of their record standing. Value labels show the number of touchdowns achieved.

The final chart (Figure 5.4) has many similarities with the first chart. Once again it maintains the same consistent definition for *framing* and it has the same *focus* as the first chart but now there is a subtle difference in *angle*.

Angle: This is now expressed as: 'How have cumulative quantitative values (NFL touchdown passes) broken down by category (quarterbacks) changed over time (age)?'. The difference is the time measure being about age, not year. This is relevant as it provides an alternative view of the time measure, switching year for age to continue pursuing the curiosity over how long

Figure 5.4
Why Peyton
Manning's Record
Will Be Hard to
Beat

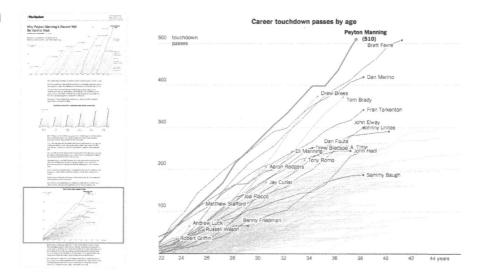

Manning's record might last. More specifically it enquires if 'the quarterback who will surpass Manning's record is playing today?'. Incidentally, as the article concludes, it is going to be a very difficult record to beat.

Influence on Design Choices

Now, let's switch the viewpoint again and look at how this visualisation's design choices are directly informed by the editorial thinking.

Data representation: As I have stated, the *angle* and *framing* dimensions are hugely influential in the reasoning of chart type requirements. In each of the charts used we are being shown different perspectives around the central theme of how touchdown passes have changed over time for each qualifying quarterback. A line chart showing cumulative values for all the players was the most appropriate way of portraying this. Naturally, the line chart belongs to the 'temporal' family of chart types. Alternative angles of analysis may have explored the relationship angle between the measures of age and total touchdown passes. A scatter plot would have been ideal to display that angle, but the inclusion of the cumulative touchdown passes statistic, as portrayed using the line, made for a much more striking display of the trajectories.

Interactivity: The only feature of interaction determined necessary here is achieved through a mouseover event in the first and third charts to reveal the names and total passes for any of the players who are presented as grey lines. This serves the interests of viewers who want to identify these background data values for 'everyone else'. By introducing value labels only through interactivity it also means the busy-ness of labelling all values by default could be elegantly – and wisely – avoided.

Annotation: This interactive labelling is a joint decision concerned with annotation. Elsewhere, the decision to include permanent annotated labels in each chart for category (player) and value (touchdown passes) provides emphasis in the first and third charts on the career achievements of Peyton Manning, the other current quarterbacks, and previous record holders. The second chart only labels the respective record holders who are the subject of each separate display.

Colour: The approach to creating focus is further achieved with colour. In the main chart, emphasis is again drawn to Peyton Manning's line, as the record holder (thick blue line), other current players (highlighted with a blue line) as well as previous record holders or noted players (dark grey line). For the second chart the light-blue coloured banding draws out the period of the records held by selected players down the years. This really helps the viewer to perceive the duration of their records.

Composition: The further influence of the editorial decisions for *focus* would be seen through the sequencing of the charts in the article. Given the rigid dimensions of space in which the article exists, the decision to order the charts in the way they are presented will have been informed by the desired narrative that was required to present analysis to support the articulated statement in the title.

A closing point to make here is that the influence of editorial thinking does not just flow forwards into the design stages. Although presented as separate, consecutive stages, 'working with data' and 'editorial thinking' are strongly related and quite iterative: working with data influences your editorial perspectives; and your editorial perspectives in turn may influence activities around working with data. In the earlier stages of your development it is useful to create this sequential distinction in activities but in reality there will be much toing and froing. The data transformation activity, in particular, is essentially the key wormhole that links these two stages. Editorial definitions may trigger the need for more data to be gathered about the specific subject matter or some consolidation in detail to support the desired angles of analysis and the framing dimensions. The acquisition of new data will always then trigger a need to repeat the data examination activity. Editorial definitions might also influence the need for further calculations, groupings or general modifications to refine its preparedness for displaying the analysis.

Summary: Establishing Your Editorial Thinking

In this chapter you learnt about the three perspectives that underpin your editorial thinking.

Angle

- Must be relevant in its potential interest for your audience.
- Must have sufficient quantities to cover all relevant views – but no more than required.

Framing

- Applying filters to your data to determine the inclusion and exclusion criteria.
- Framing decisions must provide access to the most salient content but also avoid any distorting of the view of the data.

Focus

- Which features of the display to draw particular attention to?
- How to organise the visibility and hierarchy of the content?

Tips and Tactics

- Data shapes the story, not the other way round: maintain this discipline throughout your work.
- If your data was especially riddled with gaps, perhaps consider making *this* the story: inverting attention towards the potential consequence, cause and meaning behind these gaps?
- There is *always* something interesting in your data: you just might not be equipped with sufficient domain knowledge to know this or it may not be currently relevant. Get to know the difference between relevant and irrelevant by researching and learning more about your subject.
- Communication: ask people better placed than you, who might have the subject knowledge, about what is truly interesting and relevant.
- A good title will often express the main curiosity or angle of analysis from the outset, giving viewers a clear idea about what the visualisation that follows will aim to answer or reveal.

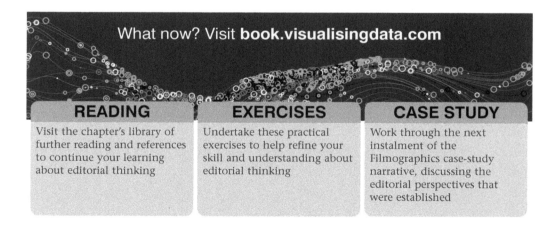

What now? Visit **book.visualisingdata.com**

READING	**EXERCISES**	**CASE STUDY**
Visit the chapter's library of further reading and references to continue your learning about editorial thinking	Undertake these practical exercises to help refine your skill and understanding about editorial thinking	Work through the next instalment of the Filmographics case-study narrative, discussing the editorial perspectives that were established

Part C

Developing Your Design Solution

The Production Cycle

Within the four stages of the design workflow there are two distinct parts. The first three stages, as presented in Part B of this book, were described as 'The Hidden Thinking' stages, as they are concerned with undertaking the crucial behind-the-scenes preparatory work. You may have completed them in terms of working through the book's contents, but in visualisation projects they will continue to command your attention, even if that is reduced to a background concern.

You have now reached the second distinct part of the workflow which involves developing your design solution. This stage follows a production cycle, commencing with rationalising design ideas and moving through to the development of a final solution.

The term **cycle** is appropriate to describe this stage as there are many loops of iteration as you evolve rapidly between conceptual, practical and technical thinking. The inevitability of this iterative cycle is, in large part, again due to the nature of this pursuit being more about optimisation rather than an expectation of achieving that elusive notion of perfection. Trade-offs, compromises, and restrictions are omnipresent as you juggle ambition and necessary pragmatism.

How you undertake this stage will differ considerably depending on the nature of your task. The creation of a relatively simple, single chart to be slotted into a report probably will not require the same rigour of a formal production cycle that the development of a vast interactive visualisation to be used by the public would demand. This is merely an outline of the most you will need to do – you should edit, adapt and participate the steps to fit with your context.

There are several discrete steps involved in this production cycle:

• Conceiving ideas across the five layers of visualisation design.
• Wireframing and storyboarding designs.
• Developing prototypes or mock-up versions.
• Testing.
• Refining and completing.
• Launching the solution.

Naturally, the specific approach for developing your design solution (from prototyping through to launching) will vary hugely, depending particularly on your skills and resources: it might be an Excel chart, or a Tableau dashboard, an infographic created using Adobe Illustrator, or a web-based interactive built with the D3.js library. As I have explained in the book's introduction, I'm not going to attempt to cover the myriad ways of implementing a solution; that would be impossible to achieve as each task and tool would require different instructions.

For the scope of this book, I am focusing on taking you through the first two steps of this cycle – conceiving ideas and wireframing/storyboarding. There are parallels here with the distinctions between architecture (design) and engineering (execution) – I'm effectively chaperoning you through to the conclusion of your design thinking.

To fulfil this, Part C presents a detailed breakdown of the many design options you will face when conceiving your visualisation design and provides you with an appreciation of the key factors that will influence the actual choices you make. The next few chapters are therefore concerned with the design thinking involved with each of these five layers of the visualisation design anatomy, namely:

Chapter 6: Data representation

Chapter 7: Interactivity

Chapter 8: Annotation

Chapter 9: Colour

Chapter 10: Composition

The sequencing of these layers is deliberate, based on the need to prioritise your attention: what will be included and how will it appear. Initially, you will need to make decisions about what choices to make around data representation (charts), interactivity and annotation. These are the layers that result in visible design content or features being included in your work. You will then complete your design thinking by making decisions about the appearance of these visible components, considering their colour and composition.

Conceiving: This will cover all your initial thinking across the various layers of design covered in the next few chapters. The focus here is on *conceiving* ideas based on the design options that seem to fit best with the preparatory thinking that has gone before during the first three stages. As you fine-tune your emerging design choices the benefit of sketching re-emerges, helping you articulate your thoughts into a rough visual form. As mentioned in Chapter 3, for some people the best approach involves sketching with the pen, for others it is best expressed through the medium of technical fluency.

Whichever approach suits you best, it is helpful to start to translate your conceptual thinking into visual thinking, particularly when collaborating. This sketching might build on your instinctive sketched concepts from stage 1, but you should now be far better informed about the realities of your challenge to determine what is relevant and feasible.

Wireframing and storyboarding: *Wireframing* involves creating a low-fidelity

'I tend to keep referring back to the original brief (even if it's a brief I've made myself) to keep checking that the concepts I'm creating tick all the right boxes. Or sometimes I get excited about an idea but if I talk about it to friends and it's hard to describe effectively then I know that the concept isn't clear enough. Sometimes just sleeping on it is all it takes to separate the good from the bad! Having an established workflow is important to me, as it helps me cover all the bases of a project, and feel confident that my concept has a sound logic.' **Stefanie Posavec, Information Designer** illustration of the potential layout for those solutions that will generally occupy a single page of space, such as a simple interactive visualisation or an infographic. There is no need to be too precise just yet, you are simply mapping out what will be on your page/screen (charts, annotations), how they will be arranged and what things (interactive functions) it will do. If your project is going to require a deeper architecture, like a complex interactive, or will comprise sequenced views, like presentations, reports or animated graphics, each individual wireframe view will be weaved together using a technique called *storyboarding*. This maps out the relationships between all the views of your content to form an overall visual structure. Sometimes you might approach things the other way round, beginning with a high-level storyboard to provide a skeleton structure within which you can then form your more detailed thinking about the specific wireframe layouts within each page or view.

Prototypes/mock-ups: Whereas wireframing and storyboarding are characterised by the creation of low-fi 'blueprints', the development of *mock-ups* (for example, Figure C.1) or *prototypes* (the terms tend to be used interchangeably) involves advancing your decisions about the content and appearance of your proposed solution. This effectively leads to the development of a first working version that offers a reasonably close representation of what the finished product might look like.

Figure C.1
Mockup
designs for
'Poppy Field'

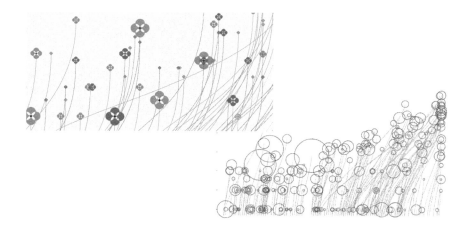

Testing: Once you have an established prototype version, you must then seek to have it tested. Firstly, you do this 'internally' (i.e. by you or by collaborators/colleagues) to help iron out any obvious immediate problems. In software development parlance, this would be generally consistent with alpha testing. Naturally, beta follows alpha and this is where you will seek others to test it, evaluate it, and feedback on it. This happens regardless of the output format; it doesn't need to be a digital, interactive project to merit being tested. There will naturally be many different aspects to your proposed solution that will need checking and evaluating. The three principles of good visualisation design that I presented earlier offer a sensible high-level structure to guide this testing:

- *Trustworthy* design testing concerns assessing the reliability of the work, in terms of the integrity of its content and performance. Are there any inaccuracies, mistakes or even deceptions? Are there any design choices that could lead to misunderstandings? Any aspects in how the data has been calculated or counted that could undermine trust? If it is a digital solution, what is the speed of loading and are there any technical bugs or errors? Is it suitably responsive and adaptable in its use across different platforms? Try out various user scenarios: multiple and concurrent users, real-time data, all data vs sample data, etc. Ask the people testing your solution to try to break it so you can find and resolve any problems now.
- *Accessible* design testing relates to how intuitive or sufficiently well explained the work is. Do they understand how to read it and what all the encodings mean? Is the viewer provided with a sufficient level of assistance that would be required as per the characteristics of the intended audience? Can testers find the answers to the questions you intended them to find and quickly enough? Can they find answers to the questions they think are most relevant?
- *Elegant* design testing relates to questions such as: Is the solution suitably appealing in design? Are there any features which are redundant or superfluous design choices that are impeding the process of using the solution?

Who you invite to test your work will vary considerably from one project to the next but generally you will have different possible people to consider participating in this task:

- *Stakeholders*: the ultimate customers/clients/colleagues who have commissioned the work may need to be included in this stage, if not for full testing then at least to engage them in receiving initial concept feedback.
- *Recipients*: you might choose a small sample of your target audience and invite those viewers to take part in initial beta testing.
- *Critical friends*: peers/team/colleagues with suitable knowledge and appreciation about the design process may offer a more sophisticated capacity to test out your work.
- *You*: sometimes (often) it may ultimately be down to you to undertake the testing, through either lack of access to other people or most typically a simple lack of time. To accomplish this effectively you have to find a way almost to detach yourself from the mindset of the creator and occupy that of the viewer: you need to see the wood *and* the trees.

The timing of *when* to seek feedback through testing/evaluation will vary across different contexts again. Sometimes the pressure from stakeholders who request to see progress will determine this. Otherwise, you will need to judge carefully the right moment to do so. You don't want to get feedback when

'We can kid ourselves that we are successful in what we "want" to achieve, but ultimately an external and critical audience is essential. Feedback comes in many forms; I seek it, listen to it, sniff it, touch it, taste it and respond.'
Kate McLean, Smellscape Mapper and Senior Lecturer Graphic Design

it is too late to change or you have invested too much effort creating a prototype that might require widespread changes in approach. Likewise, it can be risky showing far-too-undercooked concepts to stakeholders or testers when they might not have the capacity to realise this is just an early indication of the direction of travel. The least valuable form of testing feedback is when pedantic stakeholders spend time pointing out minutiae that of course need correcting but have no significance at this stage. No-one comes away with anything of value from this kind of situation.

Refining and completing: Based on the outcome of your testing process, this will likely trigger a need to revisit some of the issues that have emerged and resolve them satisfactorily. Editing your work involves:

* correcting issues;
* stripping away the superfluous content;
* checking and enhancing preserved content;
* adding extra degrees of sophistication to every layer of your design;
* improving the consistency and cohesion of your choices;
* double-checking the accuracy of every component.

As your work heads towards a state of completion your mindset will need to shift from a micro-level checking back to a macro-level assessment of whether you have truly delivered against the contextual requirements and purpose of your project.

In any creative process a visualiser is faced with having to declare work as being complete. Judging this can be quite a tough call to make in many projects. As I have discussed plenty of times, your sense of 'finished' often needs to be based on when you have reached the status of *good enough*. While the presence of a looming deadline (and at times increasingly agitated stakeholders) will sharpen the focus, often it comes down to a fingertip sense of when you feel you are entering the period of diminishing returns, when the refinements you make no longer add sufficient value for the amount of effort you invest in making them.

'You know you've achieved perfection in design, not when you have nothing more to add, but when you have nothing more to take away.' **Antoine de Saint-Exupéry, Writer, Poet, Aristocrat, Journalist, and Pioneering Aviator**

'Admit that nothing you create on a deadline will be perfect. However, it should never be wrong. I try to work by a motto my editor likes to say: No Heroics. Your code may not be beautiful, but if it works, it's good enough. A visualisation may not have every feature you could possibly want, but if it gets the message across and is useful to people, it's good enough. Being "good enough" is not an insult in journalism – it's a necessity.' **Lena Groeger, Science Journalist, Designer and Developer at ProPublica**

Launching: The nature of launching work will again vary significantly based, as always, on the context of your challenge. It may simply be emailing a chart to a colleague or you might be presenting your work to an audience. For other cases it could be a graphic going to print for a newspaper or involve an anxious go-live moment with the launch of a digital project on a website, to much fanfare and public anticipation. Whatever the context of your 'launch' stage, there are a few characteristic matters to bear in mind – these will not be relevant to all situations but over time you might need to consider their implications for your setting:

'It was intimidating to release to the public a self-initiated project on such a delicate subject considering some limitation with content and data source. But I came to appreciate that it's OK to offer a relevant way of looking at the subject, rather than provide a beginning-to-end conclusion.' **Valentina D'efilippo, Information Designer, discussing her 'Poppy Field' project that looked at the history of world conflicts and the resulting loss of life**

- Are *you* ready? Regardless of the scope of your work, as soon as you declare work completed and published you are at the mercy of your decisions. You are no longer in control of how people will interpret your work and in what way they will truly use it. If you have particularly large, diverse and potentially emotive subject matter, you will need to be ready for the questions and scrutiny that might head in your direction.
- *Communicating* your work is a big deal. The need to publicise and sell its benefits is of particular relevance if you have a public-facing project (you might promote it strongly or leave it as a slow burner that spreads through 'word of mouth'). For more modest and personal audiences you might need to consider directly presenting your work to these groups, coaching them through what it offers. This is particularly necessary on those occasions when you may be using a less than familiar representation approach.
- What ongoing *commitment* exists to support the work? This clearly refers to specific digital projects. Do you have to maintain a live data feed? Will it need to sustain operations with variable concurrent visitors? What happens if it goes viral – have you got the necessary infrastructure? Have you got the luxury of ongoing access to the skill sets required to keep this project alive and thriving?
- Will you need to revise, *update* and rerelease the project? As I discussed in the contextual circumstances, will you need to replicate this work on a repeated basis? What can you do to make the reproduction as seamless as possible?
- What is the work's likely *shelf life*? Does it have a point of expiry after which it could be archived or even killed? How might you digitally preserve it beyond its useful lifespan?

6

Data Representation

In this chapter you will explore in detail the first, and arguably the most significant, layer of the visualisation design anatomy: data representation. This is concerned with deciding in what visual form you wish to show your data.

To really get under the skin of data representation, we are going to look at it from both theoretical and pragmatic perspectives. You will start by learning about the building blocks of visual encoding, the real essence of this discipline and something that underpins all data representation thinking. Whereas visual encoding is perhaps seen as the purist 'bottom-up' viewpoint, the 'top-down' perspective possibly offers more pragmatic value by framing your data representation thinking around the notion of chart types. For most people facing up to this stage of data representation, this is conceptually the more practical entry point from which to shape their decisions.

To substantiate your understanding of this design layer you will take a tour through a gallery of 49 different chart type options, reflecting the many common and useful techniques being used to portray data visually in the field today. This gallery will then by supplemented by an overview of the key influencing factors that will inform and determine the choices you make.

6.1 Introducing Visual Encoding

As introduced in the opening chapter, data representation is the act of giving visual form to your data. As viewers, when we are perceiving a visual display of data we are *decoding* the various shapes, sizes, positions and colours to form an understanding of the quantitative and categorical values represented. As visualisers, we are doing the reverse through visual *encoding*, assigning visual properties to data values. Visual encoding forms the basis of any chart or map-based data representation, along with the components of chart apparatus that help complete the chart display.

There are many different ways of encoding data but these always comprise combinations of two different properties, namely *marks* and *attributes*. Marks are visible features like dots, lines and areas. An individual mark can represent a record or instance of data (e.g. your phone bill for a given month). A mark can also represent an aggregation of records or instances (e.g. a summation of individual phone charges to produce the bill for a given month). A set of marks would therefore represent a set of records or instances (e.g. the 12 monthly phone bills for 2015).

Attributes are variations applied to the appearance of marks, such as the size, position, or colour. They are used to represent the values held by different quantitative or categorical variables against each record or instance (or, indeed, each aggregation). If you had 12 marks, one for each phone bill during 2015, you could use the size attribute of each mark to represent the various phone bill totals.

Figure 6.1 offers a more visual illustration. In the dataset there are six records, one for each record listed. 'Gender' is a categorical variable and 'Years Since First Movie' is a quantitative variable. 'Male' and '43' are the specific values of these variables associated with Harrison Ford. In the associated chart, each actor from the table is represented by the mark of a line (or bar). This represents their record or instance in the table. Harrison Ford's bar is proportionally sized in scale to represent the 43 years since his first movie and is coloured purple to distinguish his gender as 'Male'. Each of the five other actors similarly has a bar sized according to the years since their first movie and coloured according to their gender.

Figure 6.1
Illustration
of Visual
Encoding

ACTOR	GENDER	YEARS SINCE FIRST MOVIE
Harrison Ford	Male	43
Meryl Streep	Female	38
Michael Douglas	Male	37
Arnold Schwarzenegger	Male	34
Nicole Kidman	Female	30
Sandra Bullock	Female	24

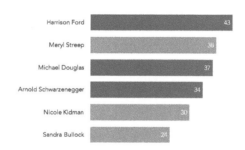

The objective of visual encoding is to find the right blend of marks and attributes that most effectively will portray the angle of analysis you wish to show your viewers. The factors that shape your choice and define the notion of what is considered 'effective' are multiple and varied in their influence. Before getting on to there, let's take a closer look at the range of different marks and attributes that are commonly found in the data representation toolkit.

It is worth noting upfront that while the organisation of the 'attributes', in particular, suggests a primary role, several can be deployed to encode both categorical (nominal, ordinal) variables and quantitative variables. Furthermore, as you see in the bar chart in Figure 6.1, combinations of several attributes are often applied to marks (such as colour and size) to encode multiple values.

Although beyond the scope of this book, there are techniques being developed in the field exploring the use of non-visual senses to portray data, using variations in properties for auditory (sound), haptic (touch), gustatory (taste) and olfactory (smell) senses.

Grasping the basics of visual encoding and its role in data visualisation is one of the fundamental pillars of understanding this discipline. However, when it comes to the reality of considering your data representation

MARK	EXAMPLE	DESCRIPTION
Point		The *point* mark has no variation ('constant') in the spatial dimension. It is largely a placeholder commonly used to represent a quantity through position on a scale, forming the basis of, for example, scatter plots.
Line		The *line* mark has one ('linear') spatial dimension. It is commonly used to represent quantitative value through variation in size, forming the basis of, for example, the bar chart.
Area		The *area* mark has two ('quadratic') spatial dimensions. It is commonly used to represent quantitative values through variation in size and position, forming the basis of, for example, bubble plots.
Form	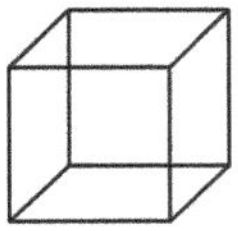	The *form* mark has three ('cubic') spatial dimensions. It might be used to represent quantitative values through variation in size (specifically, through volume), forming the basis of, for example, a 3D proportional shape chart.

Figure 6.2   List of *Mark* Encodings

ATTRIBUTE	EXAMPLE	DESCRIPTION
QUANTITATIVE ATTRIBUTES		
Position	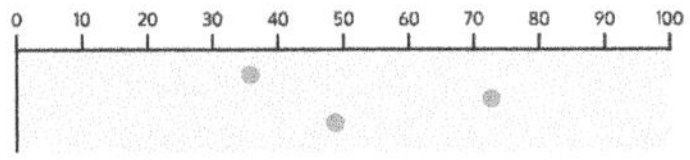	Position along a scale is used to indicate a quantitative value.
Size	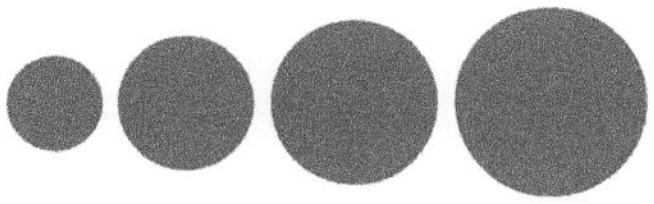	Size (length, area, volume) is used to represent quantitative values based on proportional scales where the larger the size of the mark, the larger the quantity.
Angle/Slope	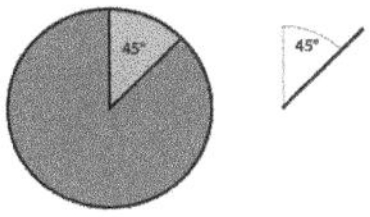	Variation in the size of angle forms the basis of pie chart sectors representing parts-of-a-whole quantitative values; the larger the angle, the larger the proportion. The slope of an incline formed by angle variation can also be used to encode values.
Quantity		The quantity of a repeated set of point marks can be used to represent a one-to-one or a one-to-many unit count.
Colour: Saturation	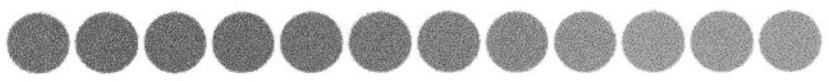	Colour saturation can be used (often in conjunction with other colour properties) to represent quantitative scales; typically, the greater the saturation, the higher the quantity.

ATTRIBUTE	EXAMPLE	DESCRIPTION
Colour: Lightness		Colour lightness can be used (often in conjunction with other colour properties) to represent quantitative scales; typically, the darker the colour, the higher the quantity.
Pattern		Variation in pattern density or difference in pattern texture can be used to represent quantitative scales or distinguish between categorical ordinal states.
Motion	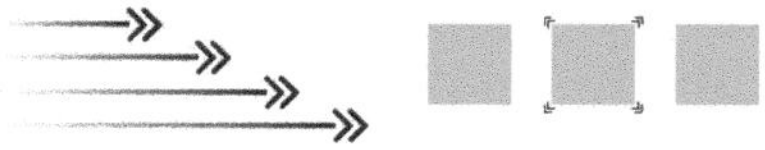	Motion is more rarely seen but it could be used as a binary indicator to draw focus (motion vs no motion) or by incorporating movement through speed and direction to represent a quantitative scale ramp.
CATEGORICAL ATTRIBUTES		
Symbol/shape		Symbols or shapes are generally used with point markers to indicate categorical association.
Colour: Hue		Colour hue is typically used for distinguishing different categorical data values but can also be used in conjunction with other colour properties to represent certain quantitative scales.
RELATIONAL ATTRIBUTES		
Connection/Edge		A connection or edge indicates a relationship between two nodes. Sometimes arrows may be added to indicate direction of relationship, but largely it is just about the presence or absence of a connection.
Containment	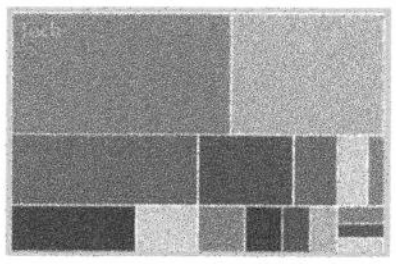	Containment is a way of indicating a grouping relationship between categories that belong to a related hierarchical 'parent' category.

Figure 6.3 List of *Attribute* Encodings

options you do not necessarily need to always approach things from this somewhat bottom-up perspective. For most people's needs when creating a data visualisation it is more pragmatic (and perhaps more comprehensible) to think about data representation from a top-down perspective in the shape of chart types.

> Recall that I am using chart type as the all-encompassing term, though this is merely a convenient singular label to cover any variation of map, graph, plot and diagram based around the representation of data.

If marks and attributes are the ingredients, a chart 'type' is the recipe offering a predefined template for displaying data. Different chart types offer different ways of representing data, each one comprising unique combinations of marks and attributes onto which specific types of data can be mapped.

Let's work through a few examples to illustrate the relationship between some selected chart types demonstrating different combinations of *marks* and *attributes*.

To begin with Figure 6.4, visualises the recent fortunes of the world's billionaires. The display shows the relative ranking of each profiled billionaire in the rich list, grouping them by the different sectors of industry in which they have developed their wealth. This data is encoded using the *point* mark and two attributes of *position*. The point in this deployment is depicted using small caricature face drawings representative of each individual – effectively unique symbols to represent the distinct 'category' of each different billionaire. Note that these are points, as distinct from area marks, because their size is constant and insignificant in terms of any quantitative implication.

The position in the allocated column signifies the industry the individuals are associated with, while the vertical position signifies the rank (higher position = higher rank towards number 1).

For reference, this is considered a derivative of the univariate scatter plot, which usually shows the dispersal of a range of absolute values rather than rank.

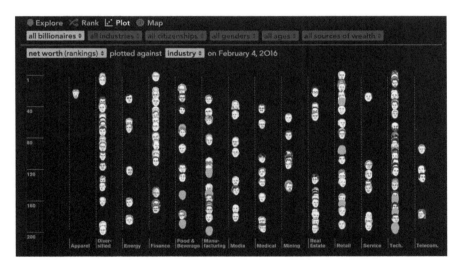

Figure 6.4
Bloomberg Billionaires

As seen in Chapter 1, the clustered bar chart in Figure 6.5 displays a series of *line* marks (normally described as bars). There are 11 pairs of bars, one for each of the football seasons included in the aggregated analysis. The attribute of *colour* is used to distinguish the bars between the two quantitative measures displayed: blue is for 'games', purple is for 'goals'. The *size* dimension of 'height' (the widths are constant) along the y-axis scale then represents the quantitative values associated with each season and each measure.

Figure 6.6 is called a bubble chart and displays a series of geometric *area* marks to represent the top 100 blog posts on my website based on their popularity over the previous 100 days.

Each circle represents an individual post and is *sized* to show the quantitative value of 'total visits' and then *coloured* according to the seven different post categories I use to organise my content.

Figure 6.5
Lionel
Messi:
Games and
Goals
for FC
Barcelona

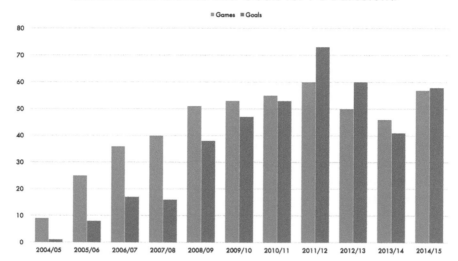

The 100 top viewed posts in the last 100 days. Select a bubble to see a preview below.

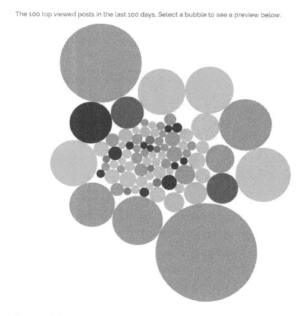

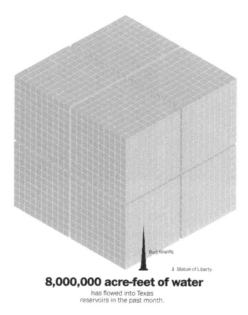

8,000,000 acre-feet of water
has flowed into Texas
reservoirs in the past month.

Figure 6.6   Image from the home page of
visualisingdata.com

Figure 6.7   How the Insane Amount of Rain in
Texas Could Turn Rhode Island Into a Lake

Figure 6.7 demonstrates the use of the *form*, which is more rarely used. My advice is that it should remain that way as it is hard for us to judge scales of volume in 2D displays. However, it can be of merit when values are extremely diverse in size as in this good example. The chart displayed contextualises the amount of water that had flowed into Texas reservoirs in the 30 days up to 27 May 2015. The *size* (volume) of a cube is used to display the amount of rain, with 8000 small cubes representing 1000 acre-feet of water (43,560,000 cubic feet or 1233.5 mega litres) to create the whole (8 million acre-feet), which is then compared against the heights of the Statue of Liberty and what was then the world's tallest building, the Burj Khalifa, to orient in height terms at least.

6.2 Chart Types

For many people, creating a visualisation involves using tools that offer chart menus: you might select a chart type and then 'map' the records and variables of data against the marks and attributes offered by that particular chart type. Different tools will offer the opportunity to work with a different range of chart types, some with more than others.

As you develop your capabilities in data visualisation and become more 'expressive' – trying out unique combinations of marks and attributes – your approach might lean more towards thinking about representation from a bottom-up perspective, considering the visual encodings you wish to deploy and arriving at a particular chart type as the destination rather than an origin. This will be especially likely if you develop or possess a talent for creating visualisations through programming languages.

As the field has matured over the years, and a greater number of practitioners have been experimenting with different recipes of marks and attributes, there is now a broad range of established chart types. Once again I hesitate to use the universal label of chart type (some mapping techniques are not chart types per se) but it will suffice. While all of us are likely to be familiar with the 'classic three' – namely, the bar, pie and line chart – there are many other chart type options to consider.

To acquaint you with a broader repertoire of charting options, over the coming pages I present you with a gallery. This offers a curated collection of some of the common and useful chart types being used across the field today. This gallery aims to provide you with a valuable reference that will directly assist your judgements, helping you to pick (conceptually, at least) from a menu of options.

I have attempted to assign each chart to one of five main families based on their primary analytical purpose. What type of angle of analysis does each one principally show? Using the five-letter mnemonic CHRTS this should provide a useful taxonomy for organising your thinking about which chart or charts to use for your data representation needs.

I know what you're thinking: 'well that's a suspiciously convenient acronym'! Honestly, if it was as intentional as that I would have tried harder to somehow crowbar in an 'A' family. OK, I did spend a lot of time, but I couldn't find it and it's now my life's ambition to do so. Only then will my time on this planet have been truly worthwhile. In the meantime, CHRTS is close enough. Besides, vowels are hugely overrated.

CATEGORICAL	Comparing categories and distributions of quantitative values
HIERARCHICAL	Charting part-to-whole relationships and hierarchies
RELATIONAL	Graphing relationships to explore correlations and connections
TEMPORAL	Showing trends and activities over time
SPATIAL	Mapping spatial patterns through overlays and distortions

Each chart type presented is accompanied by an array of supporting details that will help you fully acquaint yourself with the role and characteristics of each option.

A few further comments about what this gallery provides:

- The primary name used to label each chart type as well as some further alternative names that are often used
- An indication of which CHRTS family each chart belongs to, based on their specific primary role, as well as a sub-family definition for further classification
- An indicator for each chart type to show which ones I consider to be most useful for undertaking Exploratory Data Analysis (the black magnifying glass symbol)
- An indicator for whether I believe a chart would typically require interactive features to offer optimum usability (the black cursor symbol)
- A description of the chart's representation: what it shows and what encodings (marks, attributes) it is comprised of
- A working example of the chart type in use with a description of what it specifically shows
- A 'how to read' guide, advising on the most effective and efficient approach to making sense of each chart type and what features to look out for
- Presentation tips offering guidance on some of the specific choices to be considered around interactivity, annotation, colour or composition design
- 'Variations and alternatives' offer further derivatives and chart 'siblings' to consider for different purposes

Exclusions: It is by no means an exhaustive list: the vast permutations of different marks and attributes prevents any finite limit to how one might portray data visually. I have, however, consciously excluded some chart types from the gallery mainly because they were not different enough from other charts that have been profiled in detail. I have mentioned charts that represent legitimate derivatives of other charts where necessary but simply did not deem it worthy to assign a whole page to profile them separately. The *Voronoi treemap*, for example, is really just a circular treemap that uses different algorithms to arrange its constituent pieces. While the construction task is different, its usage is not. The *waterfall chart* is a single stacked bar chart broken down into sequenced stages.

Inclusions: I have wrestled with the rights and wrongs of including some chart types, unquestionably. The radar chart, for example, has many limitations and flaws but is not entirely without merit if deployed in a very specific way and only for certain contexts. By including profiles of partially flawed charts like these I am using the gallery as much to signpost their shortcomings so that you know to use them sparingly. There will be some purists gathering in angry mobs and foaming at the mouth in reaction to the audacity of my including the pie chart and word cloud. These have limited roles, absolutely, but a role nonetheless. Put down your pitchforks, return to your homes and have a good read of my caveats. Rather than being the poacher of all bad stuff, I think a gamekeeper role is equally important.

Although I have excluded several charts on grounds of demonstrating only a slight variation on profiled charts, there are some types included that do exhibit only small derivations from other charts (such as the bar chart and the clustered bar, or the scatter plot and the bubble plot). In these cases I felt there was sufficient difference in their practical application, and they were in common usage, to merit their separate inclusion, despite sharing many similarities with other profiled siblings.

'Interestingly, visualisations of textual data are not as developed as one would expect. There is a great need for such visualisations given the amount of textual information we generate daily, from social media to news media and so on, not to mention all the materials generated in the past and that are now digitally available. There are opportunities to contribute to the research efforts of humanists as well as social scientists by devising ways to represent not only frequencies of words and topics, but also semantic content. However, this is not at all trivial.' **Isabel Meirelles, Professor, OCAD University (Toronto), discussing one of the many remaining unknowns in visualisation**

Categorical comparisons: All chart types can feasibly facilitate comparisons between categories, so why have a separate C family? Well, the distinction is that those charts belonging to the H, R, T and S families offer an additional dimension of analysis *as well* as providing comparison between categories.

Dual families: Some charts do not fit just into a single family. Showing connected relationships (e.g. routes or flows) on a map is ticking the requirements across at least two or family groups (Relational, Spatial). In each case I have tried to best-fit the family classifications around the primary angle of analysis portrayed by each chart – what is the most prominent aspect that characterises each representation technique.

Text visualisation: As I noted in the discussion about data types, when it comes to working with textual-based data you are almost always going to need to perform some transformation, maybe through value extraction or by applying a statistical technique. The text itself can otherwise largely function only as an annotated device. Chart types used to visualise text actually visualise the properties of text. For example, the word cloud visualises the quantitative frequency of the use of words: text might be the subject, but categories (words) and their quantities (counts) are the data mappings. Varieties of network diagrams might show the relationship between word usage, such as the sequence of words used in sentences (word trees), but these are still only made possible through some quantitative, categorical or semantic property being drawn from the original text.

Dashboard: These methods are popular in corporate settings or any context where you wish to create instrumentation that offers both at-a-glance and detailed views of many different analytical and information monitoring dimensions. Dashboards are not a unique chart type themselves but rather should be considered projects that comprise multiple chart types from across the repertoire of options presented in the gallery. Some of the primary demands of designing dashboards concern editorial thinking (what angles to show and why) and composition choices (how to get it all presented in a unified page layout).

Small multiples: This is an invaluable technique for visualising data but not necessarily a chart type per se and, once again, more a concern for about editorial thinking and composition design. Small multiples involve repeated display of the same chart type but with adjustments to the framing of the data in each panel. For example, each panel may show the same angle of analysis but for different categories or different points in time. Small multiples are highly valued because they exploit the capabilities of our visual perception system when it comes to comparing charts in a simultaneous view, overcoming our weakness at remembering and recalling chart views when consumed through animated sequences or across different pages.

A note about 'storytelling': Storytelling is an increasingly popular term used around data visualisation but I feel it is often misused and misunderstood, which is quite understandable as we all have different perspectives. I also feel it is worth clarifying my take on what I believe storytelling means practically in data visualisation and especially in this discussion about data representation, which is where it perhaps most logically resides in terms of how it is used.

Stories are constructs based on the essence of movement, change or narrative. A line chart shows how a series of values have changed over a temporal plane. A flow map can reveal what relationships exist across a spatial plane between two points separated by distance – they may be evident of a journey. However, aside from the temporal and spatial families of charts, I would argue that no other chart family realistically offers this type of construct in and of itself.

The only way to create a story from other types of charts is to incorporate a temporal dimension (video/slideshow) or provide a verbal/written narrative that itself involves a dimension of time through the sequence of its delivery.

For example, a bar chart alone does not represent a story, but if you show a 'before' and 'after' pair of bar charts side by side or between slides, you have essentially created 'change' through sequence. If you show a bar chart with a stack on top of it to indicate growth between two points in time, well, you have added a time dimension. A network diagram shows relationships, but stood alone this is not a story – its underlying structure and arrangement are in abstract space. Just as you do when showing friends a photograph from your holiday, you might use this chart as a prop to explain how relationships between some of the different entities presented are significant. Making the chart a prop allows *you* to provide a narrative. In this case it is the setting and delivery that are consistent with the notion of storytelling, not the chart itself. I made a similar observation about the role of exhibitory visualisations used as props within explanatory settings.

A further distinction to make is between stories as being presented and stories as being interpreted. The famous six-word story 'for sale: baby shoes, never worn' by Ernest Hemingway is not presented as a story, the story is triggered in our mind when we dissect this passage and start to infer meaning, implication and context. The imagined bar chart I mentioned earlier in the book that could show the 43 white presidents and 1 black president is only presenting a story if it is accompanied by an explanatory narrative (in which case the chart was again really just a prop) or if you understand the meaning of the significance of this statistic without this description and are able to form the story in your own mind.

BAR CHART

ALSO KNOWN AS Column chart, histogram (wrongly)

REPRESENTATION DESCRIPTION

A bar chart displays quantitative values for different categories. The chart comprises line marks (bars) – not rectangular areas – with the size attribute (length or height) used to represent the quantitative value for each category.

EXAMPLE

Comparing the number of Oscar nominations for the 10 actors who have received the most nominations without actually winning an award.

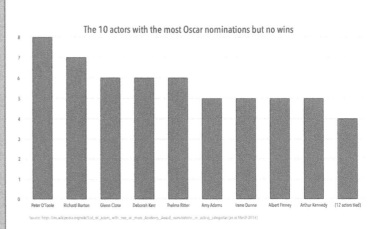

The 10 actors with the most Oscar nominations but no wins

Source: https://en.wikipedia.org/wiki/List_of_actors_with_two_or_more_Academy_Award_nominations_in_acting_categories (as at March 2016)

Figure 6.8   The 10 Actors with the Most Oscar Nominations but No Wins

161

HOW TO READ IT & WHAT TO LOOK FOR

Look at the axes so you know with which categorical value each bar is associated and what the range of the quantitative values is (min to max). Think about what high and low values mean: is it 'good' to be large or small? Glance across the entire chart to locate the big, small and medium bars and perform global comparisons to establish the high-level ranking of biggest > smallest. Identify any noticeable exceptions and/or outliers. Perform local comparisons between neighbouring bars, to identify larger than and smaller than relationships and estimate the relative proportions. Estimate (or read, if labels are present) the absolute values of specific bars of interest. Where available, compare the quantities against annotated references such as targets, forecast, last year, average, etc.

PRESENTATION TIPS

ANNOTATION: Chart apparatus devices like tick marks and gridlines, in particular, can be helpful to increase the accuracy of the reading of the quantitative values. If you have axis labels you should not need direct labels on each bar – this will lead to label overload, so generally decide between one or the other.

COMPOSITION: The quantitative value axis should always start from the origin value of zero: a bar should be representative of the true, full quantitative value, nothing more, nothing less, otherwise the perception of bar sizes will be distorted when comparing relative sizes. There is no significant difference in perception between vertical or horizontal bars though horizontal layouts tend to make it easier to accommodate and read the category labels for each bar. Unlike the histogram, there should be a gap, even if very small, between bars to keep each category's value distinct. Where possible, try to make the categorical sorting meaningful.

VARIATIONS & ALTERNATIVES

A variation in the use of bar charts is to show changes over time. You would use a bar chart when the focus is on individual quantitative values over time rather than (necessarily) the trend/change between points, for which a line-chart would be best. 'Spark bars' are mini bar charts that aim to occupy only a word's length amount of space. They are often seen in dashboards where space is at a premium and there is a desire to optimise the density of the display. To show further categorical subdivisions, you might consider the 'clustered bar chart' or a 'stacked bar chart' if there is a part-to-whole angle. 'Dot plots' offer a particularly useful alternative to the bar chart for situations where you have to show large quantitative values with a narrow range of differences.

CLUSTERED BAR CHART

ALSO KNOWN AS Clustered column chart, paired bar chart

COMPARISONS

REPRESENTATION DESCRIPTION

A clustered bar chart displays quantitative values for different major categories with additional categorical dimensions included for further breakdown. The chart comprises line marks (bars) – not rectangular areas – with the size attribute (length or height) used to represent the quantitative value for each category and colours used to distinguish further categorical dimensions.

EXAMPLE Comparing the number of Oscar nominations with the number of Oscar awards for the 10 actors who have received the most nominations.

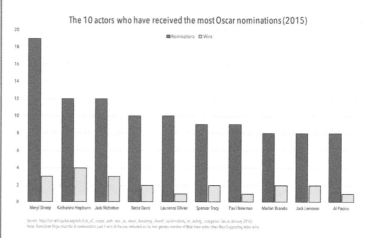

Figure 6.9   The 10 Actors who have Received the Most Oscar Nominations

HOW TO READ IT & WHAT TO LOOK FOR

Look at the axes so you know with which categorical value each bar is associated and what the range of the quantitative values is (min to max). Learn about the colour associations to understand what sub-categories the bars within each cluster represent. Glance across the entire chart to locate the big, small and medium bars and perform global comparisons to establish the high-level ranking of biggest > smallest. Identify any noticeable exceptions and/or outliers. Perform local comparisons within clusters to identify the size relationship (which is larger and by how much?) and estimate (or read, if labels are present) the absolute values of specific bars of interest.

PRESENTATION TIPS

ANNOTATION: Chart apparatus devices like tick marks and gridlines, in particular, can be helpful to increase the accuracy of the reading of the quantitative values. If you have axis labels you should not need direct labels on each bar – this will lead to label overload, so generally decide between one or the other.

COMPOSITION: The quantitative value axis should always start from the origin value of zero: a bar should be representative of the true, full quantitative value, nothing more, nothing less, otherwise the perception of bar sizes will be distorted when comparing relative sizes. If your categorical clusters involve a breakdown of more than three bars, it becomes a little too busy, so you might therefore consider giving each cluster its own separate bar chart and using small multiples to show a chart for each major category. Sometimes one bar might be slightly hidden behind the other, implying a before and after relationship, often when space is at a premium – just do not hide too much of the back bar. There is no significant difference in perception between vertical or horizontal bars though horizontal layouts tend to make it easier to accommodate and read the category labels for each bar. The individual bars should be positioned adjacent to each other with a noticeable gap and then between each cluster to help direct the eye towards the clustering patterns first and foremost. Where possible try to make the categorical sorting meaningful.

VARIATIONS & ALTERNATIVES

Clustered bar charts are also sometimes used to show how two associated sub-categories have changed over time (like the Lionel Messi bar chart discussed in Chapter 1). Alternatives would include the 'dot plot' or, if you have just two categories forming the clusters and these categories have a binary state (male, female or yes %, no %), the 'back-to-back bar chart' would be effective.

DOT PLOT

ALSO KNOWN AS Dot chart

REPRESENTATION DESCRIPTION

A dot plot displays quantitative values for different categories. In contrast to the bar chart, rather than using the size of a bar, point marks (typically circles but any 'symbol' is legitimate) are used with the position along a scale indicating the quantitative value for each category. Sometimes an area mark is used to indicate one value through position and another value through size. Additional categorical dimensions can be accommodated in the same chart by including additional marks differentiated by colour or symbol.

EXAMPLE

EXAMPLE Comparing the number and percentage of PhDs awarded by gender across different academic subjects.

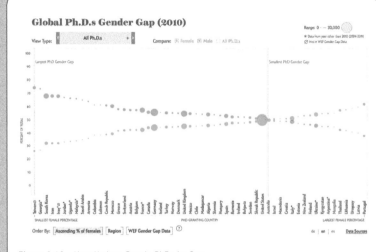

Figure 6.10 How Nations Fare in PhDs by Sex

163

HOW TO READ IT & WHAT TO LOOK FOR

For single-series dot plots (i.e. just one dot per row), look at the axes so you know with which categorical value each row is associated and what the range of the quantitative values is (min to max). Where you have multiple series dot plots (i.e. more than one dot), establish what the different colours/symbols represent in terms of categorical breakdown. Glance across the entire chart to locate the big, small and medium values and perform global comparisons to establish the high-level ranking of biggest > smallest. Identify any noticeable exceptions and/or outliers. Where you have multiple series look across each series of dot values separately and then perform local comparisons within rows to identify the relative position of each dot, observing the gaps, big and small. Estimate the absolute values of specific dots of interest. Where available, compare the quantities against annotated references such as targets, forecast, last year, average, etc.

PRESENTATION TIPS

ANNOTATION: Chart apparatus devices like tick marks and gridlines, in particular, can be helpful to increase the accuracy of the reading of the quantitative values.

COMPOSITION: Given that the quantitative value axis does not need to commence from a zero origin it is important to label clearly the axis values when the baseline is *not* commencing from a minimum of zero. There is no significant difference in perception between vertical or horizontal arrangement though horizontal layouts tend to make it easier to accommodate and read the category labels for each row. Where possible try to make the categorical sorting meaningful, maybe organising values in ascending/descending size order.

VARIATIONS & ALTERNATIVES

Alternatives would include the 'bar chart', to show the size of quantitative values for different categories. The 'connected dot plot' would be used to focus on the difference between two measures. The 'univariate scatter plot' would be used to show the range of multiple values across categories, to display the diversity and distribution of values.

REPRESENTATION DESCRIPTION

A connected dot plot displays absolute quantities and quantitative differences between two categorical dimensions for different major categories. The display is formed by two points (normally circles but any 'symbol' is legitimate) to mark the quantitative value positions for two comparable categorical dimensions. There is a row of connected dots for each major category. Colour or difference in symbol is generally used to distinguish these points. Joining the two points together is a connecting line which effectively represents the 'delta' (difference) between the two values.

EXAMPLE Comparing the typical salaries for women and men across a range of different job categories in the US.

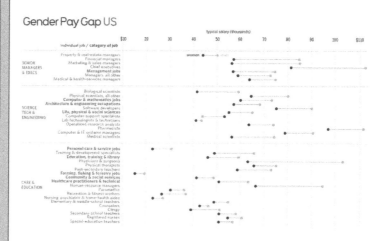

Figure 6.11   Gender Pay Gap US

HOW TO READ IT & WHAT TO LOOK FOR

Look at the axes so you know with which major categorical values each row is associated and what the range of the quantitative values is (min to max). Determine which dots resemble which categorical dimension (could be colour, symbol or a combination) and see if there is any meaning behind the colouring of the connecting bars. Think about what the quantitative values mean to determine whether it is a good thing to be higher or lower. Glance across the entire chart to locate the big, small and medium connecting bars in each direction. Perform global comparisons to establish the high-level ranking of biggest > smallest differences as well as the highest and lowest values. There may be deliberate sorting of the display based on one of the quantitative measures. Identify any noticeable exceptions and/or outliers. Estimate (or read, if labels are present) the absolute values, direction and size of differences for specific categories of interest.

PRESENTATION TIPS

ANNOTATION: Chart apparatus devices like tick marks and gridlines, in particular, can be helpful to increase the accuracy of the reading of the quantitative values. Consider labelling categories adjacent to the plotted points rather than next to the axis line (and possibly far away from the values) to make it easier for the reader to understand the category–row association.

COLOUR TIPS: Colour may be used to indicate and emphasise the directional basis of the connecting line differences.

COMPOSITION: If the two plotted measures are very similar, and the point markers effectively overlap, you will need to decide which should be positioned on top. As the representation of the quantitative values is through position along a scale and not size (it is the difference that is sized, not the absolutes) the quantitative axis does not need to have a zero origin. However, a zero origin can be helpful to establish the scale of the differences. Where possible try to make the sorting meaningful using any one of the three quantitative measures to optimise the layout.

VARIATIONS & ALTERNATIVES

Variations in the use of the 'connected dot plot' would show before and after analysis between two points in time, possibly using the 'arrow chart' to indicate the direction of change explicitly. Similarly, the 'carrot chart' uses line width tapering to indicate direction, the fatter end the more recent values. The 'univariate scatter plot' would be used to show the range of multiple values across categories, to display the diversity and distribution of values rather than comparing differences between values.

PICTOGRAM

ALSO KNOWN AS Isotype chart, pictorial bar chart, stacked shape chart, tally chart

COMPARISONS

REPRESENTATION DESCRIPTION

A pictogram displays quantitative values for different major categories with additional categorical dimensions included for further breakdown. In contrast with the bar chart, rather than using the size of a bar, quantities of point marks, in the form of symbols or pictures, are stacked to represent the quantitative value for each category. Each point may be representative of one or many quantitative units (e.g. a single shape may represent 1000 people) but note that, unless you use symbol portions, you will not be able to represent decimals. Pictograms may be used to offer a more emotive (humanising or more light-hearted) display than a bar can offer. Additional categorical dimensions can be accommodated in the same chart by using marks differentiated by variations in colour, symbol or picture. Always ensure the markers used are as intuitively recognisable as possible and consider minimising the variety as this makes it cognitively harder for the viewer to identify associations easily and make sense of the quantities.

EXAMPLE Comparing the number of players with different facial hair types across the four teams in the NHL playoffs in 2015.

Razors Are for the Regular Season

Based on recent photographs, here is how the four remaining teams in the NHL playoffs compare in terms of facial hair. Players are divided into three categories: full beard, scraggly/light beards and clean-shaven.

	Full beard	Light beard	Clean

Rangers	13	6	
Blackhawks	10	8	1
Ducks	10	6	3
Lightning	10	6	3

Note: Results reflect each team's 12 forwards, six defensemen and one goalie with most playing time.

THE WALL STREET JOURNAL

Figure 6.12   Who Wins the Stanley Cup of Playoff Beards?

HOW TO READ IT & WHAT TO LOOK FOR

Look at the major categorical axis to establish with which category each row is associated. Establish the mark associations to understand what categorical dimensions each colour/shape variation represents. Glance across the entire chart to locate the big, small and medium stacks of shapes and perform global comparisons to establish the high-level ranking of biggest > smallest. Identify any noticeable exceptions and/or outliers. Perform local comparisons between neighbouring categories, to identify larger than and smaller than relationships and estimate the relative proportions. Estimate (or read, if labels are present) the absolute values of specific groups of markers of interest.

PRESENTATION TIPS

ANNOTATION: The choice of symbol/ picture should be as recognisably intuitive as possible and locate any legends as close as possible to the display.

COLOUR TIPS: Maximise the variation in marker by using different combinations in both colour and shape, rather than just variation of one attribute.

COMPOSITION: If the quantities of markers exceed a single row, try to make the number of units per row logically 'countable', such as displaying in groups of 5, 10 or 100. To aid readability, make sure there is a sufficiently noticeable gap between rows, otherwise sometimes the eye struggles to form the distinct clusters of shapes for each category displayed. Where possible try to make the categorical sorting meaningful, maybe organising values in ascending/descending size order.

VARIATIONS & ALTERNATIVES

Extending the idea of using repeated quantities of representative symbols, some applications take this further by using large quantities of individual symbols to get across the feeling of magnitude and scale. When showing a part-to-whole relationship, the 'waffle chart' can use simple symbol devices to differentiate the constituent parts of a whole.

PROPORTIONAL SHAPE CHART

ALSO KNOWN AS Area chart (wrongly)

REPRESENTATION DESCRIPTION

A proportional shape chart displays quantitative values for different categories. The chart is based on the use of different area marks, one for each category, sized in proportion to the quantities they represent. By using the quadratic dimension of area size rather than the linear dimension of bar length or dot position, the shape chart offers scope for displaying a diverse range of quantitative values within the same chart. Typically the layout is quite free-form with no baseline or central gravity binding the display together.

EXAMPLE Comparing the market capitalisation ($) of companies involved in the legal sale of marijuana across different industry sectors.

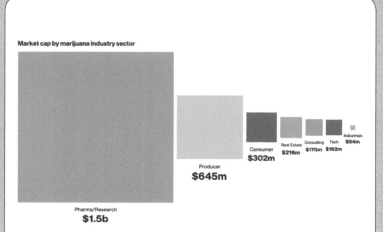

Figure 6.13   For These 55 Marijuana Companies, Every Day is 4/20

HOW TO READ IT & WHAT TO LOOK FOR

Look at the shapes and their associated labels so you know with what major categorical values each is associated. If there are only direct labels, find the largest shape to establish its quantitative value as the maximum and do likewise for the smallest – this will help calibrate the size judgements. Otherwise, if it exists, acquaint yourself with the size key. Glance across the entire chart to locate the big, small and medium shapes and perform global comparisons to establish the high-level ranking of biggest > smallest. Identify any noticeable exceptions and/or outliers. Perform local comparisons between neighbouring shapes to identify larger than and smaller than relationships and estimate the relative proportions. Estimate (or read, if labels are present) the absolute values of specific shapes of interest.

PRESENTATION TIPS

ANNOTATION: Sometimes a quantitative size key will be included rather than direct labelling (usually when there are many shapes and limited empty space) though direct labels will help overcome some of the limitations of judging area size. You will have to decide how to handle label positioning for those shapes with exceptionally small sizes.

COLOUR TIPS: Colours are not fundamentally necessary to encode category (the position/separation of different shapes achieves that already) but they can be useful as redundant encodings to make the category even more immediately distinguishable.

COMPOSITION: Estimating and comparing the size of areas with accuracy is not as easy as it is for judging bar length or dot position, so only use this chart type if you have a diverse range of quantitative values. The geometric accuracy of the size calculations is paramount. Mistakes are often made, in particular, with circle size calculations: it is the area you are modifying, not the diameter/radius. Arrangement approaches vary: sometimes you see the shapes anchored to a common baseline (bottom or central alignment) while on other occasions they might just 'float'. If you use an organic shape, like a human figure, to represent different quantities you need to adjust the entire shape area, not just the height. Often the approach for this type of display is to treat the figure as a rudimentary rectangular shape. Sometimes the volume of a shape is used rather than area to represent quantitative values (especially if there are almost exponentially different values to show) but this increases the perceptual difficulty in estimating and comparing values. Where possible try to make the categorical sorting meaningful, maybe organising values in ascending/descending size order.

VARIATIONS & ALTERNATIVES

The 'bubble chart' uses clusters of sized bubbles to compare categorical values and, sometimes, to represent part-to-whole analysis. The 'nested shape chart' might include secondary, smaller area sizes nested within each shape to display local part-to-whole relationships.

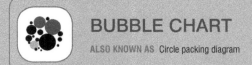

BUBBLE CHART

ALSO KNOWN AS Circle packing diagram

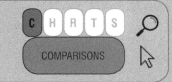

COMPARISONS

REPRESENTATION DESCRIPTION

A bubble chart displays quantitative values for different major categories with additional categorical dimensions included for further breakdown. It is based on the use of circles, one for each category, sized in proportion to the quantities they represent. Sometimes several separate clusters may be used to display further categorical dimensions, otherwise the colouring of each circle can achieve this. It is similar in concept to the proportional shape chart but differs through the typical layout being based on clustering, which therefore also enables it as a device for showing part-to-whole relationships as well.

EXAMPLE Comparing the Public sector capital expenditure (£ million) on services by function of the UK Government during 2014/15.

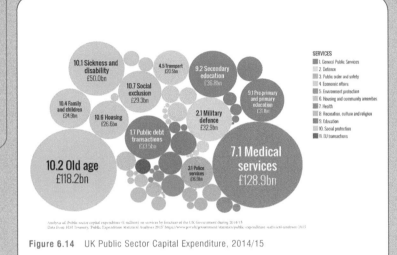

Figure 6.14   UK Public Sector Capital Expenditure, 2014/15

HOW TO READ IT & WHAT TO LOOK FOR

Look at the shapes and their associated labels so you know with what major categorical values each is associated, noting any size and colour legends to assist in forming associations. If there are multiple clusters, learn about the significance of the grouping/separation in each case. If there are direct labels, find the largest shape to establish its quantitative value as the maximum and do likewise for the smallest – this will help calibrate other size judgements. Glance across the entire chart to locate the big, small and medium shapes and perform global comparisons to establish the high-level ranking of biggest > smallest. Identify any noticeable exceptions and/or outliers. Perform local comparisons between neighbouring shapes to identify larger than and smaller than relationships and estimate the relative proportions. Estimate (or read, if labels are present) the absolute values of specific shapes of interest. If there are multiple clusters, note the general relative size and number of members in each case.

PRESENTATION TIPS

INTERACTIVITY: Bubble charts may often be accompanied by interactive features that let users select or mouseover individual circles to reveal annotated values for the quantity and category.

ANNOTATION: If interactivity is not achievable, a quantitative size key should be included or direct labelling; the latter may make the display busy (and be hard to fit into smaller circles) but will help overcome some of the limitations of judging area size.

COLOUR TIPS: Colours are sometimes used as redundant encodings to make the quantitative sizes even more immediately distinguishable.

COMPOSITION: Estimating and comparing the size of areas with accuracy is not as easy as it is for judging bar length or dot position, so only use this chart type if you have a diverse range of quantitative values. The use of this chart will primarily be about facilitating a gist, a general sense of the largest and smallest values. The geometric accuracy of the circle size calculations is paramount. Mistakes are often made with circle size calculations: it is the area you are modifying, not the diameter/radius. If you wish to make your bubbles appear as 3D spheres you are essentially no longer representing quantitative values through the size of a geometric area mark; rather the mark will be a 'form' and so the size calculation will be based on volume, not area. There is no categorical or quantitative sorting applied to the layout of the bubble chart, instead the tools that offer these charts will generally use a layout algorithm that applies a best-fit clustering to arrange the circles radially about a central 'gravity' force.

VARIATIONS & ALTERNATIVES

When the collection of quantities represents a whole, this evolves into a chart known as a 'circle packing diagram' and usually involves many parts that pack neatly into a circular layout representing the whole. Another variation of the packing diagram is when the adjacency between circle 'nodes' indicates a connected relation, offering a variation of the node–link diagram for showing networks of relationships. The bubble plot also uses differently sized circles but the position in each case is overlaid onto a scatter plot structure, based on two dimensions of further quantitative variables. Removing the size attribute (and effectively replacing area with point mark) you could simply use the quantity of points clustered together for different categories to create a 'tally chart'.

RADAR CHART

ALSO KNOWN AS Filled radar chart, star chart, spider diagram, web chart

REPRESENTATION DESCRIPTION

A radar chart shows values for three or more different quantitative measures in the same display for, typically, a single category. It uses a radial (circular) layout comprising several axes emerging from the centre-like spokes on a wheel, one for each measure. The quantitative values for each measure are plotted through position along each scale and then joined by connecting lines to form a unique geometric shape. Sometimes this shape is then filled with colour. A radar chart should only be considered in situations where the cyclical ordering (and neighbourly pairings) has some significance (such as data that might be plotted around the face of a clock or compass) and when the quantitative scales are the same (or similar) for each axis. Do not plot values for multiple categories on the same radar chart, but use small multiples formed of several radar charts instead.

EXAMPLE Comparing the global competitive scores (out of 7) across 12 'pillars' of performance for the United Kingdom.

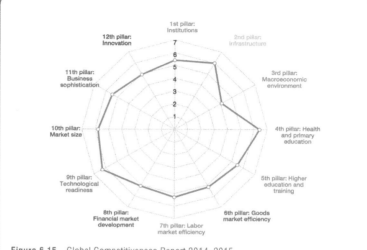

Figure 6.15   Global Competitiveness Report 2014–2015

HOW TO READ IT & WHAT TO LOOK FOR

Look around the chart and acquaint yourself with the quantitative measure represented by each axis and note the sequencing of the measures around the display. Is there any significance in this arrangement that can assist in interpreting the overall shape? Note the range of values along each independent axis so you understand what positions along the scales mean in a value sense for each measure. Scan the shape to locate the outliers both towards the outside (larger values) and inside (smaller values) of the scales. It is more important to pay attention to the position of values along an axis than the nature of the connecting lines between axes, unless the axis scales are consistent or at least if the relative position along the scale has the same implied meaning. If the variable sequencing has cyclical relevance, the spiking, bulging or contracting shape formed will give you some sense of the balance of values. Perform local comparisons between neighbouring axes to identify larger than and smaller than relationships. Estimate (or read, if labels are present) the absolute values of specific shapes of interest.

PRESENTATION TIPS

ANNOTATION: The inclusion of visible annotated features like axis lines, tick marks, gridlines and value labels can naturally aid the readability of the radar chart. Gridlines are only relevant if there are common scales across each quantitative variable. If so, the gridlines must be presented as straight lines, not concentric arcs, because the connecting lines joining up the values are themselves straight lines.

COLOUR TIPS: Often the radar shapes are filled with a colour, sometimes with a degree of transparency to allow the background apparatus to be partially visible.

COMPOSITION: The cyclical ordering of the quantitative variables has to be of optimum significance as the connectors and shape change for every different ordering permutation. This will have a major impact on the readability and meaning of the resulting chart shape. As the axes will be angled all around the radial display, you will need to make sure all the associated labels are readable (i.e. not upside down or at difficult angles).

VARIATIONS & ALTERNATIVES

A 'polar chart' is an alternative to the radar chart that removes some of the main shortcomings caused by connecting lines in the radar chart. If you have consistent value scales across the different quantitative measures, a 'bar chart' or 'dot plot' would be a better alternative. While not strictly a variation, 'parallel coordinates' display a similar technique for plotting several independent quantitative measures in the same chart. The main difference is that parallel coordinates use a linear layout and can accommodate many categories in one display.

POLAR CHART

ALSO KNOWN AS Coxcomb plot, polar area plot

REPRESENTATION DESCRIPTION

A polar chart shows values for three or more different quantitative measures in the same display. It uses a radial (circular) layout comprising several equal-angled circular sectors like slices of a pizza, one for each measure. In contrast to the radar chart (which uses position along a scale), the polar chart uses variation in the size of the sector areas to represent the quantitative values. It is, in essence, a radially plotted bar chart. Colour is an optional attribute, sometimes used visually to indicate further categorical dimensions. A polar chart should only be considered in situations where the cyclical ordering (and neighbourly pairings) has some significance (such as data that might be plotted around the face of a clock or compass) and when the quantitative scales are the same (or similar) for each axis.

EXAMPLE Comparing the quantitative match statistics across 14 different performance measures for a rugby union player.

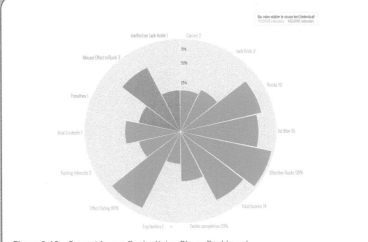

Figure 6.16   Excerpt from a Rugby Union Player Dashboard

169

HOW TO READ IT & WHAT TO LOOK FOR

Look around the chart and acquaint yourself with the quantitative measures each sector represents and note the sequencing of the measures around the display. Is there any significance in this arrangement that can assist in interpreting the overall shape? Note the range of values included on the quantitative scale and acquaint yourself with any colour associations. Glance across the entire chart to locate the big, small and medium sectors and perform global comparisons to establish the high-level ranking of biggest > smallest. Identify any noticeable exceptions and/or outliers. Perform local comparisons between neighbouring variables to identify the order of magnitude and estimate the relative sizes. Estimate (or read, if labels are present) the absolute values of specific sectors of interest. Where available, compare the quantities against annotated references such as targets, forecast, last year, average, etc. If there is significance behind the sequencing of the variables, look out for any patterns that emerge through spiking, bulging or contracting shapes.

PRESENTATION TIPS

ANNOTATION: The inclusion of visible annotated features like tick marks and value labels can naturally aid the readability of the polar chart. Gridlines are only relevant if there are common scales across each quantitative variable. If so, the gridlines must be presented as arcs reflecting the outer shape of each sector. Connecting lines joining up the values are themselves straight lines. Each sector typically uses the same quantitative scale for each quantitative measure but, on the occasions when this is not the case, each axis will require its own, clear value scale.

COLOUR TIPS: Often polar chart sectors are filled with a meaningful colour, sometimes with a degree of transparency to allow the background apparatus to be partially visible.

COMPOSITION: The cyclical ordering of the quantitative variables has to be of some significance to legitimise the value of the polar chart over the bar chart. As the sectors will be angled all around the radial display, you will need to make sure all the associated labels are readable (i.e. not upside down or at difficult angles). The quantitative values represented by the size of the sectors need to be carefully calculated. It is the area of the sector, not the radius length, that will be modified to portray the values accurately. If you make maximum quantitative value equivalent to the largest sector area, all other sector sizes can be calculated accordingly. Knowing how many different quantitative variables you are showing means you can easily calculate the angle of any given sector. The quantitative measure axes should always start from the origin value of zero: a sector should be representative of the true, full quantitative value, nothing more, nothing less, otherwise the perception of size will be distorted when comparing relative sizes.

VARIATIONS & ALTERNATIVES

Unless the radial layout provides meaning through the notion of a 'whole' or through the cyclical arrangement of measures, you might be best using a 'bar chart'. Variations in approach tend to see modifications in the sector shape with measure values represented by individual bars lengths or, in the example of the Better Life Index project, through variations in 'petal' sizes.

RANGE CHART

ALSO KNOWN AS Span chart, floating bar chart, barometer chart

DISTRIBUTIONS

REPRESENTATION DESCRIPTION

A range chart displays the minimum to maximum distribution of a series of quantitative values for different categories. The display is formed by a bar, one for each category, with the lower and upper position of the bars shaped by the minimum and maximum quantitative values in each case. The resulting bar lengths thus represent the range of values between the two limits.

EXAMPLE Comparing the highest and lowest temperatures (°F) recorded across the top 10 most populated cities during 2015.

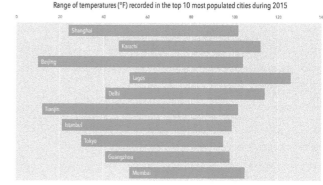

Figure 6.17 Range of Temperatures Recorded in Top 10 Most Populated Cities (2015)

HOW TO READ IT & WHAT TO LOOK FOR

Look at the axes so you know with what major categorical values each range bar is associated and what the range of the quantitative values is (min to max). Glance across the entire chart to locate the big, small and medium bars and perform global comparisons to establish the high-level ranking of biggest > smallest differences as well as the highest and lowest values. Identify any noticeable exceptions and/or outliers. Perform local comparisons between neighbouring bars, to identify larger than and smaller than relationships and estimate the relative proportions. There may be deliberate sorting of the display based on one of the quantitative measures. Estimate (or read, if labels are present) the absolute values of specific bars of interest. Where available, compare the quantities against annotated references such as targets, forecast, last year, average, etc.

PRESENTATION TIPS

ANNOTATION: Chart apparatus devices like tick marks and gridlines, in particular, can be helpful to increase the accuracy of the reading of the quantitative values. If you have axis labels you may not need direct labels on each bar – this will be lead to label overload, so generally decide between one or the other.

COMPOSITION: The quantitative value axis does not need to commence from zero, unless it means something significant to the interpretation, as the range of values themselves does not necessarily start from zero and the focus is more on the range and difference between the outer values. There is no significant difference in perception between vertical or horizontal layouts, though the latter tend to make it easier to accommodate and read the category labels. Where possible, try to make the categorical sorting meaningful, maybe organising values in ascending/descending size order.

VARIATIONS & ALTERNATIVES

'Connected dot plots' will also emphasise the difference between two selected measure values (as opposed to min/max) or where the underlying data is a change over time between two observations. 'Band charts' will often be used to show how the range of data values has changed over time, displaying the minimum and maximum bands at each time unit. These are often used in displays like weather forecasts.

BOX-AND-WHISKER PLOT

ALSO KNOWN AS Box plot

REPRESENTATION DESCRIPTION

A box-and-whisker plot displays the distribution and shape of a series of quantitative values for different categories. The display is formed by a combination of lines and point markers to indicate (through position and length), typically, five different statistical measures. Three of the statistical values are common to all plots: the first quartile (25th percentile), the second quartile (or median) and the third quartile (75th percentile) values. These are displayed with a box (effectively a wide bar) positioned and sized according to the first and third quartile values with a marker indicating the median. The remaining two statistical values vary in definition: usually either the minimum and maximum values or the 10th and 90th percentiles. These statistical values are represented by extending a line beyond the bottom and top of the main box to join with a point marker indicating the appropriate position. These are the whiskers. A plot will be produced for each major category.

EXAMPLE Comparing the distribution of annual earnings 10 years after starting school for graduates across the eight Ivy League schools.

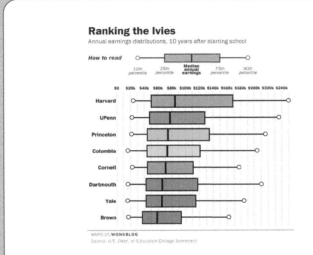

Figure 6.18   Ranking the Ivies

171

HOW TO READ IT & WHAT TO LOOK FOR

Begin by looking at the axes so you know with which category each plot is associated and what the range of quantitative values is (min to max). Establish the specific statistics being displayed, by consulting any legends or descriptions, especially in order to identify what the 'whiskers' are representing. Glance across the entire chart to locate the main patterns of spread, identifying any common or noticeably different patterns across categories. Look across the shapes formed for each category to learn about the dispersal of values: starting with the median, then observing the extent and balance of the 'box' (the interquartile range between the 25th and 75th percentiles) and then check the 'whisker' extremes. Is the shape balanced or skewed around the median? Is the interquartile range wide or narrow? Are the whisker extremes far away from the edges of the box? Then return to comparing shapes across all categories to identify more precisely any interesting differences or commonalities for each of the five statistical measures.

PRESENTATION TIPS

ANNOTATION: If you have axis labels you may not need direct labels on each bar – this will lead to label overload, so generally decide between one or the other.

COMPOSITION: The quantitative value axis does not need to commence from zero, unless it means something significant to the interpretation, as the range of values themselves do not necessarily start from zero and the focus is on the statistical properties between the outer values. There is no significant difference in perception between vertical or horizontal box-and-whisker plots, though horizontal layouts tend to make it easier to accommodate and read the category labels. Try to keep a noticeable gap between plots to enable greater clarity in reading. When you have several or many plots in the same chart, where possible try to make the categorical sorting meaningful, maybe organising values in ascending/descending order based on the median value.

VARIATIONS & ALTERNATIVES

Variations involve reducing the number of statistical measures included in the display by removing the whiskers to just show the 25th and 75th percentiles through the lower and upper parts of the box. The 'candlestick chart' (or OHLC chart) involves a similar approach and is often used in finance to show the distribution and milestone values of stock performances during a certain time frame (usually daily), plotting the opening, highest, lowest and closing prices, using colour to indicate an up or down trend.

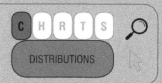

REPRESENTATION DESCRIPTION

A univariate scatter plot displays the distribution of a series of quantitative values for different categories. In contrast to the box-and-whisker plot, which shows selected statistical values, a univariate scatter plot shows all values across a series. For each category, a range of points (typically circles but any 'symbol' is legitimate) are used to mark the position along the scale of the quantitative values. From this you can see the range, the outliers and the clusters and form an understanding about the general shape of the data.

EXAMPLE Comparing the distribution of average critics score (%) from the Rotten Tomatoes website for each movie released across a range of different franchises and movie theme collections.

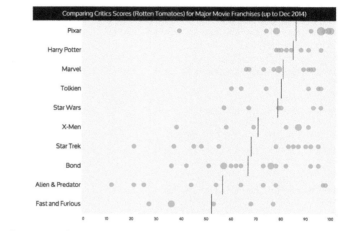

Figure 6.19 Comparing Critics Scores for Major Movie Franchises

HOW TO READ IT & WHAT TO LOOK FOR

Look at the axes so you know what each scatter row/column relates to in terms of which category it is associated with and what the range of the quantitative values is (min to max). If colour has been used to emphasise or separate different marks, establish what the associations are. Also, learn about how the design depicts multiple marks on the same value – these may appear darker or indeed larger. Glance across the entire chart to observe the main patterns of clustering and identify any noticeable exceptions and/or outliers across all categories. Then look more closely at the patterns within each scatter to learn about each category's specific dispersal of values. Look for empty regions where no quantitative values exist. Estimate the absolute values of specific dots of interest. Where available, compare the quantities against annotated references such as the average or median.

PRESENTATION TIPS

ANNOTATION: Chart apparatus devices like gridlines can be helpful to increase the accuracy of the reading of the quantitative values. Direct labelling is normally restricted to including values for specifically noteworthy points only.

COLOUR: Colour may be used to establish focus of certain points and/or distinction between different sub-category groups to assist with interpretation. When several points have the exact same value you might need to use unfilled or semi-transparent filled circles to facilitate a sense of value density.

COMPOSITION: The representation of the quantitative values is based on position and not size, therefore the quantitative axis does not need to have a zero origin. There is no significant difference in perception between vertical or horizontal arrangement, though horizontal layouts tend to make it easier to accommodate and read the category labels. Where possible try to make the categorical sorting meaningful, maybe organising values in ascending/descending size order.

VARIATIONS & ALTERNATIVES

To overcome occlusion caused by plotting several marks at the same value, a variation of the univariate scatter plot may see the points replaced by geometric areas (like circles), where the position attribute is used to represent a quantitative value along a scale and the size attribute is used to indicate the frequency of observations of similar value. Adding a second quantitative variable axis would lead to the use of a 'scatter plot'.

HISTOGRAM

ALSO KNOWN AS Bar chart (wrongly)

C H R T S

DISTRIBUTIONS

REPRESENTATION DESCRIPTION

A histogram displays the frequency and distribution for a range of quantitative groups. Whereas bar charts compare quantities for different categories, a histogram technically compares the number of observations across a range of value 'bins' using the size of lines/bars (if the bins relate to values with equal intervals) or the area of rectangles (if the bins have unequal value ranges) to represent the quantitative counts. With the bins arranged in meaningful order (that effectively form ordinal groupings) the resulting shape formed reveals the overall pattern of the distribution of observations.

EXAMPLE Comparing the distribution of movies released over time starring Michael Caine across five-year periods based on the date of release in the US.

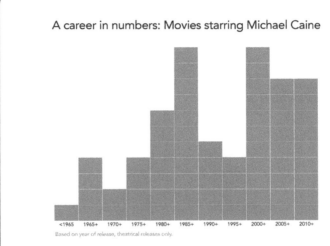

A career in numbers: Movies starring Michael Caine

| <1965 | 1965+ | 1970+ | 1975+ | 1980+ | 1985+ | 1990+ | 1995+ | 2000+ | 2005+ | 2010+ |

Based on year of release, theatrical releases only.

Figure 6.20   A Career in Numbers: Movies Starring Michael Caine

HOW TO READ IT & WHAT TO LOOK FOR

Begin by looking at the axes so you know what the chart depicts in terms of the categorical bins and the range of the quantitative values (zero to max). Glance across the entire chart to establish the main pattern. Is it symmetrically shaped, like a bell or pyramid (around a median or average value)? Is it skewed to the left or right? Does it dip in the middle and peak at the edges (known as bimodal)? Does it have several peaks and troughs? Maybe it is entirely random in its pattern? All these characteristics of 'shape' will inform you about the underlying distribution of the data.

PRESENTATION TIPS

ANNOTATION: Chart apparatus devices like tick marks and gridlines in particular can be helpful to increase the accuracy of the reading of the quantitative values. Axis labels more than direct value labels tend to be used so as not to crowd the shape of the histogram.

COMPOSITION: Unlike the bar chart there should be no (or at most a very thin) gap between bars to help the collective shape of the frequencies emerge. The sorting of the quantitative bins must be in ascending order so that the reading of the overall shape preserves its meaning. The number of value bins and the range of values covered by each have a prominent influence over the appearance of the histogram and the usefulness of what it might reveal: too few bins may disguise interesting nuances, patterns and outliers; too many bins and the most interesting shapes may be abstracted by noise above signal. There is no singular best approach, the right choice simply arrives through experimentation and iteration.

VARIATIONS & ALTERNATIVES

For analysis that looks at the distribution of values across two dimensions, such as the size of populations for age across genders, a 'back-to-back histogram' (with male on one side, female on the other), also commonly known as a 'violin plot' or 'population pyramid', is a useful approach to see and compare the respective shapes. A 'box-and-whisker plot' reduces the distribution of values to five key statistical measures to describe key dimensions of the spread of values.

WORD CLOUD

ALSO KNOWN AS Tag cloud

REPRESENTATION DESCRIPTION

A word cloud shows the frequency of individual word items used in textual data (such as tweets, comments) or documents (passages, articles). The display is based around an enclosed cluster of words with the font (not the word length) sized according to the frequency of usage. In modifying the size of font this is effectively increasing the area size of the whole word. All words have a different shape and size so this can make it quite difficult to avoid the prominence of long words, irrespective of their font size. Word clouds are therefore only useful when you are trying to get a quick and rough sense of some of the dominant keywords used in the text. They can be an option for working with qualitative data during the data exploration stage, more so as a means for reporting analysis to others.

EXAMPLE Comparing the frequency of words used in Chapter 1 of this book.

Figure 6.21   Word Cloud of the Text from Chapter 1

HOW TO READ IT & WHAT TO LOOK FOR

The challenge with reading word clouds is to avoid being drawn to the length and/or area of a word – they are simply attributes of the word, not a meaningful representation of frequency. It is the size of the font that you need to focus on. Scan the display to spot the larger text showing the more frequently used words. Consider any words of specific interest to see if you can find them; if they are not significantly visible, that in itself could be revealing. While most word cloud generators will dismiss many irrelevant words, you might still need to filter out perceptually the significance of certain dominantly sized text.

PRESENTATION TIPS

INTERACTIVITY: Interactive features that let users interrogate, filter and scrutinise the words in more depth, perhaps presenting examples of their usage in a passage, can be quite useful to enhance the value of a word cloud.

ANNOTATION: While the absolutes are generally of less interest than relative comparisons, to help viewers get as much out of the display as possible a simple legend explaining how the font size equates to frequency number can be useful.

COLOUR: Colours may be used as redundant encoding to accentuate further the larger frequencies or categorically to create useful visual separation.

COMPOSITION: The arrangement of the words within a word cloud is typically based on a layout process. Although not random, this will generally prioritise the placement of words to occupy optimum collective space that preserves an overall shape (with essentially a central gravity) over and above any arrangement that might better enable direct comparison.

VARIATIONS & ALTERNATIVES

The alternative approach would be to use any other method in this categorical family of charts that would more usefully display the counts of text, such as a bar chart.

PIE CHART

ALSO KNOWN AS Pizza chart

REPRESENTATION DESCRIPTION

A pie chart shows how the quantities of different constituent categories make up a whole. It uses a circular display divided into sectors for each category, with the angle representing each of the percentage proportions. The resulting size of the sector (in area terms) is a spatial by-product of the angle applied to each part and so offers an additional means for judging the respective values. The role of a pie chart is primarily about being able to compare a part to a whole than being able to compare one part to another part. They therefore work best when there are only two or three parts included. There are a few important rules for pie charts. Firstly, the total percentage values of all sector values must be 100%; if the aggregate is greater than or less than 100% the chart will be corrupted. Secondly, the whole has to be meaningful – often people just add up independent percentages but that is not what a pie chart is about. Finally, the category values must represent exclusive quantities; nothing should be counted twice or overlap across different categories. Despite all these warnings, do not be afraid of the pie chart – just use it with discretion.

EXAMPLE Comparing the proportion of eligible voters in the 2015 UK election who voted for the Conservative Party, for other parties and who did not vote.

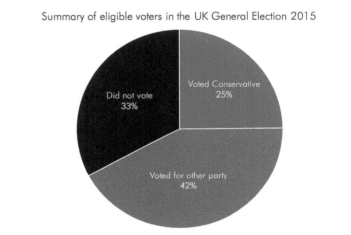

Summary of eligible voters in the UK General Election 2015

Figure 6.22 Summary of Eligible Votes in the UK General Election 2015

175

HOW TO READ IT & WHAT TO LOOK FOR

Begin by establishing which sectors relate to what categories. This may involve referring to a colour key legend or through labels directly adjacent to the pie. Quickly scan the pie to identify the big, medium and small sectors. Notice if there is any significance behind the ordering of the parts. Unless there are value labels, you next will attempt to judge the individual sector angles. This usually involves mentally breaking the pie into 50% halves (180°) or 25% quarters (90°) and using those guides to perceptually measure the category values. Comparing parts against other parts with any degree of accuracy will only be possible once you have formed estimates of the individual sector sizes. If you are faced with the task of judging the size of many parts it is quite understandable if you decide to give up quite soon.

PRESENTATION TIPS

ANNOTATION: The use of local labelling for category values can be useful but too many labels can become cluttered, especially when attempting to label very small angled sectors.

COLOUR: Colour is generally vital to create categorical separation and association of the different sectors so aim to use the difference in colour hue and not colour saturation to maximise the visible difference.

COMPOSITION: Positioning the first slice at the vertical 12 o'clock position gives a useful baseline to help judge the first sector angle value. The ordering of sectors using descending values or ordinal characteristics helps with the overall readability and allocation of effort. Do not consider using gratuitous decoration (like 3D, gradient colours, or exploding slices).

VARIATIONS & ALTERNATIVES

Sometimes a pie chart has a hole in the centre and is known as a 'doughnut chart', continuing the food-related theme. The function is exactly the same as a pie but the removal of the centre, often to accommodate a labelling property, removes the possibility of the reader judging the angles at the origin. One therefore has to derive the angles from the resulting arc lengths. If you want to display multiple parts (more than three) the bar chart will be a better option and, for many parts, the 'treemap' is best. Depending on the allocated space, a 'stacked bar chart' may provide an alternative to the pie. Unlike most chart types, the pie chart does not work well in the form of small multiples (unless there is only a single part being displayed). A 'nested shape chart', typically based on embedded square or circle areas, enables comparison across a series of one-part-to-whole relationships based on absolute numbers, rather than percentages, where the wholes may vary in size.

WAFFLE CHART

ALSO KNOWN AS Square pie, unit chart, 100% stacked shape chart

REPRESENTATION DESCRIPTION

A waffle chart shows how the quantities of different constituent categories make up a whole. It uses a square display usually representing 100 point 'cells' through a 10 × 10 grid layout. Each constituent category proportion is displayed through colour-coding a proportional number of cells. Difference in symbol can also be used. The role of the waffle chart is to simplify the counting of proportions in contrast to the angle judgements of the pie chart, though the display is limited to rounded integer values. This is easier when the grid layout facilitates quick recognition of units of 10. As with the pie chart, the waffle chart works best when you are showing how a single part compares to the whole and perhaps offers greater visual impact when there are especially small percentages of a whole. Rather than just colouring in the grid cells, sometimes different symbols will be used to associate with different categories. For example, you might see figures or gender icons used to show the makeup of a given sample population.

EXAMPLE Comparing the proportion of total browser usage for Internet Explorer and Chrome across key milestone moments.

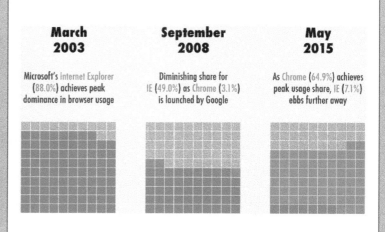

Figure 6.23 The Changing Fortunes of Internet Explorer and Google Chrome

HOW TO READ IT & WHAT TO LOOK FOR

Begin by establishing how the different shapes or colours are associated with different categories. Assess the grid layout to understand the dimension of the chart and the quantity of cell 'units' forming the display (e.g. is it a 10 x 10 grid?). Quickly scan the chart to identify the big, medium and small sectors. Notice if there is any significance behind the ordering of the parts. Unless there are value labels, you will need to count/estimate the number of units representing each category value. Comparing parts against other parts will only be possible once you have established the individual part sizes. If several related waffle charts are shown, possibly for different categories or points in time, identify the related colours/shapes in each chart and establish the patterns of size between and across the various charts, looking for trends, declines and general differences.

PRESENTATION TIPS

ANNOTATION: Direct labelling can become very cluttered and hard to incorporate elegantly without the need for long arrows.

COLOUR: Borders around each square cell are useful to help establish the individual units, but do not make the borders too thick to the point where they dominate attention.

COMPOSITION: Always start each row of values from the same side, for consistency and to make it easier for people to estimate the values. When you have several parts in the same waffle chart, where possible try to make the categorical sorting meaningful, maybe organising values in ascending/descending size order or based on a logical categorical order.

VARIATIONS & ALTERNATIVES

Sometimes the waffle chart approach is used to show stacks of absolute unit values and indeed there are overlaps in concept between this variation in the waffle chart and potential applications of the pictogram. Aside from the pie chart, a 'nested shape chart' will provide an alternative way of showing a part-to-whole relationship while also occupying a squarified layout.

STACKED BAR CHART

ALSO KNOWN AS

REPRESENTATION DESCRIPTION
A stacked bar chart displays a part-to-whole breakdown of quantitative values for different major categories. The percentage proportion of each categorical dimension or 'part' is represented by separate bars, distinguished by colour, that are sized according to their proportion and then stacked to create the whole. Sometimes the whole is standardised to represent 100%, at other times the whole will be representative of absolute values. Stacked bar charts work best when the parts are based on ordinal dimensions, which enables ordering of the parts within the stack to help establish the overall shape of the data. If the parts are representative of nominal data, it is best to keep the number of constituent categories quite low, as estimating the size of individual stacked parts when there are many becomes quite hard.

EXAMPLE Comparing the percentage of adults (16–65 year olds) achieving different proficiency levels in literacy across different countries.

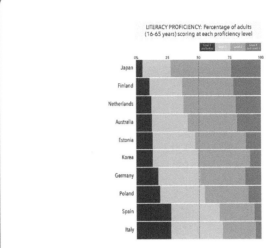

Figure 6.24 Literacy Proficiency: Adult Levels by Country

HOW TO READ IT & WHAT TO LOOK FOR
Look at the axes so you know with what major categorical values each bar is associated and what the quantitative values are, determining if it is a 100% stacked bar or an absolute stacked bar (in which case identify the min and the max). Establish the colour association to understand what categories the bars within each stack represent. Glance across the entire chart. If the categorical data is ordinal, and the sorting/colour of the stacks is intuitive, you should be able to derive meaning from the overall balance of colour patterns, especially where any annotated gridlines help to guide your value estimation. If the categorical data is nominal, seek to locate the dominant colours and the least noticeable ones. Comparing across different stacked bars is made harder by the lack of a common baseline for anything other than the bottom stack on the zero baseline (and for 100% stacked bars, those final ones at the top) and so a general sense of magnitude will be your focus. Study closer the constituent parts within each stack to establish the high-level ranking of biggest > smallest. Estimate (or read, if labels are present) the absolute values of specific stacked parts of interest.

PRESENTATION TIPS
ANNOTATION: Direct value labelling can become very cluttered when there are many parts or stacks and you are comparing several different major categories. You might be better with a table if that is your aim. Definitely include value axis labels with logical intervals and it is very helpful to annotate, through gridlines, key units such as the 25%, 50% and 75% positions when based on a 100% stacked bar chart.

COLOUR: If you are representing categorical ordinal data, colour can be astutely deployed to give a sense of the general balance of values within the whole, but this will only work if their sorting arrangement within the stack is logically applied. For categorical nominal data, ensure the stacked parts have sufficiently different colours so that their distinct bar lengths can be efficiently observed.

COMPOSITION: Across the main categories, once again consider the optimum sorting option, maybe organising values in ascending/descending size order or based on a logical categorical order. Judging the size of the stacks with accuracy is harder for those that are not on the zero baseline, so maybe consider which ones are of most importance to be more easily read and place those on the baseline.

VARIATIONS & ALTERNATIVES
The main alternative would be to use 'multi-panel bar charts', where separate bar charts each include just one 'stack'/part and they are then repeated for each subsequent constituent category. In the world of finance the 'waterfall chart' is a common approach based on a single stacked bar broken up into individual elements, almost like a step-by-step narrative of how the components of income look on one side and then how the components of expenditure look on the other, with the remaining space representing the surplus or deficit. Like their unstacked siblings, stacked bar charts can also be used to show how categorical composition has changed over time.

BACK-TO-BACK BAR CHART

ALSO KNOWN AS Paired bar chart

REPRESENTATION DESCRIPTION

A back-to-back bar chart displays a part-to-whole breakdown of quantitative values for different major categories. As with any bar chart, the length of a bar represents a quantitative proportion or absolute value for each part and across all major categories. In contrast to the stacked bar chart, where the constituent bars are simply stacked to form a whole, in a back-to-back bar chart the constituent parts are based on diverging categorical dimensions with a 'directional' essence such as yes/no, male/female, agree/disagree. The values for each dimension are therefore presented on opposite sides of a shared zero baseline to help reveal the shape and contrast differences across all major categories.

EXAMPLE Comparing the responses to a survey question asking for opinions about 'the government collection of telephone and Internet data as part of anti-terrorism efforts' across different demographic categories.

Figure 6.25   Political Polarization in the American Public

HOW TO READ IT & WHAT TO LOOK FOR

Look at the axes so you know with which major categorical values each bar is associated and what the range of the quantitative values is (min to max). Establish what categorical dimensions are represented by the respective sides of the display and any colour associations. Glance across the entire chart to locate the big, small and medium bars and perform global comparisons to establish the high-level ranking of biggest > smallest. Repeat this for each side of the display, noticing any patterns of dominance of larger values on either side. Identify any noticeable exceptions and/or outliers. Perform local comparisons for each category value to estimate the relative sizes (or read, if labels are present) of each bar.

PRESENTATION TIPS

ANNOTATION: Chart apparatus devices like tick marks and gridlines in particular can be helpful to increase the accuracy of the reading of the quantitative values.

COLOUR: The bars either side of the axis do not need to be coloured but often are to create further visual association.

COMPOSITION: The quantitative value axis should always start from the origin value of zero: a bar should be representative of the true, full quantitative value, nothing more, nothing less, otherwise the perception of bar sizes will be distorted when comparing relative sizes. There is no significant difference in perception between vertical or horizontal bars, though horizontal layouts tend to make it easier to accommodate and read the category labels. Where possible try to make the categorical sorting meaningful, maybe organising values in ascending/descending size order or based on a logical categorical order.

VARIATIONS & ALTERNATIVES

Back-to-back bar charts facilitate a general sense of the shape of diverging categorical dimensions. However, if you want to facilitate direct comparison, a 'clustered bar chart' showing adjacent bars helps to compare respective heights more precisely. For analysis that looks at the distribution values across two dimensions, such as the size of populations for age across genders, a 'back-to-back histogram' (with male on one side, female on the other), also commonly known as a 'violin plot' or 'population pyramid', is a useful approach to see and compare the respective shapes. Some back-to-back applications do not show a part-to-whole relationship but simply compare quantities for two categorical values. Further variations may appear as 'back-to-back area charts' showing mutual change over time for two contrasting states.

TREEMAP

ALSO KNOWN AS Heat map (wrongly)

PART-TO-WHOLE

REPRESENTATION DESCRIPTION

A treemap is an enclosure diagram providing a hierarchical display to show how the quantities of different constituent parts make up a whole. It uses a contained rectangular layout (often termed 'squarified') representing the 100% total divided into proportionally sized rectangular tiles for each categorical part. Colour can be used to represent an additional quantitative measure, such as an indication of amount of change over a time period. The absolute positioning and dimension of each rectangle is organised by an underlying tiling algorithm to optimise the overall space usage and to cluster related categories into larger rectangle-grouped containers. Treemaps are most commonly used, and of most value, when there are many parts to the whole but they are only valid if the constituent units are legitimately part of the same 'whole'.

EXAMPLE Comparing the relative value of and the daily performance of stocks across the S&P 500 index grouped by sectors and industries.

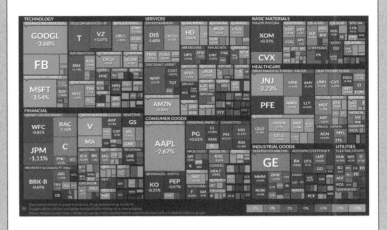

Figure 6.26 FinViz: Standard and Poor's 500 Index

HOW TO READ IT & WHAT TO LOOK FOR

Look at the high-level groupings to understand the different containing arrangements and establish what the colour association is. Glance across the entire chart to seek out the big, small and medium individual rectangular sizes and perform global comparisons to establish a general ranking of biggest > smallest values. Also identify the largest through to smallest container group of rectangles. If the colour coding is based on quantitative variables, look out for the most eye-catching patterns at the extreme end of the scale(s). If labels are provided (or offered through interactivity), browse around the display looking for categories and values of specific interest. As with any display based on the size of the area of a shape, precise reading of values is hard to achieve and so it is important to understand that treemaps can only aim to provide a single-view gist of the properties of the many components of the whole.

PRESENTATION TIPS

INTERACTIVITY: Typically, a treemap will be presented with interactive features to enable selection/mouseover events to reveal further annotated details and/or drill-down navigation.

ANNOTATION: Group/container labels are often allocated a cell of space but these are not to be read as proportional values. Effective direct value labelling becomes difficult as the rectangles get smaller, so often only the most prominent values might be annotated. Interactive features will generally offer visibility of the relevant labels where possible.

COLOUR: Colour can also be used to provide further categorical grouping distinction if not already assigned to represent a quantitative measure of change.

COMPOSITION: As the tiling algorithm is focused on optimising the dimensions and arrangement of the rectangular shapes, treemaps may not always be able to facilitate much internal sorting of high to low values. However, generally you will find the larger shapes appear in the top left of each container and work outwards towards the smaller constituent parts.

VARIATIONS & ALTERNATIVES

A variation of the treemap sees the rectangular layout replaced by a circular one and the rectangular tiles replaced by organic shapes. These are known as 'Voronoi treemaps' as the tiling algorithm is informed by a Voronoi tessellation. The 'circle packing diagram', a variation of the 'bubble chart', similarly shows many parts to a whole but uses a non-tessellating circular shape/layout. The 'mosaic plot' or 'Marimekko chart' is similar in appearance to a treemap but, in contrast to the treemap's hierarchical display, presents a detailed breakdown of quantitative value distributions across several categorical dimensions, essentially formed by varied width stacked bars.

VENN DIAGRAM

ALSO KNOWN AS Set diagram, Euler diagram (wrongly)

REPRESENTATION DESCRIPTION

A Venn diagram shows collections of and relationships between multiple sets. They typically use round or elliptical containers to represent all different 'membership' permutations to include all independent and intersecting containers. The size of the contained area is (typically) not important: what is important is in which containing region a value resides, which may be represented through the mark of a text label or 'point'.

EXAMPLE Comparing sets of permutations for legalities around marijuana usage and same-sex marriage across states of the USA.

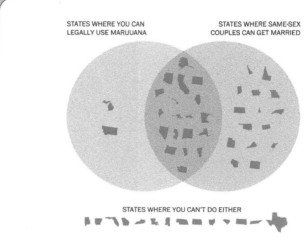

STATES WHERE YOU CAN LEGALLY USE MARIJUANA

STATES WHERE SAME-SEX COUPLES CAN GET MARRIED

STATES WHERE YOU CAN'T DO EITHER

Figure 6.27 This Venn Diagram Shows Where You Can Both Smoke Weed and Get a Same-Sex Marriage

HOW TO READ IT & WHAT TO LOOK FOR

To read a Venn diagram firstly establish what the different containers are representative of in terms of their membership. Assess the membership of the intersections (firstly 'all', then 'partial' intersections when involving more than two sets) then work outwards towards the independent container regions where values are part of one set but not part of others. Occasionally there will be a further grouping state outside of the containers that represents values that have no membership with any set at all.

PRESENTATION TIPS

ANNOTATION: Unless you are using point markers to represent membership values, clear labels are vital to indicate how many or which elements hold membership with each possible set combination.

COLOUR: Colour is often used to create more immediate distinction between the intersections and independent parts or members of each container.

COMPOSITION: As the attributes of size and shape of the containers are of no significance there is more flexibility to manipulate the display to fit the number of sets around the constraint of real estate you are facing and to get across the set memberships you are attempting to show. The complexity of creating containers to accommodate all combinations of intersection and independence states increases as the number of sets increases, especially to preserve all possible combinations of intersections between and independencies from all sets. As the number of sets increases, the symmetry of shape reduces and the circular containers are generally replaced with ellipses. While it is theoretically possible to exceed four and five set diagrams, the ability of readers to make sense of the displays diminishes and so they commonly involve only two or three different sets.

VARIATIONS & ALTERNATIVES

A common variation or alternative to the Venn (but often mistakenly called a Venn) is the 'Euler diagram'. The difference is that an Euler diagram does not need to present all possible intersections with and independencies from all sets. A different approach to visualising sets (especially larger numbers) can be achieved using the 'UpSet' technique.

DENDROGRAM

ALSO KNOWN AS Node–link diagram, layout tree, cluster tree, tree hierarchy

REPRESENTATION DESCRIPTION
A dendrogram is a node–link diagram that displays the hierarchical relationship across multiple tiers of categorical dimensions. It displays a hierarchy based on multi-generational 'parent-and-child' relationships. Starting from a singular origin root node (or 'parent') each subsequent set of constituent 'child' nodes, a tier below and represented by points, is connected by lines (curved or straight) to indicate the existence of a relationship. Each constituent node may have further sub-constituencies represented in the same way, continuing down through to the lowest tier of detail. Each 'generational' tier is presented at the same relative distance from the origin. The layout can be based on either a linear tree structure (typically left to right) or radial tree (outwards from the centre).

EXAMPLE Showing a breakdown of the 200+ beer brands belonging to SAB InBev across different countries grouped by continent.

Figure 6.28 The 200+ Beer Brands of SAB InBev

HOW TO READ IT & WHAT TO LOOK FOR
Reading a dendrogram will generally be a highly individual experience based on your familiarity with the subject and your interest in exploring certain hierarchical pathways. The main focus of attention will likely be to find the main clusters from where most constituent parts branch out and to contrast these with the thinner, lighter paths comprising fewer parts. Work left to right (linear) or in to out (radial) through the different routes that stoke your curiosity.

PRESENTATION TIPS
ANNOTATION: With labelling required for each node, depending on the number of tiers and the amount of nodes, the size of the text will need to be carefully considered to ensure readability and minimise the effect of clutter.

COLOUR: Colour would be an optional choice for accentuating certain nodes or applying some further visual categorisation.

COMPOSITION: There are several different layout options to display tree hierarchies like the dendrogram. The common choice is a cluster layout based on the 'Reingold–Tilford' tree algorithms that offers a tidying and optimisation treatment for the efficiency of the arrangement of the nodes and connections. The sequencing of sub-constituencies under each node could be logically arranged in some more meaningful way than just alphabetical, though the cataloguing nature of A–Z may suit your purpose. The choice of a linear or radial tree structure will be informed largely by the space you have to work in as well as by the cyclical or otherwise nature of the content in your data. The main issue is likely to be one of legibility if and when you have numerous layers of divisions and many constituent parts to show in a single view.

VARIATIONS & ALTERNATIVES
More advanced applications of dendrograms are used to present hierarchical clustering (in fields such as computational biology) and apply more quantitative meaning to the length of the links and the positioning of the nodes. The 'tree hierarchy diagram' offers a similar tree structure but introduces quantitative attributes to the nodes using area marks, such as circles, sized according to a quantitative value. An alternative approach to the dendrogram could involve a 'linear bracket'. This might show hierarchical structures for data-related sporting competitions with knock-out format. The outer nodes would be the starting point representing all the participating competitors/teams. Each subsequent tier would represent those participants who progressed to the next round, continuing through to the finalists and eventual victors.

SUNBURST

ALSO KNOWN AS Adjacency diagram, icicle chart, multi-level pie chart

REPRESENTATION DESCRIPTION

A sunburst chart is an adjacency diagram that displays the hierarchical and part-to-whole relationships across multiple tiers of categorical dimensions. In contrast to the dendrogram, the sunburst uses layers of concentric rings, one layer for each generational tier. Each ring layer is divided into parts based on the constituent categorical dimensions at that tier. Each part is represented by a different circular arc section that is sized (in length; width is constant) according to the relative proportion. Starting from the centre 'parent' tier, the outward adjacency of the constituent parts of each tier represents the 'parent-and-child' hierarchical composition.

EXAMPLE
Showing a breakdown of the types of companies responsible for extracting different volumes of carbon-based fuels through various activities.

Figure 6.29   Which Fossil Fuel Companies are Most Responsible for Climate Change?

HOW TO READ IT & WHAT TO LOOK FOR

Reading a sunburst chart will be a highly individual experience based on your familiarity with the subject and your interest in exploring certain hierarchical pathways. The main focus of attention will likely be to find the largest arc lengths, representing the largest single constituent parts, and those layers or tiers with the most constituent parts. Work from the centre outwards through the different routes that stoke your curiosity. Depending on the deployment of colour, this may help you identify certain additional categorical patterns.

PRESENTATION TIPS

INTERACTIVITY: Often interactive mouseover/selection events are the only way to reveal the annotations here.

ANNOTATION: Labelling can be quite difficult to fit into the narrow spaces afforded by small proportion 'parts'. If interactivity is not an option you may decide to label only those parts that can accommodate the text space.

COLOUR: Colours are often used to achieve further categorical distinction.

COMPOSITION: Sometimes the parent–child (and other generational) relationships could be legitimately reversed, so decisions need to be made about the best hierarchy sequencing to suit the curiosities of the audience. The sequencing of sub-constituencies under each node could also be logically arranged in a meaningful way, more so than just alphabetical, unless the cataloguing nature of A–Z ordering suits your purpose.

VARIATIONS & ALTERNATIVES

Where the sunburst chart uses a radial layout, the 'icicle chart' uses a vertical, linear layout starting from the top and moving downwards. The choice of a linear or radial tree structure will be informed largely by the space you have to work in as well as by the legitimacy of the cyclical nature of the content in your data. A variation on the sunburst chart would be the 'ring bracket'. This might show a reverse journey for hierarchical data based on something like sporting competitions with knock-out formats. The outer concentric partitions would represent the participant competitors/teams at the start of the process. The length of these arc line parts would be equally distributed across all constituent parts with each subsequent tier representing 'participants' who progress forward to the next 'round', continuing through to the finalists and eventual victors in the centre.

SCATTER PLOT CHART

ALSO KNOWN AS Scatter graph

CORRELATIONS

REPRESENTATION DESCRIPTION

A scatter plot displays the relationship between two quantitative measures for different categories. Scatter plots are used to explore visually the potential existence, extent or absence of a significant relationship between the plotted variables. The display is formed by points (usually a dot or circle), representing each category and plotted positionally along quantitative x- and y-axes. Sometimes colour is used to distinguish categorical dimensions across all the points. Scatter plots do not work too well if one or both of the quantitative measures has limited variation in value as this especially causes problems of 'occlusion', whereby multiple instances of the similar values are plotted on top of each other and essentially hidden from the reader.

EXAMPLE Exploring the relationship between life expectancy and the percentage of healthy years across all countries.

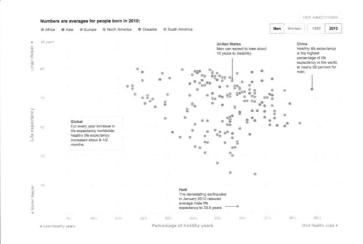

Figure 6.30   How Long Will We Live – And How Well?

183

HOW TO READ IT & WHAT TO LOOK FOR

Learn what each quantitative axis relates to and make a note of the range of values in each case (min to max). Look at what category or observation each plotted value on the chart refers to and look up any colour associations being used for categorical distinction. Scan the chart looking for the existence of any diagonal trends that might suggest a linear correlation between the variables, or note the complete absence of any pattern, to mean no correlation. Annotations will often assist in determining the significance of any patterns like this. Identify any clusters of points and also look at the gaps, which can be just as revealing. Some of the most interesting observations come from individual outliers standing out separately from others. Look out for any patterns formed by points with similar categorical colour. One approach to reading the 'meaning' of the plotted positions involves trying to break down the chart area into a 2 × 2 grid translating what marks positioned in those general areas might mean – which corner is 'good' or 'bad' to be located in? Remember that ruling out significant relationships can be just as useful as ruling them in.

PRESENTATION TIPS

ANNOTATION: Gridlines can be useful to help make the value estimates clearer and reference lines (such as a trend line of best fit) might aid interpretation. It is usually hard to make direct labelling of all values work well. Firstly, it can be tricky making it clear which value relates to which point, especially when several points may be clustered together. Secondly, it creates a lot of visual clutter. Labelling choices should be based on values that are of most interest to include editorially unless interactive features enable annotations to be revealed through selection or mouseover events. If possible, you might consider putting a number inside the marker to indicate a count of the number of points at the same position if this occurs.

COLOUR: If colours are being used to distinguish the different categories, ensure these are as visibly different as possible. On the occasion where multiple values may be plotted close to or on top of each other, you might need to use semi-transparency to enable overlapping of points to build up a recognisably darker colour compared to other points, indicating an underlying stack of values at the same location on the chart.

COMPOSITION: As the encoding of the plotted point values is based on position along an axis, it is not necessary to start the axes from a zero baseline, so just make the scale ranges as representative as possible of the range of values being plotted. Ideally a scatter plot will have a 1:1 aspect ratio (equally as tall as it is wide), creating a squared area to help patterns surface more evidently. If one quantitative variable (e.g. weight) is likely to be affected by the other variable (e.g. height), it is general practice to place the former on the y-axis and the latter on the x-axis. If you have to use a logarithmic quantitative scale on either or both axes, you need to make this clear to readers so they avoid making incorrect conclusions from the resulting patterns (that might imply correlation if the values were linear, for example).

VARIATIONS & ALTERNATIVES

A 'ternary plot' is a variation of the scatter plot through the inclusion of a third quantitative variable axis. The 'bubble plot' also incorporates a third quantitative variable, this time through encoding the size of a geometric shape (replacing the point marker). A 'scatter plot matrix' involves a single view of multiple scatter plots presenting different combinations of plotted quantitative variables, used to explore possible relationships among larger multivariate datasets. A 'connected scatter plot' compares the shifting state of two quantitative measures over time.

BUBBLE PLOT

ALSO KNOWN AS Bubble chart

REPRESENTATION DESCRIPTION

A bubble plot displays the relationship between three quantitative measures for different categories. Bubble plots are used visually to explore the potential existence, extent or absence of a significant relationship between the plotted variables. In contrast to the scatter plot, the bubble plot plots proportionally sized circular areas, for each category, across two quantitative axes with the size representing a third quantitative measure. Sometimes colour is used to distinguish categorical dimensions across all the shapes.

HOW TO READ IT & WHAT TO LOOK FOR

Learn what each quantitative axis relates to and make a note of the range of values in each case (min to max). Look at what category or observation each plotted value on the chart refers to. Establish the quantitative size associations for the bubble areas and look up any colour associations being used for categorical distinction. Scan the chart looking for the existence of any diagonal trends that might suggest a linear correlation between the variables, or note the complete absence of any pattern, to mean no correlation. Annotations will often assist in determining the significance of any patterns like this. Identify any clusters of points and also look at the gaps, which can be just as revealing. Some of the most interesting observations come from individual outliers standing out separately from others. Look out for any patterns formed by points with similar categorical colour. What can you learn about the distribution of small, medium or large circles: are they clustered together in similar regions of the chart or

184

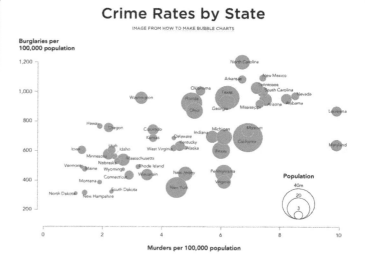

Figure 6.31 Crime Rates by State

quite randomly scattered? One approach to reading the 'meaning' of the plotted positions involves trying to break down the chart area into a 2 × 2 grid translating what marks positioned in those general areas might mean – which corner is 'good' or 'bad' to be located in? Remember that ruling out significant relationships can be just as useful as ruling them in. Estimating and comparing the size of areas is not as easy as it is for judging bar length or dot position. This means that the use of this chart type will primarily be about facilitating a gist – a general sense of the hierarchy of the largest and smallest values.

PRESENTATION TIPS

ANNOTATION: Gridlines can be useful to help make the value estimates clearer and reference lines (such as a trend line of best fit) might aid interpretation. It is usually hard to make direct labelling of all values work well. Firstly, it can be tricky making it clear which value relates to which point, especially when several points may be clustered together. Secondly, it creates a lot of visual clutter. Labelling choices should be based on values that are of most interest to include editorially unless interactive features enable annotations to be revealed through selection or mouseover events.

COLOUR: If colours are being used to distinguish the different categories, ensure these are as visibly different as possible. When a circle has a large value its size will often overlap in spatial terms with other values. The use of outline borders and semi-transparent colours helps with the task of avoiding occlusion (visually hiding values behind others).

COMPOSITION: As the encoding of the plotted area marker values is based on position along an axis, it is not necessary to start the axes from a zero baseline – just make the scale ranges as representative as possible of the range of values being plotted. Make sensible decisions about how large to make the maximum bubble size; this will usually require trial and error experimentation to find the right balance. Ideally a bubble plot will have a 1:1 aspect ratio (equally as tall as it is wide), creating a squared area to help patterns surface more evidently. If one quantitative variable (e.g. weight) is likely to be affected by the other variable (e.g. height), it is general practice to place the former on the y-axis and the latter on the x-axis. Geometric accuracy of the circle size calculations is paramount, since mistakes are often made with circle size calculations: it is the area you are modifying, not the diameter/radius. If you wish to make your bubbles appear as 3D spheres you are essentially no longer representing quantitative values through the size of a geometric area mark, rather the mark will be a 'form' and so the size calculation will be based on volume, not area.

VARIATIONS & ALTERNATIVES

If the third quantitative variable is removed, the display would just become a 'scatter plot'. Variations on the bubble plot might see the use of different geometric areas as the markers, maybe introducing extra meaning from the underlying data through the shape, size and dimensions used.

PARALLEL COORDINATES

ALSO KNOWN AS Parallel sets

CORRELATIONS

REPRESENTATION DESCRIPTION

Parallel coordinates display multiple quantitative measures for different categories in a single display. They are used visually to explore the relationships and characteristics of multi-dimensional, multivariate data. Parallel coordinates are based on a series of parallel axes representing different quantitative measures with independent axis scales. The quantitative values for each measure are plotted and then connected to form a single line. Each connected line represents a different category record. Colour may be used to differentiate further categorical dimensions. As more data is added the collective 'shape' of the data emerges and helps to inform the possibility of relationships existing among the different measures. Parallel coordinates look quite overwhelming but remember that they are almost always only used to assist in exploratory work of large and varied datasets, more so than being used for explanatory presentations of data. Generally the greater the number of measures, the more difficult the task of making sense of the underlying patterns will be, so be discerning in your choice of which variables to include. This method does not work for showing categorical (nominal) measures nor does it really offer value with the inclusion of low-range, discrete quantitative variables used (e.g. number of legs per human). Patterns will mean very little when intersecting with such axes (they may be better deployed as a filtering parameter or a coloured categorical separator).

EXAMPLE Exploring the relationship between nutrient contents for 14 different attributes across 1,153 different items of food.

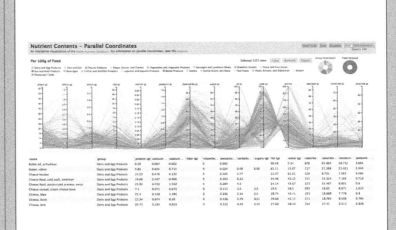

Figure 6.32   Nutrient Contents – Parallel Coordinates

HOW TO READ IT & WHAT TO LOOK FOR

Look around the chart and acquaint yourself with what each quantitative measure axis represents. Also note what kind of sequencing of measure has been used: are neighbouring measures significantly paired? Note the range of values along each independent axis so you understand what positions along the scales represent and can determine what higher and lower positions mean. If colour has been used to group related records then identify what these represent. Scan the overall mass of lines to identify any major patterns. Study the patterns in the space between each pair of adjacent axes. This is where you will really see the potential presence or absence of, and nature of, relationships between measures. The main patterns to identify involve the presence of parallel lines (showing consistent relationships), lines converging in similar directions (some correlation) and then complete criss-crossing (negative relationship). Look out for any associations in the patterns across colour groupings. Remember that ruling out significant relationships can be just as useful as ruling them in.

PRESENTATION TIPS

INTERACTIVITY: Parallel coordinates are particularly useful when offered with interactive features, such as filtering techniques, enabling the user to interrogate and manipulate the display to facilitate visual exploration. Additionally, the option to rearrange the sequence of the measures can be especially useful.

ANNOTATION: The inclusion of visible annotated features like axis lines, tick marks, gridlines and value labels can naturally aid the readability of the data but be aware of the impact of clutter.

COLOUR: When you are plotting large quantities of records, inevitably there will be over-plotting and this might disguise the real weight of values, so the variation in the darkness of colour can be used to establish density of observations.

COMPOSITION: The ordering of the quantitative variables has to be of optimum significance as the connections between adjacent axes will offer the main way of seeing the local relationships: the patterns will change for every different ordering permutation. Remember that the line directions connecting records are often inconsequential in their meaning unless neighbouring measures have a common scale and similar meaning: the connections are more about establishing commonality of pattern across records, rather than there being anything too significant behind the absolute slope direction/length.

VARIATIONS & ALTERNATIVES

The 'radar chart' has similarities with parallel coordinates in that they include several independent quantitative measures in the same chart but on a radial layout and usually only showing data for one record in the same display. A variation on the parallel coordinate would be the 'Sankey diagram', which displays categorical composition and quantitative flows between different categorical dimensions or 'stages'.

HEAT MAP

ALSO KNOWN AS Matrix chart, mosaic plot

CHRTS

CORRELATIONS

REPRESENTATION DESCRIPTION

A heat map displays quantitative values at the intersection between two categorical dimensions. The chart comprises two categorical axes with each possible value presented across the row and column headers of a table layout. Each corresponding cell is then colour-coded to represent a quantitative value for each combination of category pairing. It is not easy for the eye to determine the exact quantitative values represented by the colours, even if there is a colour scale provided, so heat maps mainly facilitate a gist of the order of magnitude.

EXAMPLE
Exploring the connections between different Avengers characters appearing in the same Marvel comic book titles between 1963 and 2015.

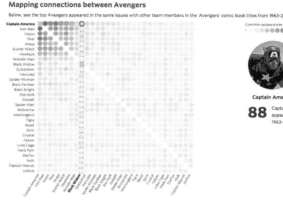

Figure 6.33 How the 'Avengers' Line-up Has Changed Over the Years

HOW TO READ IT & WHAT TO LOOK FOR

Learn what each categorical dimension relates to and make a note of the range of values in each case, paying attention to the significance of any ordering. Establish the quantitative value associations for the colour scales, usually found via a legend. Glance across the entire chart to locate the big, small and medium shades (generally darker = larger) and perform global comparisons to establish the high-level ranking of biggest > smallest. Scan across each row and/or column to see if there are specific patterns associated with either set of categories. Identify any noticeable exceptions and/or outliers. Perform local comparisons between neighbouring cell's areas, to identify larger than and smaller than relationships and estimate the relative proportions. Estimate (or read, if labels are present) the absolute values of specific colour scales of interest.

PRESENTATION TIPS

ANNOTATION: Direct value labelling is possible, otherwise a clear legend to indicate colour associations will suffice.

COLOUR: Sometimes multiple different colour hues may be used to subdivide the quantitative values into further distinct categorical groups. Decisions about how many colour-scale levels and what intervals each relates to in value ranges will affect the patterns that emerge. There is no single right answer – you will arrive at it largely through trial and error/experimentation – but it is important to consider, especially when you have a diverse distribution of values.

COMPOSITION: Logical sorting (and maybe even sub-grouping) of the categorical values along each axis will aid readability and may help surface key relationships.

VARIATIONS & ALTERNATIVES

A 'radial heat map' offers a structure variation whereby the table may be portrayed using a circular layout. As with any radial display this is only really of value if the cyclical ordering means something for the subject matter. A variation would see colour shading replaced by a measure of pattern density, using a scale of 'packedness' to indicate increasing quantitative values. An alternative approach would be the 'matrix chart' using size of a shape to indicate the quantitative or a range of point marker to display categorical characteristics.

MATRIX CHART

ALSO KNOWN AS Table chart

REPRESENTATION DESCRIPTION

A matrix chart displays quantitative values at the intersection between two categorical dimensions. The chart comprises two categorical axes with each possible value presented across the row and column headers of a table layout. Each corresponding cell is then marked by a geometric shape with its area sized to represent a quantitative value and colour often used visually to distinguish a further categorical dimension. While they are most commonly seen using circles, you can use other proportionally sized shapes.

EXAMPLE Exploring the perceived difficulty of fixtures across the season for teams in the premier league 2013–14.

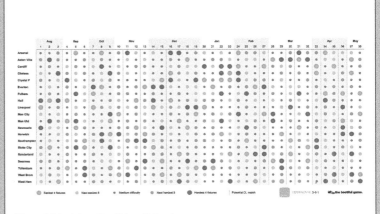

Figure 6.34   Interactive Fixture Molecules

HOW TO READ IT & WHAT TO LOOK FOR

Learn what each categorical dimension relates to and make a note of the range of values in each case, paying attention to the significance of any ordering. Establish the quantitative size associations for the area marks and look up any colour associations being used, both usually found via a legend. Glance across the entire chart to locate the big, small and medium areas and perform global comparisons to establish the high-level ranking of biggest > smallest. Scan across each row and/or column to see if there are specific patterns associated with either set of categories. Identify any noticeable exceptions and/or outliers. Perform local comparisons between neighbouring circular areas, to identify larger than and smaller than relationships and estimate the relative proportions. Estimate (or read, if labels are present) the absolute values of specific geometric areas of interest.

PRESENTATION TIPS

ANNOTATION: Direct value labelling is possible, otherwise be sure to include a clear size legend. Normally this will be more than sufficient as the reader may simply be looking to get a gist of the order of magnitude.

COLOUR: If colours are being used to distinguish the different categories, ensure these are as visibly different as possible.

COMPOSITION: If there are large outlier values there may be occasions when the size of a few circles outgrows the cell it occupies. You might editorially decide to allow this, as the striking shape may create a certain impact, otherwise you will need to limit the largest quantitative value to be represented by the maximum space available within the table's cell layout. Logical sorting (and maybe even sub-grouping) of the categorical values along each axis will aid readability and may help surface key relationships. The geometric accuracy of the circle size calculations is paramount. Mistakes are often made with circle size calculations: it is the area you are modifying, not the diameter/radius.

VARIATIONS & ALTERNATIVES

A variation may be to remove the quantitative attribute of the area marker, replacing it with a point marker to represent a categorical status to indicate simply a yes/no observation through the presence/absence of a point or through the quantity of points to represent a total. An application of this might be in calendar form whereby a marker in a date cell indicates an instance of something. It could also employ a broader range of different categorical options; in practice any kind of marker (symbol, colour, photograph) could be used to show a characteristic of the relationship at each coordinate cell. An alternative might be the 'heat map' which colour-codes the respective cells to indicate a relationship based on a quantitative measure.

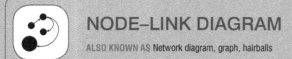

NODE–LINK DIAGRAM

ALSO KNOWN AS Network diagram, graph, hairballs

REPRESENTATION DESCRIPTION

Node–link diagrams display relationships through the connections between categorical 'entities'. The entry-level version of this type of diagram displays entities as nodes (represented by point marks and usually including a label) with links or edges (represented by lines) depicting the existence of connections. The connecting lines will often display an attribute of direction to indicate the influencer relationship. In some versions a quantitative weighting is applied to the show relationship strength, maybe through increased line width. Replacing point marks with a geometric shape and using attributes of size and colour is a further variation. Often the complexity seen in these displays is merely a reflection of the underlying complexity of the subject and/or system upon which the data is based, so oversimplifying can compromise the essence of such content.

EXAMPLE Exploring the connections of voting patterns for Democrats and Republicans across all members of the US House of Representatives from 1949 to 2012.

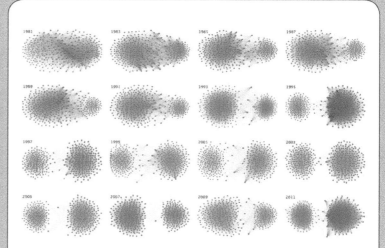

Figure 6.35 The Rise of Partisanship and Super-cooperators in the U.S.

HOW TO READ IT & WHAT TO LOOK FOR

The first thing to consider is what entity each node (point or circular area) represents and what the links mean in relationship terms. There may be several other properties to acquaint yourself with, including attributes like the size of the node areas, the categorical nature of colouring, and the width and direction of the connections. Across the graph you will mainly be seeking out the clusters that show the nodes with the most relationships (representative of influencers or hubs) and those without (including outliers). Small networks will generally enable you to look closely at specific nodes and connections and easily see the emerging relationships. When datasets are especially large, consisting of thousands of nodes and greater numbers of mutual connections, the displays can seem overwhelmingly cluttered and will be too dense to make many detailed observations at node–link level. Instead, just relax and know that your readability will be about a higher level sense-making of the clusters/hubs and main outliers.

PRESENTATION TIPS

INTERACTIVITY: Node–link diagrams are particularly useful when offered with interactive features, enabling the user to interrogate and manipulate the display to facilitate visual exploration. The option to apply filters to reduce the busy-ness of the visual and enable isolation of individual node connections helps users to focus on specific parts of the network of interest.

ANNOTATION: The extent of annotated features tends to be through the inclusion of value labels for each entity. Accommodating the relative word sizes on each node can be difficult to achieve with real elegance (once again that is where interactivity adds value, through the select/mouseover event to reveal the label).

COLOUR: Aside from the possible categorical colouring of each node, decisions need to be made about the colour of the connecting lines, especially on deciding how prominent these links will be in contrast to the nodes.

COMPOSITION: Composition decisions are where most of the presentation customisation exists. There are several common algorithmic treatments used to compute custom arrangements to optimise network displays, such as force-directed layouts (using the physics of repulsion and springs to amplify relationships) and simplifying techniques (such as edge bundling to aggregate/summarise multiple similar links).

VARIATIONS & ALTERNATIVES

There are many derivatives of the node–link diagram, as explained, based on variations in the use of different attributes. 'Hive plots' and 'BioFabric' offer alternative approaches based on replacing nodes with vertices.

REPRESENTATION DESCRIPTION

A chord diagram displays relationships through the connections between and within categories. They are formed around a radial display with different categories located around the edge: either as individual nodes or proportionally sized segments (arcs) of the circumference according to a part-to-whole breakdown. Emerging inwards from each origin position are curved lines that join with other related categorical locations around the edge. The connecting lines are normally proportionally sized according to a quantitative measure and a directional or influencing relationship is often indicated. The perceived readability of the chord diagram will always be influenced by the quantity and range of values being plotted. Small networks will enable a reader to look closely at specific categories and their connections to see the emerging relationships easily; larger systems will look busy through the network of lines but they can still provide windows into complex networks of influence. Often the complexity seen in these displays is merely a reflection of the underlying complexity of the subject and/or system upon which the data is based, so oversimplifying can compromise the essence of such content.

EXAMPLE Exploring the connections of migration between and within 10 world regions based on estimates across five-year intervals between 1990 and 2010.

Figure 6.36   The Global Flow of People

HOW TO READ IT & WHAT TO LOOK FOR

First determine how categories are displayed around the circumference, either as nodes or part-to-whole arcs, and identify each one individually. Consider the implication of the radial sorting of these categorical values and, if based on part-to-whole sizes, establish a sense of the largest > smallest arc lengths. Colour-coding may be applied to the categories so note any associations. Look inside the display to determine what relationships the connecting lines represent and check for any directional significance. Look closer at the tangled collection of lines criss-crossing this space, noting the big values (usually through line weight or width) and the small ones. Avoid being distracted by the distance a line travels, which is just a by-product of the outer categorical arrangement: a long connecting line is just as significant a relationship as a short one. For this reason, pay close attention to any connecting lines that have very short looping distances to adjacent categories. Are there any patterns of lines heading towards or leaving certain categories?

PRESENTATION TIPS

INTERACTIVITY: Chord diagrams are particularly useful when offered with interactive features, enabling the user to interrogate and manipulate the display to facilitate visual exploration. The option to apply filters to reduce the busy-ness of the visual and enable isolation of individual node connections helps users to focus on specific parts of the network of interest.

ANNOTATION: Annotated features tend to be limited to value labelling of the categories around the circumference and, occasionally, directly onto the base or ends of the connecting lines (usually just those that are large enough to accommodate them).

COLOUR: Aside from the categorical colouring of each node, decisions need to be made about the colour of the connecting lines, especially on deciding how prominent these links will be in contrast to the nodes. Sometimes the connections will match the origin or destination colours, or they will combine the two (with a start and end colour to match the relationship).

COMPOSITION: The main arrangement decisions come through sorting, firstly by generating as much logical meaning from the categorical values around the edge of the circle and secondly by deciding on the sorting of the connecting lines in the z-dimension – if many lines are crossing, there is a need to think about which will be on top and which will be below. Showing the direction of connections can be difficult as there is so little room for manoeuvring many more visual attributes, such as arrows or colour changes. One common, subtle solution is to pull the destination join back a bit, leaving a small gap between the connecting line and the destination arc. This then contrasts with connecting lines that emerge directly from the categorical arcs, showing it is their origin.

VARIATIONS & ALTERNATIVES

The main alternatives would be to consider variations of the 'node–link diagram' or, specifically, the 'arc diagram', which offers a further variation on the theme of networked displays, placing all the nodes along a baseline and forming connections using semi-circular arcs, rather than using a graph or radial layout.

SANKEY DIAGRAM

ALSO KNOWN AS Alluvial diagram

C H **R** T S

CONNECTIONS

REPRESENTATION DESCRIPTION

Sankey diagrams display categorical composition and quantitative flows between different categorical dimensions or 'stages'. The most common contemporary form involves a two-sided display, with each side representing different (but related) categorical dimensions or different states of the same dimension (such as 'before and after'). On each side there is effectively a stacked bar chart displaying proportionally sized and differently coloured (or spaced apart) constituent parts of a whole. Curved bands link each side of the display to represent connecting categories (origin and destination) with the proportionally sized band (its thickness) indicating the quantitative nature of this relationship. Some variations involve multiple stages and might present attrition through the diminution size of subsequent stacks. Traditionally the Sankey has been used as a flow diagram to visualise energy or material usage across engineering processes. It is closely related to the 'alluvial diagram', which tends to show changes in composition and flow over time, but the Sankey label is often applied to these displays also.

EXAMPLE Exploring the seat changes among political parties between the 2010 and 2015 UK General Elections.

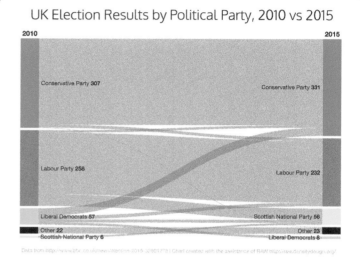

Figure 6.37   UK Election Results by Political Party, 2010 vs 2015

HOW TO READ IT & WHAT TO LOOK FOR

Based on the basic two-sided version of the Sankey diagram, look down both sides of the chart to learn what states are represented and what the constituent categories are. Pay close attention to the categorical sorting and pick out the large and small values on each side. Then look at the connecting lines, making observations about the largest and narrowest bands and noting any that seem to be mostly redistributed into a different category compared to those that just join with the same. Notice any small break-off bands that seem to cross the height of the whole chart, perhaps representing a more dramatic change or diversion between states. As with most network-type visualisations, the perceived readability of the Sankey diagram will always be influenced by the quantity and range of values being plotted, as well as the number of different states presented.

PRESENTATION TIPS

INTERACTIVITY: Sankey diagrams are particularly useful when offered with interactive features, enabling the user to interrogate and manipulate the display to facilitate visual exploration. The option to apply filters to reduce the busy-ness of the visual and enable isolation of individual node connections helps users to focus on specific parts of the network of interest.

ANNOTATION: Annotated features tend to be limited to value labelling of the categories that make up each 'state' stack.

COLOUR: Colouring is often used visually to indicate the categories of the connecting bands, though it can get a little complicated when trying to combine a sense of change through an origin category colour blending with a destination category colour when there has been a switch.

COMPOSITION: The main arrangement decisions come through sorting, firstly by generating as much logical meaning from the categorical values within the stacks and, secondly, by deciding on the sorting of the connecting lines in the z-dimension – if many lines are crossing, there is a need to think about which will be on top and which will be below. There is no significant difference between a landscape or portrait layout, which will depend on the subject matter 'fit' and the space within which you have to work. Try to ensure that the sorting of the categorical dimensions is as logical and meaningful as possible.

VARIATIONS & ALTERNATIVES

The concept of a Sankey diagram showing composition and flow can also be mapped onto a geographical projection as one of the variations of the 'flow map'. You could use a 'chord diagram' as an alternative to show how larger networks are composed proportionally and in their connections. Showing how component parts have changed over time could just be displayed using a 'stacked area chart'. A 'funnel chart' is a much simplified display to show how a single value changes (usually diminishing) across states, for topics like sales conversion. This often is based on a funnel-like shape formed by a wide bar at the top (those entering the system) and then gradually narrower bars, stage by stage towards the end state.

LINE CHART

ALSO KNOWN AS Fever chart, stock chart

REPRESENTATION DESCRIPTION
A line chart shows how quantitative values for different categories have changed over time. They are typically structured around a temporal x-axis with equal intervals from the earliest to latest point in time. Quantitative values are plotted using joined-up lines that effectively connect consecutive points positioned along a y-axis. The resulting slopes formed between the two ends of each line provide an indication of the local trends between points in time. As this sequence is extended to plot all values across the time frame it forms an overall line representative of the quantitative change over time story for a single categorical value. Multiple categories can be displayed in the same view, each represented by a unique line. Sometimes a point (circle/dot) is also used to substantiate the visibility of individual values. The lines used in a line chart will generally be straight. However, sometimes curved line interpolation may be used as a method of estimating values between known data points. This approach can be useful to help emphasise a general trend. While this might slightly compromise the visual accuracy of discrete values if you already have approximations, this will have less impact.

EXAMPLE
Showing changes in percentage income growth for the Top 1% and Bottom 90% of earners in the USA between 1917 and 2012.

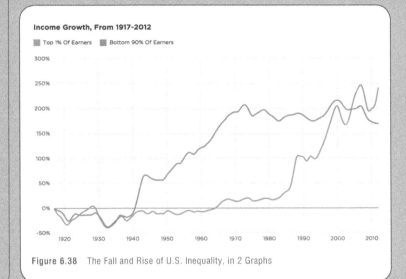

Income Growth, From 1917-2012

■ Top 1% Of Earners   ■ Bottom 90% Of Earners

Figure 6.38   The Fall and Rise of U.S. Inequality, in 2 Graphs

HOW TO READ IT & WHAT TO LOOK FOR
Firstly, learn about the axes: what is the time period range presented on the x-axis (and in what order) and what is the range of quantitative values shown on the y-axis, paying particular attention to the origin value (which may not be zero)? Inside the chart, determine what categories each line represents: for single lines this will usually be clear from the chart title, for multiple lines you might have direct labelling or a legend to learn colour associations. Think about what high and low values mean: is it 'good' to be large/small, increasing or decreasing? Glance at the general patterns (especially if there are many) looking for observations such as any trends (short or long term), any sudden moments of a rise or fall (V- or W -shapes, or inverted), any sense of seasonal or cyclical patterns, any points of interest where lines cross each other or key thresholds that are reached/exceeded. Can you mentally extrapolate from the values shown any sense of a forecasted trend? Avoid jumping to spurious interpretations if you see two line series following a similar pattern; this does not necessarily mean that one thing has caused the other, it might just be coincidence. Then look more closely at categories of interest and at patterns around specific moments in time, and pick out the peak, low, earliest and latest values for each line. Where available, compare the changing quantities against annotated references such as targets, forecast, previous time periods, range bands, etc.

PRESENTATION TIPS
INTERACTIVITY: Interactivity may be especially helpful if you have many categories and wish to enable the user to isolate (in focus terms) a certain line category of interest.

ANNOTATION: Chart apparatus devices like tick marks and gridlines in particular can be helpful to increase the accuracy of the reading of the quantitative values. If you have axis labels you should not need direct labels on each value point – this will be label overload. You might choose to annotate specific values of interest (highest, lowest, specific milestones). Think carefully about what is the most useful and meaningful interval for your time axis labelling. When several categories are being shown, if possible, try directly to label the categories shown by each line, maybe at the start or end position.

COLOUR: When many categories are shown it may be that only certain emphasised lines of interest possess a colour and a label – the rest are left in greyscale for context.

COMPOSITION: Composition choices are mostly concerned with the chart's dimensions: its aspect ratio, how high and wide to make it. The sequencing of values tends to be left to right for the sequence of the time-based x-axis and low rising to high values on the y-axis; you will need a good (and clearly annotated) reason to break this convention. Line charts do not always need the y-axis to start at zero, as we are not judging the size of a bar, rather the position along an axis. You should expect to see a zero baseline if zero has some critical significance in the interpretation of the trends. If your y-axis origin is not going to be zero, you might include a small gap between the x-axis and the minimum so that it is not implied. Be aware that the upward and downward trends on a line chart can seem more significant if the chart width is narrow and less significant if it is more stretched out. There is no single rule to follow here but a useful notion involves 'banking to 45°' whereby the average slope angle across your chart heads towards 45°. While it is impractical to actually measure this, judging by eye tends to be more than sufficient.

VARIATIONS & ALTERNATIVES
Variations of the line chart may include the 'cumulative line chart' or 'step chart'. 'Spark lines' are mini line charts that aim to occupy almost only a word's length amount of space. Often seen in dashboards where space is at a premium and there is a desire to optimise the density of the display. 'Bar charts' can also be used to show how values look over time when there is perhaps greater volatility in the quantitative values across the time period and when the focus is on the absolute values at each point in time, more so than trends. Sometimes a line chart can show quantitative trends over continuous space rather than time. For showing ranking over time, consider the 'bump chart', and for before and after comparisons, the 'slope graph'.

BUMP CHART

ALSO KNOWN AS

TRENDS

REPRESENTATION DESCRIPTION

A bump chart shows how quantitative rankings for categories have changed over time. They are typically structured around a temporal x-axis with equal intervals from the earliest to latest point in time. Quantitative rankings are plotted using joined-up lines that effectively connect consecutive points positioned along a y-axis (typically top = first). The resulting slopes formed between the two ends of each line provide an indication of the local ranking trends between points in time. As this sequence is extended to plot all values across the time frame it forms an overall line representative of the ranking story for a single categorical value. Multiple categories are often displayed in the same view, showing how rankings have collectively changed over time. Sometimes a point (circle/dot) mark is also used to substantiate the connected visibility of category lines, as is colour (for the lines and/or the points).

EXAMPLE Showing changes in rank of the most populated US cities at each census between 1790 and 1890.

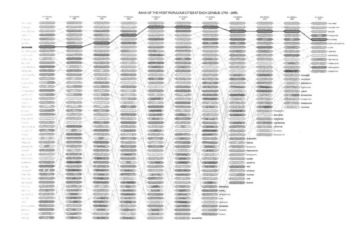

Figure 6.39 Census Bump: Rank of the Most Populous Cities at Each Census, 1790–1890

HOW TO READ IT & WHAT TO LOOK FOR

Firstly, you need to learn about the axes. What is the time period range presented on the x-axis (and in what order)? What are the range of quantitative rankings shown on the y-axis (check that the ranks start at 1 from the top downwards)? Inside the chart, determine what categories each line represents: this might be explained through direct labelling, a colour legend, interactivity or through differentiating point marker attributes of colour/shape/pattern. Think about what high and low ranks mean: is it 'good' to be high up the rankings and is it better to be moving up or down? Consider the general patterns to look for observations such as consistent trends (largely parallel lines) or completely non-relational patterns (lines moving in all directions). Are there any prominent stories of categories that have had a sudden rise or fall (V- or W-shapes, or inverted)? Is there any evidence of seasonal or cyclical patterns, any key points of interest where lines cross each other or key thresholds that are reached/exceeded? Next, look more closely at categories of interest and at patterns around specific moments in time, and pick out the peak, low, earliest and latest values for each line.

PRESENTATION TIPS

INTERACTIVITY: Interactivity is usually necessary with bump charts, especially if you have many categories and wish to enable the user to isolate (in focus terms) a certain line category of interest.

ANNOTATION: The ranking labels can be derived from the vertical position along the scale so direct labelling is usually unnecessary. You might choose to annotate specific values of interest (highest, lowest, specific milestones). Think carefully about what is the most useful and meaningful interval for your time axis labelling.

COLOUR: Often, with many categories to show in the same chart, the big challenge is to distinguish each line, especially as they likely criss-cross often with others. Using colour association can be useful for less than 10 categories, but for more than that you really need to offer the interactivity or maybe decide that only certain emphasised lines of interest will possess a colour and the rest are left in greyscale for context.

COMPOSITION: The sequencing of values tends to be left to right for the sequence of the time-based x-axis with high rankings (low number) on the y-axis moving downwards. You will therefore need a good (and clearly annotated) reason to break this convention.

VARIATIONS & ALTERNATIVES

Alluvial diagrams (similar to Sankey diagrams) can show how rankings have changed over time while also incorporating a component of quantitative magnitude. This approach is effectively merging the 'bump chart' with the 'stacked area chart'. Consider 'line charts' and 'area charts' if the ranking is of secondary interest to the absolute values.

SLOPE GRAPH CHART

ALSO KNOWN AS Slope chart

REPRESENTATION DESCRIPTION

A slope graph shows a 'before and after' display of changes in quantities for different categories. The display is based on (typically) two parallel quantitative axes with a consistent scale range to cover all possible quantitative values. A line is plotted for each category connecting the two axes together with the vertical position on each axis representing the respective quantitative values. Sometime a dot is also used to further substantiate the visibility of the value positions. These connecting lines form slopes that indicate the upward, downward or stable trend between points in time. The resulting display incorporates absolute values, reveals rank and, of course, shows change between time. Colours are often used visually to distinguish different categorical lines, otherwise this can be used to surface visibly the major trend states (up, down, no change). A slope graph works less well when all values (or the majority) are going in the same direction; consider alternatives if this is the case.

EXAMPLE Showing changes in the share of power sources across all US states between 2004 and 2014.

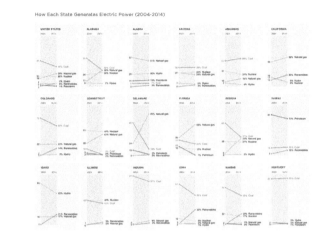

Figure 6.40   Coal, Gas, Nuclear, Hydro? How Your State Generates Power

HOW TO READ IT & WHAT TO LOOK FOR

Firstly, learn about the axes: what are the two points in time being presented and what is the possible range of quantitative values shown on the y-axis, checking that the ranks start from the top down? Inside the chart, learn what each category line relates to and determine what categories each line represents: this might be explained through direct labelling, a colour legend, or through interactivity. Think about what upward, downward and stable trends mean: is it 'good' to be moving up or down? Is it more interesting to show no change? Look at the general patterns to observe such things as consistent trends (largely parallel lines in either direction) or completely non-relational patterns (lines moving in all directions). Colour may be used to accentuate the distinction between upward and downward trends. Are there any prominent stories of categories that have had a dramatic rise or fall? Even if no values have dramatically altered, that in itself can be an important finding, especially if change was expected. Next, look more closely at categories of interest and pick out the highest and lowest values on each side to learn about those stories. Look for the gaps where there are no values, and at outlier values too, to see if some sit outside the normal value clusters.

PRESENTATION TIPS

INTERACTIVITY: Depending on the number of category values being presented, slope graphs can become quite busy, especially if there are bunches of similar values and slope transitions. This also causes a problem with accommodating multiple labels on the same value. On these occasions you might find interactive slope graphs to help filter/exclude certain values.

ANNOTATION: Labelling of each category will get busy, especially when there are shared values, so you might choose to annotate specific values of interest (highest, lowest, of editorial interest).

COLOUR: Often when you have many categories to show in the same chart the big challenge is to distinguish each line, especially as they likely criss-cross often with others. Using colour association can be useful for less than 10 categories usually with direct labelling on the left and/or right of the chart.

COMPOSITION: The aspect ratio of the slope graph (height and width) will often be determined by the space you have to work with.

VARIATIONS & ALTERNATIVES

Rather than showing a before and after story, some slope graphs are used to show the relationship between different quantitative measures for linked categories. In this case the connecting line is not indicative of a directional relationship, just the relationship itself. An alternative option would be the 'connected dot plot' which can also show before and after stories and is a better option when all values are moving in the same direction.

193

CONNECTED SCATTER PLOT

ALSO KNOWN AS Trail chart

TRENDS

REPRESENTATION DESCRIPTION

A connected scatter plot displays the relationship between two quantitative measures over time. The display is formed by plotting marks like a dot or circle for each point in time at the respective coordinates along two quantitative x- and y-axes. The collection of individual points is then connected (think of a dot-to-dot drawing puzzle) using lines joining each consecutive point in time to form a sequence of change. Generally there would only be a single connected line plotted on a chart to avoid the great visual complexity of overlaying several in one display. However, if multiple categories are to be included, colour is typically used to distinguish each series.

EXAMPLE Showing changes in the daily price and availability of Super Bowl tickets on the secondary market four weeks prior to the event across five Super Bowl finals.

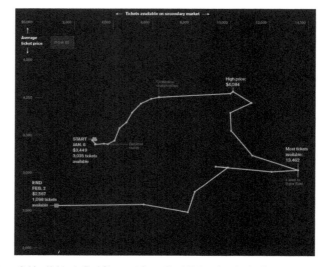

Figure 6.41 Holdouts Find Cheapest Super Bowl Tickets Late in the Game

HOW TO READ IT & WHAT TO LOOK FOR

Learn what each quantitative axis relates to and make a note of the range of values in each case (min to max). Look at what each plotted value on the chart refers to in terms of its date label and determine the meaning of line direction. It usually helps to parse your thinking by considering what higher/lower values mean for each quantitative axis individually and then combining the joint meaning thereafter. Try to follow the chart from the start to the end, mapping out in your mind the sequence of a narrative as the values change in all directions and noting the extreme values in the outer edges of your line's reach. Look at the overall pattern of the connected line: is it consistently moving in one direction? Does it ebb and flow in all directions? Does it create a spiral shape? Compare consecutive points for a more focused view of change between two points.

PRESENTATION TIPS

INTERACTIVITY: The biggest challenge is making the connections and the sequence as visible as possible. This becomes much harder when values change very little and/or they loop back almost in spiral fashion, crossing back over themselves. It is especially hard to label the sequential time values elegantly. One option to overcome this is through interactivity and particularly through animated sequences which build up the display, connecting one line at a time and unveiling the date labels as time progresses. It is often the case that only one series will be plotted. However, interactive options may allow the user to overlay one or more for comparison, switching them on and off as required.

ANNOTATION: Connected scatter plots are generally seen as one of the most complex chart types for the unfamiliar reader to work out how to read, given the amount of different attributes working together in the display. It is therefore vital that as much help is given to the reader as possible with 'how to read' guides and illustrations of what the different directions of change mean.

COLOUR: Colour is only generally used to accentuate certain sections of a sequence that might represent a particularly noteworthy stage of narrative.

COMPOSITION: As the encoding of the plotted point values is based on position along an axis, it is not necessary to start the axes from a zero baseline – just make the scale ranges as representative as possible of the range of values being plotted. Ideally a connected scatter plot will have a 1:1 aspect ratio (equally as tall as it is wide), creating a squared area to help patterns surface more evidently. If one quantitative variable (e.g. weight) is likely to be affected by the other variable (e.g. height), it is general practice to place the former on the y-axis and the latter on the x-axis.

VARIATIONS & ALTERNATIVES

The 'comet chart' is to the connected scatter plot what the 'slope graph' is to the 'line chart' – a summarised view of the changing relationships across two quantitative values between just two points in time. Naturally a reduced variation of the connected scatter plot is simply the 'scatter plot' where there is no time dimension or elements of connectedness.

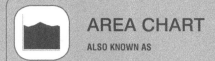

AREA CHART

ALSO KNOWN AS

TRENDS

REPRESENTATION DESCRIPTION

A line chart shows how quantitative values for different categories have changed over time. They are typically structured around a temporal x-axis with equal intervals from the earliest to latest point in time. Quantitative values are plotted using joined-up lines that effectively connect consecutive points positioned along a y-axis. The resulting slopes formed between the two ends of each line provide an indication of the local trends between points in time. As this sequence is extended to plot all values across the time frame it forms an overall line representative of the quantitative change over time story for a single categorical value. To accentuate the magnitude of the quantitative values and the change through time the area beneath the line is filled with colour. The height of each coloured layer at each point in time reveals its quantity. Area charts can display values for several categories, using stacks, to show also the changing part-to-whole relationship.

EXAMPLE Showing changes in the average monthly price ($ per barrel) of crude oil between 1985 and 2015.

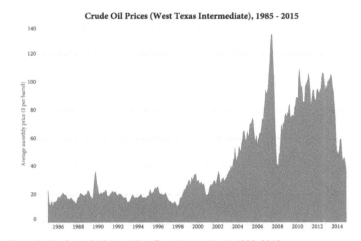

Figure 6.42   Crude Oil Prices (West Texas Intermediate), 1985–2015

195

HOW TO READ IT & WHAT TO LOOK FOR

Firstly, learn about the axes: what is the time period range presented on the x-axis (and in what order) and what is the range of quantitative values shown on the y-axis, paying particular attention to whether it is a percentage or absolute based scale? Inside the chart, determine what categories each area layer represents: for single areas this will usually be clear from the chart title, for multiple areas you might have direct labelling or a nearby legend to learn colour associations. Think about what high and low values mean: is it 'good' to be large/small, increasing or decreasing? Glance at the general patterns (especially if there are many layers), looking at the visible 'thickness' of the coloured layers. At what points are the values highest or lowest? When are they growing or shrinking as the time axis moves along? If there are multiple categories, which ones take up the largest and smallest slices of the overall total? Are there any trends (short or long term), any sudden moments of a rise or fall, any sense of seasonal or cyclical patterns? If there are multiple categories, look more closely at individual layers of interest.

PRESENTATION TIPS

ANNOTATION: Direct labelling of quantitative values will get far too busy so you might choose to annotate specific values of interest (highest, lowest, specific milestones). Think about the most useful interval for your axis labelling. As ever there is no single rule, so adopt the Goldilocks principle of not too many, not too few. If you have a stacked area chart, try directly to label the category layers shown as closely as possible (if the heights allow it) or at least ensure any colour associations are easily identifiable through a nearby legend. Think carefully about what is the most useful and meaningful interval for your time axis labelling.

COLOUR: If you are using a stacked area chart, ensure the categorical layers have sufficiently different colours so that their distinct reading can be efficiently performed.

COMPOSITION: Similar to the line chart, the area chart's dimensions should ideally utilise an aspect ratio that optimises the readability through 45° banking (roughly judging the average slope angle). The sequencing of values tends to be left to right for the sequence of the time-based x-axis and low rising to high values on the y-axis; you will need a good (and clearly annotated) reason to break this convention. Unlike the line chart, the quantitative axis for area charts must start at zero as it is the height of the coloured areas under each line that helps readers to perceive the quantitative values. Do not have overlapping categories on the same chart because it makes it very difficult to see (imagine hills behind hills, peaking out and then hiding behind each other). Rather than stacking categories you might consider using small multiples, especially as this will present the respective displays from a common baseline (and make reading sizes a little easier).

VARIATIONS & ALTERNATIVES

Like area charts, 'alluvial diagrams' display proportional stacked layers for multiple categories showing the absolute value change over time. However, they also show the evolving ranks, switching the relative ordering of each layer of values based on the current magnitude. Some deployments of the area chart are not plotted over time but over continuous dimensions of space, perhaps showing the changing nature of a given quantitative measure along a given route. When you have many concurrent layers to show and these layers start and stop at different times, a 'slope graph' is worth considering.

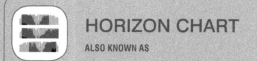

REPRESENTATION DESCRIPTION

Horizon charts show how quantitative values for different categories have changed over time. They are valuable for showing changes over time for multiple categories within space-constrained formats (such as dashboards). They are structured around a series of rows each showing changes in quantitative values for a single category. The temporal x-axis has equal intervals from the earliest to latest point in time. Quantitative values are plotted using joined-up lines that connect consecutive points positioned along a value y-axis. The resulting slopes formed between the ends of each line provide an indication of the local trends between two points in time. As this sequence is extended to plot all values across the time frame it forms an overall line representative of the quantitative changes. To accentuate the magnitude of the quantitative values the area beneath the line is filled with colour. Negative values are highlighted in one colour, positive values in another colour. Variations in colour lightness are used to indicate different degrees or bands of magnitudes, with the extremes getting darker. Negative value areas are then flipped from underneath the baseline to above it, joining the positive values but differentiated in their polarity by colour. Finally, like slicing off layers of a mountain, each distinct threshold band that sits above the imposed maximum y-axis scale is chopped off and dropped down to the baseline, in front of its foundation base. The final effect shows overlapping layers of increasingly darker colour-shaded areas all occupying the same vertical space with combinations of height, colour and shade representing the values.

EXAMPLE Showing percentage changes in price for selected food items in the USA between 1990 and 2015.

Figure 6.43 Percentage Change in Price for Select Food Items, Since 1990

HOW TO READ IT & WHAT TO LOOK FOR

Firstly, learn about the category rows: what do they represent and in what order are they presented? Next, the chart axes: what is the time period range presented on the x-axis (and in what order) and what is the range of quantitative values shown on the y-axis, paying attention to whether it is a percentage or absolute value scale? Next, what are the colour associations (for positive and negative values) and the different shaded banding thresholds? Think about what high and low values mean: is it 'good' to be large/small, increasing or decreasing? Glance at the general patterns over time, looking at the most visible dark areas of each colour polarity: where have values reached a peak in either direction? Maybe then separate your reading between looking at the positive value insights and then the negative ones: which chunks of colour are increasing in value (darker) or shrinking (getting lighter) as the time axis moves along? Where can you see most empty space, indicating low values? Are there any trends (short or long term), any sudden moments of a rise or fall, any sense of seasonal or cyclical patterns, any points of interest where lines cross each other or key thresholds that are reached/exceeded? Then look more closely at categories of interest, assessing their own patterns around specific moments in time and picking out the peak, low, earliest and latest values for each row.

PRESENTATION TIPS

ANNOTATION: The decisions around annotations are largely reduced to labelling the category rows. Such is the busy-ness of the chart areas that any direct labelling is going to clutter the display too much: horizon charts are less about precise value reading and more about getting a sense of the main patterns, so avoid the temptation to over-label. Think carefully about what is the most useful and meaningful interval for your time axis labelling.

COLOUR: Colour decisions mainly concern the choices of quantitative scale bandings to show the positive and negative value ranges.

COMPOSITION: The height of the chart area in which you can accommodate a single row of data will have an influence on the entire construction of the horizon chart. It will often involve an iterative/trial and error process, looking at the range of quantitative values across each category, establishing the most sensible and meaningful thresholds within these range and then fixing the y-axis scales accordingly. Try to ensure the sorting of the main categorical rows is as logical and meaningful as possible.

VARIATIONS & ALTERNATIVES

An alternative to the horizon chart is the entry-level single category 'area chart', which does not suffer the same constraints of restrictions to the vertical scale. For space-constrained displays, 'spark lines' would offer an option suitable to such situations and easily accommodate multiple category displays.

196

STREAM GRAPH

ALSO KNOWN AS Theme river

REPRESENTATION DESCRIPTION

A stream graph shows how quantitative values for different categories have changed over time. They are generally used when you have many constituent categories at any given point in time and these categories may start and stop at different points in time (rather than continue throughout the presented time frame). As befitting the name, their appearance is characterised by a flowing, organic display of meandering layers. They are typically structured around a temporal x-axis with equal intervals from the earliest to latest point in time. Quantitative values are plotted using joined-up lines that effectively connect consecutive points to quantify the height above a local baseline, which is not a stable zero baseline but rather a shifting shape formed out of other category layers. To accentuate the size of the category's height at any given point the area beneath the line is filled with colour. The height of each coloured layer at each point in time reveals its quantity. This colour is often used to further represent a quantitative value scale or to associate with categorical colours. The stacking arrangement of the different categorical streams goes above and below the central axis line to optimise the layout but not with any implication of polarity.

EXAMPLE Showing changes in the total domestic gross takings ($US) and the longevity of all movies released between 1986 and 2008.

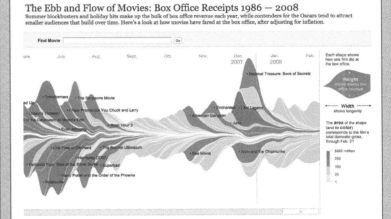

Figure 6.44 The Ebb and Flow of Movies: Box Office Receipts 1986–2008

197

HOW TO READ IT & WHAT TO LOOK FOR

Firstly, determine what is the time period presented on the x-axis (and in what order). In most stream graphs you do not see the quantitative y-axis scale because the level of reading is more about getting a gist for the main patterns in a relative sense rather than an absolute one. You might find that the colouring of layers has a quantitative scale or categorical association so look for any keys. Also, you will often find guides to help estimate the quantitative heights of each layer. Think about what high and low values mean: is it 'good' to be large/small, increasing or decreasing? Glance at the general patterns over time. Remember that above or below means nothing in the sense of polarity of values, so your focus is on the entirety of the collective shape. Look for the largest peaks and the shallowest troughs, possible seasonal patterns or the significant moments of change. Note where these patterns occur in relation to the timescale. Can you see any prominently tall (big values) or wide (long-duration) layers? Notice when layers start and end, noting times when there are many concurrent categories and when there are few. Pick out the layers of personal interest and assess their patterns over time. Do not spend too much effort trying to estimate precise values of height, but keep your focus on the bigger picture level. It is often useful to rotate the display so the streams are travelling vertically, offering a different perspective and removing the instinct to see positive values above and negative values below the central axis.

PRESENTATION TIPS

INTERACTIVITY: If interactivity is a possibility, this could enable selection or mouseover events to reveal annotated values at any given point in time or to filter the view.

ANNOTATION: Chart apparatus devices are generally of limited use in a stream graph with the priority on a general sense of pattern more than precision value reading. Direct labelling of categories is likely to be quite busy but may be required, at least to annotate the most interesting patterns (highest, lowest, specific milestones). Think carefully about what is the most useful and meaningful interval for your time axis labelling.

COLOUR: Ensure any colour associations or size guides are easily identifiable through a nearby legend.

COMPOSITION: Composition choices are firstly concerned with the landscape or portrait layout. This will largely be informed by the format and space of your outputs and the meaning of the data. The stream layers are often smoothed, giving them an aesthetically organic appearance, both individually and collectively. This is achieved via curved line interpolation.

VARIATIONS & ALTERNATIVES

The fewer categorical series you have in your data, the more likely a stacked 'area chart' is going to best-fit your needs. You could consider a stacked 'bar chart' over time also, but there is less chance of maintaining the connected visibility of continuous categorical series via a singular shape.

CONNECTED TIMELINE

ALSO KNOWN AS Relationship timeline, storyline visualisations, swim-lane chart

REPRESENTATION DESCRIPTION
A connected timeline displays the duration, milestones and categorical relationships across a range of categorical 'activities'. It represents a particularly diverse and creative way of showing changes over time and so involves many variations in approach. The structure is generally formed of time-based quantitative x-axis and categorical y-axis lanes. Each categorical activity will commence at a point in time and from within a vertical category 'family'. Over time, the line will progress, possibly switching to a different categorical lane position as the nature of the activity alters. The lines may be of fixed width or proportionally weighted to represent a quantitative measure. Some activity lines may cease, restart or merge with others to build a multi-faceted narrative. Colour can also be used to present further relevant detail. The main issue with any connected timeline approach is simply the complexity of the content and the number of moving parts crossing over the display. As there are many entry points into reading such a timeline there can be inefficiency in the reading process, but this is usually proportional simply to the subject at hand and you may not wish to see these nuances being removed.

EXAMPLE Showing changes in US major college football programme allegiance to different conferences between 1965 and 2015.

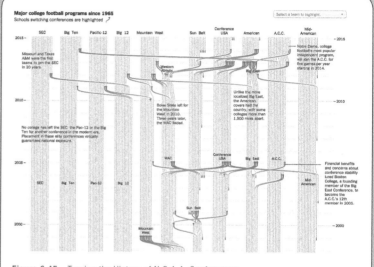

Figure 6.45 Tracing the History of N.C.A.A. Conferences

198

HOW TO READ IT & WHAT TO LOOK FOR
Look at the axes so you know what the major categorical 'lanes' represent and what the range of date values is (min to max). Then try to determine what each categorical activity line represents. As there are so many derivatives there is no single reading strategy, but generally glance across the entire chart noting the sequence of the activities; there is usually a sequential logic attached to their sorting based on the start date milestone in particular. Follow the narrative from left to right, noting observations about any big, small and medium weighted lines and spotting any moment when they connect with, overlap or detach from other activities. Are there any major convergences or divergences in pattern? Any hubs of dense activity and other sparse moments? Look for the length of lines to determine the long, medium and short durations of activity. Where available, compare the activities against annotated references about other key milestone dates that might hold some significance or influence.

PRESENTATION TIPS
ANNOTATION: Chart apparatus devices like tick marks and gridlines in particular can be helpful to increase the accuracy of the reading of both the quantitative values and the activity 'lanes', which may be coloured to help recognise divisions between categories. Direct labelling is usually seen in these timelines to help maintain associations across the display with the categories of characters or activities, perhaps annotating the consequence or cause of lines merging, etc. Think carefully about what is the most useful and meaningful interval for your time axis labelling.

COLOUR: Even if colour does not have a direct association with given activities, it can be a useful property to highlight certain features of the narrative, sometimes acting as a container device to group activities together, even if just for a momentary time period.

COMPOSITION: Where possible, try to make the categorical sorting meaningful, maybe organising values in ascending/descending size order. The vertical (y) or horizontal (x) sequencing of time will depend on the amount of data to show and the space you have to work with. Also, depending on the narrative, the past > present ordering may be reversed.

VARIATIONS & ALTERNATIVES
There are similarities with the organic nature of the 'alluvial diagram', which shows ranking and quantitative change over time for a number of concurrent categories. When there are fewer inter-activity relationships and more discrete categories are involved, then the 'Gantt chart' offers an alternative way of showing this analysis.

GANTT CHART

ALSO KNOWN AS Range chart, floating bar chart

REPRESENTATION DESCRIPTION

A Gantt chart displays the start and finish points and durations for different categorical 'activities'. The display is commonly used in project management to illustrate the breakdown of a schedule of tasks but can be a useful device to show any data based on milestone dates and durations. The chart is structured around a time-based quantitative x-axis and a categorical y-axis. Each categorical activity is represented by lines positioned according to the start moment and then stretched out to the finish point. There may be several start/finish durations within the same activity row. Sometimes points are used to accentuate the start/finish positions and the line may be coloured to indicate a relevant categorical value (e.g. separating completed vs ongoing).

EXAMPLE
Showing the events of birth, death and period serving in office for the first 44 US Presidents.

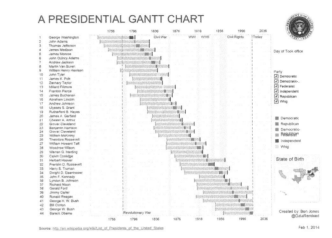

Figure 6.46   A Presidential Gantt Chart

HOW TO READ IT & WHAT TO LOOK FOR

Look at the axes so you know with what major categorical values each Gantt bar is associated and what the range of the date values is (min to max). Follow the narrative, noting the sequence of the categories – there is usually a sequential sorting based on the start date milestone. Glance across the entire chart and perform global comparisons to establish the high-level ranking of biggest > smallest durations (based on the length of the line) as well as early and late milestones. Identify any noticeable exceptions and/or outliers. Perform local comparisons between neighbouring bars to identify proportional differences and any connected dependencies. Estimate (or read, if labels are present) the absolute values for specific categories of interest. Where available, compare the activities against annotated references about other key milestone dates that might hold some significance or influence.

PRESENTATION TIPS

ANNOTATION: Chart apparatus devices like tick marks and gridlines (or row band-shading) in particular can be helpful to increase the accuracy of the reading of the start point and duration of activities along the timeline. If you have axis labels you may not need direct labels for the values shown with each duration bar – this will be label overload, so generally decide between one or the other. Think carefully about what is the most useful and meaningful interval for your time axis labelling.

COMPOSITION: There is no significant difference in perception between vertical or horizontal Gantt charts, though horizontal layouts are more metaphorically consistent with the concept of reading time. Additionally, these layouts tend to make it easier to accommodate and read the category labels. Where possible, try to sequence the categorical 'activities' in a way that makes for the most logical reading, either organised by the start/finish dates or maybe the durations (depending on which has most relevance).

VARIATIONS & ALTERNATIVES

Variations might involve the further addition of different point markers (represented by combinations of symbols and/or colours) along each activity row to indicate additional milestone details, using the 'instance chart'. An emerging trend in technique terms involves preserving the position of activity lines adjacent to other concurrent activities, rather than fixing them to stay within discrete rows. Sometimes there is much more fluidity and less 'discreteness' in the relationships between activity, so approaches like the 'connected timeline' may be more fitting.

199

INSTANCE CHART

ALSO KNOWN AS Milestone map, barcode chart, strip plot

REPRESENTATION DESCRIPTION

An instance chart displays individual moments or instances of categorical 'activities'. There are many variations in approach for this kind of display but generally you will find a structure based on a time-based quantitative x-axis and a categorical y-axis. For each categorical activity, instances of note are represented by different point markers that indicate along the timeline when something has happened. The point markers may have different combinations of symbols and colours to represent different types of occurrences, but avoid having too many different combinations so that viewers do not have to learn an entirely new alphabet of meaning.

EXAMPLE Showing the instances of different Avengers characters appearing in Marvel's comic book titles between 1963 and 2015.

Figure 6.47   How the 'Avengers' Line-up Has Changed Over the Years

HOW TO READ IT & WHAT TO LOOK FOR

Look at the axes so you know with what major categorical values each row of instances is associated and what the range of the date values is (min to max). Look up any legend that will explain what (if any) associations exist between the instance markers and their colour/symbol. Glance down the y-axis noting the sequence of the categories; there is usually a sequential logic attached to their sorting based on the start date milestone in particular. Follow the narrative, noting observations about the type and frequency of instances being plotted. Look across the entire chart to locate the headline patterns of clustering and identify any noticeable exceptions and/or outliers. Look across the patterns within each row individually to learn about each category's dispersal of instances. Look for empty regions where no marks appear. How do all these patterns relate to the time frame displayed? Where available, compare the activities against annotated references about other key milestone dates that might hold some significance or influence.

PRESENTATION TIPS

ANNOTATION: The main annotation properties will be used to serve the role of explaining the associations between marks and attributes through clear legends/keys.

COMPOSITION: Where possible, try to sequence the categorical 'activities' in a way that makes for the most logical reading, either organised by the start/finish dates or maybe the durations (depending on which has most relevance).

VARIATIONS & ALTERNATIVES

Some variations may see the size of a geometric shape used instead of just a point to indicate also a quantitative measure to go with the instance. The marking of an instance through a 'when' moment could also be based on data that talks about positional moments within a sequence. If the basic activity is reduced to a start/finish moment then the 'Gantt chart' will be the best-fit option.

200

CHOROPLETH MAP

ALSO KNOWN AS Heat map

REPRESENTATION DESCRIPTION

A choropleth map displays quantitative values for distinct, definable spatial regions on a map. Each geographic region is represented by a polygonal area based on its outline shape, with each distinct shape then collectively arranged to form the entire landscape. (Note that most tools for mapping have a predetermined reference between a region name and the dimensions of the regional polygon.) Each area is colour-coded to represent a quantitative value based on a scale with colour variation intervals that (typically) go from a light tint for smaller values to a dark shade for larger values. Choropleth maps should only be used when the quantitative measure is directly associated with and continuously relevant across the spatial region on which it will be displayed. Similarly, if your quantitative measure is about or related to the consequence of more people living in an area, interpretations may be distorting, so consider transforming your data to per capita or per acre (or other spatial denominator) to standardise the analysis accordingly.

EXAMPLE Mapping the percentage change in the populations of Berlin's districts across new and native Berliners since the fall of the Berlin Wall.

Figure 6.48   Native and New Berliners – How the S-Bahn Ring Divides the City

201

HOW TO READ IT & WHAT TO LOOK FOR

Acquaint yourself with the geographic region you are presented with and carefully consider the quantitative measure that is being represented. Establish the colour-scale value associations, usually found via a legend. Glance across the entire chart to locate the dark, light and medium shades (generally darker = larger) and perform global comparisons to establish the high-level ranking of biggest values > smallest. Identify any noticeable exceptions and/or outliers. Beware making judgements about the significance of prominent large geographical areas: size is an attribute of the underlying region, not the significance of the measure displayed. Gradually zoom in your focus to perform increasingly local comparisons between neighbouring regional areas to identify any noticeable consistencies or inconsistencies between their values. Estimate (or read, if labels are present) the absolute values of specific regions of interest.

PRESENTATION TIPS

ANNOTATION: Directly labelling the regional areas with geographical details and the value they hold is likely to lead to too much clutter. You might include only a limited number of regional labels to provide spatial context and orientation.

COLOUR: Legends explaining the colour scales should ideally be placed as close to the map display as possible. The border colour and stroke width for each spatial area should be distinguishable to define the shape but not so prominent as to dominate attention – usually a subtle grey- or white-coloured thin stroke will be fine. As well as variation in colour scales, sometimes pattern or textures may add an extra layer of detail to the value status of each region. When including a projected mapping layer image in the background, ensure it is not overly competing for visual prominence by making it light in colour and possibly semi-transparent. Do not include any unnecessary geographical details that add no value to the spatial orientation or interpretation and clutter the display (e.g. roads, building structures).

COMPOSITION: With Earth being a sphere, there are many different mapping projections for representing the regions of the world on a plane surface. Be aware that the transformation adjustments made by some map projections can distort the size of regions of the world, inflating their size relative to other regions.

VARIATIONS & ALTERNATIVES

Some choropleth maps may be used to indicate categorical association rather than quantitative measurements. Alternative thematic mapping approaches to representing quantitative values might include the 'proportional symbol map' and the 'dot density map'. This is a variation that involves plotting a representative quantity of dots equally (but randomly) across and within a defined spatial region. The position of individual dots is therefore not to be read as indicative of precise locations but used to form a measure of quantitative density. This offers a useful alternative to the choropleth map, especially when categorical separation of the dots through colour is of value. 'Dasymetric mapping' is similar in approach to choropleth mapping but breaks the constituent regional areas into much more specific, almost custom-drawn, sub-regions to better represent the realities of the distribution of human and physical phenomena within a given spatial boundary.

ISARITHMIC MAP

ALSO KNOWN AS Contour map, isopleth map, isochrone map

OVERLAYS

REPRESENTATION DESCRIPTION

An isarithmic map displays distinct spatial surfaces on a map that share the same quantitative classification. All spatial regions (transcending geo-political boundaries) that share a certain quantitative value or interval are formed by interpolated 'isolines' connecting points of similar measurement to form distinct surface areas. Each area is then colour-coded to represent the relevant quantitative value. The scale of colour variation intervals differs between deployments but will typically range from a light tint for smaller values to a dark shade for larger values. An isarithmic map would be used in preference to a choropleth map when the patterns of data being displayed transcend the distinct regional polygons. They could be used to show temperature bandings or smoothed regions of political attitudes.

EXAMPLE Mapping the degree of dialect similarity across the USA.

Figure 6.49 How Y'all, Youse and You Guys Talk

HOW TO READ IT & WHAT TO LOOK FOR

Acquaint yourself with the geographic region you are presented with and carefully consider the quantitative measure that is being represented. Establish the colour scale value associations, usually found via a legend. Glance across the entire chart to locate the dark, light and medium shades (generally darker = larger) and perform global comparisons to establish the high-level ranking of biggest values > smallest. Identify any noticeable exceptions and/or outliers, including regions that appear in isolation from their otherwise related values and notable for their position adjacent to very different shaded regions. Note that any interpolation used to smooth the joins between data points to form organic surfaces will inevitably reduce the precision of the surfaces in their relationship to land position. Gradually zoom in your focus to perform increasingly local comparisons between neighbouring regional areas to identify any noticeable consistencies or inconsistencies between their values. Estimate the absolute values of specific regions of interest.

PRESENTATION TIPS

ANNOTATION: Directly labelling the surface areas to show the quantitative value or range they represent will be too cluttered. You might include only a limited number of regional labels to provide spatial context and orientation.

COLOUR: Legends explaining the colour scales should ideally be placed as close to the map display as possible. If using visible contour or boundary lines there is a clear implication of a location being inside or outside the line, so make these lines as prominent in colour as possible according to the precision of their representation. If the smoothing of the surface locations has been applied the representation of these areas should similarly avoid looking definitive. You therefore might consider subtle colour gradation/overlapping between different regions to capture appropriately the underlying 'fuzziness' of the data. As well as colour scales, sometimes pattern or textures may add an extra layer of detail to the value status of each surface region. When including a projected mapping layer image in the background, ensure it is not overly competing for visual prominence by making it light in colour and possibly semi-transparent. Do not include any unnecessary geographical details that add no value to the spatial orientation or interpretation and clutter the display (e.g. roads, building structures).

COMPOSITION: Be aware that the transformation adjustments made by some map projections can distort the size of regions of the world, inflating their size relative to other regions.

VARIATIONS & ALTERNATIVES

There are specific applications of isarithmic maps used for showing elevation ('contour maps'), atmospheric pressure ('isopleth maps') or travel–time distances ('isochrone maps'). Sometimes you might use isarithmic maps to show a categorical status (perhaps even a binary state) rather than a quantitative scale.

PROPORTIONAL SYMBOL MAP

ALSO KNOWN AS Graduated symbol map

REPRESENTATION DESCRIPTION

A proportional symbol map displays quantitative values for locations on a map. The values are represented via proportionally sized areas (usually circles), which are positioned with the centre midpoint over a given location coordinate. Colour is sometimes used to introduce further categorical distinction.

EXAMPLE Mapping the origin and size of funds raised across the 22 major candidates running for US President during the first half of 2015.

$10 $100 $1K $10K $100K $1M $10M

Figure 6.50   Here's Exactly Where the Candidates' Cash Came From

HOW TO READ IT & WHAT TO LOOK FOR

Acquaint yourself with the geographic region you are presented with and carefully consider the quantitative measure that is being represented. Establish the area size value associations, usually found via a legend. Glance across the entire chart to locate the large, medium and small shapes and perform global comparisons to establish the high-level ranking of biggest values > smallest. Identify any noticeable exceptions and/or outliers. Gradually zoom in your focus to perform increasingly local comparisons between neighbouring regional areas to identify any noticeable consistencies or inconsistencies between their values. Estimate (or read, if labels are present) the absolute values of specific regions of interest. Also note where there are no markers. If colour is being used to further break down the categories of the values shown, identify any grouped patterns that emerge.

PRESENTATION TIPS

INTERACTIVITY: Interaction may be helpful to reveal location and value labels through selection or mouseover events.

ANNOTATION: Directly labelling the shapes with geographical details and the value they hold is likely to lead to too much clutter. You might therefore include only a limited number of regional labels to provide spatial context and orientation. Legends explaining the size scales – and any colour associations – should ideally be placed as close to the map display as possible. Avoid including unnecessary geographical details that add no value to the spatial orientation or interpretation and clutter the display (e.g. roads, building structures).

COLOUR: Sometimes the circular shapes are filled, at other times they remain unfilled. If colours are being used to distinguish the different categories, ensure these are as visibly different as possible. When a circle has a large value its shape will transgress well beyond the origin of its geographical location, intruding on and overlapping with other neighbouring values. The use of outline borders and semi-transparent colours helps with the task of avoiding occlusion (visually hiding values behind others). When including a projected mapping layer image in the background, ensure it is not overly competing for visual prominence by making it light in colour and possibly semi-transparent.

VARIATIONS & ALTERNATIVES

Variations may see the typical circle replaced by squares and geographical space replaced by anatomical regions. Alternatives to the proportional symbol map include the 'choropleth map', which colour-codes regions, or the 'dot map', which uses a dot to represent an instance of something. Avoid the temptation to turn the circle symbols into pie charts; it is not a good look. If you absolutely positively have to show a part-to-whole relationship, only show two categories, as per the recommended practice for pies.

203

PRISM MAP

ALSO KNOWN AS Isometric map, spike map, datascape

REPRESENTATION DESCRIPTION

A prism map displays quantitative values for locations on a map. The values are represented via proportionally sized lines, appearing as 3D bars, that typically cover a fixed surface area of space and are just extended in height proportionally to represent the quantitative value for that location. Being able to judge the dimensions of 3D forms in a 2D view is very difficult, so they are only ever really used to create a gist of the profile of values, enabling recognition of the main peaks in particular.

EXAMPLE Mapping the population of trees for each 180 square km of land across the globe.

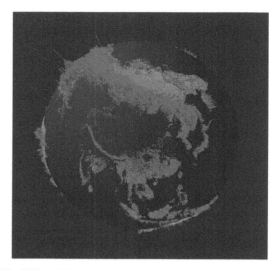

Figure 6.51 Trillions of trees

HOW TO READ IT & WHAT TO LOOK FOR

Acquaint yourself with the geographic region you are presented with and carefully consider the quantitative measure that is being represented. Establish the area size value associations, usually found via a legend. Glance across the entire chart to locate the large, medium and small shapes and perform global comparisons to establish the high-level ranking of biggest values > smallest. Identify any noticeable exceptions and/or outliers. Gradually zoom in your focus to perform increasingly local comparisons between neighbouring regional areas to identify any noticeable consistencies or inconsistencies between their values. Estimate (or read, if labels are present) the absolute values of specific regions of interest. Also note where there are no bars emerging from the surface.

PRESENTATION TIPS

INTERACTIVITY: Ideally prism maps would be provided with interactive features that allow panning around the map region to offer different viewing angles to overcome the perceptual difficulties of judging the dimensions of 3D forms in a 2D view. Without this, smaller values will be hidden behind the larger forms, just as smaller buildings are hidden by skyscrapers in a city.

ANNOTATION: Directly labelling the prism shapes is infeasible – at most you might include only a limited number of labels to provide spatial context and orientation against the largest forms. Legends explaining the size scales should ideally be placed as close to the map display as possible.

COLOUR: Most tools that enable this type of mapping will likely have visual property settings for a faux light effect, helping the physical shapes to emerge more prominently through light and shadow. Ensure colour assist in helping the shape of the forms to be as visible as possible, maybe with opacity to enable smaller values to be not entirely hidden behind any larger ones. When including a mapping layer image on the surface, ensure it is not overly competing for visual prominence by making it light in colour and possibly semi-transparent. Do not include any unnecessary geographical details that add no value to the spatial orientation or interpretation and clutter the display (e.g. roads, building structures).

COMPOSITION: Be aware that the transformation adjustments made by some map projections can distort the size of regions of the world, inflating their size relative to other regions.

VARIATIONS & ALTERNATIVES

Alternatives to the prism map, especially to avoid 3D form, include the 'proportional symbol map', which uses proportionally sized geometric shapes, and the 'choropleth map', which colour-codes regional shapes.

DOT MAP

ALSO KNOWN AS Dot distribution map, pointillist map, location map, dot density map

REPRESENTATION DESCRIPTION

A dot map displays the geographic density and distribution of phenomena on a map. It uses a point marker to indicate a categorical 'observation' at a geographical coordinate, which might be plotting instances of people, notable sites or incidences. The point marker is usually a filled, small dot. Colour can be used to distinguish categorical classifications. Sometimes a dot represents a one-to-one phenomenon (i.e. a single record at that location) and sometimes a dot will represent one-to-many phenomena (i.e. for an aggregated statistic whereby the location represents a logical mid-point). As the proliferation of GPS recording devices increases, the accuracy and prevalence of detailed location marked incidences are leading to increased potential for this type of approach. However, think carefully about the potential sensitivity of directly plotting a phenomenon or data incidence at a given location.

EXAMPLE Mapping each resident of the USA based on the location at which they were counted during the 2010 Census across different ethnicities.

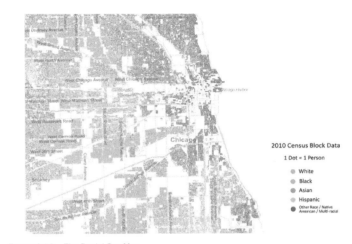

Figure 6.52   The Racial Dot Map

HOW TO READ IT & WHAT TO LOOK FOR

Acquaint yourself with the geographic region you are presented with and carefully consider the phenomenon that is being represented. Establish the unit of this measure (is it a one-to-one relationship or one-to-many?) by referring to a legend. If categorical colours have been deployed, establish the different classifications and associations. Scan the chart looking for the existence of noticeable clusters as well as the widely dispersed (and maybe empty) regions. Some of the most interesting observations come from individual outliers that stand out separately from others. Are there any patterns between the presence of dots and their geographical location? Are there any patterns across the points with similar categorical colour? Gradually zoom in your focus to perform increasingly local assessments between neighbouring regional areas to identify any noticeable consistencies or inconsistencies between their patterns.

PRESENTATION TIPS

INTERACTIVITY: One method for dealing with plotting high quantities of observations is to provide interactive semantic zoom features, whereby each time a user zooms in by one level of focus, the unit quantity represented by each dot decreases, from a one-to-many towards a one-to-one relationship.

ANNOTATION: Direct labelling is not necessary, just provide a limited number of regional labels to offer spatial context and orientation. Legends explaining the dot unit scale and any colour associations should ideally be placed as close to the map display as possible.

COLOUR: If colours are being used to distinguish the different categories, ensure these are as visibly different as possible. When including a mapping layer image in the background, ensure it is not overly competing for visual prominence by making it light in colour and possibly semi-transparent. Do not include any unnecessary geographical details that add no value to the spatial orientation or interpretation and clutter the display (e.g. roads, building structures).

COMPOSITION: Dot maps must always be displayed on a map that demonstrates an equal-area projection as the precision of the plotted locations is paramount. From a readability perspective, try to find a balance between making the size of the dots small enough to preserve their individuality but not too tiny to be indecipherable.

VARIATIONS & ALTERNATIVES

A 'dot density map' is a variation that involves plotting a representative quantity of dots equally (but randomly) across and within a defined spatial region. The position of individual dots is therefore not to be read as indicative of precise locations but used to form a measure of quantitative density. This offers a useful alternative to the choropleth map, especially when categorical separation of the dots through colour is of value. Plotting the location of an incidence of a phenomenon can transcend geographical mapping to any spatial display, such as the seat layout and availability at a theatre or on a flight, or showing the key patterns of play across a sports pitch.

FLOW MAP

ALSO KNOWN AS Connection map, route map, stream map, particle flow map

OVERLAYS

REPRESENTATION DESCRIPTION

A flow map shows the characteristics of the movement or flow of a phenomenon across spatial regions. It is often formed using line marks to map flow and combinations of attributes to display the characteristics of this flow. Examples might include the patterns of traffic and travel across or between given routes, the dynamics of the patterns of weather, or the movement patterns of people or animals. There is no fixed template for a flow map but it generally displays characteristics of origin and destination (positions on a map), route (using organic or vector paths), direction (arrow or tapered line width), categorical classification (colour) and some quantitative measure (line weight or motion speed).

EXAMPLE Mapping the average number of vehicles using Hong Kong's main network of roads during 2011.

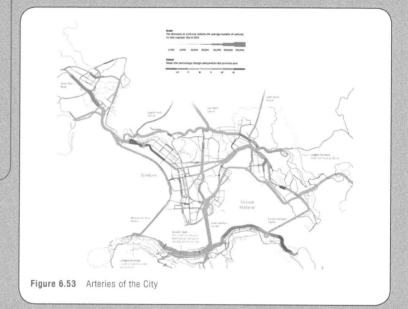

Figure 6.53   Arteries of the City

HOW TO READ IT & WHAT TO LOOK FOR

Acquaint yourself with the geographic region you are presented with and carefully consider the phenomenon that is being displayed. Establish the association of all visible attributes to understand fully their classification and representation, such as the use of quantitative scales (colour, line size or width) or categorical associations (colour). Scan the chart looking for the existence of patterns of movement, maybe through clustering or common direction, and identify any main hubs and densities within the network. Find the large and the small, the dense and the sparse, and draw out any patterns formed by colour classifications. Gradually zoom in your focus to perform increasingly local assessments between neighbouring regional areas to identify any noticeable consistencies or inconsistencies between their patterns.

PRESENTATION TIPS

INTERACTIVITY: Animated sequences will be invaluable to convey motion if the nature of the flow being presented has the relevant physics of movement.

ANNOTATION: Annotation needs will be unique to each approach and the inherent complexity or otherwise of the display. Often the general patterns may offer the sufficient level of readability without the need for imposing amounts of value labels.

COLOUR: The colour relationship needs careful consideration to get the right balance between the intricacies of the foreground data layer and the background mapping layer image. Ensure the background is not overly competing for visual prominence by making it light in colour and possibly semi-transparent. Do not include any unnecessary geographical details that add no value to the spatial orientation or interpretation, but do include those features that have a direct association with the subject matter (such as roads, routes, etc.).

COMPOSITION: Some degree of geographic distortion of routes or connecting lines may be required practically to display flow data. Choices like interpolation of lines to smooth an activities route or the merging of relatively similar pathways may be entirely legitimate but ensure that this is made clear to the reader.

VARIATIONS & ALTERNATIVES

There are naturally many variations in how you might show flow. It generally differs between whether you are showing point A to point B 'connection maps', more nuanced 'route maps' or surface phenomena such as 'particle flow maps'.

AREA CARTOGRAM

ALSO KNOWN AS Contiguous cartogram, density-equalizing map

REPRESENTATION DESCRIPTION

An area cartogram displays the quantitative values associated with distinct definable spatial regions on a map. Each geographic region is represented by a polygonal area based on its outline shape with the collective regional shapes forming the entire landscape. (Note that most tools for mapping have a predetermined reference between a region name and the dimensions of the regional polygon.) Quantitative values are represented by proportionately distorting (inflating or deflating) the relative size of and, to some degree, shape of the respective regional areas. Traditionally, area cartograms strictly aim to preserve the neighbourhood relationships between different regions. Colour is sometimes used to further represent the same quantitative value or to associate the region with a categorical classification. Area cartograms require the reader to be relatively familiar with the original size and shape of regions in order to be able to establish the degree of relative change in their proportions. Without this it is almost impossible to assess the degree of distortion and indeed to identify the regions themselves.

EXAMPLE Mapping the measures of climate change responsibility compared to vulnerability across all countries.

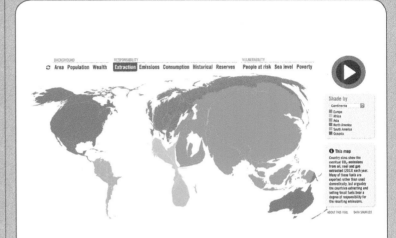

Figure 6.54 The Carbon Map

HOW TO READ IT & WHAT TO LOOK FOR

Acquaint yourself with the geographic region you are presented with and carefully consider the quantitative measure that is being represented. Establish the quantitative value scales or categorical classifications associated with the colour scale, usually found via a legend. Glance across the entire chart to locate the big-, small- and medium-sized shapes according to their apparent distortion. Identify any noticeable exceptions and/or outliers. Gradually zoom in your focus to perform increasingly local comparisons between neighbouring regional areas to identify any noticeable consistencies or inconsistencies between their values. Estimate (or read, if labels are present) the absolute values of specific regions of interest.

PRESENTATION TIPS

INTERACTIVITY: Animated sequences enabled through interactive controls can help to better identify instances and degrees of change but usually only over a small set of regions and only if the change is relatively smooth and sustained. Manual animation will help provide more control over the experience.

ANNOTATION: Directly labelling the regional areas with geographical details and the value they hold is likely to lead to too much clutter. You might include only a limited number of regional labels to provide spatial context and orientation.

COLOUR: Legends explaining any colour scales should ideally be placed as close to the map display as possible. The border colour and stroke width for each spatial area should be distinguishable to define the shape but not so prominent as to dominate attention, usually a subtle grey- or white-coloured thin stroke will be fine.

COMPOSITION: To aid the readability of the size of the distortions, it can be useful to present a thumbnail view of the undistorted original geographical layout to help the readers orient themselves with the changes.

VARIATIONS & ALTERNATIVES

Unlike contiguous cartograms, non-contiguous cartograms tend to preserve the shape of the individual polygons but modify the size and the neighbouring connectivity to other adjacent regional polygon areas. The best alternative ways of showing similar data would be to consider using the 'choropleth map' or 'Dorling cartogram'.

DORLING CARTOGRAM

ALSO KNOWN AS Demers cartogram

DISTORTIONS

REPRESENTATION DESCRIPTION

A Dorling cartogram displays the quantitative values associated with distinct, definable spatial regions on a map. Each geographic region is represented by a circle which is proportionally sized to represent a quantitative value. The placement of each circle generally resembles the region's geographic location with general preservation of neighbourhood relationships between adjacent shapes. Colour is used to associate the region with a categorical classification.

EXAMPLE Mapping the predicted electoral voting results for each state in the 2012 Presidential Election.

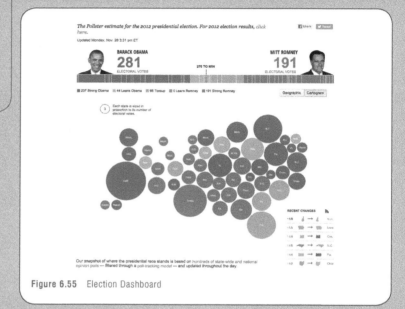

Figure 6.55   Election Dashboard

HOW TO READ IT & WHAT TO LOOK FOR

Acquaint yourself with the geographic region you are presented with and carefully consider the quantitative measure that is being represented. Establish the quantitative value scales or categorical classifications associated with the colour scale, usually found via a legend. Glance across the entire chart to locate the big-, small- and medium-sized shapes. Identify any noticeable exceptions and/or outliers. Gradually zoom in your focus to perform increasingly local comparisons between neighbouring regional areas to identify any noticeable consistencies or inconsistencies between their values. Estimate (or read, if labels are present) the absolute values of specific regions of interest.

PRESENTATION TIPS

INTERACTIVITY: Interactive features that enable annotation for category and value labelling can be useful to overcome the difficulties associated with the geographic distortion.

ANNOTATION: Directly labelling the shapes with geographical details and the value they hold is common, though you might restrict this to the circles that have sufficient size to hold such annotation. Otherwise you will need to decide how to handle the labelling of small values.

COLOUR: Legends explaining the size scales and colour associations should ideally be placed as close to the map display as possible. If colours are being used to distinguish the different categories, ensure these are as visibly different as possible.

COMPOSITION: Remember that preserving the adjacency with neighbouring regions is important. Dorling cartograms tend not to allow circles to overlap or occlude, so some accommodation of large values might result in location distortion.

VARIATIONS & ALTERNATIVES

A variation on the approach, called the 'Demers cartogram', involves the use of squares or rectangles instead of circles, which offers an alternative way of connecting adjacent shapes. Other approaches would be through the 'area cartogram' and the 'choropleth map'.

GRID MAP

ALSO KNOWN AS Cartogram, bin map, equal-area cartogram, hexagon bin map

REPRESENTATION DESCRIPTION

A grid map displays the quantitative values associated with distinct definable spatial regions on a map. Each geographic region (or a statistically consistent interval of space, known as a 'bin') is represented by a fixed-size uniform shape, sometimes termed a 'tile'. The shapes used tend to be squares or hexagons, though any tessellating shape would work in theory in order to help arrange all the regional tiles into a collective shape that roughly fits the real-world geographical adjacency. Colours are applied to each regional tile either to represent a quantitative value or to associate the region with a categorical classification. Note that the mark used for this chart type is a point rather than an area mark as its size attributes are constant.

EXAMPLE Showing the percentage of household waste recycled in each council region across London between April 2013 to March 2014.

London Squared Map ©2015 www.aftertheflood.co

Figure 6.56 London is Rubbish at Recycling and Many Boroughs are Getting Worse

HOW TO READ IT & WHAT TO LOOK FOR

Acquaint yourself with the geographic region you are presented with and carefully consider the quantitative measure that is being represented. Identify the general layout of the constituent tiles to determine how good a fit they are with their adjacent regions in absolute and relative geographical terms. Establish the categorical or quantitative classifications associated with the colour scale, usually found via a legend. Glance across the entire chart to locate the big, small and medium shaded tiles (if quantitative) or the main patterns formed by the categorical colouring. Identify any noticeable exceptions and/or outliers. Gradually zoom in your focus to perform increasingly local comparisons between neighbouring regional areas to identify any noticeable consistencies or inconsistencies between their values. Estimate (or read, if labels are present) the absolute values of specific regions of interest.

PRESENTATION TIPS

INTERACTIVITY: Interactive features that enable annotation for category and value labelling can be useful to overcome the difficulties associated with the geographic distortion.

ANNOTATION: Directly labelling the shapes with geographical details is usually too hard. Some versions of the 'grid map' will include abbreviated labels, maybe two digits, to indicate the region they represent and to aid orientation. Otherwise it may require interactivity to facilitate such annotations. Legends explaining the colour associations should ideally be placed as close to the map display as possible.

COLOUR: If colour is being used to distinguish the different categories, ensure they are as visibly different as possible.

COMPOSITION: The main challenge is to find the most appropriate and representative tile–region relationship (what is the right amount and geographical level for each constituent tile?) and to optimise the best-fit collective layout that preserves as many of the legitimate neighbouring regions as possible.

VARIATIONS & ALTERNATIVES

'Hexagon bin maps' are specific deployments of the grid map that offer a layout formed by a high resolution of smaller hexagons to preserve localised details. Beyond geographical space, the grid map approach is applicable to any spatial analysis such as in sports.

209

6.3 Influencing Factors and Considerations

Having covered the fundamentals of visual encoding and profiled many chart type options that deploy different encoding combinations you now need to consider the general factors that will influence your specific choices for which chart or charts to use for your data representation.

Choosing which chart type(s) to use is, inevitably, not a single-factor decision. Rather, as ever with data visualisation, it is an imperfect recipe made up of many ingredients. A pragmatic balance has to be found somewhere between taking on board the range of influencing factors that shape selections and not becoming frozen with indecision caused by the burden of having to consider so many different issues.

Firstly, you need to reflect on the relevant factors that emerge from the first three 'preparatory' stages of the design process and then supplement this by addressing the guidance offered by the three visualisation design principles introduced in Chapter 1. It must be emphasised that there are no direct answers provided for you here, simply guidance. How you might resolve the unique challenges posed by your project has to be something you arrive at yourself.

Formulating Your Brief

'The capability to cope with the technological dimension is a key attribute of successful students: coding - more as a logic and a mindset than a technical task - is becoming a very important asset for designers who want to work in Data Visualization. It doesn't necessarily mean that you need to be able to code to find a job, but it helps a lot in the design process. The profile in the (near) future will be a hybrid one, mixing competences, skills and approaches currently separated into disciplinary silos.' **Paolo Ciuccarelli, discussing students on his Communication Design Master Programme at Politecnico di Milano**

Skills and resources, frequency: What charts can you actually make and how efficiently can you create them? This is the big question. Having the ability to create a broad repertoire of different chart types is the vocabulary of this discipline, judging when to use them is the literacy. What will have a great influence on the ambitions of the type of charts you might employ is the 'expressiveness' of your abilities and that of the technology (applications, programs, tools) you have access to. Expressiveness is a term I first heard used in this context by Arvind Satyanarayan, a Computer Science PhD candidate at Stanford University. It describes the amount of variety and extent of control you are provided with by a given technology in the construction of your visualisation solution, so long as you also possess the necessary skills to exploit such features, of course:

- In a data representation context, maximum expressiveness means you can create any combination of mark and attribute encoding to display your data – that is, you can create many different charts. Programming libraries like D3.js and open source tools like R offer broad libraries of different chart options and customisations. The drawing-by-hand nature of

Adobe Illustrator would similarly enable you to create a wide range of solutions (though unquestionably more manual in effort and less replicable).

- Restricted expressiveness means you have much more limited scope to adapt different mark and attribute encodings. Indeed you might be faced with assigning data to the fixed encoding options afforded by a modest menu of chart types. A tool like Excel has a relatively limited range of (useful) chart types in its menu. While there are ways of enhancing the options through plugins and different 'workaround' techniques that broaden its scope, it is a relatively limited tool. It may, however, suffice for most people's visualisation ambitions. Elsewhere, there are many web-based visualisation creation tools which are of value for those who want quick and simple charting, though they certainly reduce the range of options and the capability to customise their appearance.

As you reflect on the gallery of charts, my advice would be to perform an assessment of the charts you can make using a scoring system as follows:

3 points	Charts you can personally create relatively easily
2	Charts you can make but involve a greater amount of time and effort, perhaps through your lack of confidence with a certain tool, and possibly involving some innovative workaround solution
1	Charts you can get collaborators or colleagues to create for you, but put you at the mercy of their capacity and availability to do so
0	Charts, currently at least, you might not be able to create at all

For any of the charts that fail to score 3 points, here are some strategies to dealing with this:

- Tools are continually being enhanced. The applications you use now that cannot create, for example, a Sankey diagram, may well offer that in the next release. So wait it out!
- For those charts that currently score 1 or 0 points, look around the web for examples of workaround approaches that will help you achieve them. For example, you might use conditional formatting in an Excel worksheet to create a rudimentary heat map. This is not a chart type offered as standard within the tool but represents an innovative solution through appropriating existing features intended to serve other purposes. Any such solutions, though, have to be framed by the frequency of your work – will this work realistically need to be replicable and repeatable (for example, every month) and does my solution make that achievable?
- Invest time in developing skills in the other tools to broaden your repertoire. Tools like R have a large community of users sharing code, tutorials and examples, resources that would greatly help to facilitate your learning.
- Lower your ambitions. Sometimes the most significant discipline to demonstrate is acknowledging what you cannot do and accepting that (at least, for now) you might need to sacrifice the ideal choices you would make for more pragmatic ones.

Purpose: Should you even seek to represent you data in chart form? Will it add any value, enabling new insights or greater perceptual efficiency compared with its non-visualised form?

> 'I was in the middle of this huge project, juggling as fast and as focused as I could, and I had this idea of a set of charts stuck in my head that kept resurfacing. And then, as we were heading close to deadline, I realized I couldn't do it. I failed. I couldn't make it work. Because we had pictures of the children, and that was enough … I had to let it go.' **Sarah Slobin, Visual Journalist, discussing a project profiling a group of families with children who have a fatal disease**

Will portraying your data via an elegantly presented table, offering the viewer the ability to look up and reference values, actually offer a more suitable solution? Do not rule out the value of a table. Additionally, perhaps you are trying to represent something in chart form that would actually be better displayed through information-based (rather than data-based) explanations using imagery, textual anecdotes, video and photos? Most of the time the charting of data will be fit for purpose, but just keep reminding yourself that you do not have to chart everything – just make sure you are doing it to add value.

Purpose map: In defining the 'tone' of the project, your were determining what the optimum perceptibility of your data would be for your audience. Your definitions were based on whether you were aiming to facilitate the *reading* of the data or more a general *feeling* of the data? Were you concerned with enabling precise and accurate perceptions of values or is it more about the sense-making of the big, medium and small judgments – getting the 'gist' of values more than reading back the values? Were there emotional qualities that you wanted to emphasise perhaps at the compromise of perceptual efficiency? Maybe there was a balance between the two?

How these tonal definitions apply specifically to data representation requires our appreciation of some fundamental theory about data visualisation. In his book *Semiology Graphique*, published in 1967, Jacques Bertin was the first, most notable author to propose the idea that different ways of encoding data might offer varying degrees of effectiveness in perception. In 1984 William Cleveland and Robert McGill published a seminal paper, 'Graphical Perception: Theory, Experimentation, and Application to the Development of Graphical Methods', that offered more empirical evidence of Bertin's thoughts. They produced a general ranking that explained which attributes used to encode quantitative values would facilitate the highest degree of perceptual accuracy. In 1986, Jock Mackinlay's paper, 'Automating the Design of Graphical Presentations of Relational Information', further extended this to include proposed rankings for encoding categorical nominal and categorical ordinal data types as well as quantitative ones. The table shown in Figure 6.57, adapted from Mackinlay's paper, presents the 'Ranking of Perceptual Tasks'.

In a nutshell, this ancestry of studies reveals that certain attributes used to encode data may make it easier, and others may make it harder, to judge accurately the values being portrayed. Let's illustrate this with a couple of examples. Looking at Figure 6.58, ask yourself: if A is 10, how big is B in the respective bar and circular displays?

In both cases the answer is B = 5, but while the B 'bar' being 5 feels about right, the idea that the B 'circle' is 5 does not feel quite right. That is because our ability to perform relative judgements for the length of bars is far more precise and accurate than the relative judgements for the area of circles. This is explained by the fact that when judging the variation in size of a line (bar) you are detecting change in a linear dimension, whereas the variation in size of a geometric area

Figure 6.57
The Ranking of
Perceptual Tasks

Qualitative **Nominal**	Qualitative **Ordinal**	Quantitative **Interval, Ratio**
Position	Position	Position
Colour (Hue)	Pattern (Density)	Size (Length)
Pattern (Texture)	Colour (Lightness)	Angle/Slope
Connection/Edge	Colour (Hue)	Size (Area)
Containment	Pattern (Texture)	Size (Volume)
Pattern (Density)	Connection/Edge	Pattern (Density)
Colour (Lightness)	Containment	Colour (Lightness)
Symbol/Shape	Size (Length)	Colour (Hue)
Size (Length)	Angle/Slope	Pattern (Texture)
Angle/Slope	Size (Area)	Connection/Edge
Size (Area)	Size (Volume)	Containment
Size (Volume)	Symbol/Shape	Symbol/Shape

Note that the attribute of 'Motion' was not included in this study. For the purposes of this display,
'Angle' and 'Slope' are combined whereas they were distinguished as separate in the study

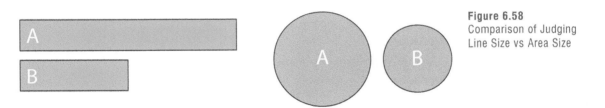

Figure 6.58
Comparison of Judging
Line Size vs Area Size

(circle) occurs across a quadratic dimension. If you look at the rankings in Figure 6.57 in the 'Quantitative' column, you will see the encoding attribute of *Length* is ranked higher than the attribute of *Area*.

Now let's consider an example (Figure 6.59) that shows the relative accuracy of using different dimensions of colour variation to represent categorical nominal values. In the next pair of charts you can see different attributes being used to represent the categorical groupings of the points in the respective scatter plots. On the left you can see variation in the attribute of colour hue (blue, orange and green) to separate the categories visually; on the right you will see the attribute of shape (diamond, circle and square) applied to the same category groupings. What you should be experiencing is a far more immediate, effortless and accurate sense of the groupings of the coloured category markers compared with the shaped category markers. It is simply easier to spot the associations through variation in colour than variation in shape. This explains why *colour hue* is much higher in the proposed rankings for nominal data than *shape*.

Figure 6.59
Comparison of
judging related
items using
variation in
colour (hue)
vs variation in
shape

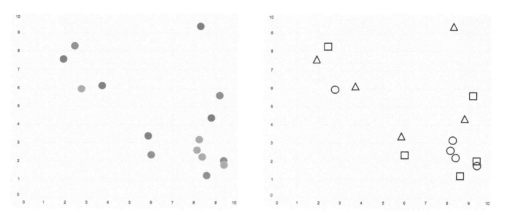

So you can see from these simple demonstrations that there are clearly ways of encoding data that will make it easier to read values accurately and efficiently. However, as Cleveland and McGill stress in their paper, this ranking should be taken as only one ingredient of guidance: 'The ordering does not result in a precise prescription for displaying data but rather is a framework within which to work'.

This is important to note because you have to take into account other factors. You have to decide whether precise perceiving is actually what you need to facilitate for your readers. If you do, then the likes of the bar chart – through the variation in length of a bar – will evidently offer a very precise approach. As stated in Chapter 3, that is why they are such an important part of your visual artillery.

However, sometimes getting a 'gist' of the data is sufficient. A few pages ago I presented an image of a bubble chart on my website's home page, showing the popularity of my blog posts over the previous 100-day period. The purpose of this display was purely to give visitors a sense of the general order of magnitude from the most popular to the relative least popular posts. I do not need visitors to form a precise understanding of absolute values or exact rankings. I just want them to get a sense of the ranking hierarchy. I can therefore justify moving down the quantitative attribute rankings proposed and deploy a series of circles that encode the visitor totals through the size of their area (colour is used to represent different article categories). The level of perceptibility (accuracy and efficiency) that I need to facilitate is adequately achieved by the resulting 'frogspawn'-like display. Furthermore, it offers an appealing and varied display that suits the purpose of this front-page navigation device.

In practice, what all this shows is that chart types vary in the relative efficiency and accuracy of perception offered to a viewer. Moreover, many of the charts shown in the gallery can therefore only ever facilitate a gist of the values of data due to the complexity of their mark and attribute combinations and the amount of data values they might typically contain (e.g. the treemap often has many parts of a whole in a single display). It is up to you to judge what the right threshold is for your purpose.

Working With Data

Data examination: Inevitably, the physical characteristics of your data are especially influential. *What* types of data you are trying to display will have a significant impact on *how* you are able to show them. Only certain types of data can fit into certain chart types; only certain chart types can accommodate certain types of data. That is why it is often most useful practically to think of this task in terms of chart types and particularly in terms of these as templates, able to accommodate specific types of data.

For example, representing data through a bar chart requires one categorical variable (e.g. department) and one quantitative variable (e.g. maximum age). If you want to show a further categorical variable (let's say, to break down departments by gender) you are going to need to switch 'template' and use something like a clustered bar chart which can accommodate this extra dimension.

I explained earlier how the shape of data influenced the viability of the flower metaphor used in the 'Better Life Index'. The range of categorical and quantitative values will certainly influence the most appropriate chart type choice. For example, suppose you want to show some part-to-whole analysis and you have only three parts (three sub-categories

> 'Effective graphics conform to the Congruence Principle according to which the content and format of the graphic should correspond to the content and format of the concepts to be conveyed.'
> **Barbara Tversky and Julie Bauer Morrison, taken from *Animation: Can it Facilitate?***

belonging to the major category or whole) then a treemap really does not make a great deal of sense – they are better at representing many parts to a whole. The unloved pie chart would probably suffice if the percentage values were quite diverse otherwise the bar chart would be best.

Beyond the size and shape of your data you also might be influenced by its inherent meaning. Sometimes, you will have scope in your encoding choices to incorporate a certain amount of visual immediacy in accordance with your topic. The flowers of the Better Life Index feel consistent in metaphor with the idea of better life: the more in bloom the flowers, the more colourful and proud each petal appears and the better the quality of life in that country. There is a congruence between subject matter and visual form. Think about the billionaires' project from earlier in the chapter, with rankings displayed by industry. Each point marking each billionaire was a small caricature face. This is not necessary – a small circular mark for each person would have been fine – but by using a face for the mark it creates a more immediate recognition that the subject matter is about people.

Data exploration: One consistently useful pointer towards how you might visually communicate your data to others is to consider which techniques helped *you* to unearth key insights when you were visually exploring the data. What chart types have you already tried out and maybe found to reveal interesting patterns? Exploratory data analysis is, in many ways, a bridge to visual communication: the charts you use to inform yourself often represent prototype thinking on how you might communicate with others. The design execution may end up being different once you introduce the influence of audience characteristics into your thinking, naturally, but if a method is already working, why not utilise the same approach again?

Establishing Your Editorial Thinking

Angle: When articulating the angles of analysis you intend to portray to your viewers, you are effectively dictating which chart types might be most relevant. If you intend to show how quantities have changed over time, for example, there will be certain charts best placed to portray that and many others that will not. By expressing your desired editorial angles of analysis in language terms, this will be extremely helpful in identifying the primary families of charts across the CHRTS taxonomy that will provide the best option.

It is vital to treat every representation challenge on its own merits – do not fall into the trap of going through the motions. Just because you have spatial data does not mean that the most useful portrayal of that data will be via a map. If the interesting insights are not regionally and spatially significant, then the map may not provide the most relevant window on that data. The composition of a map – the shape, size and positioning of the world's regions – is so diverse, inconsistent and truly non-uniform that it may hinder your analysis rather than illuminate it. So always make sure you have carefully considered the relevance of your chosen angle through your editorial thinking.

Trustworthy Design

Avoiding deception: In the discussion about tone I explained how variations in the potential precision of perception may be appropriate for the purpose and context of your work. Precision in perception is one thing, but precision in design is another. Being truthful and avoiding deception in how you portray data visually are fundamental obligations.

There are many ways in which viewers can be deceived through incorrect and inappropriate encoding choices. The main issues around deception tend to concern encoding the size of quantities. For beginners, these mistakes can be entirely innocent and unintended but need to be eradicated immediately.

- *Geometric calculations* – When using the area of shapes to represent different quantitative values, the underlying geometry needs to be calculated accurately. One of the common mistakes when using circles, for example, is simply to modify the diameters: if a quantitative value increases from 10 to 20, just double the diameter, right? Wrong. That geometric approach would be a mistake because, as viewers, when perceiving the size of a circle, it is the area, not the width, of the circle upon which we base our estimates of the quantitative value being represented.

Figure 6.60
Illustrating the correct and incorrect circle size encoding

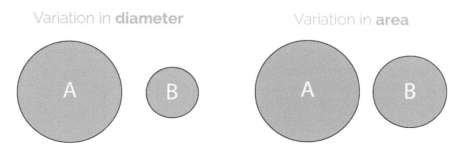

The illustration in Figure 6.60 shows the incorrect and correct ways of encoding two quantitative values through circle size, where the value of A is twice the size of B. The orange circle for B has half the *diameter* of A, the green circle for B has half the *area* of A. The green circle area calculations are the correct way to encode these two values, whereas the orange circle calculations disproportionately shrink circle B by halving the diameter rather than halving the area. This makes it appear much smaller than its true value.

- *3D decoration* – In the vast majority of circumstances the use of 3D charts is at best unnecessary and at worst hugely distorting in the display of data. I have some empathy for those who might volunteer that they have made and/or like the look of 3D charts. In the past I did too. Sometimes we don't know not to do something until we are told. So this is me, here and now, telling you.

The presence of 3D in visualisation tends to be motivated by a desire to demonstrate technical competence with the features of a tool in terms of 'look how many things I know how to do with this tool!' (users of Excel, I am pointing an accusatory finger at you right now). It is also driven by the appetite of rather unsophisticated viewers who are still attracted by the apparent novelty of 3D skeuomorphic form. (Middle and senior management of the corporate world, with your 'make me a fancy chart' commands, my finger of doom is now pointing in your direction.)

Using psuedo-3D effects in your charts when you have only two dimensions of data means you are simply decorating data. And when I say 'decorating', I mean this with the same sneer that would greet memories of avocado green bathrooms in 1970s Britain. A 3D visualisation of 2D data is gratuitous and distorts the viewer's ability to read values within any degree of acceptable accuracy. As illustrated in Figure 6.61, in perceiving the value estimates of the angles and segments in the respective pie charts, the 3D version makes it much harder to form accurate judgements. The tilting of the isometric plane amplifies the front part of the chart and diminishes the back. It also introduces a raised 'step' which is purely decorative, thus embellishing the judgement of the segment sizes.

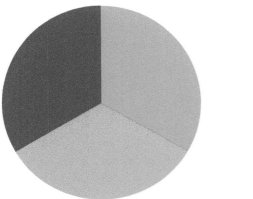 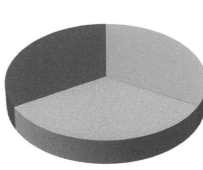

Figure 6.61
Illustrating the Distortions Created by 3D Decoration

- Furthermore, for charts based on three dimensions of data, 3D effects should only be considered if – and only if – the viewer is provided with means to move around the chart object to establish different 2D viewing angles *and* the collective representation of all the 3D of data makes sense in showing a whole 'system'.

- *Truncated axis scales* – When quantitative values are encoded through the height or length components of size (e.g. for bar charts and area charts), truncating the value axis (not starting the range of quantitative values from the true origin of zero) distorts the size judgements. I will look at this in more detail in the chapter on composition because it is ultimately more about the size considerations of scales and deployment of chart apparatus than necessarily just the representation choices.

Accessible Design

> The bullet chart is a derivative of the bar chart – the older, more sophisticated brother of the idiot gauge chart – but I didn't think it was necessary to profile as a separate chart type.

Encoded overlays: Beyond the immediate combinations of marks and attributes that comprise a given chart type, you may find value in incorporating additional detail to help viewers with the perceiving and interpretation task. *Encoded overlays* are useful to help explain further the context of values and amplify the interpretation of the good and the bad, the normal and the exceptional. In some ways these features might be considered forms of annotation, but as they represent data values (and therefore require encoding choices) it makes sense to locate these options within this chapter. There are many different types of visual overlays that may be useful to include:

Figure 6.62   Example of a Bullet Chart Using Banding Overlays

Figure 6.63   Excerpt from 'What's Really Warming the World?'

- *Bandings* – These are typically shaded areas that provide some sense of contrast between the main data value marks and contextual judgements of historic or expected values. In a bullet chart (Figure 6.62) there are various shaded bands that might help to indicate whether the bar's value should be considered bad, average or good. In the line chart (Figure 6.63) here you can see the observed rise in global temperatures. To facilitate comparison with potentially influencing factors, in the background there is a contextual overlay showing the change in greenhouse gases with banding to indicate the 95% confidence interval.

- *Markers* – Adding points to a display might be useful to show comparison against a target, forecast, a previous value, or to highlight actual vs budget. Figure 6.64 shows a chart that facilitates comparisons against a maximum value marker.
- *Reference lines* – These are useful in any display that uses position or size along an axis as an attribute for a quantitative value. Line charts or scatter plots (Figure 6.65) are particularly enhanced by the inclusion of reference lines, helping to direct the eye towards calculated trends, constants or averages and, with scatter plots specifically, the lines of best fit or correlation.

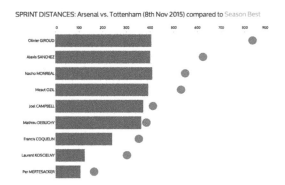

Figure 6.64   Example of Using Markers Overlays

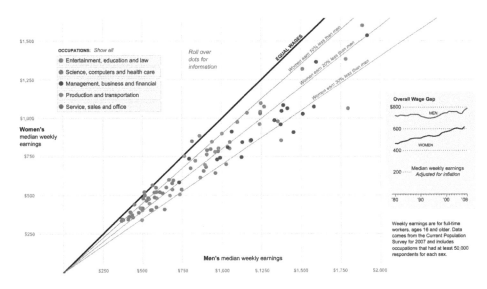

Figure 6.65
Why Is Her
Paycheck
Smaller?

Elegant Design

Visual appeal: This fits again with the thinking about 'tone' and may also be informed by some of the mental visualisations that might have formed in the initial stages of the process. Although you should not allow yourself to be consumed by ideas over the influence of the data, sometimes there is scope to squeeze out an extra sense of stylistic association between the visual and the content. For example, the 'pizza' pie chart in Figure 6.66 presents analysis about the political contributions made by companies in the pizza industry. The decision to use pizza slices as the basis of a pie chart makes a lot of sense. The graphic in Figure 6.67

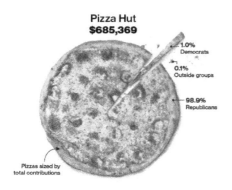

Counting the Dough

U.S. pizza companies made political contributions totaling $1.5 million in the 2012 and 2014 elections, with 88 percent going to Republican candidates and groups.

Pizza Hut
$685,369

1.0%
Democrats

0.1%
Outside groups

98.9%
Republicans

Pizzas sized by
total contributions

Smooth Sales
The online men's razor and blade market in the U.S. is growing, threatening traditional retail sales.

$111M
2013

$189M
2014

$141M
2015, through May

Source: Slice Intelligence   Photo: F. Martin Ramin/The Wall Street Journal; styling by Anne Cardenas   THE WALL STREET JOURNAL.

Figure 6.66   Inside the Powerful Lobby Fighting for Your Right to Eat Pizza

Figure 6.67   Excerpt from 'Razor Sales Move Online, Away From Gillette'

displays the growth in online sales of razors. Like the pizzas, the notion of creating bar charts by scraping away lengths of shaving foam offers a clever, congruent and charming solution.

Summary: Data Representation

Visual Encoding All charts are based on combinations of marks and attributes:

- Marks: represent records (or aggregation of records) and can be points, lines, areas or forms.
- Attributes: represent variable values held for each record and can include visual properties like position, size, colour, connection.

Chart Types If visual encoding is the fundamental theoretical understanding of data representation, chart types are the practical application. There are five families of chart types (CHRTS mnemonic):

CATEGORICAL	Comparing categories and distributions of quantitative values
HIERARCHICAL	Charting part-to-whole relationships and hierarchies
RELATIONAL	Graphing relationships to explore correlations and connections
TEMPORAL	Showing trends and activities over time
SPATIAL	Mapping spatial patterns through overlays and distortions

Influencing Factors and Considerations

- Formulating the brief: skills and resources – what charts can you make and how efficiently? From the definitions across the 'purpose map' what 'tone' did you determine this project might demonstrate?
- Working with data: what is the shape of the data and how might that impact on your chart design? Have you already used a chart type to explore your data that might prove to be the best way to communicate it to others?
- Establishing your editorial thinking: what is the specific angle of the enquiry that you want to portray visually? Is it relevant and representative of the most interesting analysis of your data?
- Trustworthy design: avoid deception through mistaken geometric calculations, 3D decoration, truncated axis scales, corrupt charts.
- Accessible design: the use of encoded overlays, such as bandings, markers, reference lines, can aid readability and interpretation.
- Elegant design: consider the scope of certain design flourishes that might enhance the visual appeal through the form of your charts whilst also preserving their function.

Tips and Tactics

- Data is your raw material, not your ideas, so do not arrive at this stage desperate and precious about wanting to use a certain data representation approach.
- Be led by the preparatory work (stages 1 to 3) but do use the chart type gallery for inspiration if you need to unblock!
- Be especially careful in how you think about representing instances of zero, null (no available data) and nothing (no observation).
- Do not be too proud to acknowledge when you have made a bad call or gone down a dead end.

What now? Visit **book.visualisingdata.com**

READING
Visit the chapter's library of further reading and references to continue your learning about data representation

EXERCISES
Undertake these practical exercises to help refine your skill and understanding about making effective data representation choices

CASE STUDY
Work through the next instalment of the Filmographics case-study narrative, discussing the data representation choices that were made

7

Interactivity

The advancement of technology has entirely altered the nature of how we consume information. Whereas only a generation ago most visualisations would have been created exclusively for printed consumption, developments in device capability, Internet access and bandwidth performance have created an incredibly rich environment for digital visualisation to become the dominant output. The potential now exists for creative and capable developers to produce powerful interactive and engaging multimedia experiences for cross-platform consumption.

Unquestionably there is still an fundamental role for static (i.e. not interactive) and print-only work: the scope offered by digital simply enables you to extend your reach and broaden the possibilities. In the right circumstances, incorporating features of interactivity into your visualisation work offers many advantages:

- It expands the physical limits of what you can show in a given space.
- It increases the quantity and broadens the variety of angles of analysis to serve different curiosities.
- It facilitates manipulations of the data displayed to handle varied interrogations.
- It increases the overall control and potential customisation of the experience.
- It amplifies your creative licence and the scope for exploring different techniques for engaging users.

The careful judgements that distinguish this visualisation design process must be especially discerning when handling this layer of the anatomy. Well-considered interactivity supports, in particular, the principle of 'accessible' design, ensuring that you are adding value to the experience, not obstructing the facilitation of understanding. Your main concern in considering potential interactivity is to ensure the features you deploy are useful. This is an easy thing to say about any context but just because you *can* does not mean to say you *should*. For some who possess a natural technical flair, there is often too great a temptation to create interactivity where it is neither required nor helpful.

Having said that, beyond the functional aspects of interactive design thinking, depending on the nature of the project there can be value attached to the sheer pleasure created by thoughtfully conceived interactive features. Even if these contribute only ornamental benefit there can be merit in creating a sense of fun and playability so long as such features do not obstruct access to understanding.

There is a lot on your menu when it comes to considering potential interaction design features. As before, ahead of your decision making about what you *should* do, you will first consider what you *could* do. To help organise your thinking, your options are divided into two main groups of features:

- Data adjustments: Affecting what data is displayed.
- Presentation adjustments: Affecting how the data is displayed.

> There is an ever-increasing range of interfaces to enable interaction events beyond the mouse/ touch through gesture interfaces like the Kinect device, oculus rift, wands, control pads. These are beyond the scope of this book but it is worth watching out for developments in the future, especially with respect to the growing interest in exploring the immersive potential of virtual reality (VR).

When considering potential interactive features you first need to recognise the difference between an *event*, the *control* and the *function*. The event is the input interaction (such as a click), applied to a control (maybe a button) or element on your display, with the function being the resulting operation that is performed (filter the data).

Where once we were limited to the mouse or the trackpad as the common peripheral, over the past few years the emergence of touch-screens in the shape of smartphones and tablets has introduced a whole new event vocabulary. For the purposes of this chapter we focus on the language of the mouse or trackpad, but here is a quick translation of the equivalent touch events. Note that arguably the biggest difference in assigning events to interactive data visualisations exists in the inability to register a mouseover (or 'hover') action with touch-screens.

Mouse/trackpad event	Touch event
Left click, right click	Single-finger tap, two-fingered tap
Double click	Double tap
Click, drag and drop	Tap, drag and drop
'Mouseover' or pointer 'hover'	Tap
Wheel scroll	Swipe (move), pinch/reverse pinch (for zoom)
Unique: keyboard controls	Unique: rotate

7.1 Features of Interactivity: Data Adjustments

> I will temporarily switch nomenclature to 'user' in this chapter because a more active role is needed than 'viewer'.

This first group of interactive features covers the various ways in which you can enable your users to adjust and manipulate your data. Specifically, they influence *what* data is displayed at a given moment.

Framing: There is only so much one can show in a single visualisation display and thus giving users the ability to modify criteria to customise what data is visible at any given point is a strong advantage. Going back to the discussion on editorial thinking, in Chapter 5, this set of adjustments would specifically concern the 'framing' of what data to isolate, include or exclude from view.

> For those of you familiar with databases, think of this group of features as similar in scope to modifying the criteria when querying data in a database.

Example events/controls	Example functions
Select a button or link	Apply a categorical data filter (one or several combinations)
Select an item from a menu list	
Select multiple items from a check-box or menu list	Apply a quantitative data filter (one value or range of values)
Select to alter the state of a toggle or radio button	Modify the data representation (chart type or encodings)
Alter the position of a handle along a scale slider	
Alter the position of two handles along a scale slider (to create a range)	Modify the values that form the basis of calculated results
Type a value into an input box	Reset all values to their original state

In 'Gun Deaths' (Figure 7.1), you can use the filters in the pop-up check-box lists at the bottom to adjust the display of selected categorical data parameters. The filtered data is then shown in isolation above the line from all non-selected groups, which are shown below the line. The 'Remove filters' link can be used to reset the display to the original settings.

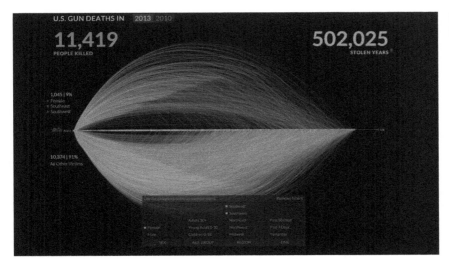

Figure 7.1
US Gun Deaths

Notice the subtle transparency of the filter menu (in Figure 7.1) so that it doesn't entirely occlude the data displayed beneath.

In the bubble map view of the 'FinViz' stock market analysis site, you can change the values of the handles along the axes to modify the maximum and minimum axis range, which allows you effectively to zoom in on

Figure 7.2
FinViz: Standard and Poor's 500 Index

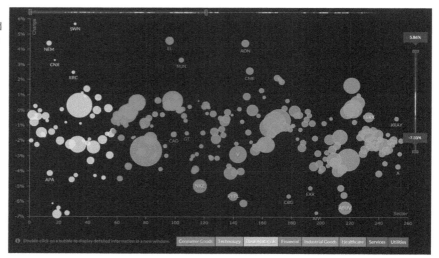

You will see that many of these interactive projects include links to share the project (or view of the project) with others via social media or through offering code to embed work into other websites. This helps to mobilise distribution and open up wider access to your work.

the records that match this criterion. You can also select the dropdown menus to change the variables plotted on each axis.

Navigating: There are dynamic features that enable users to expand or explore greater levels of detail in the displayed data. This includes lateral movement and vertical drill-down capabilities.

Example events/controls	Example functions
Select a mark from within a chart	Expand to reveal the sub-category value
Scroll to modify zoom level	Increase or decrease the level of detail of the data (its 'granularity')
Select zoom level from a scale	Zoom in and out of a view level
Select a button or link	Move ('pan') around a display
Select and drag	Access an underlying dataset
	Link to data sources

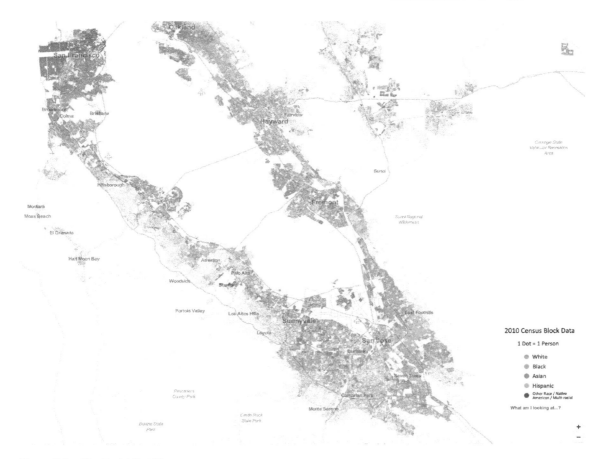

Figure 7.3 The Racial Dot Map

The dot map in Figure 7.3, showing the 2010 Census data, displays population density across the USA. As a user you can use a scrollable zoom or scaled zoom to zoom in and out of different map view levels. The map can also be navigated laterally to explore different regions at the same resolution.

This act of zooming to increase the magnification of the view is known as a geometric zoom. This is considered a data adjustment because through zooming you are effectively re-framing the window of the included and excluded data at each level of view.

In the 'Obesity Around the World' visualisation (Figure 7.4), selecting a continent connector expands the sub-category display to show the marks for all constituent countries. Clicking on the same connector collapses the countries to revert back to the main continent-level view.

The 'Social Progress Imperative' project (Figure 7.5) provides an example of features that enable users to view the tabulated form of the data – the highest level of detail – by selecting the 'Data

Figure 7.4
Obesity Around
the World

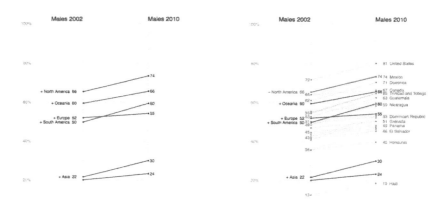

Table' tab. The data adjustment taking place here is through providing access to the data in a non-visual form. Users can also export the data by clicking on the relevant button to conduct further local analysis.

Figure 7.5
Excerpt
from 'Social
Progress
Index 2015'

Countries	Social Progress...	Basic Human Nee...	Foundations of ...	Opportunity
Norway	88.36	94.80	88.46	81.82
Sweden	88.06	94.83	86.43	82.93
Switzerland	87.97	95.66	86.50	81.75
Iceland	87.62	95.00	86.11	81.73
New Zealand	87.08	92.87	82.77	85.61
Canada	86.89	94.89	79.22	86.58
Finland	86.75	95.05	82.58	82.63
Denmark	86.63	96.03	82.63	81.23
Netherlands	86.50	94.80	83.81	80.88
Australia	86.42	93.73	79.98	85.55
United Kingdom	84.68	92.22	79.04	82.78
Ireland	84.66	93.68	76.34	83.97
Austria	84.45	95.04	82.53	75.77
Germany	84.04	94.12	81.50	76.49
Japan	83.15	95.01	78.78	75.66
United States	82.85	91.23	75.15	82.18

● Social Progress Index

● Basic Human Needs
● Foundations of Wellbeing
● Opportunity

Add aspect to compare

Group by country
Group by region

Display scores
Display ranks

Animating: Data with a temporal component often lends itself to being portrayed via animated sequences. The data adjustment taking place here involves the shifting nature of the timeframe in view at any given point. Operations used to create these sequences may be automatic and/or manual in nature.

Example events/controls	Example functions
Alter the position of a single handle along a scale slider	Automatically triggered animation
Alter the position of two handles along a scale slider (to create a range)	Automatic controlled animation (using buttons)
Select a button (play, pause, stop and reset, speed buttons)	Manually controlled animation (using a slider)
Land on the web page	

This next project (Figure 7.6) plots NFL players' height and weight over time using an animated heat map. When you land on the web page the animation automatically triggers. Once completed, you can also select the play button to recommence the animation as well as moving the handle along the slider to manually control the sequence. The gradual growth in the physical characteristics of players is clearly apparent through the resulting effect.

Sequencing: In contrast to animated sequences of the same phenomena changing over time, there are other ways in which a more discrete sequenced experience can suit your needs. This commonly exists by letting users navigate through predetermined, different angles of analysis about a subject. As you navigate through the sequence a narrative is constructed. This is a quintessential example of storytelling with data exploring the metaphor of the anecdote: 'this happened' and then 'this happened'...

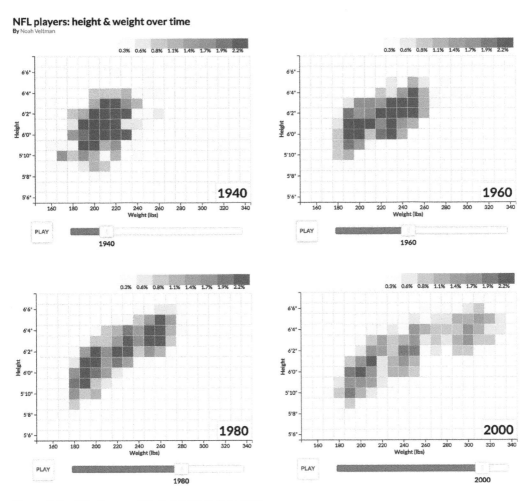

Figure 7.6 NFL Players: Height & Weight Over Time

Example events/controls	Example functions
Select tabs	Navigate through a sequence of pages
Select pagination elements (such as a dot stepper)	Navigate through a sequence of displays (within the page)
Select buttons	
Alter the position of a single handle along a scale slider	Manually controlled reveal/fade (using a slider)
Sideward scroll (unique to trackpads, Mac Mouse)	

The project 'How Americans Die' (Figure 7.7) offers a journey through many different angles of analysis. Clicking on the series of 'pagination' dots and/or the navigation buttons will take you through a pre-prepared sequence of displays to build a narrative about this subject.

Figure 7.7
Excerpt from 'How Americans Die'

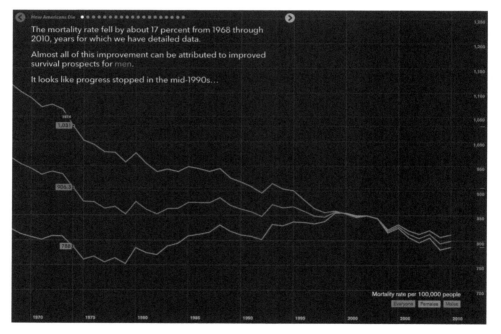

Sometimes data exists in only two states: a before and after view. Using normal animated sequences would be ineffective – too sudden and too jumpy – so one popular technique, usually involving two images, employs the altering of the position of a handle along a slider to reveal/fade the respective views. This offers a more graduated sequence between the two states and facilitates comparisons far more effectively as exhibited by the project shown in Figure 7.8.

A different example of sequencing – and an increasingly popular trend – is the vertical sequence. This article from the *Washington Post* (Figure 7.9) profiles the beauty of baseball

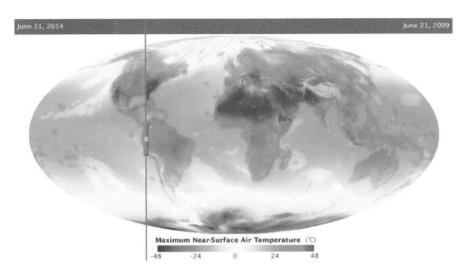

Figure 7.8 Model Projections of Maximum Air Temperatures Near the Ocean and Land Surface

player Bryce Harper's swing and uses a very slick series of illustrations to break down four key stages of his swing action. As you scroll down the page it acts like a lenticular print or flip-book animation. Notice also how well judged the styles of the illustrations are.

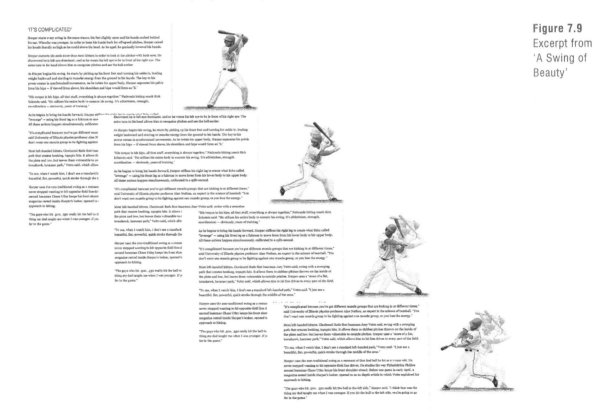

Figure 7.9 Excerpt from 'A Swing of Beauty'

Contributing: So far the features covered modify the criteria of what data is included/ excluded, that then help you dive deeper into the data, and move through sequenced views of that data. The final component of 'data adjustment' concerns contributing data. Sometimes there are projects that require user input, either for collecting further records to append and save to an original dataset or just for temporary (i.e. not held beyond the moment of usage) participation. Additionally, there may be scope to invite users to modify certain data in order to inform calculations or customise a display. In each case, the events and controls associated with this kind of interaction are designed to achieve one function: input data.

Example events/controls	Example functions
Select a button or link	Input data values
Select an item from a menu list	
Select multiple items from a check-box or menu list	
Select to alter the state of a toggle or radio button	
Select a mark from within a chart	
Alter the position of a handle along a scale slider	
Type a value into an input box	

The first example 'How well do you know your area?' (Figure 7.10) by ONS Digital, employs simple game/quiz dynamics to challenge your knowledge of your local area in the UK. Using the handle to modify the position along the slider you input a quantitative response to the

Figure 7.10
How Well Do
You Know
Your Area?

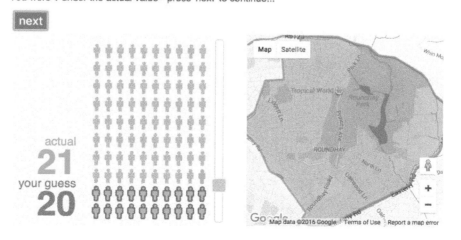

questions posed. Based on your response it then provides feedback revealing the level of accuracy of your estimation.

In the next project (Figure 7.11), by entering personal details such as your birth date, country and gender into the respective input boxes you learn about your place in the world's population with some rather sobering details about your past, present and future on this planet.

Figure 7.11   Excerpt from 'Who Old Are You?'

Figure 7.12 shows an excerpt from '512 Paths to the White House'. In this project the toggle buttons are used to switch between three categorical data states (unselected, Democratic and Republican) to build up a simulated election outcome based on the user's predictions for the winners in each of the key swing states. As each winner is selected, only the remaining possible pathways to victory for either candidate are shown.

Adjusting the position of the handle along the slider in the Better Life Index project (Figure 7.13) modifies the quantitative data value representing the weighting of importance you would attach to each quality of life topic. In turn, this modifies the vertical positioning of the country flowers based on the recalculated average quality of life.

> Inevitably data privacy and intended usage are key issues of concern for any project that involves personal details being contributed, so be careful to handle this with integrity and transparency.

Figure 7.12   512 Paths to the White House

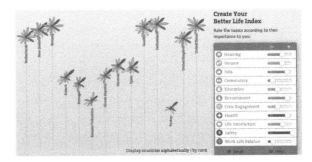

Figure 7.13   OECD Better Life Index

7.2 Features of Interactivity: Presentation Adjustments

In contrast to the features of 'data adjustment', this second group of interactive features does not manipulate the data but rather lets you configure the presentation of your data in ways that facilitate assistance and enhance the overall experience.

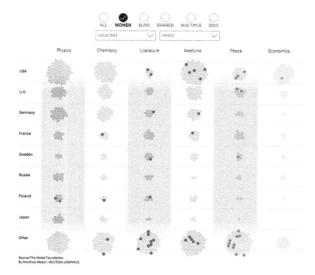

Figure 7.14   Nobel Laureates

Figure 7.15   Geography of a Recession

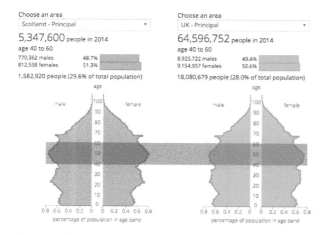

Figure 7.16   How Big Will the UK Population be in 25 Years' Time?

Focusing: Whereas the 'framing' features outlined previously modified what data would be included and excluded, 'focus' features control what data is visually emphasised and, sometimes, how it is emphasised. Applying such filters helps users select the values they wish to bring to the forefront of their attention. This may be through modifying the effect of depth through colour (foreground, mid-ground and background) or a sorting arrangement. The main difference with the framing features is that no data is eliminated from the display but simply relegated in its contrasting prominence or position.

The example in Figure 7.14 provides a snapshot of a project which demonstrates the use of a focus filter. It enables users to select a radio button from the list of options to emphasise different cohorts of all Nobel Laureates (as of 2015). As you can see the selections include filters for women, shared winners and those who were still living at the time. The selected Laureates are not coloured differently, rather the unselected values are significantly lightened to create the contrast.

The project shown in Figure 7.15 titled 'Geography of a Recession' allows users to select a link from the list of filters provided on the left to emphasise different cohorts of counties across the USA. Once again, the selected counties are not coloured differently here, the unselected regions are de-emphasised by washing-out their original shades.

'Brushing' data is another technique used to apply focus filters. In this next example (Figure 7.16), looking at the UK Census estimates for 2011, you use the cursor to select a range of marks from within the 'violin plot' display in order to view calculated statistics of those chosen values below the chart.

The next example (Figure 7.17), portraying the increase or cuts in Workers' Compensation benefits by US state, demonstrates a technique known as 'linking', whereby hovering over a mark in one chart display will then highlight

Example events/controls	Example functions
Select a button or link	Applying contrasting colours to emphasise selected data
Select an item from a menu list	
Select multiple items from a check-box or menu list	Rearrange the order of the data values
Select to alter the state of a toggle or radio button	Choose values to form statistical calculations
Alter the position of a handle along a scale slider	Highlight associated data values across charts
Alter the position of two handles along a scale slider (to create a range)	
Select a mark from within a chart	
Mouseover a mark from within a chart	
Select a range of marks from within a chart ('brushing')	
Type a value into an input box	

an associated mark in another chart to draw attention to the relationship. In this case, hovering over a state circle in any of the presented 'grid maps' highlights the same state in the other two maps to draw your eye to their respective statuses. You might also see this technique combined with a brushing event to choose multiple data marks and then highlight all associations between charts, as also demonstrated in the population 'violin plot' in Figure 7.16.

Figure 7.17
Excerpt from 'Workers' Compensation Reforms by State'

Sorting is another way of emphasising the presentation of data. In Figure 7.18, featuring work by the Thomson Reuters graphics team, 'ECB bank test results', you see a tabular display with sorting features that allow you to reorder columns of data by clicking on the column headers. For categorical data this will sort values alphabetically; for quantitative data, by value order. You can also hand-pick individual records from the table to promote them to the top of the display to facilitate easier comparisons through closer proximity.

> Linking and brushing are particularly popular approaches used for exploratory data analysis where you might have several chart panels and wish to see how a single record shows up within each display.

Annotating: As you saw in the previous chapter on data representation, certain combinations of marks and attributes may only provide viewers with a sense of the order of magnitude of the values presented. This might be entirely consistent with the intended tone of the project. However, with interactivity, you can at least enable viewers to interact with marks to view more details momentarily. This temporary display is especially useful because most data

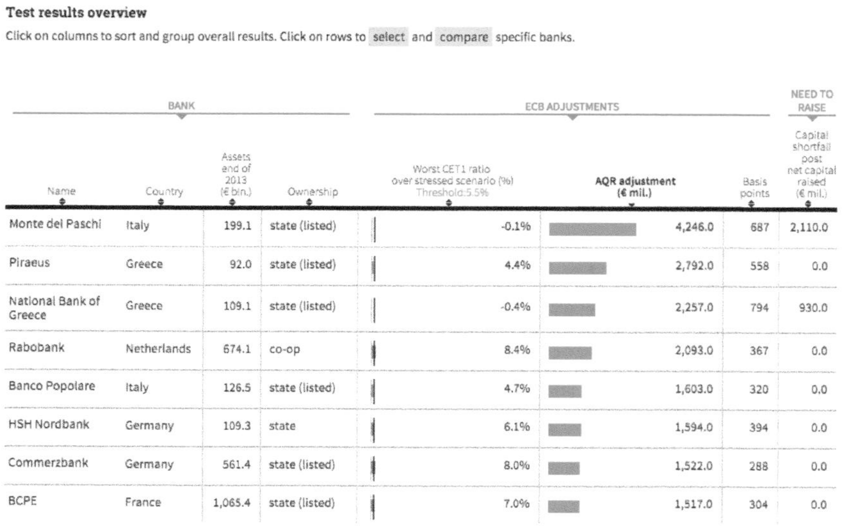

Figure 7.18
Excerpt from
'ECB Bank Test
Results'

Test results overview

Click on columns to sort and group overall results. Click on rows to `select` and `compare` specific banks.

Name	Country	Assets end of 2013 (€ bln.)	Ownership	Worst CET1 ratio over stressed scenario (%) Threshold:5.5%	AQR adjustment (€ mil.)		Basis points	Capital shortfall post net capital raised (€ mil.)
Monte dei Paschi	Italy	199.1	state (listed)	-0.1%		4,246.0	687	2,110.0
Piraeus	Greece	92.0	state (listed)	4.4%		2,792.0	558	0.0
National Bank of Greece	Greece	109.1	state (listed)	-0.4%		2,257.0	794	930.0
Rabobank	Netherlands	674.1	co-op	8.4%		2,093.0	367	0.0
Banco Popolare	Italy	126.5	state (listed)	4.7%		1,603.0	320	0.0
HSH Nordbank	Germany	109.3	state	6.1%		1,594.0	394	0.0
Commerzbank	Germany	561.4	state (listed)	8.0%		1,522.0	288	0.0
BCPE	France	1,065.4	state (listed)	7.0%		1,517.0	304	0.0

representations are already so busy that permanently including certain annotated apparatus (like value labels, gridlines, map layers) would overly clutter the display.

Example events/controls	Example functions
Select a link or button	Reveal annotations in a local tooltip/pop-up
Select a mark from within a chart	Reveal annotations in a separate panel
Mouseover a mark from within a chart	
Select to alter the state of a toggle or radio button	
Alter the position of a handle along a scale slider	

The example in Figure 7.19, profiles the use of language throughout the history of US Presidents' State of the Union addresses, using circle sizes to encode the frequency of different word mentions, giving a gist of the overall quantities and how patterns have formed over time. By hovering over each circle you get access to a tooltip dialogue box which reveals annotations such as the exact word-use quantities and extra contextual commentary.

One issue to be aware of when creating pop-up tooltips is to ensure the place they appear does not risk obstructing the view of important data in the chart beneath. This can be especially intricate to handle when you have a lot of annotated detail to share. One tactic is to utilise otherwise-empty space on your page display, occupying it with temporary annotated captions only when triggered by a select or hover event from within a chart.

Orientating: A different type of interactive annotation comes in the form of orientation devices, helping you to make better sense of your location within a display – where you are or what values you are looking at. Some of these functions naturally supplement features listed in the previous section about 'data adjustment' specifically for navigation support.

Rhetoric

The absence of "God" from earlier addresses surprised Fields, who said earlier references framed God as a "divine majesty," but in later political rhetoric, God has been treated more like an old buddy, one who understands and likes us and one whom we like and understand."

"Must" was a favorite rallying word of Franklin D. Roosevelt, who used his addresses to assert confidence and assured determination to the nation. The trend continued to blossom in subsequent decades.

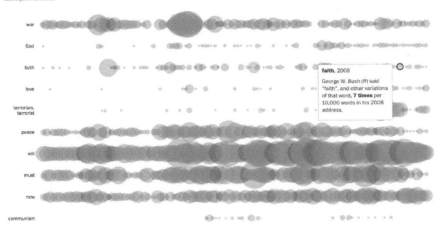

faith, 2008

George W. Bush (R) said "faith", and other variations of that word, **7 times** per 10,000 words in his 2008 address.

Figure 7.19
Excerpt from 'History Through the President's Words'

Example events/controls	Example functions
Select a link or button	Display values for current position
Select a mark from within a chart	Show visual guides for current position
Mouseover a mark from within a chart	Reveal layer of chart apparatus
Select to alter the state of a toggle or radio button	Highlight changes
Scroll to move	

This snapshot, again from the 'How Americans Die' project (Figure 7.20), dynamically reveals the values of every mark (both x and y values) in this line chart depending on the hover position of the cursor. This effect is reinforced by visual guides extending out to the axes from the current position.

Figure 7.21 displays the language of tweets posted over a period of time from the New York City area. Given the density and number of data points, displaying the details of the mapping layer would be quite cluttered, yet this detail would provide useful assistance for judging the location of the data patterns. The effective solution employed

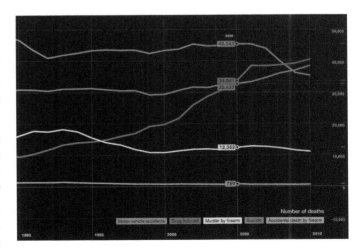

Figure 7.20   Excerpt from 'How Americans Die'

Figure 7.21
Twitter NYC:
A Multilingual
Social City

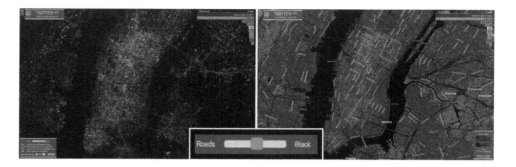

Figure 7.22   Killing the Colorado: Explore the Robot River

lets you access both views by providing an adjustable slider that allows you to modify the transparency of the network of roads to reveal the apparatus of the mapping layer.

Finally, as mentioned in the previous section, navigating through digital visualisation projects increasingly uses a vertical landscape to unfold a story (some term this 'scrollytelling'). Navigation is often seamlessly achieved by using the scroll wheel to move up and down through the display. To assist with orientation, especially when you have a limited field of view of a spatial display, a thumbnail image might be used to show your current location within the overall journey to give a sense of progress. The project featured in Figure 7.22 is a great example of the value of this kind of interface, providing a deep exploration of some of the issues impacting on the Colorado River.

7.3 Influencing Factors and Considerations

You now have a good sense of the possibilities for incorporating interactive features into your work, so let's turn to consider the factors that will have most influence on which of these techniques you might need to or choose to apply.

Formulating Your Brief

Skills and resources: Interactivity is unquestionably something that many people aspire to create in their visualisation work, but it is something greatly influenced by the skills possessed, the technology you have access to and what they offer. These will be the factors that ultimately shape your ambitions. Remember, even in common desktop tools like Excel and Powerpoint, which may appear more limited on this front, there are ways to incorporate interactive controls (e.g. using VBA in Excel) to offer various adjustment features (e.g. links within Powerpoint slides to create sequences and navigate to other parts of a document).

Timescales: It goes without saying that if you have a limited timeframe in which to complete your work, even with extensive technical skills you are going to be rather pushed in undertaking any particularly ambitious interactive solutions. Just because you want to does not mean that you will be able to.

Setting: Does the setting in which the visualisation solution will be consumed lend itself to the inclusion of an interactive element to the experience? Will your audience have the time and know-how to take full advantage of multi-interactive features or is it better to look to provide a relatively simpler, singular and more immediate static solution?

Format: What will be the intended output format that this project needs to be created for? What device specifications will it need to work across? How adaptable will it need to be?

The range and varied characteristics of modern devices present visualisers (or perhaps more appropriately, at this stage, developers) with real challenges. Getting a visualisation to work consistently, flexibly and portably across device types, browsers and screen dimensions (smartphone, tablet, desktop) can be something of a nightmare. Responsive design is concerned with integrating automatic or manually triggered modifications to the arrangement of contents within the display and also the type and extent of interactive features that are on offer. Your aim is to preserve as much continuity in the core experience as possible but also ensure that the same process and outcome of understanding can be offered to your viewers.

While the general trend across web design practice is heading towards a mobile-first approach, for web-based data visualisation developments there is still a strong focus on maximising the capabilities of the desktop experience and then maybe compromising, in some way, the richness of the mobile experience.

For ProPublica's work on 'Losing Ground' (Figure 7.23), the approach to cross-platform compatibility was based around the rule of thumb 'smallify or simplify'. Features that worked on

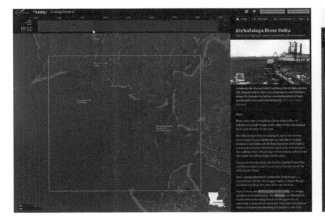 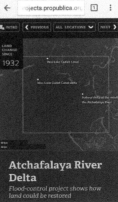

Figure 7.23
Losing Ground

ProPublica's primary platform of the desktop would have to be either simplified to function practically on the smartphone or simply reduced in size. You will see in the pair of contrasting images how the map display is both shrunk and cropped, and the introductory text is stripped back to only include the most essential information.

Other format considerations include whether your solution will be primarily intended for the Web, but will it also need to work in print? The proverb 'horses for courses' comes to mind here: solutions need to be created as fit for the format it will be consumed in. The design features that make up an effective interactive project will unlikely translate directly as a static, print version. You might need to pursue two parallel solutions to suit the respective characteristics of each output format.

Another illustration of good practice from the 'History through the Presidents' words' (Figure 7.24) includes a novel 'Download graphic' function which, when selected, opens up an entirely different static graphic designed to suit a printable, pdf format.

Figure 7.24

Excerpt from 'History Through the President's Words'

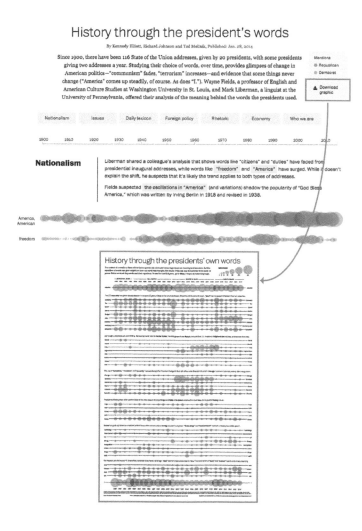

Purpose map: Interactivity does not only come into your thinking when you are seeking to create 'Exploratory' experiences. You may also employ interactive features for creating 'Explanatory' visualisations, such as portraying analysis across discrete sequenced views or interactively enabling focus filters to emphasise certain characteristics of the data. The general position defined on the purpose map will not singularly define the need for interactivity, rather it will inform the type of interactivity you may seek to incorporate to create the experience you desire.

There will also often be scope for an integrated approach whereby you might lead with an explanatory experience based around showing headline insights and then transitions into a more exploratory experience through offering a set of functions to let users interrogate data in more detail.

Working With Data

Data examination: As profiled with the functions to facilitate drill-down navigation, one of the keen benefits of interactivity is when you have data that is too big and too broad to show in one view. To repeat, you can only show so much in a single-screen display. Often you will need to slice up views across and within the various hierarchies of your data.

One particular way the physical properties of the data will inform your interaction design choices is with animation. To justify an animated display over time, you will need to consider the nature of the change that exists in your data. If your data is not changing much, an animated sequence may simply not prove to be of value. Conversely, if values are rapidly changing in all dimensions, an animated experience will prove chaotic and a form of change blindness will occur. It may be that the intention is indeed to exhibit this chaos, but the value of animated sequences is primarily to help reveal progressive or systematic change rather than random variation.

The speed of an animation is also a delicate matter to judge as you seek to avoid the phenomenon of change blindness. Rapid sequences will cause the stimulus of change to be missed; a tedious pace will dampen the stimulus of change and key observations may be lost. The overall duration will, of course, be informed by the range of values in your temporal data variable. There is no right or wrong here, it is something that you will get the best sense of by prototyping and trialling different speeds.

Establishing Your Editorial Thinking

Angle, framing and focus: If you have multiple different angles of analysis you wish to portray then these will have to be accommodated within the space allocated. Alternatively, using interactivity, you could provide access to them via sequenced views or menus enabling their selection. The value of incorporating the potential features to achieve this – and the specific range of different options you do wish to facilitate – will be informed by the scope of the decisions you made in the editorial thinking stages.

Thinking again about animations, you must consider whether an animated sequence will ulti-mately convey the clearest answer to an angle of interest about how something has changed over time. This really depends on what it is you want to show: the dynamics of a 'system' that changes over time or a comparison between different states over time?

The animated project in Figure 7.25 shows the progressive clearing of snow across the streets of New York City during the blizzard of February 2014. The steady and connected fluidity of progress of the snow-clearing is ideally illustrated through the intervals of change across the 24 hours shown.

Figure 7.25
Plow: Streets
Cleared of Snow
in New York City

Streets cleared of snow in New York City as of
2:00 p.m. on **February 8th**

A blizzard came through the northeast during the first week of February 2013. The NYC Department of Sanitation posted a map showing when roads are plowed, updating every 30 minutes. The maps shown here illustrate 24 hours of that data, which I scraped starting just after noon on February 8th.

Dark lines indicate roads that were cleared of snow within the previous hour; lighter lines have gone longer since being plowed.

Sometimes, you might wish to compare one moment directly against another. With ani-mated sequences, there is a reliance on memory to conduct this comparison of change. However, our ability to recall is fleeting at best and weakens the further apart (in time) the basis of the comparison has occurred. Therefore, to facilitate such a comparison you ideally need to juxtapose individual frames within the same view. The most common technique used to achieve this is through *small multiples*, where you repeat the same representation for each moment in time of interest and present them collec-tively in the same view, often through a grid layout. This enables far more incisiv

'Generations of masterpieces portray the legs of galloping horses incorrectly. Before stop-gap photography, the complex interaction of horses' legs simply happened too fast to be accurately apprehended ... but in order to see the complex interaction of moving parts, you need the motion.' [Paraphrasing] **Barbara Tversky and Julie Bauer Morrison, taken from *Animation: Can it Facilitate?***

comparisons, as you can see through 'The Horse in Motion' work by Eadward Muyrbidge, which was used to learn about the galloping form of a horse by seeing each stage of the motion through individually framed moments.

Figure 7.26
The Horse in
Motion

Data Representation

Chart type choice: Some charts are inherently visually complex and ideally need interactivity to make them more accessible and readable for the viewer. The bump chart, chord diagram, and Sankey diagram are just a few of the charts that are far more readable and, by extension, usable if they can offer users the means to filter or focus on certain selected components of the display through interactivity.

Trustworthy Design

Functional performance: Faith in the reliability, consistency and general performance of a visualisation is something that impacts on the perception of a project as 'trustworthy'. Does it do what it promises and can I trust the functions that it performs? Projects that involve the collection of user-inputted data will carry extra risk around trust: how will the data be used and stored? You need to alleviate any such concerns upfront.

'Confusing widgets, complex dialog boxes, hidden operations, incomprehensible displays, or slow response times … may curtail thorough deliberation and introduce errors.' **Jeff Heer and Ben Schneiderman**, taken from *Interactive Dynamics for Visual Analysis*

Accessible Design

Useful: Does it add value? Resort to interactivity only when you have exhausted the possibility of an appropriate and effective static solution. Do not underestimate how effective a well-conceived and executed static presentation of data can be. This is not about holding a draconian view about any greater merits offered by static or print work, but instead recognising that the brilliance of interactivity is when it introduces new means of engaging with data that simply could not be achieved in any other way.

Unobtrusive: As with all decisions, an interactive project needs to strive for the optimum ease of usability: minimise the friction between the act of engaging with interactive features and the understanding they facilitate. Do not create unnecessary obstacles that stifle sparks of curiosity and the scent of intrigue that stirs within the user. The main watchword here is affordance, making interactive features seamless and either intuitive or at least efficiently understandable.

Visual accessibility: To heighten the accessibility levels of your work you may offer different presentations of it. For people with visual impairments you might offer options to magnify the view of your data and all accompanying text. For those with colour deficiencies, as you will learn about shortly, you could offer options to apply alternative, colour-blind friendly palettes. A further example of this is seen with satellite navigation devices whereby the displayed colour combinations change to better suit the surrounding lightness or darkness at a given time of day.

Elegant Design

Feature creep: The discipline required to avoid feature creep is indisputable. The gratuitous interactive operation of today is the equivalent of the flashy, overbearing web design trends of the late 1990s and early 2000s. People were so quick and so keen to show how competent and expressive they could be through this (relatively) new technology that they forgot to judge if it added value.

If your audience is quite broad you may be (appropriately) inclined to cover more combinations of features than are necessary in the hope of responding to as many of the anticipated enquiries as well as possible and serving the different types of viewer. Judging the degree of flexibility is something of a balancing act within a single project: you do not want to overwhelm the user with more adjustments than they need, nor do you want to narrow the scope of their likely interrogations. For a one-off project you have to form your own best judgement; for repeatedly used projects you might have scope to accommodate feedback and iteration.

Minimise the clicks: With visualisation you are aiming to make the invisible (insights) visible. Conversely, to achieve elegance in design you should be seeking to make visible design features as seamlessly inconspicuous as possible. As Edward Tufte stated, 'the best design is invisible; the viewer should not see your design. They should only see your content'.

Fun: A final alternative influence is to allow yourself room for at least a little bit of fun. So long as the choices do not gratuitously interrupt the primary objective of facilitating understanding, one should not downplay the heightened pleasure that can be generated by interactive features that might incorporate an essence of playability.

Summary: Interactivity

Data adjustments affect what data is displayed and may include the following features:

- Framing: isolate, include or exclude data.
- Navigating: expand or explore greater levels of detail in the displayed data.
- Animating: portray temporal data via animated sequences.
- Sequencing: navigate through discrete sequences of different angles of analysis.
- Contributing: customising experiences through user-inputted data.

Presentation adjustments affect how the data is displayed and may include the following features:

- Focusing: control what data is visually emphasised.
- Annotating: interact with marks to bring up more detail.
- Orientating: make better sense of your location within a display.

Influencing Factors and Considerations

- Formulating the brief: skills and resources, timescales, setting, and format will all influence the scope of interactivity. What experience are you facilitating and how might interactive options help achieve this?
- Working with data: what range of data do you wish to include? Large datasets with diverse values may need interactive features to help users filter views and interrogate the contents.
- Establishing your editorial thinking: choices made about your chosen angle, as well as definitions for framing and focus will all influence interactive choices, especially if users must navigate to view multiple angles of analysis or representations portrayed through animated sequences.
- Data representation: certain chart choices may require interactivity to enable readability.
- Trustworthy design: functional performance and reliability will substantiate the perception of trust from your users.
- Accessible design: any interactive feature should prove to be useful and unobtrusive. Interactivity can also assist with challenges around visual accessibility.
- Elegant design: beware of feature creep, minimise the clicks, but embrace the pleasure of playability.

Tips and Tactics

- Initial sketching of concepts will be worth doing first before investing too much time jumping into prototype mode.
- Project management is critical when considering the impact of development of an interactive solution.
- Backups, contingencies, version control.
- Do not be precious about – nor overly impressed with – 'cool'-sounding interaction features that will disproportionately divert precious resources (time, effort, people).
- Beware of feature creep: keep focusing on what is important and relevant. A technical achievement is great for you, but is it great for the project?
- Version control and file management will be important here.

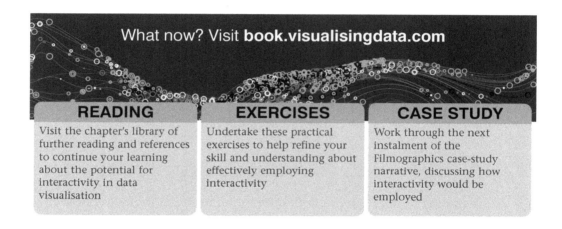

What now? Visit book.visualisingdata.com

READING	EXERCISES	CASE STUDY
Visit the chapter's library of further reading and references to continue your learning about the potential for interactivity in data visualisation	Undertake these practical exercises to help refine your skill and understanding about effectively employing interactivity	Work through the next instalment of the Filmographics case-study narrative, discussing how interactivity would be employed

8

Annotation

Annotation is the third layer of the visualisation design anatomy and is concerned with the simple need to explain things: what is the right amount and type of help your viewers will need when consuming the visualisation?

Annotation is unquestionably the most often neglected layer of the visualisation anatomy. Maybe this is because it involves the least amount of pure design thinking relative to the other matters requiring attention, like interactivity and colour. More likely, it is because effective annotation requires visualisers truly to understand their intended audience. This can be a hard frame of mind to adopt, especially when your potential viewers are likely to have a diverse knowledge, range of interests and capability.

In contrast to the greater theoretical and technical concerns around data representation, colour and interactivity, I find thinking about annotation relatively refreshing. It is not only uncomplicated and based on a huge dose of common sense, but also hugely influential, especially in directly facilitating understanding.

Annotation choices often conform to the Goldilocks principle: too much and the display becomes cluttered, overwhelming, and potentially unnecessarily patronising; too little and the viewers may be inappropriately faced with the prospect of having to find their own way around a visualisation and form their own understanding about what it is showing.

Later in this chapter we will look at the factors that will influence your decision making but to begin with here is a profile of some of the key features of annotated design that exist across two main groups:

- Project annotations: helping viewers understand what the project is about and how to use it.
- Chart annotations: helping viewers perceive the charts and optimise their potential interpretations.

8.1 Features of Annotation: Project Annotation

This collection of annotation options is related to decisions about how much and what type of help you might need to offer your audiences in their understanding of the background, function and purpose of your project.

Headings: The *titles* and *subtitles* occupy such prime real estate within your project's layout, yet more often than not visualisers fail to exploit these to best effect. There are no universal practices for what a heading should do or say; this will vary considerably between subject areas and industries, but should prove fundamentally useful.

Figure 8.1   A Sample of Project Titles

Tracking Super Bowl Tickets: Daily Price, Supply on Secondary Market

Presidential Approval, Ike to Obama

Why Peyton Manning's Record Will Be Hard to Beat

How well do you know your area?

How Y'all, Youse and You Guys Talk

Black Students Are Underrepresented On Campus

Song Structure

How did the form of Beatles songs evolve?

Which companies caused global warming?

wind map

Lunge Feeding

SPOTLIGHT ON PROFITABILITY

Counting the Dough

THE COUNTRIES WITH THE MOST LAND NEIGHBOURS

Arteries of the city

Global Ph.D.s Gender Gap (2010)

Razors Are for the Regular Season

Comparing Critics Scores (Rotten Tomatoes) for major movie franchise (Dec 2014)

'Avengers' characters' appearances over time

The primary aim of a title (and often subtitle combination) is to inform viewers about the immediate topic or display, giving them a fair idea about what they are about to see. You might choose to articulate the essence of the curiosity that has driven the project by framing it around a question or maybe a key finding you unearthed following the work.

Subheadings, *section headings* and *chart titles* will tend to be more functional in their role, making clear to the viewer the contents or focus of attention associated with each component of the display. Your judgement surrounds the level of detail and the type of language you use in each case to fit cohesively with the overall tone of the work.

Introductions: Essentially working in conjunction with titles, *introductions* typically exist as short paragraphs that explain, more explicitly than a title can, what the project is about. The content of this introduction might usefully explain in clear language terms some of the components you considered during the editorial thinking activity, such as:

• details of the reason for the project (source curiosity);
• an explanation of the relevance of this analysis;
• a description of the analysis (angle, framing) that is presented;
• expression of the main message or finding that the work is about to reveal (possibly focus).

Some introductions will extend beyond a basic description of the project to include thorough details of where the data comes from and how it has been prepared and treated in advance of its analysis (including any assumptions, modifications or potential shortcomings). There may also be further links to 'read more' detail or related articles about the subject.

Figure 8.2
Excerpt from
'The Color
of Debt'

Introductions may be presented as fixed text located near the top (or start) of a project (usually underneath a title) as in Figure 8.2 or, through interactivity, may be hidden from view and brought up in a separate window or pop-up to provide the details upon request.

User guides: As you have seen, some projects can incorporate many different features of interactivity. While they may not necessarily be overly technical – and therefore not that hard to learn how to use them – the full repertoire of features may be worth walking through, as in Figure 8.3. This is important to consider so that, as a visualiser, you can be sure your users are acquainted with the entire array of options they have to explore, interrogate and control their experience. You should want people to fully utilise all the different features you have carefully curated and created, so it is in everyone's interest to think about including these types of *user guides*.

Multimedia: There is increasing potential and usage of broader media assets in visualisation design work beyond charts, such as video and imagery. In visualisation this is perhaps a relatively contemporary trend (infographics have incorporated such media but visualisations generally have done so far less) and, in some ways, reflects the ongoing blurring of boundaries between this and other related fields. Incorporating good-quality and sympathetically styled assets like illustrations or photo-imagery can be a valuable complementary device alongside your data representation elements.

In the 'Color of Debt' (Figure 8.4) project, different neighbourhoods of Chicago that have been hardest hit by debt are profiled using accompanying imagery to show more graphic context of the communities affected, including a detailed reference map of the area and an animated panel displaying a sequence of street view images.

Imagery, in particular, will be an interesting option to consider when it adds value to help exhibit the subject matter in tangible form, offering an appealing visual hook to draw people in or simply to aid immediate

Figure 8.3   Excerpt from 'Kindred Britain'

Figure 8.4
Excerpt from 'The
Color of Debt'

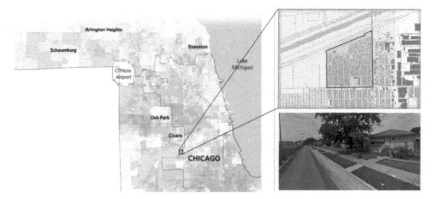

recognition of the topic. In Bloomberg's billionaires project (Figure 8.5), each billionaire is represented by a pen-and-ink caricature. This is elegant in choice and also dodges the likely flaws of having to compose the work around individual headshot photographs that would have been hard to frame and colour consistently.

It was worth Bloomberg investing in the time/cost involved in commissioning these illustrations, given that the project was not a one-off but something that would be an ongoing, updated daily resource.

'Although all our projects are very much data driven, visualisation is only part of the products and solutions we create. This day and age provides us with amazing opportunities to combine video, animation, visualisation, sound and interactivity. Why not make full use of this? ... Judging whether to include something or not is all about editing: asking "is it really necessary?". There is always an aspect of "gut feel" or "instinct" mixed with continuous doubt that drives me in these cases.' **Thomas Clever, Co-founder CLEVER°FRANKE, a data driven experiences studio**

Problems with the integration of such media within a visualisation project will occur when unsuitable attempts are made to combine imagery within the framework of a chart. Often the lack of cohesion creates a significant hindrance whereby the data representations are obscured or generally made harder to read, as the inherent form and colour clashes undermine the functional harmony.

Researching, curating, capturing or creating assets of imagery requires skill and a professional approach, otherwise the resulting effect will look amateurish. Incorporating these media into a data visualisation is not about quickly conducting some Google Image fishing exercise. Determining what imagery you will be able to use involves careful considerations around image suitability, quality and, critically, usage rights. Beware the client or colleague who thinks otherwise.

A frequent simple example of incorporated imagery is when you have to include logos according to the needs of the organisation for whom your work is being created. Remember to consider this early so you at least know in advance that you will have to assign some space to accommodate this component elegantly.

Footnotes: Often the final visible feature of your display, *footnotes* provide a convenient place to share important details that further substantiate the explanation of your work. Sometimes this information might be stored within the introduction component (especially if that is interactively hidden/revealed to allow it more room to accommodate detail):

Figure 8.5 Excerpt from 'Bloomberg Billionaires'

- *Data sources* should be provided, ideally in close proximity to the relevant charts.

- *Credits* will list the authors and main contributors of the work, often including the provision of contact details.

- *Attribution* is also important if you wish to recognise the influence of other people's work in shaping your ideas or to acknowledge the benefits of using an open source application or free typeface, for example.

- *Usage* information might explain the circumstances in which the work can be viewed or reused, whether there are any confidentialities or copyrights involved.

- *Time/date stamps* are often forgotten but they will give an indication to viewers of the moment of production and from that they might be able to ascertain the work's current accuracy and contextualise their interpretations accordingly.

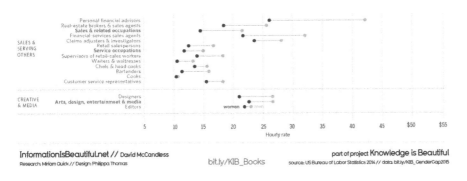

Figure 8.6
Excerpt from 'Gender Pay Gap US'

8.2 Features of Annotation: Chart Annotation

This second group of annotated features concerns the ways you provide viewers with specific assistance for perceiving and interpreting the charts. Think of these as being the features that refer directly to your charts or exist directly within or in immediate proximity to each chart.

Reading guides: These are written or visual instructions that provide viewers with a guide for how to read the chart or graphic and offer greater detailed assistance than a legend (see later). The idea of learnability in visualisation is an important consideration. It is a two-way commitment requiring will and effort from the viewer and sufficient assistance from the visualiser. This is something to be discussed in Chapter 11 under 'Visualisation literacy'.

Recognising that their readership may not necessarily understand connected scatter plots, Bloomberg's visual data team offer a 'How to Read this Graphic' guide immediately as you land on the project shown in Figure 8.7. This can be closed but a permanent 'How to' button remains for those who may need to refer to it again. The connected scatter plot was the right choice for this angle of analysis, so rather than use a different 'safer' representation approach (and therefore

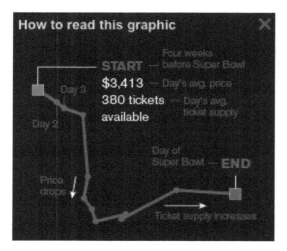

Figure 8.7   Excerpt from 'Holdouts Find Cheapest Super Bowl Tickets Late in the Game'

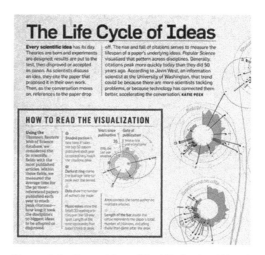

Figure 8.8   Excerpt from 'The Life Cycle of Ideas'

alter what analysis was shown) it is to their credit that they respected the capacity of their viewers to be willing to learn how to read this unfamiliar graphical form.

The second example shown (Figure 8.8) is from the 'How to Read' guide taken from the 'Life Cycle of Ideas' graphic created by Accurate, a studio renowned for innovative and expressive visualisation work. Given the relative complexity of the encodings used in this piece, it is necessary to equip the viewer with as much guidance as possible to ensure its potential is fully realised.

Chart apparatus: Options for *chart apparatus* relate to the structural components found in different chart types. Every visualisation displayed in this book has different elements of chart apparatus (Figure 8.9), specifically visible axis lines, tick marks or gridlines to help viewers orient their judgements of size and position. There is no right or wrong for including or excluding these features, it tends to be informed by your tonal definitions based on how much precision in the perceiving of values you wish to facilitate. I will discuss the range of different structures underlying each chart type (such as Cartesian, Radial or Spatial) in Chapter 10 on composition, as these have more to do with issues of shape and dimension.

> 'Labelling is the black magic of data visualization.' **Gregor Aisch, Graphics Editor, The *New York Times***

Labels: There are three main labelling devices you will need to think about using within your chart: axis titles, axis labels and value labels:

- *Axis titles* describe what values are being referenced by each axis. This might be a single word or a short sentence depending on what best fits the needs of your viewers. Often the role of an axis is already explained (or implied) by *project annotations* elsewhere, such as titles or sub-headings, but do not always assume this will be instantly clear to your viewers.
- *Axis labels* provide value references along each axis to help identify the categorical value or the date/quantitative value associated with that scale position. For categorical axes

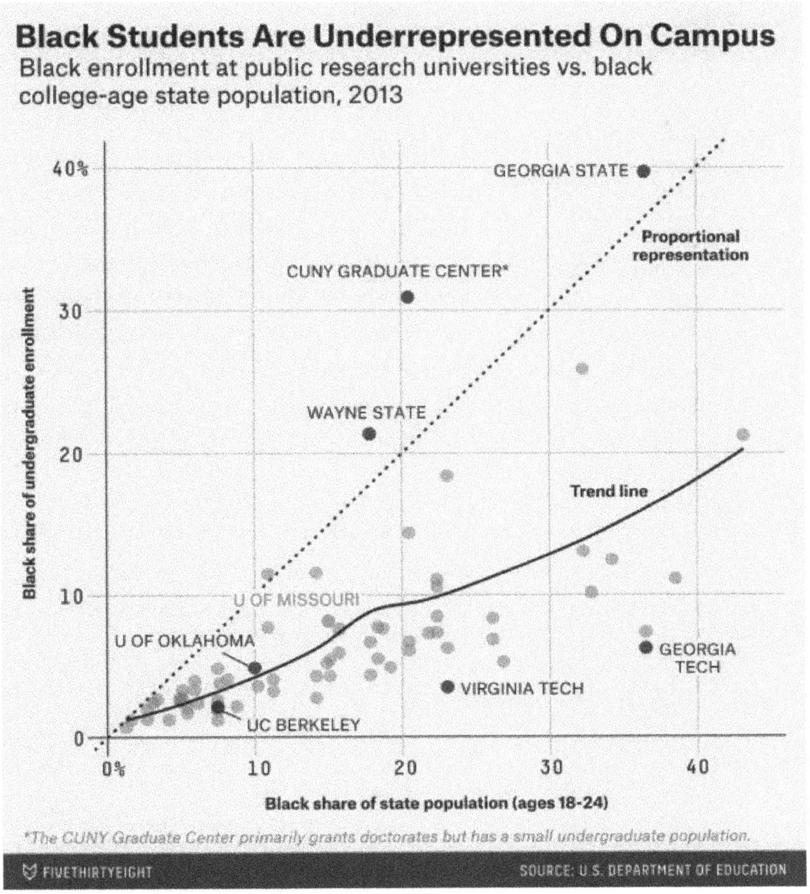

Figure 8.9
Mizzou's Racial Gap Is
Typical On College Campuses

(as seen in bar charts and heat maps, for example) one of the main judgments relates to the orientation of the label: you will need to find sufficient room to fit the label but also preserve its readability. For non-categorical data the main judgement will be what scale intervals to use. This has to be a combination of what is most useful for referencing values by your viewer, what is the most relevant interval based on the nature of the data (e.g. maybe a year-level label is more relevant than marking each month), and also what feels like it achieves the best-looking visual rhythm along the chart's edge. This will be another matter that is discussed more in the composition chapter.

- *Value labels* will appear in proximity to specific mark encodings inside the chart. Typically, these labels will be used to reveal a quantity, such as showing the percentage sizes of the sectors in a pie chart or the height of bars. Judging whether to include such annotations will refer back to your definition of the appropriate tone: will viewers need to read off exact values or will their perceived estimates of size and/or relationship be sufficient? The need to include categorical labels will be a concern for maps (whether to label locations?) or charts like the scatter plot seen in Figure 8.9, where you may wish to draw focus to a select sample of the categories plotted across the display.

> Redundancy in labelling occurs when you include value labelling of quantities for all marks whilst also including axis-scale labelling. You are effectively unnecessarily doubling the assistance being offered and so, ideally, you should choose to include one or the other.

As you have seen, one way of providing detailed value labels is through interaction, maybe offering a pop-up/tooltip annotation that is triggered by a hover or click event on different mark encodings. Having the option for interactivity here is especially useful as it enables you to reduce clutter from your display that can develop as more annotated detail is added.

Legend: A legend is an annotated feature within or alongside your chart that presents one or several keys to help viewers understand the categorical or quantitative meaning of different attributes.

Figure 8.10
Excerpt from 'The Infographic History of the World'

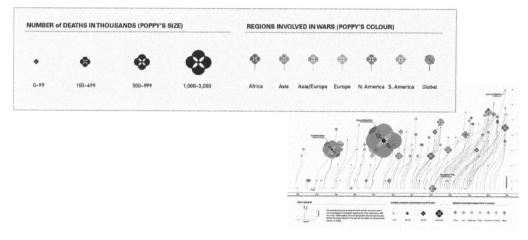

For quantitative data the main role for a legend will be if the attribute of area size has been used to encode values, as found on the bubble plot chart type. The keys displayed there will provide a reference for the different size scales. Which selection of sizes to show needs careful thought: what is the most useful guide to help your viewers make their perceptual judgements from a chart? This might not entail showing only even interval sizes (50, 100, 150 etc.); rather, you might offer viewers a indicative spread of sizes to best represent the distribution of your data values. The example in Figure 8.10 shows logical interval sizes to reflect the range of values in the data and also helpfully includes reference to the maximum value size to explain that no shape will be any larger than this. For categorical data you also see a key showing the meaning of different colours and shapes and their associated values.

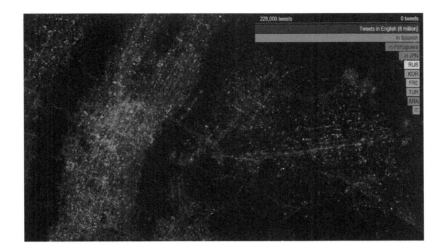

Figure 8.11
Twitter NYC:
A Multilingual
Social City

A nice approach to getting more out of your legends is shown in Figure 8.11. Here you will see a key explaining the colour associations combined with a bar chart to display the distribution of quantities for each language grouping from this analysis of tweets posted around New York City.

Captions: These exist typically as small passages of written analysis that bring to the surface some of the main insights and conclusions from the work. These might be presented close to related values inside the chart or in separate panels to provide commentary outside the chart.

In 'Gun Deaths' (Figure 8.12), there is a nice solution that combines annotated captions with interactive data adjustments. Below the main chart there is a 'What This Data Reveals' section which some of the main findings from the analysis of the gun death data. The captions double up as clickable shortcuts so that you can quickly apply the relevant framing filters and update the main display to see what the captions are referring to.

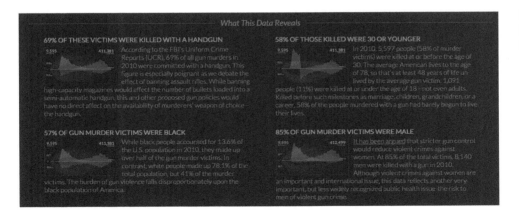

Figure 8.12
Excerpt from 'US
Gun Deaths'

As creative tools become more ubiquitous the possibility for incorporating non-visual data in you work increases. As an alternative to the written caption there is greater scope to consider using audio as a means of verbally narrating a subject and explaining key messages. Over the past few years one of the standout projects using this feature was the video profiling 'Wealth

Figure 8.13
Image taken
from 'Wealth
Inequality in
America'

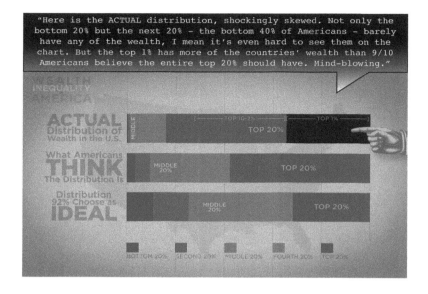

Inequality in America' (Figure 8.13), as introduced in Chapter 3, where the voiceover provides a very compelling and cohesive narrative against the backdrop of the animated visuals that present the data being described.

8.3 Typography

As you have seen, many features of annotation utilise text. This means your choices will be concerned not just with *what* text to include, but also with *how* it will look. This naturally merits a brief discussion about how typography will have a significant role in the presentation of your work.

Firstly, some clarity about language. A *typeface* is a designed collection of glyphs representing individual letters, numbers and other symbols of language based on a cohesive style. A *font* is the variation across several physical dimensions of the typeface, such as weight, size, condensation and italicisation. A typeface can have one or many different fonts in its family. *Type* effectively represents the collective appearance formed by the choice of typeface and the font.

I discussed earlier the distinction between definitions of data visualisation and other related fields. I mentioned how the person creating their design is not necessarily conscious or concerned about what label is attached to their work, they are simply doing their work regardless. The same could be applied to people's interchangeable use of and meaning of the terms typeface and font, the clarity of which has been irreparably confused by Microsoft's desktop tools in particular.

Tahoma and Century Gothic are different typefaces. This *font* and this **font** both belong to the Georgia typeface family but display variations in size, weight and italicisation.

Serif typefaces add an extra little flourish in the form of a small line at the end of the stroke in a letter or symbol. Garamond is an example of a serif font. Serif typefaces are generally considered to be easier to read for long sequences of text (such as the full body text) and are especially used in print displays.

Sans-serif typefaces have no extra line extending the stroke for each character. **Verdana** is an example of a sans-serif typeface. These typefaces are commonly used for shorter sections of text, such as axis or value labels or titles, and for screen displays.

In making choices about which type to use, there are echoes with the thinking you are about to face on using colour. As you will see, colour decisions concern legibility and meaning first, decoration last. With typeface choices you are not dressing up your text, you are optimising its readability and meaning across your display. The desired style of typeface only comes into your thinking after legibility and meaning.

In terms of *legibility*, you need to choose a typeface and font combination that will be suitable for the role of each element of text you are using. Viewers need to be able to read the words and numbers on display without difficulty. Quite obvious, really. Some typefaces (and specifically fonts) are

> Typeface decisions will often be taken out of your hands by the visual identity guidelines of organisations and publications, as well as by technical reasons relating to browser type, software compatibility and availability.

more easily read than others. Some work better to make numbers as clearly readable as possible, others work better for words. There are plenty of typefaces that might look cool and contemporary but if they make text indecipherable then that is plain wrong.

Just as variation in colour implies *meaning*, so does variation in typeface and font. If you make some text capitalised, large and bold-weight this will suggest it carries greater significance and portrays a higher prominence across the object hierarchy than any text presented in lower case, with a smaller size and thinner weight. So you should seek to limit the variation in font where possible.

Text-based annotations should be considered part of the supporting cast and the way you consider typeface and font choices should reflect this role. Typography in visualisation should be seen but really not heard. Deciding on the most suitable type is something that can ultimately

> 'Never choose Times New Roman or Arial, as those fonts are favored only by the apathetic and sloppy. Not by typographers. Not by you.' **Matthew Butterick, Typographer, Lawyer and Writer**

come down to experience and influence through exposure to other work. Every individual has their own relied-upon preferences. In practice, I find there is a good chunk of trial and error as well as viewer testing that goes into resolving the final selection. Across the spectrum of data visualisation work being produced there are no significant trends to be informed by largely because judging the most suitable typography choices will be unique to the circumstances influencing each project.

Typography is just another of the many individual ingredients relevant to data visualisation that exists as a significant subject in its own right. It is somewhat inadequate to allocate barely two pages of this book to discussing its role in visualisation, but these will at least offer you a bite-sized window into the topic.

8.4 Influencing Factors and Considerations

Having become familiar with the principal options for annotating, you now have to decide which features to incorporate into your work and how you might deploy these.

Formulating Your Brief

> 'Think of the reader – a specific reader, like a friend who's curious but a novice to the subject and to data-viz – when designing the graphic. That helps. And I rely pretty heavily on that introductory text that runs with each graphic – about 100 words, usually, that should give the new-to-the-subject reader enough background to understand why this graphic is worth engaging with, and sets them up to understand and contextualize the takeaway. And annotate the graphic itself. If there's a particular point you want the reader to understand, make it! Explicitly! I often run a few captions typeset right on the viz, with lines that connect them to key elements in the design.' **Katie Peek, Data Visualisation Designer and Science Journalist, on making complex and/ or complicated subject matter accessible and interesting to her audience**

Audience: Given that most annotations serve the purpose of viewer assistance, your approach will inevitably be influenced by the characteristics of your intended audience. Having an appreciation of and empathy towards the knowledge and capabilities of the different cohorts of viewers is especially important with this layer of design. How much help will they need to understand the project and also the data being portrayed? You will need to consider the following:

- *Subject:* how well acquainted will they be with this subject matter? Will they understand the terminology, acronyms, abbreviations? Will they recognise the relevance of this particular angle of analysis about this subject?
- *Interactive functions:* how sophisticated are they likely to be in terms of being able to understand and utilise the different features of interactivity made possible through your design?
- *Perceiving:* how well equipped are they to work with this visualisation? Is it likely that the chart type(s) will be familiar or unfamiliar; if the latter, will they need support to guide them through the process of perceiving?
- *Interpreting:* will they have the knowledge required to form legitimate interpretations of this work? Will they know how to understand what is good or bad, what big and small mean, what is important, or not? Alternatively, will you need to provide some level of assistance to address this potential gap?

Purpose map: The defined intentions for the *tone* and *experience* of your work will influence the type and extent of annotation features required.

If you are working towards a solution that leans more towards the 'reading' tone you are placing an emphasis on the perceptibility of the data values. It therefore makes sense that you should aim to provide as much assistance as possible (especially through extensive chart annotations) to maximise the efficiency and precision of this process.

If it is more about a 'feeling' tone then you may be able to justify the absence of the same annotations. Your intent may be to provide more of a general sense – a 'gist' – of the order of magnitude of values.

If you are seeking to provide an 'explanatory' experience it would be logical to employ as many devices as possible that will help inform your viewers about how to read the charts (assisting with the 'perceiving' stage of understanding) and also bring some of the key insights to the surface, making clear the meaning of the quantities and relationships displayed (thus assisting with the stage of 'interpreting'). The use of captions and visual overlays will be particularly helpful in achieving this, as will the potential for audio accompaniments if you are seeking to push the explanatory experience a step further.

'Exploratory' experiences are less likely to include layers of insight assistance, instead the focus will be more towards project-level annotation, ensuring that viewers (and particularly here, users) have as much understanding as possible about how to use the project for their exploratory benefit. You might find, however, that devices like 'How to read this graphic' are still relevant irrespective of the definition of your intended experience.

Characteristically, 'exhibitory' work demonstrates far less annotated assistance because, by intention, it is more about providing a visual display of the data rather than offering an explanatory presentation or the means for exploratory interrogation. The assumptions here are that audiences will have sufficient domain and project knowledge not to require extensive additional assistance. Common chart annotations like value labels and legends, and project annotations like titles and introductions, are still likely to be necessary, but these might reflect the extent required.

Establishing Your Editorial Thinking

Focus: During your editorial thinking you considered focus and its particular role in supporting explanatory thinking. Are there specific value labels that you wish to display over others? Rather than labelling *all* values, for example, have you determined that only certain marks and attributes will merit labelling? As you saw earlier in the example scatter plot about the under-representation of black students in US colleges, only certain points were labelled, not all. These would have been judged to have been the most relevant and interesting elements to emphasise through annotation.

Trustworthy Design

Transparency: Annotation is one of the most important aids to ensure that you secure and sustain trust from your viewers by demonstrating integrity and openness:

- Explain what the project is and is not going to show.
- Detail where the data came from and what framing criteria were used during the process of acquisition, and also make what has been ultimately included in the chart(s).
- Outline any data transformation treatments, assumptions and calculations. Are there any limitations that viewers need to be aware of?
- Highlight and contextualise any findings to ensure accuracy in interpretation.
- With digital projects in particular, provide access to coding repositories to lay open all routines and programmatic solutions.

Accessible Design

Understandable: If you recall, in the section profiling circumstances you considered what the characteristics were of the setting or situation in which your audience might consume your visualisation. Well-judged project and chart annotations are entirely concerned with providing a sufficient level of assistance to achieve understanding. The key word there is 'sufficient' because there is a balance: too much assistance makes the annotations included feel overburdening; too little and there is far more room for wrong assumptions and misconceptions to prosper. A setting that is consistent with the need to deliver immediate insights will need suitable annotations to fulfil this. There will be no time or patience for long introductions or explanations in that setting. Conversely, a visualisation about a subject matter that is inherently complex may warrant such assistance.

Elegant Design

Minimise the clutter: A key concern about annotations is judging the merits of including structural or textual assistance against the potential disruption and obstruction caused by these to the view of the data. Any annotation device added to your display has a spatial and visual consequence that needs to be accommodated. Of course, as mentioned, with the benefit of interactivity it is possible to show and hide layers of detail. Overall, you will have to find the most elegant solution for presenting your annotations to ensure you do not inadvertently undermine the help you are trying to provide.

Summary: Annotation

Project annotations help viewers understand what the project is about and how to use it, and may include the following features:

- Headings: titles, sub-titles and section headings.
- Introductions: providing background and aims of the project.
- User guides: advice or instruction for how to use any interactive features.
- Multimedia: the potential to enhance your project using appropriate imagery, videos or illustrations.
- Footnotes: potentially includes data sources, credits, usage information, and time/date stamps.

Chart annotations help viewers perceive the charts and optimise their potential interpretations and may include the following features:

- Chart apparatus: axis lines, gridlines, tick marks.
- Labels: axis titles, axis labels, value labels.
- Legend: providing detailed keys for colour or size associations.
- Reading guides: detailed instructions advising readers how to perceive and interpret the chart.
- Captions: drawing out key findings and commentaries.

Typography Most of the annotation features you include are based on text and so you will need to consider carefully the legibility of the typeface you choose and the logic behind the font-size hierarchy you display.

Influencing Factors and Considerations

- Formulating the brief: consider the characteristics and needs of the audience. Certain chart choices and subjects may require more explanation. From the 'purpose map' what type of tone and experience are you trying to create and what role might annotation play?
- Establishing your editorial thinking: what things do you want to emphasise or direct the eye towards (focus)?
- Trustworthy design: maximise the information viewers have to ensure all your data work is transparent and clearly explained.
- Accessible design: what is the right amount and type of annotation suitable to the setting and complexity of your subject?
- Elegant design: minimise the clutter.

Tips and Tactics

- Attention to detail is imperative: all instructions, project information, captions and value labels need to be accurate. Always spell-check digitally and manually, and ask others to proofread if you are too 'close' to see.
- Do not forget to check on permission to use any annotated asset, such as imagery, photos, videos, quotations, etc.

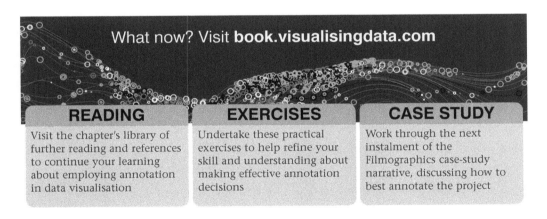

What now? Visit book.visualisingdata.com

READING	EXERCISES	CASE STUDY
Visit the chapter's library of further reading and references to continue your learning about employing annotation in data visualisation	Undertake these practical exercises to help refine your skill and understanding about making effective annotation decisions	Work through the next instalment of the Filmographics case-study narrative, discussing how to best annotate the project

9

Colour

Having established which charts you will use, the potential interactive functions that might be required and the annotation features that will be especially useful, you have effectively determined all the visible elements that will be included in your project. The final two layers of design concern not *what* elements will be included or excluded, but *how* they will appear. After this chapter you will look at issues on composition, but before that the rather weighty matter of colour.

As one of the most powerful sensory cues, colour is a highly influential visual property. It is arguably the design decision that has the most immediate impact on the eye of the viewer. All the design features of your visualisation display hold some attribute of colour, otherwise they are invisible:

- Every mark and item of apparatus in your *charts* will be coloured; indeed colour in itself may be an attribute that represents your data values.
- *Interactive* features do not always have an associated visible property (some are indeed invisible and left as intuitively discoverable). However, those features that involve buttons, menus, navigation tabs and value sliders will always have a colour.
- *Annotation* properties such as titles, captions and value labels will all be coloured.
- *Composition* design mainly concerns the arrangement of all the above features, though you might use colour to help achieve a certain design layout. As you will see, emptiness is a useful organising device – leaving something blank is a colour choice.

Thankfully, there is a route through all of this potential complexity relying on just a little bit of science mixed in with lots of common sense. By replacing any arbitrary judgements that might have been previously based on

> 'Colors are perhaps the visual property that people most often misuse in visualization without being aware of it.' **Robert Kosara, Senior Research Scientist at Tableau Software**

taste, and through increasing the sensitivity of your choices, colour becomes one of the layers of visualisation design that can be most quickly and significantly improved.

The key factor in thinking about colour is to ensure you establish meaning first and decoration last. That is not to rule out the value of certain decorative benefits of colour, but to advise that these should be your last concern. Besides, in dealing with meaningful applications of colour you will already have gone a long way towards establishing the 'decorative' qualities of your project's aesthetic appearance.

This chapter begins with a look at some of the key components of colour science, offering a foundation for your understanding about this topic. After that you will learn about the ways and places in which colour could be used. Finally, you will consider the main factors that influence colour decisions.

Colour thinking begins from inside the chart(s), working outwards across the rest of the visualisation anatomy:

* Data legibility.
* Editorial salience.
* Functional harmony.

9.1 Overview of Colour Theory

Colour in visualisation is something of a minefield. As with many of these design layer chapters, an introduction to colour involves judging the right amount of science and the right amount of practical application. What does justice to the essence of the subject and gives you the most relevant content to work with is a delicate balance.

When you lift the lid on the science behind colour you open up a world of brain-ache. When this chapter is finalised I will have spent a great deal of time agonising over how to explain this subject and what to leave in or leave out because there is so much going on with colour. And it is tricky. Why? Because you almost come face to face with philosophical questions like 'what is white?' and the sort of mathematical formulae that you really rather hoped had been left behind at school. You learn how the colours you specify in your designs as X might be perceived by some people as Y and others as Z. You discover that you are not just selecting colours from a neat linear palette but rather from a multi-dimensional colour space occupying a cubic, cylindrical or spherical conceptual shape, depending on different definitions.

The basis of this topic is the science of optics – the branch of physics concerned with the behaviour and properties of light – as well as colorimetry – the science and technology used to quantify and describe human colour perception. Two sciences, lots of maths, loads of variables, endless potential for optical illusions and impairment: that is why colour is tricky and why you need to begin this stage of thinking with an appreciation of some colour theory.

The most relevant starting point is to recognise that when dealing with issues of colour in data visualisation you will almost always be creating work on some kind of computer. Unless you are creating something by hand using paints or colouring pencils, you will be using software viewed through an electronic display.

This is important because a discussion about colour theory needs to be framed around the RGB (Red, Blue, Green) colour model. This is used to define the combination of light that forms the colours you see on a screen, conceptually laid out in a cubic space based on variations across these three attributes.

The output format of your work will vary between screen display and print display. If you are creating something for print you will have to shift your colour output settings to CMYK (Cyan, Magenta, Yellow and Black). This is the model used to define the proportions of inks that make up a printed colour. This is known as a subtractive

When you are creating work to be consumed on the Web through screen displays, you will often program using HEX (Hexadecimal) codes to specify the mix of red, green and blue light (in the form #RRGGBB using codes 00 to FF).

model, which means that combining all four inks produces black, whereas RGB is additive as the three screen colours combine to produce white.

While CMYK communicates from your software to a printer, telling it what colours to print as an output, it does not really offer a logical model to think about the input decisions you will make about colour. Neither, for that matter, does RGB: it just is not realistic to think in those terms when considering what choices are needed in a visualisation design. There are different levers to adjust and different effects being sought that require an alternative model of thinking.

I share the belief with many in the field that the most accessible colour model – in terms of considering the application of colour in data visualisation – is HSL (Hue, Saturation, Lightness), devised by Albert Munsell in the 1980s. These three dimensions combine to make up what is known as a cylindrical-coordinate colour representation of the RGB colour model (I did warn you about the cylinders).

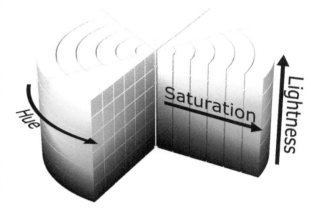

Figure 9.1 HSL Colour Cylinder

Hue is considered the *true* colour. With hue there are no shades (adding black), tints (adding whites) or tones (adding grey) – a consideration of these attributes follows next. When you are describing or labelling colours you are most commonly referring to their hue: think of the colours of the rainbow ranging through various mixtures of red, orange, yellow, green, blue, indigo and violet. Hue is considered a qualitative colour attribute because it is defined by difference and not by scale.

Figure 9.2
Colour Hue Spectrum

Saturation defines the purity or colourfulness of a hue. This does have a scale from intense pure colour (high saturation) through increasing tones (adding grey) to the no-colour state of grey (low saturation). In language terms think *vivid* through to *muted*.

Figure 9.3
Colour Saturation
Spectrum

Technically speaking, black, white and grey are not considered colours.

Lightness defines the contrast of a single hue from dark to light. It is not a measure of brightness – there are other models that define that – rather a scale of light tints (adding white) through to dark shades (adding black). In language terms I actually think of lightness more as degrees of darkness, but that is just a personal mindset.

Figure 9.4
Colour Lightness
Spectrum

I have deliberately described these dimensions separately because, as you will see when looking at the applications of colour in visualisation, your decisions will often be defined by how you might employ these distinct dimensions of colour to form your visual display. The main choices tend to fall between employing difference in hue and variation in lightness, with the different levels of saturation often being a by-product of the definitions made for the other two dimensions.

Alternative models exist offering variations on a similar theme, such as HSV (Hue, Saturation, Value), HSI (Hue, Saturation, Intensity), HSB (Hue, Saturation, Brightness) and HCL (Hue, Chroma, Luminance).

These are all primarily representations of the RGB model space but involve differences in the mathematical translation into/from RGB and offer subtle differences in the meaning of the same terms (local definitions of hue and saturation vary). The biggest difference relates to their emphasis as a means of specifying either a colour quality (in an input, created sense) or a colour perception (in how a colour is ultimately experienced).

Pantone is another colour space that you might recognise. It offers a proprietary colour-matching, identifying and communicating service for print, essentially giving 'names' to colours based on the CMYK process.

The argument against using the HSL model for defining colour is that, while it is fine for colour setting (i.e. an intuitive way to think about and specify the colours you want to set in your visual-

isation work), the resulting colours will not be uniformly perceived the same, from one device to the next. This is because there are many variables at play in the projection of light to display colour and the light conditions present in the moment of perception. That means the same perceptual experience will not be guaranteed. It is argued that more rigorous models (such as CIELAB) offer an absolute (as opposed to a relative) definition of colour for both input and output. My view is that they are just a little bit too hard to easily translate into visualisation design thinking. Furthermore, trying to control for all the subtleties of variation in consumption conditions is an extra burden you should ideally avoid.

At this stage, it is important to be pragmatic about colour as much as possible. The vast majority of your colour manipulating and perceptual needs should be nicely covered by the HSL model. As and when you develop a deeper, purist interest in colour you should then seek to learn more about the nuances in the differences between the definitions of these models and their application.

9.2 Features of Colour: Data Legibility

Data legibility concerns the use of the attribute of colour to encode data values in charts. The objective here is to make the data being represented by differences in colour as clearly readable and as meaningful as possible.

While you have probably already decided by now the chart or charts you intend to use, you still need to take think carefully – and separately – about how you will specifically employ colour. To do this we first need to revisit the classification of data types and consider how best to use colour for representing each different type.

Nominal (Qualitative)

With nominal data colour is used to classify different categorical values. The primary motive for the choice of colour is to create a visible distinction between each unique categorical association, helping the eye to discern the different categories as efficiently and accurately as possible.

Creating contrast is the main aim of representing nominal data. What you are *not* seeking to show or even imply is any sense of an order of magnitude. You want to help differentiate one category from the next – and make it easily identifiable – but to do so in a way that preserves the sense of equity among the colours deployed.

Variation in hue is typically the colour dimension to consider using for differentiating categories. Additionally, you might explore different tones (variations in saturation across the hues). You should not, though, consider using variations in the lightness dimension. That is because the result is insufficiently discernible. As you can see demonstrated in Figure 9.5, the lightness variation of a blue tone makes it quite hard to connect the colour scale presented in the key at the top with the colours displayed in the

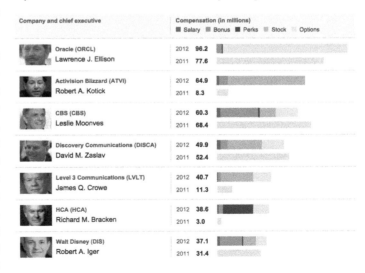

Figure 9.5 Excerpt from 'Executive Pay by the Numbers'

stacked bars underneath. With the shading in the column header and the 2011 grey bar also contributing similar tones to the overall aesthetic of the table our visual processing system has to work much harder to determine the associations than it should need to do.

Often the categories you will be differentiating with colour will be relatively few in number, maybe two or three, such as in the separation between political parties or plotting different values for gender, as seen in Figure 9.6.

Figure 9.6
How Nations Fare in PhDs by Sex

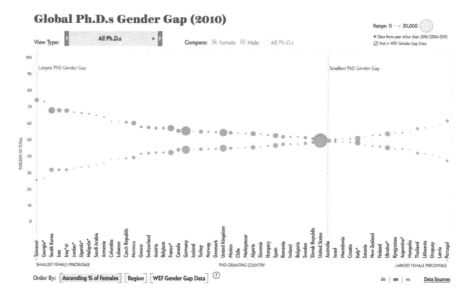

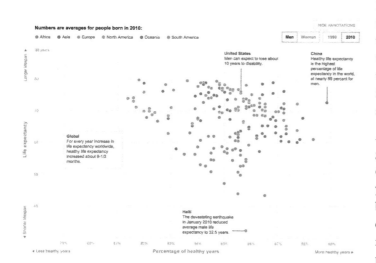

Figure 9.7   How Long Will We Live – And How Well?

Beyond these small numbers, you still typically might only need to contend with assigning colours to around four to six categories, perhaps in analysis that needs to visually distinguish values for different continents of the world, as seen in the scatter plot in Figure 9.7.

As the range of different categories grows, the ability to preserve clear differentiation becomes harder. In expanding your required palette, the colours used become decreasingly unique. The general rule of thumb is that once you have more than 12 categories it will not be possible to find a sufficiently different colour to assign to categories from 13 upwards. Additionally, you are really increasing the demands of learning and recognition for viewers. This then becomes quite a cognitive burden and delays the process of understanding.

Two approaches for dealing with this. Firstly, consider offering interactive filters to modify what categories are displayed in a visualisation – thus potentially reducing the impact of so many being available. Secondly, think about transforming your data by excluding or combining categories in to a reduced number of aggregate groupings.

Depending on the subject of your data, sometimes you can look to supplement the use of colour with texture or pattern to create further visible distinctions. In Figure 9.8 you can see two patterns being used occasionally as additive properties to show the structure of tracks on The Beatles' album.

Figure 9.8 Charting the Beatles: Song Structure

Ordinal (Qualitative)

With ordinal data you are still dealing with categories but now they have a natural hierarchy or ordering that can be exploited. The primary motive for using colour in this case is not only to create a visible distinction between each unique category association but also to imply some sense of an order of magnitude through the colour variation. The colour dimensions used to achieve this tend to employ variations of either the saturation or the lightness (or a combination of both).

You might also introduce different hues when dealing with *diverging* (dual-direction) scales rather than simply *converging* (single-direction) ones.

Figure 9.9 displays a simple example of colour used to display a converging ordinal variable. This is the teacup that I use in my office. On the inside you can see it has a colour guide to help ascertain how much milk you might need to add: going through Milky, Classic British, Builder's Brew, and finally Just Tea (zero milk).

A typical example of a diverging ordinal scale might be seen in the stacked bar chart showing the results of a survey question (Figure 9.10). The answers are based on the strength of feeling: strongly agree, agree, neutral, disagree, strongly disagree. By colouring the agreement in red ('hot' sometimes used to represent 'good') and the disagreement in blue ('cold' to mean 'bad') means a viewer can quickly perceive the general balance of feelings being expressed.

Figure 9.9 Photograph of MyCuppa Mug

Figure 9.10
Example of a Stacked
Bar Chart Based on
Ordinal Data

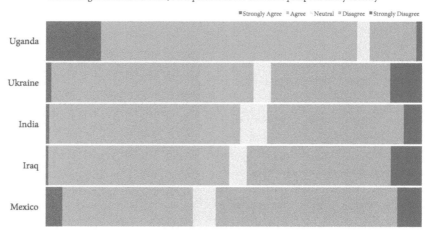

Another example of ordinal data might be to represent the notion of recency. In Figure 9.11 you see a display plotting the 2013 Yosemite National Park fire. Colour is used to display the recorded day-by-day progress of the fire's spread. The colour scale is based on a recency scale with darker = recent, lighter = furthest away (think faded memory).

Figure 9.11
The Extent of
Fire in the Sierra
Nevada Range and
Yosemite National
Park, 2013

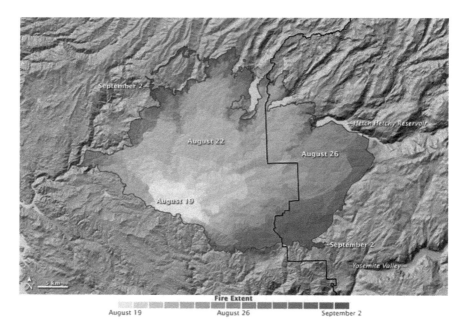

Interval and Ratio (Quantitative)

With quantitative data (ratio and interval) your motive, as it is with ordinal data, is to demonstrate the difference between and of a set of values. In the choropleth map in Figure 9.12, showing the variation in electricity prices across Switzerland, the darker shades of blue indicate the higher values, the lighter tints the lower prices. This approach makes the viewer's perception of the map's values immediate – it is quite intuitive to recognise the implication of the general patterns of light and dark shades.

Wie hoch die Strompreise in den Gemeinden sind

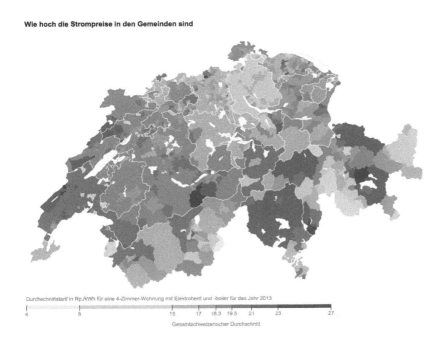

Durchschnittstarif in Rp./kWh für eine 4-Zimmer-Wohnung mit Elektroherd und -boiler für das Jahr 2013

Gesamtschweizerischer Durchschnitt

Figure 9.12
What are the Current Electricity Prices in Switzerland [Translated]

Typically, using colour to represent quantitative data will involve breaking up your data values into discrete classifications or 'bins'. This makes the task of reading value ranges from their associated colour shade or tone a little easier than when using a continuous gradient scale. While our capacity to judge exact variations in colour is relatively low (even with a colour key for reference), we are very capable of detecting local variations of colour through differences in tint, shade or tone. Assessing the relative contrast between two colours is generally how we construct a quantitative hierarchy.

Look at the fascinating local patterns that emerge in the next map (Figure 9.13), comparing increases in the percentage of people gaining health insurance in the USA (during 2013–14). The data is broken down to county level detail with a colour scale showing a darker red for the higher percentage increases.

Some of the most relevant colour practices for data visualisation come from the field of cartography (as do many of the most passionate colour purists). Just consider the amount of quantitative and categorical detail shown in a reference map that relies on colour to differentiate types of land, indicate the depth of water or the altitude of high ground, present route features of road and rail networks, etc. The best maps pack an incredible amount of detail into a single display and yet somehow they never feel disproportionately overwhelming.

Figure 9.13
Excerpt from
'Obama's Health
Law: Who Was
Helped Most'

Obama's Health Law: Who Was Helped Most

By KEVIN QUEALY and MARGOT SANGER-KATZ   OCT. 29, 2014

A new data set provides a clearer picture of which people gained
health insurance under the Affordable Care Act.

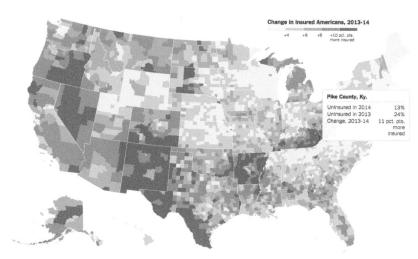

Aside from the big-picture observations of the darker shades in the west and the noticeably lighter tints to the east and parts of the mid-west, take a closer look at some of the interesting differences at a more local level. For example, notice the stark contrast across state lines between the dark regions of southern Kentucky (to the left of the annotated caption) and the light regions in the neighbouring counties of northern Tennessee. Despite their spatial proximity there are clearly strong differences in enrolment on the programme amongst residents of these regions.

Both of these previous examples use a *convergent* colour scale, moving through discrete variations in colour lightness to represent an increasing scale of quantitative values, from zero or small through to large. As illustrated with the stacked bar chart example shown earlier, portraying the range of feelings from an ordinal dataset, sometimes you may need to employ a

Figure 9.14
Daily Indego
Bike Share
Station Usage

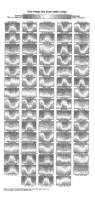

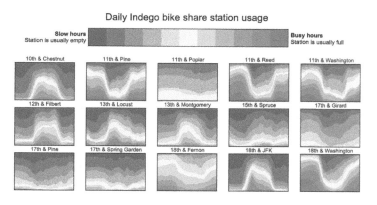

divergent colour scale. This is when you want to show how values are changing in two directions either side of a set breakpoint.

Figure 9.14 shows a cropped view of a larger graphic comparing the relative peaks and troughs of usage across all bike share stations in Philadelphia over a 24-hour period. The divergent colour scale uses two hues and variations in lightness to show the increasingly busy and increasingly slow periods of station activity either side of a breakpoint, represented by a very light grey to indicate the average point. The darkest red means the station is full, the darkest blue means the station is empty.

Regardless of whether you are plotting a converging or diverging scale, judging how you might divide up your colour scales into discrete value bins needs careful thought. The most effective colour scales help viewers perceive not just the relative order of magnitude – higher or lower – but also a sense of the absolute magnitude – how different a value might be compared to another value.

There is no universal rule about the number of value bins. Indeed, it is not uncommon to see entirely continuous colour scales. However, a general rule of thumb I use is that somewhere between between four and nine meaningful – and readable – value intervals should suffice. There are two key factors to consider when judging your scales:

- Are you plotting *observed* data or *observable* data? You might only have collected data for a narrow range of quantities (e.g. 15 to 35) so will your colour classifications be based on this observed range or on the potentially observable data range i.e. the values you know would/ could exist with a wider sample size or on a different collection occasion (e.g. 0 to 50)?

- What are the range and distribution of your data? Does it make sense to create equal intervals in your colour classifications or are there more meaningful intervals that better reflect the shape of your data and the nature of your subject? Sometimes, you will have legitimate outliers that, if included, will stretch your colour scales far beyond the meaningful concentration of most of your data values.

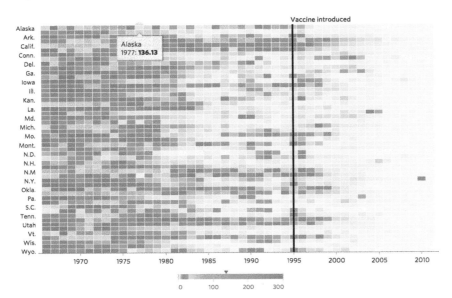

Figure 9.15
Battling Infectious Diseases in the 20th Century: The Impact of Vaccines

You can see this effect in Figure 9.15, showing the incidence of Hepatitis A per 100,000 population. There are only three values that exceed 100 (you can see them on the top line for Alaska in the late 1970s). To accommodate these outliers the colour scale becomes somewhat stretched-out, with a wide range of potential values being represented by a dark yellow to red colour. With 99.9% of the values being under 100 there is little discernibly in the blue/green shades used for the lower values. If outliers are your focus, it makes sense to include these and colour accordingly to emphasise their exceptional quality. Otherwise if they risk compromising the discrete detail of the lower values you might look to create a broad classification that uses a single colour for any value beyond a threshold of maybe 75, with even value intervals of maybe 15 below that help to show the patterns of smaller values.

For diverging scales, the respective quantitative shades either side of a breakpoint need to imply parity in both directions. For example, a shade of colour that means +10% one side of the breakpoint should have an equal shade intensity in a different hue on the other side to indicate the same interval, i.e. −10%. Additionally, the darkest shades of hues at the extreme ends of a diverging scale must still be discernible. Sometimes the darkest shades will be so close to black that you will no longer be able to distinguish the differences in their underlying hues when plotted in a chart or map.

As well as considering the most appropriate discrete bins for your values, for diverging scales one must also pay careful attention to the role of the breakpoint. This is commonly set to separate values visually above or below zero or those either side of a meaningful threshold, such as target, average or median.

One of the most common mistakes in using colour to represent quantitative data comes with use of the much-derided rainbow scale. Look at Figure 9.16, showing the highest temperatures across Australia during the first couple of weeks in 2013. Consider the colour key to the right

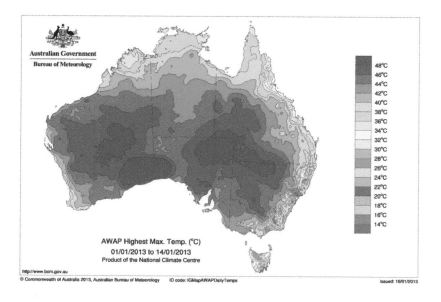

Figure 9.16
Highest Max
Temperatures in
Australia

of the map and ask yourself if this feels like a sufficiently intuitive scale. If the key was not provided, would you be able to perceive the order of magnitude relationship between the colours on the map? If you saw a purple colour next to a blue colour, which would you expect to mean hotter and which colder?

While the general implication of blue = 'colder' through to red = 'hotter' is included within sections of this temperature colour scale, it is the presence of many other hues that obstructs the accessibility and creates inconsistency in logic. For instance, do the colours used to show 24°C (light blue) jumping to 26°C (dark green) make sense as a means for showing an increasing temperature? How about 18°C (grey) to 20°C (dark blue), or the choice of the mid-brown used for 46°C which interrupts the increasingly dark red sequence? If you saw on the map a region with the pink tone as used for 16°C would you be confident that you could easily distinguish this from the lighter pink used to represent 38°C? Unless there are meaningful thresholds within your quantitative data – justifiable breakpoints – you should only vary your colour scales through the lightness dimension, not the hue dimension.

One of the interesting recurring challenges faced by visualisers is how to represent *nothing*. For example, if a *zero* quantity or *no* category is a meaningful state to show, you still need to represent this visually somehow, even though it might possess no size, no position and no area. How do you distinguish between no data and a zero value?

Typically, using colour is one of the best ways to portray this. Figure 9.17 shows one solution to making 'no data' a visible value. This map displays the population trends of the polar bear. Notice those significant areas of grey representing 'data deficient'. A subtle but quite effective political point is being made here by including this status indicator. As I mentioned before, sometimes the absence of data can be the message itself.

When considering colour choices for quantitative classifications, you will need to think especially carefully about the lowest value grouping: is it to be representative of zero, an interval starting from zero up to a low value, or an interval starting only from the minimum value and never including zero? In this choropleth map (Figure 9.18) looking at the unemployment rate across

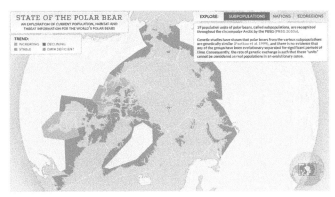

Figure 9.17 State of the Polar Bear

Figure 9.18 Excerpt from 'Geography of a Recession'

the counties of the USA, no value is as low as zero. There might be value that are close, but nowhere is the unemployment rate at 0%. As you can see, the lowest tint used in this colour key is not white, rather a light shade of orange, so as not to imply zero. Whilst not relevant to this example, if you wanted to create a further distinction between the lowest value interval and the 'null' or 'no data' state you could achieve this by using a pure white/blank.

9.3 Features of Colour: Editorial Salience

Having considered options for the application of colour in facilitating data legibility, the next concern is colour used for *editorial salience*. Whereas data legibility was concerned with helping to represent data, using colour for editorial salience is about drawing the viewer's attention to the significant or meaningful features of your display. Colour offers such a potent visual stimulus and an influential means for drawing out key aspects of your data and project that you might feel are sufficiently relevant to make prominent.

Consider again the idea of photography and the effect of taking a photograph of a landscape. You will find the foreground objects are darker and more prominent than the faded view of the background in the distance as light and colour diminish. Using colour to achieve editorial salience involves creating a similar effect of depth across your visualisation's contents: if everything is shouting, nothing is heard.

The goal of using colour to facilitate editorial salience is a suitable contrast. For things to stand out, you are in turn determining which other things will not.

The degree of contrast you might seek to create will vary. Often you will be seeking to draw a significant contrast, maximising the emphasis of a value or subset of values so the viewer can quickly home in on what you have elevated for their attention relative to everything else.

For this reason, grey will prove to be one of your strongest allies in data visualisation. When contrasted with reasonably saturated hues, grey helps to create depth. Elements coloured in greyscale will sit quietly at the back of the view, helping to provide a deliberately subdued context that enables the more emphasised coloured properties to stand proudly in the foreground.

In Figure 9.19, the angle of analysis shows a summary of the most prevalent men's names featuring among the CEOs of the S&P 1500 companies. As you can see there are more guys named 'John' or 'David' than the percentage of *all* the women CEOs combined. With the emphasis of the analysis on this startling statement of inequality the bar for 'All women' is emphasised in a burgundy colour, contrasting with the grey bars of all the men's names. Notice also that the respective axis and bar value labels are both presented using a bold font, which further accentuates this emphasis. It is also editorially consistent with the

Figure 9.19   Fewer Women Run Big Companies Than Men Named John

overriding enquiry of the article. As discussed in Chapter 3, bringing to the surface key insights from data displays in this way contributes towards facilitating an 'explanatory' experience.

Sometimes, only noticeable contrast – not shouting, just being slightly more distinguishable – may be appropriate. Compared with the previous bar chart example, Figure 9.20 creates a more subtle distinction between the slightly darker shade of green (and emboldened text) emphasising the New York figures compared to the other listed departments in a slightly lighter green. As with the CEOs' example, the object

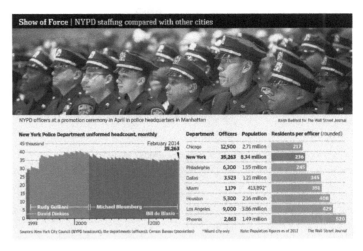

Figure 9.20   NYPD, Council Spar Over More Officers

of our attention is the subject of focus in the analysis, in this case regarding a drive for more NYPD officers. This does not need to be any more contrasting; it is just as sufficiently noticeable as the visualiser wishes it to be.

Sometime you will seek to create several levels of visual 'urgency' in the relative contrast of your display. The colour choices in Figure 9.21 gives foreground prominence to the yellow coloured markers and values (the dots are also larger) and then mid-ground/ secondary prominence to the slightly muted red markers. In perceiving the values of the yellow markers, the viewer is encouraged to concentrate on primarily comparing these with the red markers. The subtle grey markers are far less visible – closer in

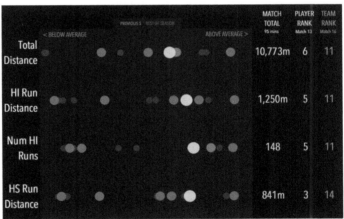

Figure 9.21   Excerpt from a Football Player Dashboard

shade to the background than the foreground – and deliberately relegated to a tertiary level so they do not clutter up the display and cause unwarranted attention. They provide further context for the distribution of the values but do not need to be any more prominent in their relationship with the foreground and mid-ground colours.

I touched on the use of encoded overlays earlier where coloured areas or bandings can be used to help separate different regions of a display in order to facilitate faster interpretation of the meaning of values. In the bubble plot in Figure 9.22, you can see the circle markers are colour coded to help viewers quickly ascertain the significance of each location on the chart according to the quadrants in which they fall. Notice how in the background the diagonal shading further emphasises the distinction between above the line 'improvement' and below the line 'worsening', a very effective approach.

Figure 9.22
Elections
Performance
Index

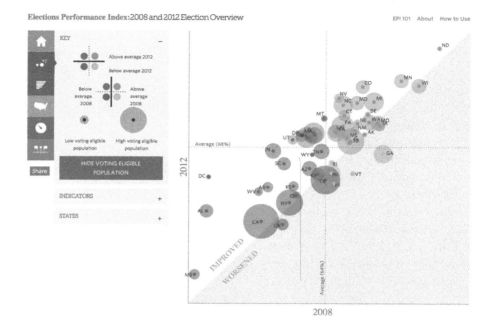

9.4 Features of Colour: Functional Harmony

After achieving data legibility and editorial salience through astute colour choices, functional harmony is concerned with ensuring that any remaining colour choices will aid, and not hinder, the functional effectiveness and elegance of the overall visualisation.

> 'When something is not harmonious, it's either boring or chaotic. At one extreme is a visual experience that is so bland that the viewer is not engaged. The human brain will reject under-stimulating information. At the other extreme is a visual experience that is so overdone, so chaotic, that the viewer can't stand to look at it. The human brain rejects what it can not organise, what it cannot understand.' **Jill Morton, Colour Expert and Researcher**

You must judge the overall balance of and suitability of your collective colour choices and not just see these as isolated selections. This is again primarily a judgement about contrast – what needs to be prominent and what needs to be less so. Such an apparent calming quality about a well-judged and cohesive colour palette is demonstrated by Stefanie Posavec's choices in visualising the structure of Walter Benjamin's essay 'Art in the age of mechanical reproduction'

(Figure 9.23). There is effortless harmony here between the colour choices extending across the entire anatomy of design: the petals, branches, labels, titles, legend, and background.

A reminder that any and every design feature you incorporate into your display will have a property of colour otherwise they will be invisible. In looking at data legibility and editorial salience you have considered your colour choices for representing data. A desire to achieve functional harmony means considering further colour decisions that will help establish visual

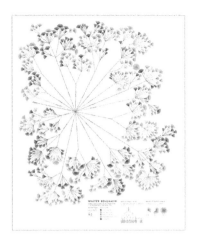 

Figure 9.23
Art in the Age
of Mechanical
Reproduction:
Walter Benjamin

relationships across and between the rest of your visualisation's anatomy: its interactive features, annotations and composition.

Interactive features: Visible interactive features will include controls such as dropdown menus, navigation buttons, time sliders and parameter selectors. The colour of every control used will need to be harmonious with the rest of the project but also, critically, must be functionally clear. How you use colour to help the user discern what is selected and what is not will need to be carefully judged.

To illustrate this, Figure 9.24 shows an interactive project that examines the connected stories of the casualties and fatalities from the Iraqi and Afghan conflicts. Here you can see that there are several interactive features, all of which are astutely coloured in a way that feels both

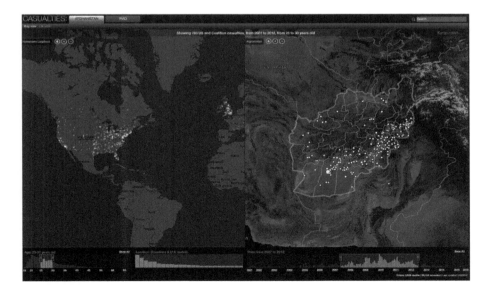

Figure 9.24
Casualties

consistent with the overall tone of the project but also makes it functionality evident what each control's selected status or defined setting is. This is achieved through very subtle but effective combinations of dark and light greys that help create intuitive clarity about which values the user has selected or highlighted. When a button has a toggle setting (on/off, something/something else), such as the 'Afghanistan' or 'Iraq' tabs at the top, the selected tab is highlighted in bright grey and the unselected tab in a more subdued grey. Filters can either frame (include/exclude) or focus (highlight/relegate) the data. The same approach to using brighter greys for the selected parameter values makes it very clear what you have chosen, but also what you have excluded (while making evident the other currently-unselected values from which you can potentially choose).

Annotations: Chart annotations such as gridlines, axis lines and value labels all need colouring in a way that will be sympathetic to the colour choices already made for the data representation and, possibly, editorial contrasting. As mentioned in the last chapter, many annotation devices exist in the form of text and so the relative font colour choices will need to be carefully considered. For any annotation device the key guiding decision is to find the level at which these are suitably prominent. Not loud, not hidden, just at the right level. This will generally take a fair amount of trial and error to get right but once again, depending on your context, your first thought should be to consider the merits offered by different shades of grey.

You might be starting to suspect I'm a lobbyist for the colour grey. Nobody wants to live in a world of only grey. The point is more about how its presence enables other colours to come alive. The great Bill Shankly once said 'Football is like a piano, you need 8 men to carry it and 3 who can play the damn thing'. In data visualisation, grey does the heavy lifting so the more vibrant colours can bring the energy and vibrancy to your design.

Figure 9.25 First Fatal Accident in Spain on a High-speed Line [Translated]

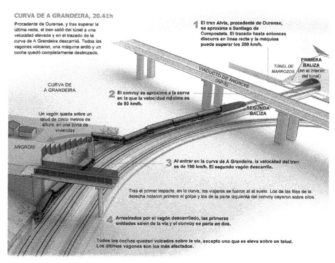

Another example of the role of greyscale is demonstrated by Figure 9.25, illustrating key aspects of the tragic rail crash in Spain in 2013. The sense of foreground and background is clearly achieved by the prominence of the scarlet-coloured annotations and visual cues offset against the backdrop of an otherwise greyscale palette.

There are other features of annotation that will have an impact on functional harmony through their colouring. Multimedia assets like photos, embedded videos, images and illustrations need to be consistent in tone accord-

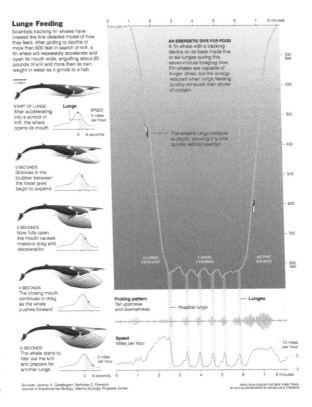

Figure 9.26
Lunge Feeding

ing to their relative role on the display. If they are to dominate the page then unleash the vibrancy of their colours to achieve this; if they are playing more of a secondary or supporting role then relegate their constituent colours to allow other primary features due prominence.

Figure 9.26 includes small illustrations of a whale, showing how it goes through the stages of lunge feeding. The elegance of the colours used in these illustrations is entirely harmonious with the look and feel of the overall piece. They are entirely at one with the rest of the graphic.

Composition: The clarity in layout of a project will often be achieved by the use of background colour to create logical organisation. In the 'Lunge Feeding' graphic the shading of the blue sea getting darker as it moves down is not attempting to offer a precise representation of the sea, but it gives a sense of depth and draws maximum attention to that panel. It is also naturally congruent with the subject matter.

In general, there are no fixed rules on the benefits of any particular colour for background

Figure 9.27 Examples of Common Background Colour Tones

shading. Your choices will depend mostly on the circumstances and conditions in which your viewers are consuming the work. Usually, when there is no associated congruence for a certain background colour, your options will tend to come from one of the selection of neutral and/or non-colours (Figure 9.27). This is because they particularly help to aid accentuation in combination with foreground colours.

Typically, though, a white background (at least for your chart area) gives viewers the best chance of being able to accurately perceive the different colour attributes used in your data representation and the contrasting nature of your editorial contrast.

'The single most overlooked element in visual design is emptiness. Space must look deliberately used.' **Alex White, Author,** *The Elements of Graphic Design*

White – or more specifically emptiness – is one of your most important options for creating functional meaning for *nothingness*, something I touched on earlier. The emptiness of uncoloured space can be used very effectively to direct the eye's attention. It organises the relationship between space on a page without the need for visible apparatus, as seen in the left hand column of the lunge feeding graphic. It can also be used to represent or emphasise values that might have the state of 'null' or 'zero' to maximise contrast.

9.5 Influencing Factors and Considerations

Having mapped out the ways and places where colour *could* be used, you will now need to consider the factors that will influence your decisions about how colour *should* be used.

Formulating Your Brief

Format: This is a simple concern but always worth pointing out: if you are producing something for screen display you will need to set your colour output to RGB; if it is for print you will need CMYK. Additionally, when you are preparing work for print, running off plenty of proofs before finalising a design is imperative. What you are preparing digitally is a step away from the form of its intended output. What looks like a perfect colour palette on screen may not ultimately look the same when printed.

We all refer to black and white printing, but technically printers do not actually print using white ink, it is just less black or no black.

Print quality and consistency is also a factor. Graphics editors who create work for print newspapers or magazines will often consider using colours as close in tone as possible to pure CMYK, especially if their work is quite intricate in detail. This is because the colour plates used in printing presses will not always be 100% aligned and thus mixtures of colours may be slightly compromised.

As black and white printing is still commonplace, you need to be aware of how your work might look if printed without colour. If you are creating a visualisation that might possibly be printed by certain users in black and white, the only colour property that you can feasibly utilise will be the lightness dimension. Sometimes, as a designer or author, you will be unaware of this intent and the colourful design that you worked carefully towards will end up not being remotely readable.

Furthermore, there is an important difference in how colours appear when published in *colour* and how they appear when published in *black and white*. Hues inherently possess different levels of brightness: the purest blue is darker than the purest yellow. If these were printed in black and white, blue would therefore appear a darker, more prominent shade of grey. If your printed work will need to be compatible for both colour and black and white output, before finalising your decisions check that the legibility and intended meaning of your colour choices are being maintained across both forms.

Setting: For digital displays, the conditions in which the work will be consumed will have some influence over the choice between light and dark backgrounds. The main factor is the relative contrast and the stresses this can place on the eye to adjust against the surroundings. If your work is intended for consumption in a light environment, lighter backgrounds tend to be more fitting; likewise darker backgrounds will work best for consuming in darker settings. For tablets/smartphones, the bordering colour of the devices can also influence the most suitable choice of background tone to most sympathetically contrast with the surroundings.

Colour rules and identities: In some organisations there are style guidelines or branding identities that require the strict use of only certain colour options. Similar guidelines may exist if you are creating work for publication in a journal, magazine, or on certain websites. Guidelines like these are well intended, driven by a desire to create conformity and consistency in style and appearance. However, in my experience, the basis of such colour guides rarely incorporates consideration for the subtleties of data visualisation. This means that the resulting palettes are often a bad fit for ideal visualisation colour needs, providing limited scope for the variation and salience you might seek to portray.

Your first task should always be to find out if there is any compromise – any chance of not having these colour restrictions imposed. If there is no flexibility, then you will just have to accept this and begin acquainting yourself with the colours you do have to work with. Taking a more positive view, achieving consistency in the use of colour for visualisation within an organisation does have merits if the defined palettes offer suitably rich variety. Developing a recognisable 'brand' and not having to think from scratch about what colours to use every time you face a new project is something that can be very helpful, especially across a team.

Purpose map: Does it need to be utilitarian or decorative? Should it be functional or appealingly seductive? Does it lend itself to being vivid and varied in colour or more muted and distinguished? Colour is the first thing we notice as viewers when looking at a visualisation, so your choices will play a huge part in setting the visible tone of voice. How you define your thinking across the vertical dimension of your purpose map will therefore have an influence on your colour thinking.

Along the horizontal dimension, the main influencing consideration will be a desire to offer an 'explanatory' experience. As mentioned, some of the tactics for incorporating editorial salience will be of specific value if you are seeking to emphasise immediately apparent, curated insights.

Ideas and inspiration: In the process of sketching out your ideas and capturing thoughts about possible sources of influence, maybe there were already certain colours you had identified as being consistent with your thinking about this subject? Additionally, you might have already identified some colours you wish to avoid using.

Working With Data

Data examination: The characteristics of your data will naturally have a huge impact, on the decisions you make around data legibility. Firstly, the type of data you are displaying (primarily nominal vs all other types) will require a different colour treatment, as explained. Secondly, the range of categorical colour associations (limits on discernible hues) and the range and distribution of quantitative values (numbers of divisions and definition of the intervals across your classification scale) will be directly shaped by the work you did in the examination stage.

In Figure 9.28 you can see a census of the prevalence and species of trees found around the boroughs of New York City. This initial big-picture view creates a beautiful tapestry made up of tree populations across the region (notice the big void where JFK Airport is located).

Figure 9.28
Excerpt from 'NYC Street Trees by Species'

'If using colour to identify certain data, be careful to not accidentally apply the same identity to a nearby part of the graphic. Don't allow colour to confuse just for the sake of aesthetics. I also like to use colour to highlight. A single colour highlight on a palette of muted colours can be a strong way to draw attention to key information.' **Simon Scarr, Deputy Head of Graphics, ThomsonReuters**

To observe patterns for individual tree types is harder: with 52 different tree species there are simply too many classifications to be able to allocate sufficiently unique colours to each. To overcome this, the project features a useful pop-up filter list which then allows you to adjust the data on view to reveal the species you wish to explore.

It is often the case when thinking about colour classifications that you may need to revisit the data transformation actions to find new ways of grouping your data to create better-fit quantitative value classifications or to look at ways of grouping your categories. For the latter, actions such as combining less important categories in an 'other' bin to reduce the variability or eliminating certain values from your analysis may be necessary.

Establishing Your Editorial Thinking

Focus: When considering the perspective of 'focus' in the editorial thinking stage, you were defining which, if any, elements of content would merit being emphasised. Are there features of your analysis that you might wish to accentuate? How might colour be used to accentuate key insights in the foreground and push other (less important) features into the background? What are the characteristics of your data that you might want to emphasise through changes in colour? For example, are there certain threshold values that will need to be visually amplified if exceeded? Your decisions here will directly influence your thinking about using colour to facilitate editorial salience.

Data Representation

Chart type choice: Specifically in relation to data legibility, depending on which chart type you selected to portray your data, this may have attributes requiring decisions about colour. The heat map and choropleth map are just two examples that use variation in colour to encode quantitative value. Almost every chart has the potential to use colour for categorical differentiation.

Trustworthy Design

Data classification: The decisions you make about how to encode data through colour have a great bearing on the legibility and accuracy of your design, especially with quantitative data. You will need to ensure the classifications present a true reflection of the shape and characteristics of your data and do not suppress any significant interpretations.

Meaningful: Eliminating arbitrary decisions is not just about increasing the sophistication of your design thinking, it is also an essential part of delivering a trustworthy design. If something looks visually significant in its data or editorial colouring it

> 'Start with black and white, and only introduce color when it has relevant meaning. In general, use color very sparingly.' **Nigel Holmes, Explanation Graphic Designer**

will be read as such, so make sure it is significant, otherwise remove it. You especially want to avoid any connotation of significant meaning across your functional or decorative colour choices. This will be confusing at best, or will appear deceptive at worst.

Do not try to make something look more interesting than it fundamentally is. Colour should not be used to decorate data. You might temporarily boost the apparent appeal of your work in the eye of the viewer but this will be short-lived and artificial.

Illusions: The relationship between a foreground colour and a background one can create distorting illusions that modify the perceived judgement of a colour. You saw an effect of this earlier with the inverted area chart showing 'Gun deaths in Florida', whereby the rising white mountain was seen by some as the foreground data, when in fact it was the background emptiness framed by the red area of data and the axis line. Illusions can affect all dimensions of colour perception. There are simply too many to mention here and they are hard to legislate for entirely; it is really more about mentioning that you need to be aware of these as a consequence of your colour choices.

Accessible Design

Consistency: Consistency in the use of colours helps to avoid visual chaos and confusion and minimises cognitive effort. When you establish association through colour you need to maintain that meaning for as long as possible. Once a viewer has allocated time and effort to learn what colours represent, that association becomes locked down in the eye and the mind. However, if you then allocate the same colour(s) to mean something different (within the same graphic or on a different page/screen view) this creates an additional cognitive burden. The viewer has almost to disregard the previous association and learn the new one. This demands effort that undermines the accessibility of your design.

Sometimes this can prove difficult, especially if you have a restricted colour palette. The main advice here is to try to maximise the 'space' between occasions of the same colour meaning different things. This space may be physical (different pages, interactive views), time (the simple duration of reading between the associations being changed) or editorial (new subject matter, new angle of analysis). Such space effectively helps to clean the palate (pun intended). Of course, at the point of any new assignment in your colour usage, clear explanations are mandatory.

Visual accessibility: Approximately 5% of the population have visual impairments that compromise their ability to discern particular colours and colour combinations. Deuteranopia is the most common form, often known as red–green colour blindness, and is a particular genetic issue

Figure 9.29
Demonstrating the Impact of Red-green Colour Blindness (deuteranopia)

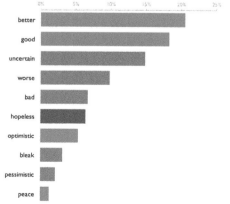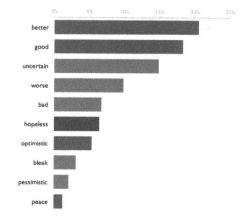

associated with men. The traffic light scheme of green = 'good', red = 'bad' is a widespread approach for using colour as an indicator. It is a convenient and common metaphor and the reasons for its use are entirely understandable. However, as demonstrated in the pair of graphics in Figure 9.29, looking at some word-usage sentiment analysis, the reds and greens that most of us would easily discern (from the left graphic) are often not at all distinguishable for those with colour blindness (simulated on the right).

Of course, if you have a particularly known, finite and fixed audience then you can easily discover if any colour-blindness issues do in fact exist. However, if your audience is much larger and undefined you are going to alienate potentially 1 person in every 14, in which case the use of the default red–green colour combination is not acceptable. Be more sensitive to your viewers by considering other options:

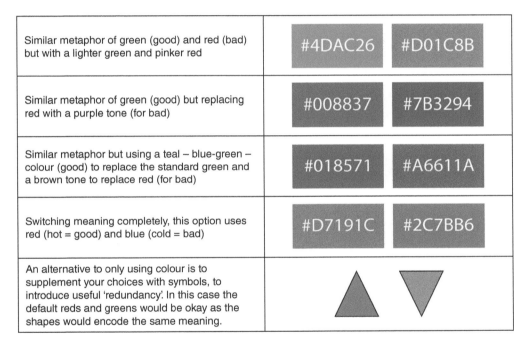

Similar metaphor of green (good) and red (bad) but with a lighter green and pinker red	#4DAC26 #D01C8B
Similar metaphor of green (good) but replacing red with a purple tone (for bad)	#008837 #7B3294
Similar metaphor but using a teal – blue-green – colour (good) to replace the standard green and a brown tone to replace red (for bad)	#018571 #A6611A
Switching meaning completely, this option uses red (hot = good) and blue (cold = bad)	#D7191C #2C7BB6
An alternative to only using colour is to supplement your choices with symbols, to introduce useful 'redundancy'. In this case the default reds and greens would be okay as the shapes would encode the same meaning.	

Figure 9.30
Colour-blind Friendly Alternatives to Green and Red

If you are working on an interactive solution, you may consider having a toggle option to switch between different colour modes. For print outputs you might normally have reduced flexibility, but in certain circumstances the option of creating dual versions (second output for colour-impaired viewers) may be legitimate.

Connotations and congruence: Whether it is in politics, sport, brands or in nature, there are many subjects that already have established colour associations you can possibly look to exploit. This association may sit directly with the data, such as the normal colour associations for political party categories, or more through the meaning of the data, such as perhaps through the use of green to present analysis about ecological topics.

In support of accessible design, exploiting pre-existing colour associations in your work can create more immediacy in subject recognition. You might also benefit from the colour learning experiences your viewers may already have gone through. This provides a shortcut to understanding through familiarity.

However, while some colour connotations can be a good thing, in some cases they can be a bad thing and possibly should be avoided. You need to be considerate of and sensitive to any colour usage to ensure that you do not employ connotations that may have a negative implication and may evoke strong emotions and reactions from people.

Sometimes a colour is simply incongruent with a subject. You would not use bright, happy colours if you were portraying data about death or disease. Earlier, in the 'Vision: Ideas' section, I described a project context where I knew I wanted to avoid the use of blue colours in a particular project about psychotherapy treatment in the Arctic, because it would carry an unwelcome clichéd association given the subject matter. The use of 'typical' skin colours to represent ethnic groups in a visualisation is something that would be immediately clumsy (at best) and offensive (at worst).

Cultural sensitivities and inconsistencies are also important to consider. In China, for example, red is a lucky colour and so the use of red in their stock market displays, for example, indicates the rising values. A sea of red on the FTSE or Dow Jones implies the opposite. In Western society red is often the signal for a warning or danger.

Occasionally established colour associations are out of sync with contemporary culture or society. For example, when you think about colour and the matter of gender, because it has been so endlessly utilised down the years, it is almost impossible not to think instinctively about the use of blue (boys) and pink (girls). My personal preference is to avoid this association entirely. I agree with so many commentators out there that the association of pink to signify the female gender, in particular, is clichéd, outdated and no longer fit for purpose. It is not too much to expect viewers to learn the association of – at most – two new colours for representing gender.

Elegant Design

Unity: As I alluded to in the discussion about using colours for editorial salience, colour choices are always about contrast. The effect of using one colour is not isolated to just that instance of colour: choosing one colour will automatically create a relationship with another. There is always a minimum of two colours in any visualisation – a foreground and background colour – but generally there are many more.

We notice the impact of colour decisions more when they are done badly. Inconsistent and poorly integrated colour combinations create jarring and discordant results. If we do not consciously notice colour decisions this probably means they have been seamlessly blended into the fabric of the overall communication.

Neutral colouring: Even if there is no relevance in the use of colour for quantitative or categorical classifications, you still have to give your chart some colour, otherwise it will be invisible. The decision you make will depend again on the relative harmony with other colour features but should also avoid unnecessarily 'using up' a useful colour. Suppose you colour your bars in blue but then elsewhere across your visualisation project blue would have been a useful colour to show something meaningful; you then have unnecessarily taken blue out of the reckoning. My default choice is to go with grey to begin with (Figure 9.31) and only use a colour if there is a suitable and available colour not used elsewhere or if it needs to be left as a back- or mid-ground artefact to preserve prominence elsewhere in the display.

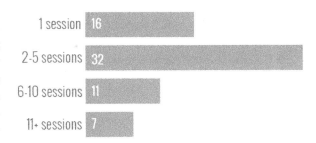

Figure 9.31 Excerpt from 'Pyschotherapy in The Arctic'

Justified: Achieving elegant design is about eliminating the arbitrary. In thinking about colour usage I often get quite tough with myself. If I want to show any feature on my visualisation display I have to seek permission from myself to unlock access to the more vibrant colours by justifying why I should be allowed to use and apply that colour (I know what you're thinking, 'what a fun existence this guy leads'). Elegance in visualisation design is often about using only the colours you need to use and avoiding the temptation to inject unnecessary decoration. The Wind Map project (Figure 9.32) demonstrates unquestionable elegance and yet uses only a monochromatic palette. There is no colouring of the sea, no topographic detail, no emphasising of any extreme wind speed thresholds being reached. The resulting elegance is quite evident: the map has artistic *and* functional beauty.

To emphasise again, I am not advocating a need to pursue minimalism: while you can create incredibly elegant and detailed works from a limited palette of colours, justifying the use of colours is not the same as unnecessarily restricting the use of colour.

Feels right: The last component of influence is yourself. Sometimes you will just find colours that feel right and look good when you apply them to your work. There is maybe no underlying

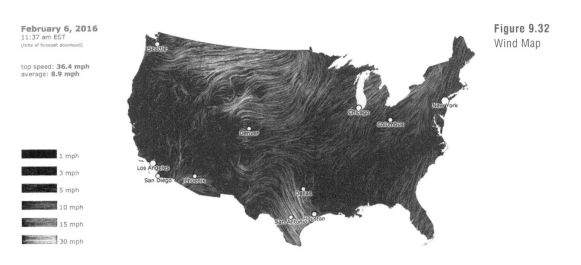

Figure 9.32 Wind Map

science behind such choices, and as such you will simply need to back your own instinctive judgement as an astute visualiser and know when something looks good. Creating the right type of visual appeal, something that is pleasing to the eye and equally fit for purpose in all the functional ways I have outlined, is a hard balance to achieve, but you will find that weighing up all these different components of influence alongside your own flair for design judgement will give you the best chance of getting there.

Summary: Colour

Data legibility involves using colours to represent different types of data. The most appropriate colour association or scale decisions will depend on the data type: nominal (qualitative), ordinal (qualitative), interval and ratio (quantitative).

Editorial salience is about using colour to direct the eye. For which features and to what degree of emphasis do you want to create contrast?

Functional harmony concerns deciding about every other colour property as applied to all interactive features, annotations and aspects of your composition thinking.

Influencing Factors and Considerations

- Formulating the brief: format, setting, colour rules and imposed guidelines all have a significant impact. Your definitions about both tone and and experience, on the purpose map, will lead to specific choices being more suitable than others. What initial ideas did you form? Have any sources of inspiration already implanted ideas inside your head about which colours you could use?
- Working with data: what type of data and what range of values/number of classifications have you got?
- Establishing your editorial thinking: what things do you want to emphasise or direct the eye towards (focus)?
- Data representation: certain chart type choices will already include colour as an encoded attribute.
- Trustworthy design: ensure that your colour choices are faithful to the shape of your data and the integrity of your insights. If something looks meaningful it should be, otherwise it will confuse or deceive.
- Accessible design: once you've committed colour to mean something preserve the consistency of association for as long as possible. Be aware of the sensitivities around visual accessibility and positive/negative colour connotations.
- Elegant design: the perception of colours is relative so the unity of your choices needs to be upheld. Ensure that you can justify every dot of colour used and, ultimately, rely on your own judgment to determine when your final palette feels right.

Tips and Tactics

- Use the squint test: shrink things down and/or half close your eyes to see what coloured properties are most prominent and visible – are these the right ones?
- Experimentation: trial and error is still often required in colour, despite the common sense and foundation of science attached to it.
- Developing a personal style guide for colour usage saves you the pain of having to think from scratch every time and will help your work become more immediately identifiable (which may or may not be an important factor).
- Make life easier by ensuring your preferred (or imposed) colour palettes are loaded up into any tool you are using, even if it is just the tool you are using for analysis rather than for the final presentation of your work.
- If you are creating for print, make sure you do test print runs of the draft work to see how your colours are looking – do not wait for the first print when you (think you) have finished your process.

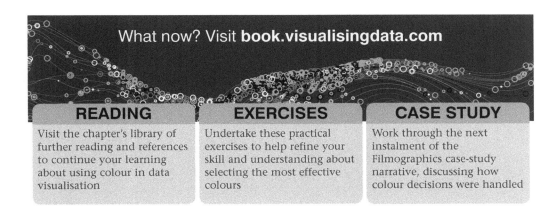

What now? Visit **book.visualisingdata.com**

READING
Visit the chapter's library of further reading and references to continue your learning about using colour in data visualisation

EXERCISES
Undertake these practical exercises to help refine your skill and understanding about selecting the most effective colours

CASE STUDY
Work through the next instalment of the Filmographics case-study narrative, discussing how colour decisions were handled

10

Composition

Composition concerns making careful decisions about the physical attributes of, and relationships between, every visual property to ensure the optimum readability and meaning of the overall, cohesive project.

Composition is the final layer of your design anatomy, but this should not imply that it is the least important part of your design workflow. Far from it. It is simply that now is the most logical time to think about this, because only at this point will you have established clarity about what content to include in your work. As I explained, this final layer of design thinking, along with colour, is no longer about *what* elements will be included but *how* they will appear. Composition is a critical component of any design discipline. The care and attention afforded in the precision of your composition thinking will continue until the final dot or pixel has been considered.

Visual assets such as your chart(s), interactive controls and annotations all occupy space. In this chapter you will be judging what is the best way to use space in terms of the position, size and shape of every visible property. In many respects these individual dimensions of thought are inseparable and so, similar to the discussion about annotation, the division in thinking is separated between project- and chart-level composition options:

- Project composition: defining the layout and hierarchy of the entire visualisation project.
- Chart composition: defining the shape, size and layout choices for all components within your charts.

10.1 Features of Composition: Project Composition

This first aspect of composition design concerns how you might lay out and size all the visual content in your project to establish a meaningful hierarchy and sequence. Content, in this case, means all of your charts, interactive operations and elements of annotation.

Where will you put all of this, what size will it be and why? How will the hierarchy (across views) and sequencing (within a view) best fit the space you have to work in? How will you convey the relative importance and provide a connected narrative where necessary?

I will shortly run through all the key factors that will influence your decisions, but it is worth emphasising that so much about composition thinking is rooted in common sense and involves

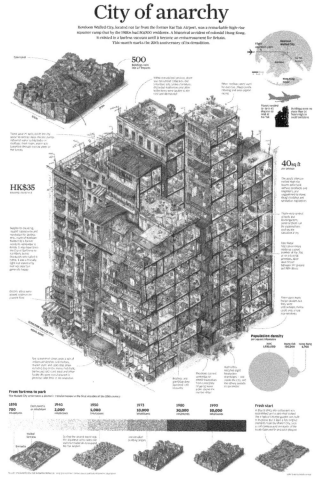

City of anarchy

Kowloon Walled City, located not far from the former Kai Tak Airport, was a remarkable high-rise
squatter camp that by the 1980s had 50,000 residents. A historical accident of colonial Hong Kong,
it existed in a lawless vacuum until it became an embarrassment for Britain.
This month marks the 20th anniversary of its demolition.

Figure 10.1   City of Anarchy

a process of iteration towards what *feels* like an optimum layout. Of course, there are certain established conventions, such as the positioning of titles first or at the top (usually left or centrally aligned). Introductions are inevitably useful to offer early, whereas footnotes detailing data sources and credits might be of least importance, relatively speaking. You might choose to show the main features first, exploiting the initial attention afforded by your audience, or you may wish to build up to this, starting off with contextual content before the big 'reveal'.

The hierarchy of content is not just a function of relative position through layout design, it can also be achieved through the relative variation in size of the contents. Just as variation in colour implies significance, so too does variation in size: a chart that is larger than another chart will imply that the analysis it is displaying carries greater importance.

The 'City of anarchy' infographic demonstrates a clear visual hierarchy across its design. There is a primary focal point of the main subject 'cutaway' illustration in the centre with a small thumbnail image above it for orientation. At the bottom there are small supplementary illustrations to provide further information. It is clear through their relative placement at the bottom of the page and their more diminutive stature that they are of somewhat incidental import compared with the main detail in the centre.

There are generally two approaches for shaping your ideas about this project-level composition activity, depending on your entry-point perspective: **wireframing** and **storyboarding**. I profiled these at the start of this part of the book, but it is worth reinforcing their role now you are focusing on this section of design thinking.

Wireframing involves sketching the potential layout and size of all the major contents of your design thinking across a single-page view. This might be the approach you take when working on an infographic or any digital project where all the interactive functions are contained within a single-screen view rather than navigating users elsewhere. Any interactive controls included would have a description within the wireframe sketch to explain the functions they would trigger.

Figure 10.2 is an early wireframe drawn by Giorgia Lupi when shaping up her early thoughts about the potential layout of a graphic exploring various characteristics of Nobel prizes and laureates between 1901 and 2012.

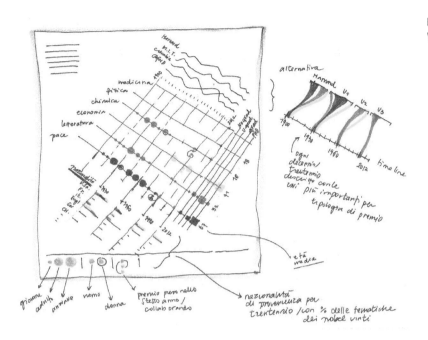

Figure 10.2
Wireframe Sketch

Storyboarding is something you would undertake *with* wireframing if you have a project that will entail multiple pages or many different views and you want to establish a high-level feel for the overall architecture of content, its navigation and sequencing. This would be an approach relevant for linear outputs like discrete sequences in reports, presentation slides or video graphics, or for non-linear navigation around different pages of a multi-faceted interactive. The individual page views included as cells in this big-picture hierarchy will each merit more detailed wireframing versions to determine how their within-page content will be sized and arranged, and how the navigation between views would operate.

With both wireframing and storyboarding activities all you are working towards, at this stage, are low-fidelity sketched concepts. Whether this sketching is on paper or using a quick layout tool does not matter; it just needs to capture with moderate precision the essence of your early thinking about the spatial consequence of bringing all your design choices together. Gradually, through further iteration, the precision and finality of your solution will emerge.

10.2 Features of Composition: Chart Composition

After establishing your thoughts about the overall layout, you will now need to go deeper in your composition thinking and contemplate the detailed spatial matters local to each chart, to optimise its legibility and meaning. There are many different components to consider.

Chart size: Do not be afraid to shrink your charts. The eye can still detect at quite small resolution and with great efficiency chart attributes such as variation in size, position, colour, shape and pattern. This supports the potential value of the small-multiples technique, an approach that tends to be universally loved in data visualisation. As I explained earlier, this technique offers an ideal solution for when you are trying to display the same analysis for multiple categories or multiple points in time. Providing all the information in a simultaneous view means that viewers can efficiently observe overall patterns as well as perform a more detailed inspection. Figure 10.3 provides a single view of a rugby team's match patterns across the first 12 matches of a season. Each line chart panel portrays the cumulative scoring for the competing teams across the 80 minutes of a match. The 12 match panels are arranged in chronological order, from top left to bottom right, based on the date of the match.

Figure 10.3
Example of the
Small Multiples
Technique

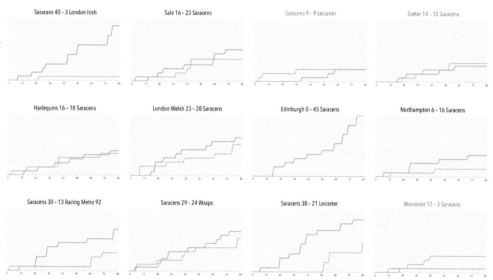

The main obstacle to shrinking chart displays is the impact on text. The eye will not cope too well with small fonts for value or category labels, so there has to be a trade-off, as always, between the amount of detail you show and the size you show it.

Chart scales: When considering your chart-scales try to think about how you might use these to tell the viewer something meaningful. This can be achieved through astute choices around the maximum value ranges and also in the choice of suitable intervals for labelling and gridline guides.

The maximum values that you assign to your chart scales, informed by decisions around editorial framing, can be quite impactful in surfacing key insights. You may recall the chart from earlier that looked at the disproportionality of women CEO's amongst the S&P 1500 companies. Figure 10.4 is another graphic on a similar subject, which contextualises the relative progress in the rise of women CEOs amongst the Fortune 500 companies. By setting the maximum y-axis value range to reflect the level at which equality would exist, the resulting empty space emphasises the significant gap that still persists.

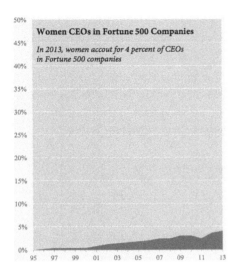

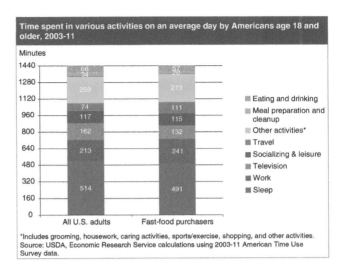

Figure 10.4 Reworking of 'The Glass Ceiling Persists'

Figure 10.5 Fast-food Purchasers Report More Demands on Their Time

Figure 10.5 shows how the lack of careful thought about your scales can undermine the ease of readability. This chart shows how American adults spend their time on different activities. The analysis is broken down into minutes and so the maximum is set at 1440 minutes in a day. For some reason, the y-axis labels and the associated horizontal gridlines are displayed at intervals of 160 minutes. This is an entirely meaningless quantity of time so why divide the day up into nine intervals? To help viewers perceive the significance and size of the different stacked activities it would have been far more logical to use 60-minute time intervals as that is how we tend to think when dividing our daily schedule.

Chart orientation: Decisions about the orientation of your chart and its contents can sometimes help squeeze out an extra degree of readability and meaning from your display.

The primary concern about chart orientation is towards the legibility of labels along the axis. A vertical bar chart, with multiple categories along the x-axis, will present a challenge of making the labels legible and avoiding them overlapping. Ideally you would want to preserve label reading in line with the eye, but you might need to adjust their orientation to either 45° or 90°. My preference for handling this with bar charts is to switch the orientation of the chart and to then have much more compatible horizontal space to accommodate the labels.

The meaning of your subject's data may also influence your choice. While there may have been constraints on the dimension of space in its native setting, Figure 10.6, portraying the split of political parties in Germany, feels like a missed opportunity to display a political axis of the Left and the Right through using a landscape rather than portrait layout.

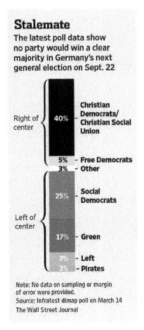

Figure 10.6 Illustrating the Effect of Chart orientation Decisions

As you saw earlier, the graphic about 'Iraq's bloody toll' (Figure 1.11) uses an inverted bar chart to create a potent display of data that effectively conveys the subject matter, but importantly does so without introducing any unnecessary obstacles in readability.

In the previous section I presented a wireframe sketch of a graphic about Nobel prize winners. Figure 10.7 shows the final design. Notice how the original concept of the novel diagonal orientation was accomplished in the final composition, exploiting the greater room that this dimension of space offers within the page. It feels quite audacious to do this in a newspaper setting.

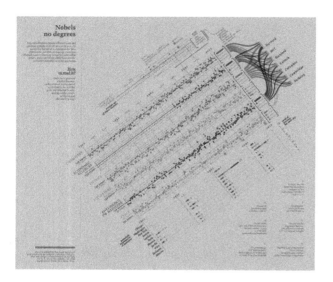

Figure 10.7   Nobels no Degrees

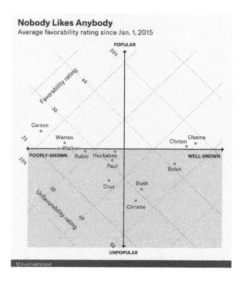

Figure 10.8   Kasich Could Be The GOP's Moderate Backstop

Figure 10.8, from FiveThirtyEight, rotates the scatter plot by 45° and then overlays a 2 × 2 grid which helps to guide the viewer's interpretation by making it easier to observe which values are located in each quadrant. It is also used to emphasise the distinction between location in the top and bottom halves of the chart along the axis of popularity, essentially the primary focus of the analysis.

Although the LATCH and CHRTS acronyms share some similarities, the application of each concerns entirely different aspects of your design thinking. They are independent of one another. A bar chart, which belongs to the categorical (C) family of charts, could have its data potentially sorted by location, alphabet, time, category or hierarchy.

Chart value sorting: Sorting content within a chart is important for helping viewers to find and compare quickly the most relevant content. One of the best ways to consider the options for value sorting comes from using the LATCH acronym, devised by Richard Saul Wurman, which stands for the five ways of organising displays of data: Location, Alphabet, Time, Category or Hierarchy.

Location sorting involves sequencing content according to the order of a spatial dimension. This does not refer to sorting data on a map locations are fixed, rather it could be sorting data by geographical spatial relationships (such as presenting data for all the stops along a subway route)

or a non-geographical spatial relationship (like a sequence based on the position of major parts of the body from head to toe). You should order by location only when you believe it offers the most logical sequence for the readability of the display or if there is likely to be interest or significance in the comparison of neighbouring values. An example of location sorting is displayed in 'On Broadway' (Figure 10.9) on the following page, an interactive installation that stitches together a sequenced compilation of data and media related to 30 metre intervals of life along the 13 miles (21 km) of Broadway that stretches across the length of Manhattan. This continuous narrative offers compelling views of the fluctuating characteristics as you transport yourself down the spine of the city.

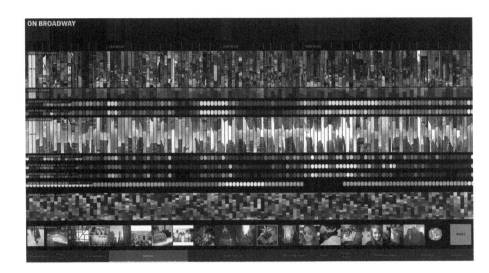

Figure 10.9
On Broadway

Alphabetical sorting is a cataloguing approach that facilitates efficient lookup and reference. Only on rare occasions, when you are especially keen to offer convenient ordering for looking up categorical values, will you find that alphabetical sorting alone offers the best sequence. In Figure 10.10, investigating different measures of waiting times in emergency rooms across the United States, the bar charts are presented based on the alphabetical sorting of each state. This is the default setting but users can also choose to reorder the table hierarchically based on the increasing/decreasing values across the four columns.

> Data representation techniques that display overlapping connections, like Sankey diagrams, slope graphs and chord diagrams, also introduce the need to contemplate value sorting in the z-dimension: that is, which of these connections will be above and which will be below, and why.

Alphabetical sorting might be seen as a suitably diplomatic option should you not wish to imply any ranking significance that would be displayed when sorting by any other dimension. Additionally, there is a lot of sense in employing alphabetical ordering for values listed in dropdown menus as this offers the most immediate way for viewers to quickly find the options they are interested in selecting.

Figure 10.10
ER Wait
Watcher: Which
Emergency
Room Will See
You the Fastest?

▲ State	‡ Waiting Time	‡ Time Until Sent Home	‡ Broken Bone	‡ Transfer Time
	Average time patients spent in the emergency room before being seen by a doctor	Average time patients spent in the emergency room before being sent home	Average time patients with broken bones had to wait before receiving pain meds	Among patients admitted, additional time spent waiting before being taken to their room
Nat Avg.	24 min	135 min	54 min	96 min
Alaska	24	132	53	124
Alabama	30	127	66	73
Arkansas	26	121	64	64
Arizona	28	166	54	96
California	28	161	60	126
Colorado	17	139	45	93
Connecticut	27	139	54	153
Dist. of Columbia	54	187	69	223
Delaware	35	165	67	200
Florida	23	145	54	108
Georgia	30	N/A	59	94
Hawaii	20	128	52	114
Iowa	20	111	45	82
Idaho	20	125	46	76
Illinois	25	141	50	88
Indiana	18	121	49	79
Kansas	17	105	44	65
Kentucky	22	129	53	78
Louisiana	25	125	55	87
Massachusetts	35	161	57	122
Maryland	46	191	67	134
Maine	27	127	48	109
Michigan	21	132	52	99
Minnesota	25	123	42	62
Missouri	23	136	49	80
Mississippi	27	112	65	62

Time-based sorting is used when the data has a relevant chronological sequence and you wish to display and compare how changes have progressed over time. In Figure 10.11, you can see a snapshot of a graphic that portrays the rain patterns in Hong Kong since 1990. Each row of data represents a full year of 365/366 daily readings running from left to right. The subject matter and likely interest in the seasonality of patterns make chronological ordering a common-sense choice.

Figure 10.11
Rain Patterns

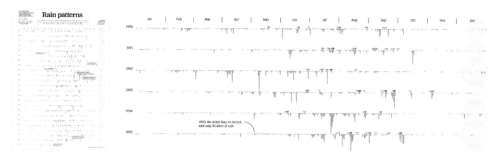

Categorical sorting can be usefully applied to a sequence of categories that have a logical hierarchy implied by their values or unique to the subject matter. For example, if you were presenting analysis about football players you might organise a chart based on the general order of their typical positions in a team (goalkeeper > defenders > midfielders > forwards) or use seniority levels as a way to present analysis about staff numbers. Alternatively, if you have ordinal data you can logically sort the values according to their inherent hierarchy. In Figure 10.12, that you saw earlier in the profile of ordinal colours, the columns are

Outcome status for clients undergoing multiple-sessions of treatment

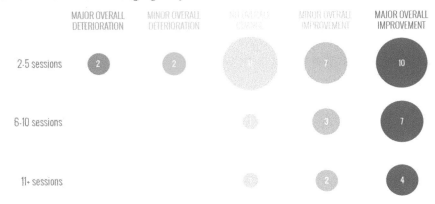

Figure 10.12
Excerpt from
'Pyschotherapy in The
Arctic'

sequenced left to right in order from 'major deterioration' to 'major improvement', to help reveal the balance of treatment outcomes from a sample of psychotherapy clients.

Hierarchical sorting organises data by increasing or decreasing quantities so a viewer can efficiently perceive the size, distribution and underlying ranking of values. In Figure 10.13, showing the highest typical salaries for women in the US, based on analysis of data from the US Bureau of Labour Statistics, the sorting arrangement presents the values by descending quantity to reveal the highest rankings values.

In Figure 10.12 the bubbles in each column do not need to be coloured as their position already provides a visual association with the 'deterioration' through to 'improvement' ordinal categories. The attribute of colour, specifically, can therefore be considered *redundant encoding*. However, you might still choose to include this redundancy if you believed it aided the immediacy of association and distinction. In this case, the chart was part of a larger graphic that employed the same colour associations across several different charts and therefore it made sense to preserve this association.

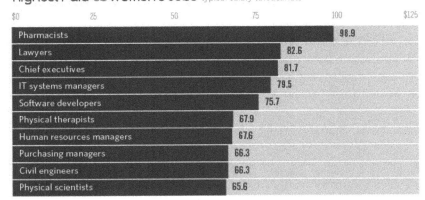

Figure 10.13
Excerpt from 'Gender
Pay Gap US'

10.3 Influencing Factors and Considerations

You are now familiar with the array of various aspects of composition thinking. At this point you will need to weigh up your decisions on how you might employ these in your own work. Here are some of the specific factors to bear in mind.

Formulating Your Brief

Format: Naturally, as composition is about spatial arrangement, the nature and dimensions of the canvas you have to work with will have a fundamental bearing on the decisions you make. There are two concerns here: what will be the shape and size of the primary format and how transferable will your solution be across the different platforms on which it might be used or consumed?

Another factor surrounding format concerns the mobility of viewing the work. If the form of your output enables viewers to easily move a display or move *around* a display in a circular plane (such as looking at a printout or work on a tablet) this means that issues such as label orientation can be largely cast aside. If your output is going to be consumed in a relatively fixed setting (desktop/laptop or via a presentation) the flexibility of viewing positions will be restricted.

Working With Data

Data examination: Not surprisingly, the shape and size of your data will directly influence your chart composition decisions. When discussing physical properties in Chapter 4, I described the influence of quantitative values with legitimate outliers distorting ideal scale choices. One solution for dealing with this is to use a non-linear logarithmic (often just known as a 'log') scale. Essentially, each major interval along a log scale increases the value at that marked position by a factor of 10 (or by one order of magnitude) rather than by equal increments. In Figure 10.14, looking at ratings for thousands of different board games, the x-axis is presented on a log scale in order to accommodate the wide range of values for the 'Number of ratings' measure and to help fit the analysis into a square-chart layout. Had the x-axis remained as a linear scale, to preserve a square layout would have meant squashing values below 1000 into such a tightly packed space that you would hardly see the patterns. Alternatively, a wide rectangular chart would have been necessary but impractical given the limitations of the space this chart would occupy.

I have great sympathy for the challenges faced by designers like Zimbabwe-based Graham van de Ruit, when working on typesetting a book titled *Millions, Billions, Trillions: Letters from Zimbabwe, 2005–2009* in 2014. The book was all text, apart from one or two tables. One of the tables of data supplied to Graham showed Zimbabwe's historical monthly inflation rates, which, as you can see (Figure 10.15), included some incredibly diverse values.

I love the subtle audacity of Graham's solution. Even though it is presented in tabular form there is a strong visual impact created by allowing the sheer spatial consequence of the exceptional mid-2008 numbers to cause the awkward widening of the final column. I think this makes the point much more effectively than a chart might, in this case.

'I thought that a graph might be more effective, but I quickly realised that the scale would be a big challenge… The whole point of graphing would have been to show the huge leap in 2008, something that I felt the log scale would detract from and was impractical with the space constraints. I also felt that a log scale might not be intuitive to the target audience.' **Graham van de Ruit, Editorial and Information Designer**

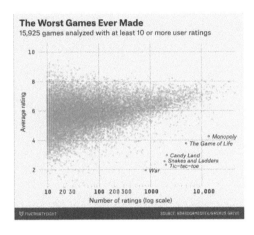

The Worst Games Ever Made
15,925 games analyzed with at least 10 or more user ratings

Figure 10.14 The Worst Board Games Ever Invented

Month on month inflation % 2000–2008

	2000	2001	2002	2003	2004	2005	2006	2007	2008
Jan	55	57	116	208	628	133	613	1593	100,580
Feb	48	57	116	220	602	127	782	1729	165,000
Mar	50	55	113	228	583	123	913	2200	355,000
Apr	53	56	114	269	505	129	1092	3714	736,604
May	58	55	122	300	448	144	1193	4530	1,800,000
Jun	59	64	114	364	394	164	1184	7251	
Jul	53	70	123	399	362	254	993	7634	220,000,000
Aug	53	76	135	426	314	265	1204	6592	231,000,000
Sept	62	86	139	455	251	359	1023	7892	
Oct	60	97	144	525	209	411	1070	14840	
Nov	56	103	175	619	149	502	1098	26470	
Dec	55	112	198	598	132	585	1281	66000	

Figure 10.15 From *Millions, Billions, Trillions: Letters from Zimbabwe, 2005–2009*

Establishing Your Editorial Thinking

Angles: The greater the number of different angles of analysis you wish to cover in your work, the greater the challenge will be to seamlessly accommodate the resulting chart displays in one view. The more content you include increases the need to contemplate reductions in the size of charts or a non-simultaneous arrangement, perhaps through multi-page sequences with interactive navigation.

In defining your editorial perspectives, you will have likely established some sense of hierarchy that might inform which angles should be more prominent (regarding layout position and size) and which less so. There might also be some inherent narrative binding each slice of analysis that lends itself to being presented in a deliberate sequence.

Data Representation

Chart type choice: Different charts have different spatial consequences. A treemap generally occupies far more space than a pie chart simply because there are many more 'parts' being shown.

A polar chart is circular in shape, whereas a waffle chart is squared. With each chart you include you will have a uniquely shaped piece that will form part of the overall jigsaw puzzle. Inevitably there will be some shuffling of content to find the right size and placement balance.

The table in Figure 10.16 summarises the main chart structures and the typical shapes they occupy. This list is based only on the charts included in the Chapter 6 gallery but still offers a reasonable compilation of the main structures. These are ordered in descending frequency as per the distribution of the different structures of charts in the gallery.

Structure	Description	Shape
Cartesian	These are effectively rectangular structures based on a coordinate system with magnitudes or positions along an x (horizontal) and y (vertical) dimension. The bar and line charts use this structure.	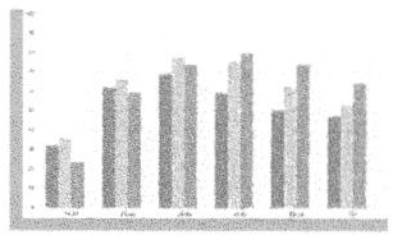
Spatial	These are mapping projections used to display thematic mapping, where values are plotted according to longitude–latitude or associated with the polygonal shapes of geographic units.	
Radial	Radial structures are characterised by a central or circular layout usually based on the division of angular parts or axes radiating outwards. They are used for polar and pie charts. Certain hierarchical and relational charts also demonstrate a similar graphical structure, whereby concentric layers or nodes and edges emanate from a natural centre. For example, node–link diagrams use this structure.	
Columnar	These structures are associated with table-like layouts based on associated x and y cell positions (like the heat map) or layouts that have different tiers or states (such as the Sankey diagram or the linear dendrogram).	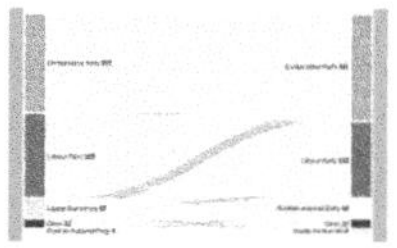
Enclosure	Enclosure charts are based around a fixed shaped container within which data is arranged optimally. This would be seen in the treemap and the waffle chart.	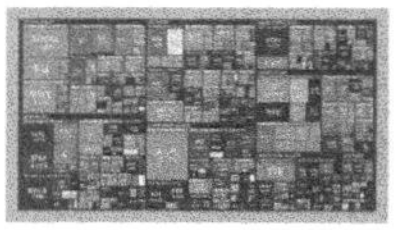

Figure 10.16   List of chart structures

Trustworthy Design

Chart-scale optimisation: Decisions about chart scales concern the maximum, minimum and interval choices that ensure integrity through the representation as well as optimise readability.

Firstly, let's look at decisions around minimum values used on the quantitative value axis, known as the origin, and the reasons why it is not OK for you to truncate the axis in methods like the bar chart. Any data representation where the attribute of *size* is used to encode a quantitative value needs to show the full, true size, nothing more and nothing less. The origin needs to be zero. When you truncate a bar chart's quantitative value axis you distort the perceived length or height of the bar. Visualisers are often tempted to crop axis scales when values are large and the differences between categories are small. However, as you can see in Figure 10.17, the consequence is that it creates the impression of highly noticeable relative difference between values when the absolute values do not support this.

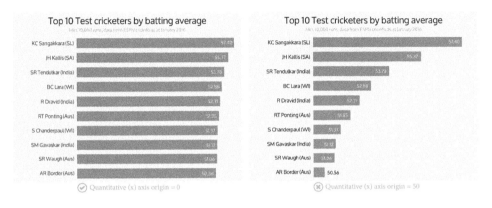

Figure 10.17
Illustrating the Effect of Truncated Bar Axis Scales

The single instance in which it is remotely reasonable to truncate an axis would be if you had a main graphic which effectively offered a thumbnail view of the whole chart for orientation positioned alongside a separate associated chart (similar to that on the right). This separate chart might have a truncated axis that would provide a magnified view of the main chart, showing just the tips of the bar, to help viewers see the differences close up.

In contrast to the bar chart, a line chart does not necessarily need always to have a zero origin for the value axis (normally the y-axis). A line chart's encoding involves a series of connected lines (marks) joining up continuous values based on their absolute position along a scale (attribute). It therefore does not encode quantitative values through size, like the bar chart does, so the truncation of a value axis will not unduly impact on perceiving the relative values against the scale and the general trajectory. For some data contexts the notion of a zero quantity might be impossible to achieve. In Figure 10.18, showing 100m sprint record times, no human is ever going to be able to run 100m in anywhere near zero seconds. Times have improved, of course, but there is a physical limit to what can be achieved. To show this analysis with the y-axis starting from zero would be unnecessary and even more so if you plotted similar analysis for longer distance races.

However, if you were to plot the 100m results and the 400m results on the same chart, you would need to start from zero to enable orientation of the scale of comparable values. This sense of comparable scale is missing from the next chart, whereby including the full quantitative value range down to zero would be necessary to perceive the relative scale of attitudes towards same-sex marriage. The chart's y-axis appears to start from an origin of 20 but as we are looking at part-to-whole analysis, the y-axis should really be displayed from an origin of

Figure 10.18
Excerpt from
'Doping under
the Microscope'

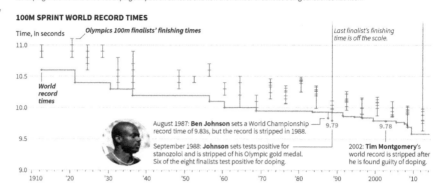

Doping under the microscope

Tuesday marks the 25th anniversary of Ben Johnson's victory in the Seoul Olympics 100m final and his subsequent disqualification for doping. Here we take a look at doping's impact on athletics and how the number of athletes being sanctioned has risen.

zero. The maximum doesn't need to go up to 100%, the highest observed value is fine in this case, but it could be interesting to set the maximum range to 100% in order to create a similar sense of the gap to be bridged before 100% of respondents are in agreement.

Figure 10.19
Record-high 60%
of Americans
Support Same-sex
Marriage

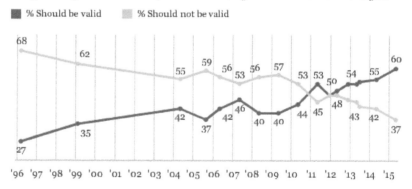

Aspect ratios: The aspect ratio of a line chart, as derived from the height and width dimensions of the chart area, can have a large impact on the perceived trends presented. If the chart is too narrow, the steepness of connections will be embellished and look more significant; if the chart is stretched out too wide, the steepness of slopes will be much more dampened and key trends may be somewhat disguised. There is no absolutely right or wrong approach here but clearly there is a need for sensitivity to avoid the possibility of unintended deception. A general rule of thumb is to seek a chart area that enables the average slope to be presented at 45°, though this is not something that can be easily and practically applied, especially as there are many other variables at play, such as the range of quantitative and time values and the scales being used. My advice is just to make a pragmatic judgement by eye to find the ratio that you think is faithful to the significance of the trends in your data.

Mapping projections: One of the most contentious matters in the visual representation of data relates to thematic mapping and specifically to the choice of map projection used. The Earth is not flat (hopefully no contention there, otherwise this discussion is rather academic), yet the dominant form through which maps are presented portrays the Earth as being just that. Features such as size, shape and distance can be measured accurately on Earth but when projected on a flat surface a compromise has to occur. Only some of these qualities can be preserved and represented accurately.

There are lots of exceptionally complicated calculations attached to the variety of spatial projections. The main things you need to know about projection mapping are that:

> I qualify this with 'dominant' because, increasingly, advances in technology (such as WebGL) mean we can now interact with spherical portrayals of the Earth within a 2D space.

- every type of map projection has some sort of distortion;
- the larger the area of the Earth portrayed as a flat map, the greater the distortion;
- there is no single right answer – it is often about choosing the least-worst case.

Thematic mapping (as opposed to mapping spatially for navigation or reference purposes) is generally best portrayed using mapping projections based on 'equal-area' calculations (so the sacrifice is more on the shape, not the size). This ensures that the phenomena per unit – the values you are typically plotting – are correctly represented by proportion of regional area. For choosing the best specific projection, in the absence of perfect, damage limitation is often the key: that is, which choice will distort the spatial truth the least given the level of mapping

> Many tools that offer rudimentary mapping options will tend to only come with a default (non-adjustable) projection, often the Mercator (or Web Mercator). The more advanced geospatial analysis tools will offer pre-loaded or add-in options to broaden and customise the range of projections. Hopefully, in time, an increasing range of the more pragmatic desktop tools will enhance projection customisations.

required. There are so many variables at play, however, based on the scope of view (world, continent, or country/sub-region), the potential distance from the equator of your region of focus and whether you are focusing on land, sea or sky (atmosphere), to name but a few. As with many other topics in this field, a discussion about mapping projections requires a dedicated text but let me at least offer a brief outline of five different projections to begin your acquaintance:

Mercator While the Mercator has been widely discredited in its role as a means of portraying the world (due to the vast distortions at the poles) it is still the most common projection found in mapping tools (where it is often termed Web Mercator). This is largely because of its rectangular dimensions that support seamless zooming. If you are determined to use this projection, you should not use it for a global view; stick to a lower regional level so the distortions are minimised, especially for regions around the equator.	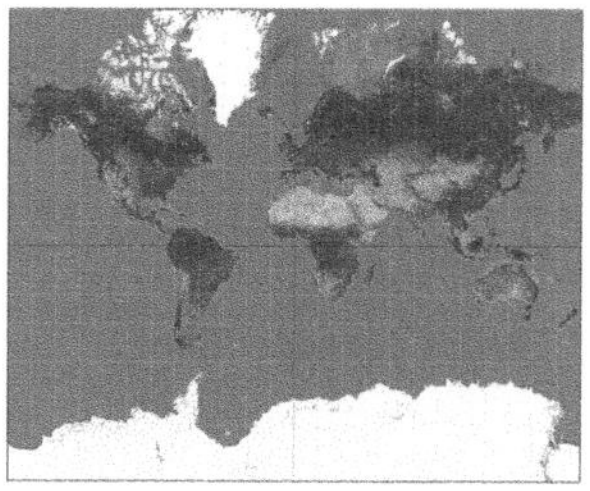
Albers Equal-area Conic This unusual looking conic projection is most highly recommended for presenting maps at a lower regional level, such as a country or subcontinent view.	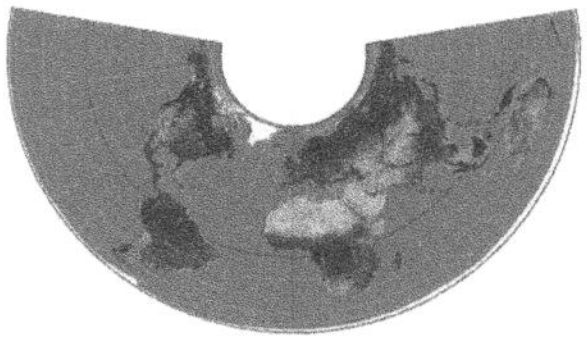
Lambert Azimuthal Equal-area This spherical projection is most commonly recommended for hemisphere- or continent-level views. The European Environment Agency, for example, recommends its usage for any European mapping purpose.	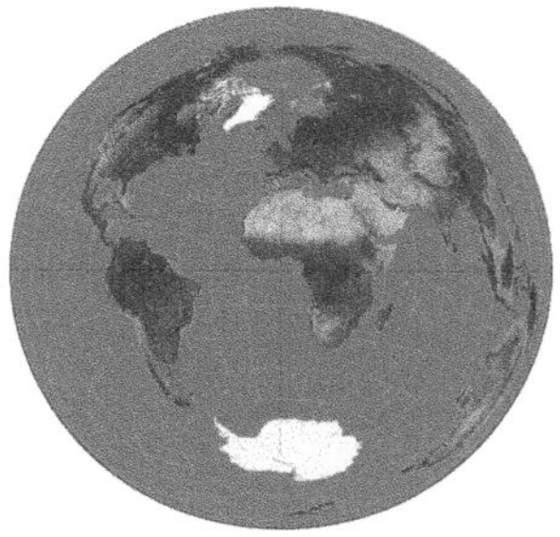
Winkel–Tripel Most of the important people who are far better informed about mapping projections than I tend to speak in glowing terms about the Winkel–Tripel projection as the best choice for viewing the world. Indeed, as the most ringing endorsement of its credentials, it represents the modern standard world map adopted by *National Geographic*.	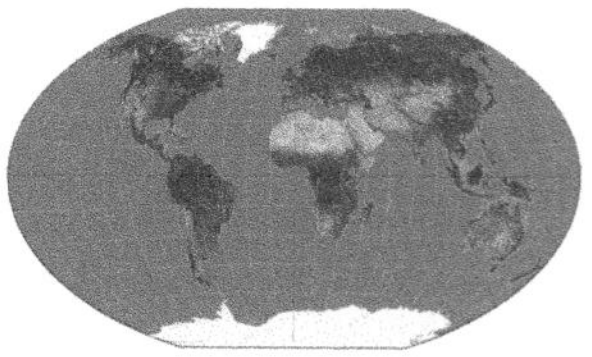
Mollweide In contrast to the Winkel–Tripel, the Mollweide (equal-area) projection offers greater emphasis on the accuracy of ocean areas and can be useful for atmospheric mapping (e.g. flight paths).	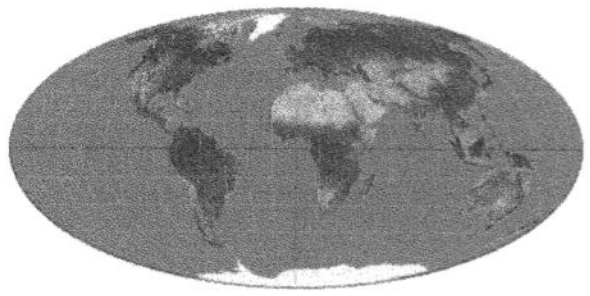

Figure 10.20   A Selection of Commonly Deployed Mapping Projections

Accessible Design

Good design is unobtrusive: One of the main obstructions to facilitating understanding through a visualisation design is when viewers are required to rely on their memory to perform comparisons between non-simultaneous views.

When the composition layout requires viewers to flick between pages or interactively generated views, they have to try store one view in their mind and then mentally compare that against the live view that has arrived on the screen. This is too hard and too likely to fail given the relatively weak performance of the brain's working memory.

> 'Using our eyes to switch between different views that are visible simultaneously has much lower cognitive load than consulting our memory to compare a current view with what was seen before.' **Tamara Munzner taken from** *Visualization Analysis and Design*

Content that warrants direct comparison should be enabled through proximity to and alignment with related items. I mentioned in the section on animation that if you want to compare different states over time, rather than see the connected system of change, you will need to have access to the 'moment' views simultaneously and without a reliance on memory.

Elegant Design

Unity: As I discussed with colour, composition decisions are always relative: an object's place and its space occupied within a display immediately create a relationship with everything else in the display. Unity in composition provides a similar sense of harmony and balance between all objects on show as was sought with colour. The flow of content should feel logical and meaningful.

> 'I'm obsessed with alignments. Sloppy label placement on final files causes my confidence in the designer to flag. What other details haven't been given full attention? Has the data been handled sloppily as well? … On the flip side, clean, layered and logically built final files are a thing of beauty and my confidence in the designer, and their attention to detail, soars.' **Jen Christiansen, Graphics Editor at** *Scientific American*

The enduring idea that elegance in design is most appreciated when it is absent is just as relevant with composition. Look around and open your eyes to composition that works and does not work, and recognise the solutions that felt effortless as you read them and those that felt punctured and confusing. This is again quite an elusive concept and one that only comes with a mixture of common-sense judgement, experience and exposure to inspiration from elsewhere.

Thoroughness: Precision positioning is the demonstration of thoroughness and care that is so important in the pursuit of elegance. You should aim to achieve pixel-perfect accuracy in the position and size of every single property.

Think of the importance of absolute positioning in the context of detailed architectural plans that outline the position of every fine detail down to power sockets, door handles and the arc of a window's opening manoeuvre. A data visualiser has to commit to ultimate precision and consistency because any shortcomings will be immediately noticeable and will fundamentally impact on the function of the work. If you do not feel a warm glow from every emphatic snap-to-grid resize operation or upon seeing the results of a mass alignment of page objects, you are not doing it right. (Honestly, I am loads of fun to be around.

Summary: Composition

Project composition defines the layout and hierarchy of the entire visualisation project and may include the following features:

- Visual hierarchy – layout: how to arrange the position of elements?
- Visual hierarchy – size: how to manage the hierarchy of element sizes?
- Absolute positioning: where specifically should certain elements be placed?

Chart composition defines the shape, size and layout choices for all components within your charts and may include the following features:

- Chart size: don't be afraid to shrink charts, so long as any labels are still readable, and especially embrace the power of small multiple.
- Chart scales: what are the most meaningful range of values given the nature of the data?
- Chart orientation: which way is best?
- Chart value sorting: consider the most meaningful sorting arrangement for your data and editorial focus, based on the LATCH acronym.

Influencing Factors and Considerations

- Formulating the brief: what space have you got to work within?
- Working with data: what is the shape and size of your data and how might this affect your chart design architecture?
- Establishing your editorial thinking: how many different angles (charts) might you need to include? Is there any specific focus for these angles that might influence a sequence or hierarchy between them?
- Data representation: any chart has a spatial consequence – different charts have different structures that will create different dimensions that will need to be accommodated.
- Trustworthy design: the integrity and meaning of your chart scale, chart dimensions, and (for mapping) your projection choices are paramount.
- Accessible design: remember that good design is unobtrusive – if you want to facilitate comparisons between different chart displays these ideally need to be presented within a simultaneous view.
- Elegant design: unity of arrangement is another of the finger-tip sense judgments but will be something achieved by careful thinking about the relationships between all components of your work.

Tips and Tactics

- You will find that as you reach the latter stages of your design process, the task of nudging things by fractions of a pixel and realigning features will dominate your attention. As energy and attention start to diminish you will need to maintain a commitment to thoroughness and a pride in precision right through to the end!

- Empty space is like punctuation in visual language: use it to break up content when it needs that momentary pause, just as how a *comma* or *full stop* is needed in a sentence. Do not be afraid to use empty space more extensively across larger regions as a device to create impact. Like the notes not played in jazz, effective visualisation design can also be about the relationship between something and nothing.

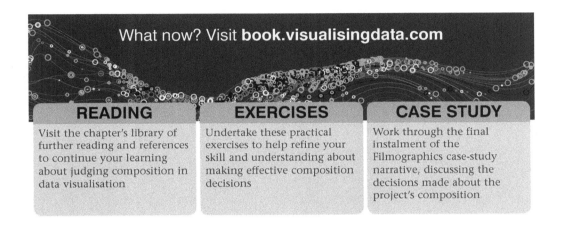

READING

Visit the chapter's library of further reading and references to continue your learning about judging composition in data visualisation

EXERCISES

Undertake these practical exercises to help refine your skill and understanding about making effective composition decisions

CASE STUDY

Work through the final instalment of the Filmographics case-study narrative, discussing the decisions made about the project's composition

Part D

Developing Your Capabilities

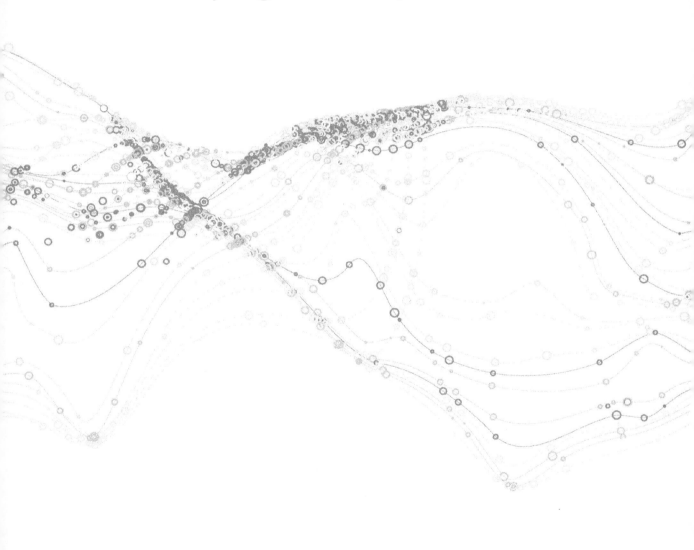

11

Visualisation Literacy

This final chapter explores some of the important ingredients and tactics that will help you continue to develop and refine your data visualisation literacy. By definition, literacy is the ability to read and write. Applied to data visualisation, this means possessing the literacy both to create visualisations (write) and consume them (read).

Data visualisation literacy is increasingly an essential capability regardless of the domain in which we work and the nature of our technical skills. Just as computer literacy is now a capability that is expected of everyone, one can imagine a time in the not-too-distant future when having data visualisation capabilities will be viewed as a similarly 'assumed' attribute across many different roles.

In exploring the components of visualisation literacy across this chapter we will look at two sides of the same coin: the competencies that make up the all-round talents of a visualiser but, first, the tactics and considerations required to be an effective and efficient viewer of data visualisation.

11.1 Viewing: Learning to See

Learning how to understand a data visualisation, as a viewer, is not a topic that has been much discussed in the field until recently. For many the idea that there are possible tactics and efficient ways to approach this activity is

Many of the ideas for this section emerged from the Seeing Data visualisation literacy research project (seeingdata.org) on which I collaborated.

rarely likely to have crossed their mind. We just *look* at charts and *read* them, don't we? What else is there to consider?

The fact is we are all viewers. Even if you never create a visualisation again you will always be a viewer and you will be widely exposed to different visual forms of data and information across your daily life. You cannot escape them. Therefore, it seems logical that optimising visualisation literacy as a consumer is a competency worth developing,

Let's put this into some sort of context. As children we develop the ability to read numbers and words. These are only understandable because we are taught how to recognise the association between numeric digits and their representation as numbers and the connection between alphabetical characters with letters and words. From there we begin to understand sentences and eventually, as we build up a broader vocabulary, we acquire the literacy of language. This is all a big effort. We are not born knowing a language but we are born with the capacity to learn one.

Beyond written language, something as simple and singular as, for example, the Wi-Fi symbol is now a universally recognised form of visual language but one that only exists in contemporary culture. For millions of people today, this symbol is a signal of relief and tangible celebration – 'Thank God, Wi-Fi is available here!' The context of the use of this symbol would have meant nothing to people in the 1990s: it is a symbol of its time and we have learnt to recognise its use and understand its meaning.

Across all aspects of our lives, there are things that once seemed complicated and inaccessible but are now embedded within us as automatic competencies: driving a car, using a keyboard, cooking a meal. I often think back to growing up as a kid in the 1980s and my first (functioning) computer, the mighty Commodore 64 (C64). One of the most famous games in the UK from this period was *Daley Thompson's Decathlon*. Of particular nostalgic fame was the brutally simple operation of maniacally waggling the single joystick arm left and right to control the running events (if memory serves me correctly, the single button came into use when there were hurdles to jump over).

Consider the universally and immediately understandable control configuration of that game with the frankly ludicrous number of options and combinations that exist on the modern football games, such as the FIFA series on contemporary consoles like the Xbox or PS4. The control combinations required to master the array of attacking moves alone require an entire page of instruction and remarkable levels of finger dexterity. Yet young kids today are almost immediate masters of this game. I should know – I have been beaten by some awfully young opponents. It hurts. But they have simply utilised their capacity to learn through reading and repeated practice.

As discussed in Chapter 1 when looking at the principle of 'accessible' design, many data visualisations *will* be intended – and designed – for relatively quick consumption. These might be simple to understand and offer immediately clear messages for viewers to easily comprehend. They are the equivalent of the C64 joystick controls. However, there will be occasions when you as a viewer are required to invest a bit more time and effort to work through a visualisation that might be based on subject matter or analysis of a more complex nature, perhaps involving many angles of analysis or numerous rich features of interactivity. This is the equivalent prospect of mastering the Xbox controls. Without having the confidence or capability to extract as *much* understanding from the viewing experience as possible and doing so as *efficiently* as possible, you are potentially missing out.

'Though I consider myself a savvy consumer of bar charts, line graphs, and other traditional styles of data display, I'm totally at sea when trying to grasp what's going on in, say, arc diagrams, circular hierarchy graphs, hyperbolic tree charts, or any of the seemingly outlandish visualisations … I haven't thought much about this flip side, except that I do find I now view other people's visualisations with a more critical eye.' **Marcia Gray, Graphic Designer**

As viewers, we therefore need to acknowledge that there might be a need to learn and a reward from learning. We should not expect every type of visualisation to signpost every pearl of insight that is relevant to us. We might have to work for it. And we have to work for it because we are not born with the ability or the right to understand everything that is presented to us. Few of us will have ever been taught how to go about effectively consuming charts and graphics. We might be given some guidance on how to read charts and histograms, maybe even a scatter plot, if we study maths or the sciences at school. Otherwise, we get by.

But 'getting by' is not really good enough, is it? Even if, through exposure and repetition, we hope gradually to become more familiar with the most common approaches to visualising data, this does not sufficiently equip us with the breadth and range of literacy that will be required.

I mentioned earlier the concept, proposed by Daniel Kahneman, of System 1 and System 2 thinking. The distinctions of these modes of thought manifest themselves again here. Remember how System 1 was intuitive and rapid whereas System 2 was slow, deliberate and almost consciously undertaken? For example, you are acutely aware of thinking when trying to run a mathematical calculation through your mind. That is System 2 at work. In part, due to the almost hyperactive and instinctive characteristics of System 1, when there is a need for System 2 thinking to kick into action, we might try to avoid whatever that activity entails. We get lazy and resort to shortcut solutions or decisions based on intuition. System 1 almost persuades System 2 to sit back and let it look after things. Anything to avoid having to expend effort thinking deeply and rationally.

The demands of learning anything new or hard can trigger that kind of response. It is understandable that somebody facing a complex or unfamiliar visualisation that needs learning might demonstrate antipathy towards the effort required to learn.

Of course, there are other factors involved in learning, such as having the time, receiving assistance or tuition, and recognising the incentive. These are all enablers and therefore their absence can create obstacles to learning. Without assistance from the visualiser, viewers are left to fend for themselves. The role of this book has primarily been to try to raise the standard of the design choices that visualisers make when creating visualisations. Visualisers do not want to obstruct viewers from being able to read, interpret and comprehend. If work is riddled with design errors and misjudgements then viewers are naturally going to be disadvantaged.

However, even with a technically perfect design, as I explained in the definition section of the first chapter, we as visualisers can only do so much to control this experience. There are things we can do to make our work as accessible as possible, but there is also a partial expectation of the viewer to be willing to make some effort (so long as it is 'proportional') to get the most out of the experience. The key point, however, is that this effort should be rewarded.

Many of the visualisations that you will have seen in this book, particularly in Chapter 6, may have been unfamiliar and new to you. They need learning. Your confidence in being able to read different types of charts is something that will develop through practice and exposure. It will be slow and deliberate at first, probably a little consciously painful, but then, over time, as the familiarity increases and the experiential benefits kick in, perceiving these different types of representations will become quite effortless and automatic. System 2 thinking will then transform into a reliably quick form of System 1 thinking.

Over the next few pages I will present a breakdown of the components of effectively working with a visualisation from the perspective of being a viewer. This demonstration will provide you with a strategy for approaching any visualisation with the best chance of understanding *how* to read it and ensure you gain the benefit of understanding from being *able* to read it.

To start with I will outline the instinctive thoughts and judgements you will need to make *before you begin* working with a visualisation. I will then separate the different features of a visualisation, first by considering the common components that sit *outside the chart* and then some pointers for how to go about perceiving what is presented *inside the chart*. This part will also connect with the content included in the chart type gallery found in Chapter 6 describing how to read each unique chart type. Finally, I will touch on the attributes that will lead you, in the longer term, to becoming a *more sophisticated* viewer.

It is important to note that not all data visualisation and infographic designs will have *all* the design features and apparatus items that I describe over the next few sections. There may be good reasons for this in each case, depending on the context. However, if you find there are significant gaps in the work you are consuming, or features of assistance have been deployed without real care or quality, that would point to flawed design. In these cases the viewer is not really being given all the assistance required: the visualiser has failed to facilitate understanding.

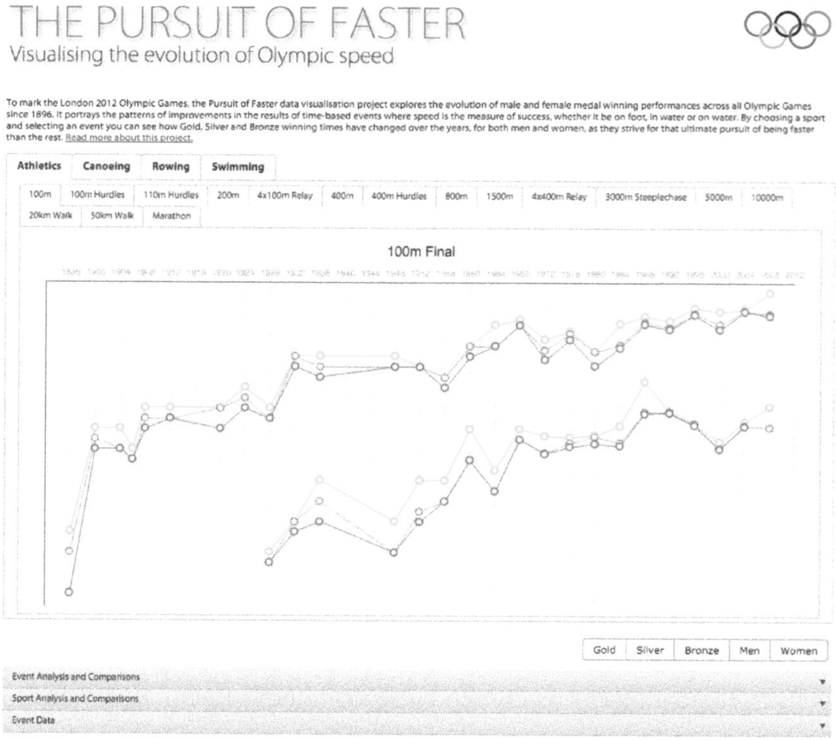

Figure 11.1
The Pursuit of Faster

To illustrate this process I will refer to a case-study project titled 'The Pursuit of Faster: Visualising the Evolution of Olympic Speed'. As the title suggests, the focus of this work was to explore how results have changed (improved or declined) over the years of the Olympics for those events where speed (as measured by a finishing time) was the determinant of success.

Before You Begin

Here are some of the instinctive, immediate thoughts that will cross your mind as soon as you come face to face with a data visualisation. Once again, these are consistent with the impulsive nature of the System 1 thoughts mentioned earlier.

Setting: Think about whether the setting you are in is conducive to consuming a visualisation at that moment in time. Are you under any pressure of time? Are you on a bumpy train trying to read this on your smartphone?

Visual appeal? In this early period of engaging with the work you will be making a number of rapid judgements to determine whether you are 'on board'. One of the ingredients of this is to consider whether the look and feel (the 'form') of the visualisation attract you and motivate you to want to spend time with it.

Relevance? In addition to the visual appeal, the second powerful instinct is to judge whether the subject matter interests you. You might have decided you are on board with your instinctive reaction to the visuals but the key hurdle is whether it is even interesting or relevant to you. Ask yourself if this visualisation is going to deliver some form of useful understanding that confirms, enlightens or thrills you about the topic.

If you respond positively to both those considerations you will likely be intent on continuing to work with the visualisation. Even if you are just positive about one of these factors (form or subject) you will most probably persevere despite the indifference towards the other. If your thoughts are leaning towards a lack of interest in both the relevance of this work and its visual appeal then, depending on circumstances, your tolerance may not be high enough to continue and it will be better to abandon the task there and then.

Initial scan? It is inevitable that your eyes will be instinctively drawn to certain prominent features. This might be the title or even the chart itself. You may be drawn to a strikingly large bar or a sudden upward rise on a line chart. You might see a headline caption that captures your attention or maybe some striking photo imagery. It is hard to fight our natural instincts, so don't. Allow yourself a brief glance at the things you feel compelled to look at – these are likely the same things the visualiser is probably hoping you are drawn to. Quickly scanning the whole piece, just for an initial period of time, gives you a sense of orientation about what is in store.

In 'The Pursuit of Faster' project you might find yourself only drawn to this if you have a passing interest in the Olympics and/or the history of athletic achievement. On the surface, the visuals might look quite analytical in nature, which might turn some people off. The initial scan probably focuses on elements like the Olympic rings and the upward direction of the lines in the chart which might offer a degree of intrigue, as might the apparent range of interactive controls.

Outside the Chart

Before getting into the nuts and bolts of understanding the chart displays, you will first need to seek assistance from the project at large to understand in more detail what you are about to take on and how you might need to go about working with it.

The Proposition

Considering the proposition offered by the visualisation is about determining how big a task of consuming and possibly interacting you have ahead of you. What is its shape, size and nature?

Format: Is it presented in a print, physical or digital format and what does this make you feel about your potential appetite and the level of your engagement? Is it static or interactive and what does this present in terms of task?

- If it is a static graphic, how large and varied is the content – is it a dense display with lots of charts and text, or quite a small and compact one? Does the sequence of content appear logical?
- If it is interactive, how much potential interactivity does there appear to be – are there many buttons, menus, options, etc.? Where do the interactive events take you? Are there multiple tabs, pages or layers beneath this initial page? Have a click around.

Shape and size: Do you think you will probably to have to put in a lot of work just to scan the surface insights? Is there a clear hierarchy or sequence derived through the size and position of elements on the page? Does it feel like there is too much or too little content-wise? If the project layout exceeds the dimensions of your screen display, how much more scrolling or how many different pages will you have to look through to see the whole?

This initial thinking helps you establish how much work and effort you are going to be faced with to explore the visualisation thoroughly. In 'The Pursuit of Faster' project, it does not feel like there is too *much* content and all the possible analysis seems to be located within the boundaries of the immediate screen area. However, with a number of different selectable tabs, interactive options and collapsible content areas lurking beneath the surface, it could be more involving than it first appears.

What's this Project About?

Although you have already determined the potential relevance of this subject matter (or otherwise) you will now look to gain a little more insight into what the visualisation is specifically about.

Title: You will have probably already glanced at the title but now have another look at it to see if you can learn more about the subject matter, the specific angle of enquiry or perhaps a headline finding. In the sample project (Figures 11.2 and 11.3), the presence of the Olympic rings logo on the right provides an immediate visual cue about the subject matter, as you might have observed in the initial scan. The title, 'The Pursuit of Faster', is quite ambiguous, but as the supporting subtitle reveals, 'Visualising the evolution of Olympic speed' helps to explain what the visualisation is about.

Figure 11.2 Excerpt from 'The Pursuit of Faster'

Source: If it is a web-based visualisation the URL is worth considering. You might already know where you are on the Web, but if not you can derive plenty from the site on which this project is being hosted. An initial sense about trust in the data, the author and the possible credibility of insights can be drawn from this single bit of information. This particular project is hosted on my website, visualisingdata.com, and so may not carry the same immediate recognition that an established Olympics or sport-related site might command. There is nothing provided in the main view of the visualisation that informs the viewer who created the project. Normally this might have been detailed towards the bottom of the display or underneath the title, but in this case viewers have to click on a 'Read more...' link to find this out. If there are no details provided about the author/visualiser, as a viewer, this anonymity might have any affect on your trust in the work's motives and quality.

Introduction: While some visualisation projects will be relatively self-explanatory, depending on the familiarity of the audience with the subject matter, others will need to provide a little extra guidance. The inclusion of introductory text will often help 'set the scene', providing some further background about the project. If, as the viewer, the introduction fails to equip you with all the information you feel you need about the visualisation, then the visualiser has neglected to include all the assistance that might be necessary.

In 'The Pursuit of Faster' project, the introductory text provides sufficient initial information about the background of the project based on a curiosity about what improvements in speed have been seen throughout the history of the Olympics. As mentioned, there is a 'Read more...'

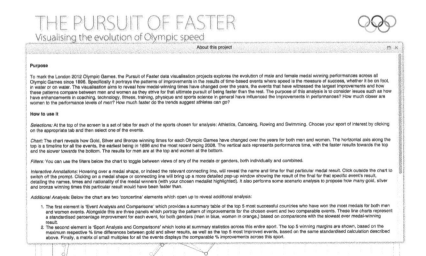

Figure 11.3 Excerpt from 'The Pursuit of Faster'

link to find more information that was perhaps too much to include in the main opening paragraph. This includes a comprehensive 'How to use it' guide providing a detailed account about the content and role of each section of the project, including advice on how to read the chart and utilise the interactive features.

What Data?

Any visualisation of data should include clear information to explain the origin of the data and what has been done with it in preparation for its visual portrayal.

Data source: Typically, details of the data source will be located in the introduction, as a footnote beneath a chart or at the bottom of a page. It is important to demonstrate transparency and give credit to the origin of your data. If none is provided, that lowers trust.

Data handling: It is also important to explain how the data was gathered and what, if any, criteria were applied to include or exclude certain aspects of the subject matter. These might also mention certain assumptions, calculations or transformations that have been undertaken on the data and are important for the reader to appreciate.

In 'The Pursuit of Faster' project, the link you saw earlier to 'Read more ...' provides details about the origin of the data and the fact that it only includes medal winners from summer Olympic events that have a time-based measure.

What Interactive Functions Exist?

As you have seen in Chapter 8, interactive visualisations (typically hosted on the Web or in an app) aim to provide users with a range of features to interrogate and customise the presentation of the data.

Sometimes, interactive features are enabled but not visible on the surface of a project. This might be because visualisers feel that users will be experienced enough to expect certain interactive capabilities without having to make these overly conspicuous by labelling or signposting their presence. For example, rather than show all the value labels on a bar chart you might be able to move the mouse over a bar of choice and a pop-up will reveal the value. The project might not tell you that you can do this, but you may intuitively expect to. Always fully explore the display with the mouse or through touch in order to gain a sense of all the different visible and possibly invisible ways you can interact with the visualisation.

In 'The Pursuit of Faster' project (Figure 11.4), you will see multiple tabs at the top, one for each of the four sports being analysed. Clicking on each one opens up a new set of sub-tabs beneath for each specific event within the chosen sport.

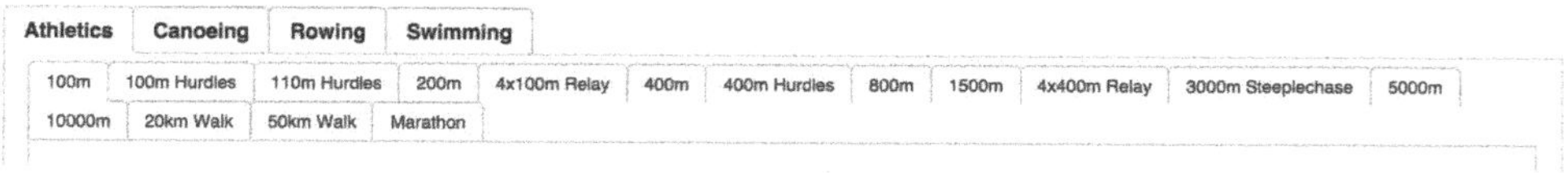

Figure 11.4
Excerpt from 'The Pursuit of Faster'

Athletics	Canoeing	Rowing	Swimming									
100m	100m Hurdles	110m Hurdles	200m	4x100m Relay	400m	400m Hurdles	800m	1500m	4x400m Relay	3000m Steeplechase	5000m	
10000m	20km Walk	50km Walk	Marathon									

Choosing an event will present the results in the main chart area (Figure 11.5). Once a chart has loaded up, you can then filter for male/female and also for each of the medals using the buttons immediately below the chart. Within the chart, hovering above a marker on the chart will reveal the specific time value for that result. Clicking on the marker will show the full race results and offer further analysis comparing those results with the all-time results for context.

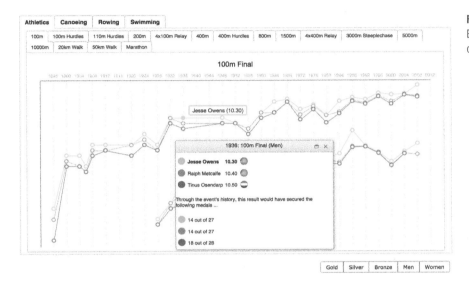

Figure 11.5
Excerpt from 'The Pursuit of Faster'

Finally, the collapsible menus below the chart show further detailed analysis and comparisons within and between each sporting event (Figure 11.6). The location of this implies that it is of lower relative importance than the chart or maybe is a more detailed view of the data.

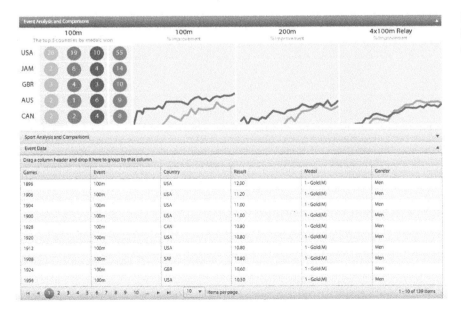

Figure 11.6
Excerpt from 'The Pursuit of Faster'

Inside the Chart

Now you have acquainted yourself with the key features of a visualisation outside the chart, the next stage is to start the process of deriving understanding from the chart.

The process of consuming a chart varies considerably between different chart types: the approach to drawing observations from a chart showing trends over time is very different from how you might explore a map-based visualisation. The charts I profiled in Chapter 6 were each accompanied by detailed information on the type of observations you should be looking to extract in each case.

In Chapter 1 you learnt how there were three elements involved in the achievement of under-standing a chart: *perceiving*, *interpreting* and *comprehending*. Let's work through these steps by looking at the analysis shown for the 100m Finals.

Perceiving: The first task in perceiving a chart is to establish your understanding about the role of every aspect of the display. Here we have a line chart (Figure 11.7) which shows how quantitative values for categories have changed over time. This chart is structured around a horizontal x-axis showing equal intervals from the earliest Olympics (1896) on the left through to the most recent (2012) on the right, although the latest values in the data only seem to reach 2008. Depending on your interest in this topic, the absence of data for the more recent Olympics may undermine your sense of its completeness and representativeness.

Figure 11.7
Excerpt from 'The
Pursuit of Faster'

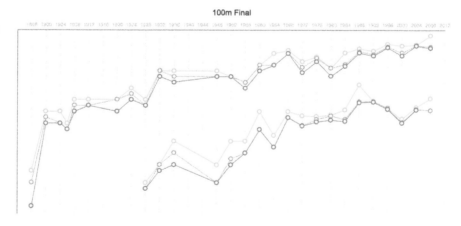

100m Final

The vertical y-axis is different from what you might normally see for two reasons. Firstly, it moves downwards below the x-axis (rather than upwards, as is more common), and secondly, there is no labelling, either of the variable plotted or of scale values.

I can see that the encoding is formed by points (marking the race results) and connecting lines showing the change over time. Through the use of colour there are plotted lines for the gold, silver and bronze medal winning times for each Olympics. There are two sets of medal lines but there is no obvious distinction to explain what these are. With no direct labelling of the values I hover over the point ('medal') markers and a tooltip annotation comes up with the athlete's name and time in a medal-coloured box. I compare tooltip info for the lines at the top and those below and discover the lower lines are the women's results and the upper lines are the men's results.

From the tooltip info I can determine that the quicker times (the gold medal line) are at the top so this suggests that the y-axis scale is inverted with quicker (smaller) times at the top and slower (larger) times at the bottom. This also reveals that there is no origin of zero in the vertical axis; rather the quickest time is anchored just below the top of the chart, the slowest stretches down to the bottom of the chart, and then all the values in between are distributed proportionally.

> Interjecting as the visualiser responsible for this project, let me explain that the focus was on patterns of relative change over time, not necessarily absolute result times. As every different event has a different distance and duration behind the final timed results, a common scale for all results needed to be established, which is why this decision was taken to standardise all results and plot them across the vertical chart space provided.

Inside the chart I now try clicking on the markers and this brings up details about the event (for that gender), including the three medal winners, their times and small flags for the countries they represented. I can also read an interesting statistic that explains if the time for the medallist I selected had been achieved throughout the event's history, it would have secured gold, silver or bronze medals on x number of occasions.

I now know enough about the chart's structure and encodings to be able to start the process of perceiving the patterns to make some observations about what the data is showing me:

- I can see that there is a general rise across all Olympics for the event in both men's and women's results.
- It feels like the women's times are getting closer to the men's, with Florence Griffith Joyner's victory time in 1988 being the closest that the respective times have been – her result there would have been good enough for a men's bronze in 1956.
- There are no real patterns between medal times; they are neither always more packed closely together, nor always spread out – it changes on each occasion.
- I notice the gaps where there were no events, during the First and Second World Wars, and also the presence of an obscure 1906 event, the only Olympic Games that did not follow the four-year interval.

Interpreting: As someone who follows a lot of sport and, like most people, is particularly familiar with the 100m event, I feel there is a lot of information I can get out of this display at both a general level, looking at the relative patterns of change, and a local level, checking up on individual medallists and their absolute values. Thinking about what these patterns mean, on looking at the times from the first Olympic Games in 1896 until the 1960s there was a lot of improvement and yet, since the 1960s, there is generally a much flatter shape – with only a gradual improvement in the times for both genders. This tells me that maybe the threshold for the capacity of athletes to run faster is getting closer. Even with all the contributions of sports science over the past few generations, the increase in speed is only ever marginal. That was until Usain Bolt blew the world away in 2008 and, likewise for women, Shelly-Ann Fraser improved the women's results for the first time in 20 years.

Comprehending: What does this all mean to me? Well it is interesting and informative and, while I have no direct investment in this information in terms of needing to make decisions or it triggering any sense of emotion in me, in outcome terms I feel I have learnt more about a topic through this chart than I would have done just looking at the data. My understanding of the history of the Olympic 100m final has been expanded and, in turn, I have a better appreciation of the advancements in speed across and between both genders.

Becoming a More Sophisticated Consumer

Effective visualisation requires the visualiser and viewer to operate in harmony, otherwise the possibility of facilitating understanding is compromised. Beyond the mechanics of perceiving a visualisation, there are softer 'attitudinal' differences you can make to give yourself even more of a chance of gaining understanding. This is about modifying your mindset to be more critically appreciative of the challenges faced by the visualiser responsible for producing the work as well as its intended purpose. It is about showing empathy in your critical evaluation which will markedly help you become an increasingly sophisticated consumer.

Appreciation of context: When consuming a visualisation try to imagine some of the circumstances and constraints that might have influenced the visualiser's decisions:

- You might not find the subject matter interesting, but other people might. You have the right not to read or interact with a visualisation that has no relevance to you. If it *should* have relevance, then that's when there may be some problems!
- If you are struggling to understand a visualisation it could be that the project was aimed more at specialists, people with specific domain knowledge. Your struggles are possibly not a reflection of an ineffective visualisation or any deficit in your expected knowledge – it just was not intended for you.
- If the size of the text is frustratingly tiny on your screen, maybe it was intended primarily for printing as a poster and would have been the right size if consumed in its native format?
- When criticising a work, spare a thought for what could have been done differently. How would you imagine an alternative way to represent the data? What other design solutions would you have tried? Sometimes what is created is a reflection of crippling constraints and might more closely resemble the least-worst solution than the best.

Overview first, details if provided: Sometimes a visualiser only aims to offer a sense of the big picture – the big values, the medium and the small ones. Just because we cannot instantly read precise values from a chart it is important to avoid getting frustrated. Our default state as viewers is often to want every detail available. Sometimes, we just need to accept the idea that a gist of the hierarchy of values is of more worth than the precise decimal point precision of specific values. It may be that it was not feasible to use a chart that would deliver such detailed reading of the data – many charts simply cannot fulfil this. We might not even realise that we are just a mouseover or click away from bringing up the details we desire.

False consciousness: Do you *really* like the things you like? Sometimes we can be too quick to offer a 'wow' or a 'how cool is that?' summary judgement before even consuming the visualisation properly. It is quite natural to be charmed by a superficial surface appeal (occasionally, dare I say it, following the crowd?). Ask yourself if it is the subject, the design or the data you like? Could *any* portrayal of that compelling data have arrived at an equally compelling presentation of that content?

Curiosities answered, curiosities not answered: Just because the curiosity you had about a subject is not answerable does not make the visualisation a bad one. Statements like 'This is great but I wish they'd shown it by year ...' are valid because they express your own curiosity, to which you are entirely entitled. However, a visualiser can only serve up responses to a limited number of different angles of analysis in one project. The things you wanted to know about, which might be missing, may simply have not been possible to include or were deemed less interesting than the information provided. If you are thinking 'this would have been better on a map', maybe there was no access to spatial data? Or maybe the geographical details were too vague or inaccurate to generate sufficient confidence to use them?

11.2 Creating: The Capabilities of the Visualiser

Now that you are reaching the end of this journey, it will be quite evident that data visualisation design is truly multidisciplinary. It is the variety that fuels the richness of the subject and makes it a particularly compelling challenge. To prepare you for your ongoing development, the second part of this final chapter aims to help you reflect on the repertoire of skills, knowledge and mindsets required to achieve excellence in data visualisation design.

The Seven Hats of Data Visualisation

Inspired by Edward de Bono's *Six Thinking Hats*, the 'Seven hats of data visualisation' is a breakdown of the different capabilities that make up the multi-talented visualiser. The attributes listed under each of these hats can be viewed as a wish-list of personal or team capabilities, depending on the context of your data visualisation work.

Project Manager

The **coordinator** – oversees the project

Initiates and leads on formulating the brief

Identifies and establishes definitions of key circumstances

Organises the resources according to the ambition of a project

Manages progress of the workflow and keeps it cohesive

Has a 'thick skin', patience and empathy

Gets things done: checks, tests, finishes tasks

Pays strong attention to detail

Communicator

The **broker** – manages the people relationships

Helps to gather and understand requirements

Manages expectations and presents possibilities

Helps to define the perspective of the audience

Is a good listener with a willingness to learn from domain experts

Is a confident communicator with laypeople and non-specialists

Possesses strong copy-editing abilities

Launches and promotes the final solution

Scientist

The **thinker** – provides scientific rigour

Brings a strong research mindset to the process

Understands the science of visual perception

Understands visualisation, statistical and data ethics

Understands the influence of human factors

Verifies and validates the integrity of all data and design decisions

Demonstrates a *system's thinking* approach to problem solving

Undertakes reflective evaluation and critique

Data Analyst

The **wrangler** – handles all data work

Has strong data and statistical literacy

Has the technical skills to acquire data from multiple sources

Examines the physical properties of the data

Undertakes initial descriptive analysis

Transforms and prepares the data for its purpose

Undertakes exploratory data analysis

Has database and data modelling experience

Journalist

The **reporter** – pursues the scent of an enquiry

Defines the trigger curiosity and purpose of the project

Has an instinct to research, learn and discover

Driven by a desire to help others understand

Possesses or is able to acquire salient domain knowledge

Understands the essence of the subject's data

Has empathy for the interests and needs of an audience

Defines the editorial angle, framing and focus

Designer

The **conceiver** – provides creative direction

Establishes the initial creative pathway through the purpose map

Forms the initial mental visualisation: ideas and inspiration

Has strong creative, graphic and illustration skills

Understands the principles of user interface design

Is fluent with the full array of possible design options

Unifies the decision-making across the design anatomy

Has a relentless creative drive to keep innovating

Technologist

The **developer** – constructs the solution

Possesses a repertoire of software and programming capabilities

Has an appetite to acquire new technical solutions

Possesses strong mathematical knowledge

Can automate otherwise manually intensive processes

Has the discipline to avoid feature creep

Works on the prototyping and development of the solution

Undertakes pre- and post-launch testing, evaluation and support

Assessing and Developing Your Capabilities

Data visualisation is not necessarily a hard subject to master, but there are plenty of technical and complicated matters to handle. A trained or natural talent in areas like graphic design, computer science, journalism and data analysis is advantageous, but very few people have all these hats. Those that do cannot be exceptional at everything listed, but may be sufficiently competent at most things and then brilliant at some. Developing mastery across the full collection of attributes is probably unachievable, but it offers a framework for guiding an assessment of your current abilities and a roadmap for the development of any current shortcomings.

'Invariably, people who are new to visualisation want to know where to begin, and, frankly, it's understandably overwhelming. There is so much powerful work now being done at such a high level of quality, that it can be quite intimidating! But you have to start somewhere, and I don't think it matters where you start. In fact, it's best to start wherever you are now. Start from your own experience, and move forward. One reason I love this field is that everyone comes from a different background – I get to meet architects, designers, artists, coders, statisticians, journalists, data scientists ... Data vis is an inherently interdisciplinary practice: that's an opportunity to learn something about everything! The people who are most successful in this field are curious and motivated. Don't worry if you feel you don't have skills yet; just start from where you are, share your work, and engage with others.' **Scott Murray, Designer**

I am painfully aware of the things I am simply not good enough at (programming), the things I have no direct education in (graphic design) and the things I do not enjoy (finishing, proofreading, note-taking). Compromise is required with the things you do not like – there are always going to be unattractive tasks, so just bite the bullet and get on with them. Otherwise, you must seek either to address your skills gap through learning and/or intensive practice, finding support from elsewhere through collaboration, or to simply limit your ambitions based on what you *can* do.

Regardless of their background or previous experience, everyone has something to contribute to data visualisation. Talent is important, of course, but better *thinking* is, in my view, the essential foundation to focus on first. Mastering the demands of a systems' thinking approach to data visualisation – being aware of the options and the mechanics behind making choices – arguably has a greater influence on effective work. Thereafter, the journey from *good* to *great*, as with anything, involves hard work, plenty of learning, lots of guidance and, most importantly, relentless practice.

The Value of the Team

The idea of team work is important. There are advantages to pursuing data visualisation solutions collaboratively, bringing together different abilities and perspectives to a shared challenge. In workplaces across industries and sectors, as the field matures and becomes more embedded, I would expect to see a greater shift towards recognising the need for interdisciplinary teams to fulfil data visualisation projects collectively.

The best functioning visualisation team will offer a collective blend of skills across all these hats, substantiating some inevitably, but also, critically, avoiding skewing the sensibilities towards one dominant talent. Success will be hard to achieve if a team comprises a dominance in technologists or a concentration of 'ideas' people whose work never progresses past the sketchbook. You need the right blend in any team.

We have seen quite a lot of great examples of visualisation and infographic work from newspaper and media organisations. In the larger organisations that have the fortune of (relatively) large graphics departments, team working is an essential ingredient behind much of the success they have had. Producing relentlessly high-quality, innovative and multiple projects in parallel, within the demands of the news environment, is no mean feat. Such organisations might have the most people and also some of the best people, but their output is still representative of their punching above their weight, no matter how considerable that base.

Developing Through Evaluating

There are two components in evaluating the outcome of a visualisation solution that will help refine your capabilities: what was the *outcome* of the work and how do you reflect on *your performance*?

Outcome: Measuring effectiveness in data visualisation remains an elusive task – in many ways it is the field's 'Everest' – largely because it must be defined according to local, contextual measures of success. This is why establishing an early view of the intended 'purpose', and then refining it if circumstances change, was necessary to guide your thinking throughout this workflow.

Sometimes effectiveness is tangible, but most times it is entirely intangible. If the purpose of the work is to further the debate about a subject, to establish one's reputation or voice of authority, then those are hard things to pin down in terms of a yes/no outcome. One option may be to flip the measure of effectiveness on its head and seek out evidence of tangible ineffectiveness. For example, there may be significant reputation-based impacts should decisions be made on inaccurate, misleading or inaccessible visual information.

There are, of course, some relatively free quantitative measures that are available for digital projects, including web-based measures such as visitor counts and social media metrics (likes, retweets, mentions). These, at least, provide a surface indicator of success in terms of the project's apparent appeal and spread. Ideally, however, you should aspire also to collect more reliable qualitative and value-added feedback, even if this can, at times, be rather expensive to secure. Some options include:

- capturing anecdotal evidence from comments submitted on a site, opinions attributed to tweets or other social media descriptors, feedback shared in emails or in person;
- informal feedback through polls or short surveys;
- formal case studies which might offer more structured interviews and observations about documented effects;
- experiments with controlled tasks/conditions and tracked performance measures.

Your performance: A personal reflection or assessment of your contribution to a project is important for your own development. The best way to learn is by considering the things you enjoyed and/or did well (and doing more of those things) and identifying the things you did not enjoy/do well (and doing less of those things or doing them better). So look back over your project experience and consider the following:

- Were you satisfied with your solution? If yes, why; if no, why and what would you do differently?
- In a different context, what other design solutions might you have considered?

- Were there any skill or knowledge shortcomings that restricted your process and/or solution?
- Are there aspects of this project that you might seek to recycle or reproduce in other projects? For instance, ideas that did not make the final cut but could be given new life in other challenges?
- How well did you utilise your time? Were there any activities on which you feel you spent too much time?

> 'There is not one project I have been involved in that I would execute exactly the same way second time around. I could conceivably pick any of them – and probably the thing they could all benefit most from? More inter-disciplinary expertise.' **Alan Smith OBE, Data Visualisation Editor,** *Financial Times*

Developing effectiveness and efficiency in your data visualisation work will take time and will require your ongoing efforts to learn, apply, reflect and repeat again. I am still learning new things every day. It is a journey that never stops because data visualisation is a subject that has no ending.

However, to try offer a suitable conclusion to this book, at least, I will leave you with this wonderful bit of transcribed from a video of Ira Glass, host and producer of 'This American Life'.

Nobody tells this to people who are beginners, I really wish someone had told this to me. All of us who do creative work, we get into it because we have good taste… [but] there is this gap and for the first couple of years that you're making stuff, what you're making is just not that good… It's trying to be good, it has potential, but it's not. But your taste, the thing that got you into the game, is still killer. And your taste is why your work disappoints you. A lot of people never get past this phase, they quit. Most people I know who do interesting, creative work went through years of this. We know our work doesn't have this special thing that we want it to have. We all go through this. And if you are just starting out or you are still in this phase, you gotta know it's normal and the most important thing you can do is do a lot of work. Put yourself on a deadline so that every week you will finish one story. It is only by going through a volume of work that you will close that gap, and your work will be as good as your ambitions. And I took longer to figure out how to do this than anyone I've ever met. It's gonna take awhile. It's normal to take awhile. You've just gotta fight your way through.

Summary: Visualisation Literacy

Viewing: Learning to See

Before You Begin

- Setting: is the situation you are in conducive to the task of consuming a visualisation? In a rush? Travelling?
- Visual appeal: are you sufficiently attracted to the appearance of the work?

- Relevance: do you have an interest or a need to engage with this topic?
- Initial scan: quickly orientate yourself around the page or screen, and allow yourself a brief moment to be drawn to certain features.

Outside the Chart

- The proposition: what task awaits? What format, function, shape and size of visualisation have you got to work with?
- What's the project about?: look at the titles, source, and read through any introductory explanations.
- What data?: look for information about where the data has originated from and what might have been done to it.
- What interactive functions exist?: if it is a digital solution browse quickly and acquaint yourself with the range of interactive devices.

Inside the Chart Refer to the Chart Type Gallery in Chapter 6 to learn about the approaches to perceiving and interpreting different chart types.

- Perceiving: what does it show?
- Interpreting: what does it mean?
- Comprehending: what does it mean to me?

Becoming a More Sophisticated Consumer

- Appreciation of context: what circumstances might the visualiser have been faced with that are hidden from you as a viewer?
- Overview first, details if provided: accept that sometimes a project only aims to (or maybe only can) provide a big-picture gist of the data, rather than precise details.
- False consciousness: don't be too quick to determine that you like a visualisation. Challenge yourself, do you *really* like it? Do you *really* gain understanding from it?
- Curiosities answered, curiosities not answered: just because it does not answer your curiosity, it might answer those of plenty of others.

Creating: The Capabilities of the Visualiser

The Seven Hats of Data Visualisation Design

- Project Manager: the coordinator – oversees the project.
- Communicator: the broker – manages the people relationships.
- Scientist: the thinker – provides scientific rigour.
- Data analyst: the wrangler – handles all the data work.
- Journalist: the reporter – pursues the scent of enquiry.
- Designer: the conceiver – provides creative direction.
- Technologist: the developer – constructs the solution.

Assessing and Developing Your Capabilities

The importance of reflective learning: evaluating the outcome of the work you have created and assessing your own performance during its production.

Tips and Tactics

- The life and energy of data visualisation are online: keep on top of blogs, the websites of major practitioners and agencies creating great work. On social media (especially Twitter, Reddit) you will find a very active and open community that is willing to share and help.
- Practise, practise, practise: experience is the key – identify personal projects to explore different techniques and challenges.
- Learn about yourself: take notes, reflect, self-critique, recognise your limits.
- Learn from others: consume case studies and process narratives, evaluate the work of others ('what would I do differently?').
- Expose yourself to the ideas and practices of other related creative and communication fields: writing, video games, graphic design, architecture, cartoonists.

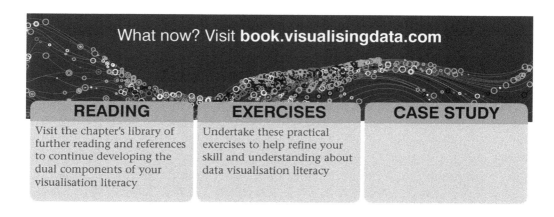

What now? Visit **book.visualisingdata.com**

READING	EXERCISES	CASE STUDY
Visit the chapter's library of further reading and references to continue developing the dual components of your visualisation literacy	Undertake these practical exercises to help refine your skill and understanding about data visualisation literacy	

References

These references relate to content mentioned in the body text and/or attributed quotes that do not come from individual interviews with the author. Extensive further reading lists to support each chapter's content are provided in the companion digital resources.

Bertin, Jacques (2011) *Semiology of Graphics: Diagrams, Networks, Maps*. Redlands, CA: ESRI Press.

Beveridge, Harriet and Hunt-Davis, Ben (2011) *Will it Make the Boat Go Faster? Olympic-winning Strategies for Everyday Success*. Leicester: Matador.

Booker, Christopher (2004) *The Seven Basic Plots: Why We Tell Stories*. New York: Continuum.

Buckle, Catherine (2014) *Millions, Billions, Trillions: Letters from Zimbabwe, 2005–2009*. http://www.cathybuckle.com/Millions-Billions-Trillions.php

Butterick, Matthew (2013) Practical Typography. http://practicaltypography.com

Buxton, Bill (2007) *Sketching User Experiences*. San Francisco, CA: Elsevier.

Cairo, Alberto (2012) *The Functional Art*. San Francisco, CA: Peachpit.

Chimero, Frank (2012) *The Shape of Design*. http://shapeofdesignbook.com/

Cleveland, William S. and McGill, Robert M. (1984) 'Graphical Perception: Theory, Experimentation, and Application to the Development of Graphical Methods'. *Journal of the American Statistical Association*, vol. 79, no. 387, pp. 531–54.

Coats, Emma (2011) Originally via Twitter, collated via http://www.aerogrammestudio.com/2013/03/07/pixars-22-rules-of-storytelling/

Cox, Amanda (2013) *Harvard Business Review*. https://hbr.org/2013/03/power-of-visualizations-aha-moment/

Crawford, Kate (2013) *Harvard Business Review*. http://blogs.hbr.org/cs/2013/04/the_hidden_biases_in_big_data.html

de Bono, Edward (1985) *Six Thinking Hats*. New York: Little, Brown.

Dilnott, Andrew (2013) Presented at a conference about the Office for National Statistics. https://twitter.com/GuardianData/status/313965008478425089

Fernandez, Manny (2013) *New York Times*. http://www.nytimes.com/2013/06/30/us/from-americas-busiest-death-chamber-a-catalog-of-last-rants-pleas-and-apologies.html?_r=0

Glass, Ira (2009) Open Culture. http://www.openculture.com/2009/10/ira_glass_on_the_art_of_story_telling.html

Gore, Al (2006) Presentation from *An Inconvenient Truth*, directed by Davis Guggenheim.

Heer, Jeffrey and Schneiderman, Ben (2012) 'Interactive Dynamics for Visual Analysis'. *ACM Queue*, vol. 10, no. 2, p. 30.

Ive, Jonny, Kemp, Klaus and Lovell, Sophie (2011) *Dieter Rams: As Little Design As Possible*. London: Phaidon Press.

Jordan, Chris (2006) TEDtalk. http://www.ted.com/talks/chris_jordan_pictures_some_shocking_stats.html

Kahneman, Daniel (2011) *Thinking Fast and Slow*. New York: Farrar, Straus & Giroux.

Kosara, Robert (2013) eagereyes: How The Rainbow Color Map Misleads. http://eagereyes.org/basics/rainbow-color-map

Lupi, Giorgia (2014) *Green Futures Magazine*. https://www.forumforthefuture.org/greenfutures/articles/why-i-draw-giorgia-lupi-art-visual-understanding

Mackinlay, Jock (1986) 'Automating the Design of Graphical Presentations of Relational Information'. *ACM Transactions on Graphics (TOG)*, vol. 5, no. 2, pp. 110–41.

Meyer, Robinson (2014) 'The *New York Times*' Most Popular Story of 2013 Was Not an Article'. *The Atlantic*. http://www.theatlantic.com/technology/archive/2014/01/-em-the-new-york-times-em-most-popular-story-of-2013-was-not-an-article/283167/

Morton, Jill (2015) Color Matters. http://www.colormatters.com/color-and-design/basic-color-theory

Munzner, Tamara (2014) *Visualization Analysis and Design*. Boca Raton, FL: CRC Press.

Reichenstein, Oliver (2013) Information Architects. https://ia.net/know-how/learning-to-see

Rosling, Hans (2006) TEDtalk. https://www.ted.com/talks/hans_rosling_shows_the_best_stats_you_ve_ever_seen

Rumsfeld, Donald (2002) US DoD News Briefing. https://en.wikipedia.org/wiki/There_are_known_knowns

Satyanarayan, Arvind and Heer, Jeffrey (2014) 'Lyra: An Interactive Visualization Design Environment'. *Computer Graphics Forum* (*Proceedings of EuroVis, 2014*).

Shneiderman, Ben (1996) 'The Eyes Have It: A Task by Data Type Taxonomy for Information Visualizations'. *Proceedings of the IEEE Symposium on Visual Languages*. Washington, DC: IEEE Computer Society Press, pp. 336–43.

Slobin, Sarah (2014) Source. https://source.opennews.org/en-US/learning/what-if-data-visualization-actually-people

Stefaner, Moritz (2014) Well-Formed Data. http://well-formed-data.net/archives/1027/worlds-not-stories

Tukey, John W. (1980) 'We Need Both Exploratory and Confirmatory'. *The American Statistician*, vol. 34, no. 1, pp. 23–5.

Tversky, Barbara and Bauer Morrison, Julie (2002) 'Animation: Can it facilitate?'. *International Journal of Human-Computer Studies* – Special issue: Interactive graphical communication, vol. 57, no. 4, pp. 247–62.

Vitruvius Pollio, Marcus (15 BC) 'De architectura'.

White, Alex (2002) *The Elements of Graphic Design*. New York: Allworth Press.

Wolfers, Justin (2014) TheUpshot. http://www.nytimes.com/2014/04/23/upshot/what-good-marathons-and-bad-investments-have-in-common.html

Wooton, Sir Henry (1624) *The Elements of Architecture*. London: Longmans, Green.

Wurman, Richard Saul (1997) *Information Architects*. New York: Graphis.

Yau, Nathan (2013) *Data Points*. Chichester: Wiley.

Index

Titles of charts are printed in italics